HEALTH LIBRARIANSHIP

An Introduction

Jeffrey T. Huber and Feili Tu-Keefner, Editors

Foreword by Fred W. Roper

LIBRARIES UNLIMITED

AN IMPRINT OF ABC-CLIO, LLC
Santa Barbara, California • Denver, Colorado • Oxford, England

Library of Congress Cataloging-in-Publication Data

   Health librarianship : an introduction / Jeffrey T. Huber and Feili Tu-Keefner, editors ; foreword by
Fred W. Roper.
      pages cm
   Includes bibliographical references and index.
   ISBN 978–1–61069–321–9 (pbk : alk. paper) — ISBN 978–1–61069–887–0 (ebook)
   1. Medical librarianship. 2. Medical librarianship—United States. 3. Medical libraries. 4. Medical libraries—
United States. I. Huber, Jeffrey T. II. Tu-Keefner, Feili.
   Z675.M4H43   2014
   026′.61—dc23   2014013267

ISBN: 978–1–61069–321–9
EISBN: 978–1–61069–887–0

18 17 16 15 14   1 2 3 4 5

This book is also available on the World Wide Web as an eBook.
Visit www.abc-clio.com for details.

Libraries Unlimited
An Imprint of ABC-CLIO, LLC

ABC-CLIO, LLC
130 Cremona Drive, P.O. Box 1911
Santa Barbara, California 93116-1911

This book is printed on acid-free paper ∞

Manufactured in the United States of America

CONTENTS

ILLUSTRATIONS

FIGURES

TABLES

FOREWORD

It is a pleasure to be asked to say a few words about this important new publication. I have great respect for the two editors and have been involved with them in other arenas. Jeff Huber and I have been most closely associated with *Introduction to Reference Sources in the Health Sciences*. Feili Tu-Keefner was the last person I employed while Dean of the School of Library and Information Science at the University of South Carolina. My valued colleagues, Jeff and Feili, are among the small number of full-time faculty members involved with the teaching of health sciences librarianship; their experience in education for the health sciences librarian eminently qualifies them to prepare this publication. That experience is complemented by the distinguished group of professionals who have made contributions to the book.

This textbook should be a great boon to the whole area of education for health sciences librarianship. Although it is certainly prepared with the library and information science student in mind, it will be important for the entire continuum of learning—from the introduction to health sciences librarianship, to preparation for the Academy of Health Information Professionals, to continuing education for practitioners, to career changes as those may occur, and to the need for refreshing and reviewing.

It has been said that necessity is the mother of invention, and this has been the case with more than one textbook/manual in library and information science. Frustration with not having a publication that defined and explained health science reference sources and that would be appropriate for a reference course brought about the publication of the first edition of *Introduction to Reference Sources in the Health Sciences* in 1980. Now the sixth edition is being prepared and is being edited by Jeffrey Huber and Susan Swogger. A similar situation was the impetus for preparation of *Health Librarianship: An Introduction*, which, I believe, will fill a void in the education of health sciences information professionals.

I view this publication as being complementary to the Medical Library Association's remarkable array of publications. Those books present more detail than is possible in a single monograph, and they will make excellent sources for further insight into a particular area.

In an environment where the only constant seems to be change, faculty and students alike will need to adjust continuously to new resources, new technologies, and new delivery methods, both for information and for education. A starting point will be an overview and understanding of the current environment, as provided by *Health Librarianship: An Introduction*. The editors will need to be vigilant in providing updates as changes occur.

I am pleased that our field will now have an important new resource. I am even more pleased that so many of my friends and colleagues have been involved in the preparation of this new textbook/resource and that I have been allowed to play a small role.

Fred W. Roper
Columbia, South Carolina

PREFACE

Health Librarianship: An Introduction is an introductory textbook that takes a holistic approach toward the professional qualifications required by today's health sciences librarians.

It was developed to serve as an introductory text to the field. Health librarianship, or health sciences librarianship, is concerned with information resources and services specific to health and biomedical sciences. In general, health sciences library and information professionals are experts in this domain. The environments in which they work include academic health science center libraries, hospital libraries, special libraries, consumer health or patient libraries, and public libraries that offer consumer health services.

This text consists of 15 chapters, and the contents provide thorough coverage of current developments in the field, as well as cutting-edge information services concepts in a variety of health information settings. The chapters in this book encompass three broad areas: (I) the environment, (II) health sciences libraries, and (III) special topics. The following chapters are focused on the environment: 1. Overview of Health Librarianship and Health Sciences Libraries, 2. Overview of the Healthcare Environment, 3. Situating Health Librarianship within the Healthcare Environment, 4. Evidence-Based Healthcare/Evidence-Based Practice, and 5. Government Agency and Professional Association Resources and Services. The chapters on the area of health sciences libraries include the following: 6. Health Librarianship: Management and Administration, 7. Technical Services in Health Sciences Libraries, 8. Public Services in Health Sciences Libraries, 9. Information Retrieval, and 10. Historical Collections in Health Sciences Libraries. Lastly, the chapters on special topics include the following: 11. Interpersonal Skills to the Fore: Consumer Health Librarianship, 12. Health Literacy, 13. Outreach Services, 14.

Special Populations, and 15. Health and Biomedical Informatics. Chapter authors represent both health sciences library and information professional practitioners and academic faculty members who specialize in health sciences librarianship.

An overview of the profession of health sciences librarianship is covered in the chapters included on the area of the environment. The content centers on types of current health information environments and how librarians position themselves as leaders and change agents in the various systems. Because the concept of patient-centered healthcare has become an important influence on physician-patient relationships and the quality of healthcare outcomes, a description of evidence-based healthcare and evidence-based practice is also covered. In addition, a number of professional agencies and organizations that have been instrumental in guiding innovations in health information services, and the development of health librarians' networks are also discussed.

In the chapters related to health sciences libraries, the detailed information related to health sciences librarians' operations (or services) are provided. In-depth descriptions of health librarians' professional responsibilities and daily operations are described. These chapters carefully document how health information professionals share their vision and provide various types of services in their environments. In addition, the descriptions in each chapter can serve as guidance for the development of professional qualifications by the individual librarian and facilitate career advancement.

The chapters on special topics include descriptions of several special topics related to health sciences information services. The chapters on consumer health, health literacy, and special populations are essential in helping the audience better understand the concepts and delivery of consumer health information services, and these chapters can serve as a cornerstone for the creation of critical health information services for non–health professionals. The chapter about outreach services describes various aspects of the design and delivery of community outreach programs and services in different types of environments for a variety of users. This group of chapters ends with an introduction of topics related to health and biomedical informatics and provides a well-rounded overview of them.

Each chapter concludes with a comprehensive list of all reference sources cited in the chapter. With its overview of current topics of health librarianship, this book is designed to be not only an introductory text for students, but also a continual learning resource for practitioners already in the field.

ACKNOWLEDGMENTS

We have many people to thank for their work in bringing this book to fruition. We offer our deep appreciation to the contributing authors—the senior professional librarians, health sciences library managers, and faculty members in library and information science programs from all over the nation. It was a privilege to work with this elite group. We express our gratitude to Dr. Fred Roper, who kindly wrote the foreword for this book. Our thanks also go to Heather Burke, who assisted in copyediting and preparing the chapters for publishing. Her thoroughness and efficiency helped us finish the project on time. Finally, Jeff wants to thank family members, friends, and colleagues who have inspired him throughout his career. Feili thanks Joanne Madsen for her advice and encouragement and Paul R. Keefner for his unconditional understanding and support. Feili also wishes to acknowledge the warm support over the years of the late Dr. Helen A. Bush.

Jeffrey T. Huber
Director and Professor
School of Library and Information Science
University of Kentucky

Feili Tu-Keefner
Associate Professor
School of Library and Information Science
University of South Carolina

INTRODUCTION

Practitioners of health librarianship, or health sciences librarianship, are concerned with the provision of information resources and services specific to health and bio-medical sciences. The environments in which these CKOs (chief knowledge offi-cers) work include academic health science center libraries, hospital libraries, special libraries, consumer health or patient libraries/learning centers, and public libraries that offer consumer health services.

Academic health sciences libraries serve healthcare providers, faculty members, students, and researchers. In addition to general collections, historical collections play an important role in health librarianship, particularly in larger academic health science center libraries. The services are vital to successful teaching and learning, and are critical to producing a competent future healthcare workforce. Some aca-demic health science center libraries also serve healthcare consumers, while others refer them to patient libraries or learning centers.

In hospital settings, clinical-based information services provided by information specialists may be a matter of a patient's life and death. In addition to healthcare providers, hospital libraries serve students completing residencies, internships, or clinical rotations. Depending on the size of the hospital, there may be separate patient libraries or learning centers.

Special libraries, such as those in biomedical and biotechnological research set-tings, may focus on business aspects of the enterprise or research and development initiatives. Knowledge-based information management and services are essential to the discovery of therapeutic innovations.

In environments providing information services to the general public, librarians are responsible for promoting health awareness, wellness, and health literacy. These public libraries or health information centers may exist in academic health science centers or hospitals; they may be found within a community-based organization that provides health-related or social support services; or they may be stand-alone entities. In addition, many public libraries offer consumer health services by including health-related materials or programming that targets a specific audience. However, the environment, to some extent, will dictate the nature, scope, and availability of collections, resources, and services.

As with other types of libraries and information centers, traditional areas of work include management and administration, technical services, and public services. One of the distinguishing features of health librarianship is information retrieval. The National Library of Medicine (NLM) has been a driving force behind health librarianship. The NLM is responsible for the development and maintenance of MEDLINE (the premier health and biomedical sciences literature database for the Americas). The controlled vocabulary used to index MEDLINE, Medical Subject Headings (MeSH), is one of the strongest examples of sets of terms naming descriptors in a hierarchical structure that permits searching at various levels of specificity. Extending the notion of information retrieval, the NLM has also been a driving force behind advancing health and biomedical informatics (using technology to provide relevant information at the point and time of need to support sound decision making).

Outreach to various constituents is often a focus of health sciences libraries/information centers. As indicated previously, healthcare consumers are often targeted specifically since they comprise a large portion of individuals seeking health information. Special populations such as adolescents, senior citizens, and minorities all have their own issues. One challenge that cuts across the healthcare consumer population is that of health literacy. Health literacy is concerned with individuals being able to make *informed* healthcare decisions. This involves issues associated with literacy, numeracy, cultural belief systems, communication styles, and so on.

Health Librarianship: An Introduction provides broad coverage of each of these topics. Its focus on current trends and issues in the field includes the design and delivery of health information services, the foundations of health librarianship, current healthcare systems, embedded knowledge-based information services, librarians' professional status, and professional networks. This book contains well-rounded discussions that move from theory to application and demonstrate examples of best practices in technology access. The coverage is well balanced and extends to almost every aspect of the profession of health librarianship. The goal is to help the audience better understand the profession of health librarianship, inspire their quest for knowledge, stimulate health librarians' creativity in advancing health information services, and motivate them to expand their professional knowledge through continued learning and development.

Chapter 1

OVERVIEW OF HEALTH SCIENCES LIBRARIES AND LIBRARIANSHIP

Katherine Schilling

WHO HEALTH SCIENCES LIBRARIANS ARE

Health Sciences Librarianship Defined

In ancient Alexandria, there was a legendary library with vast collections of diverse material. If an ancient scholar or researcher wanted access to the knowledge contained there, the librarian would need to know something about what the scholar wanted. This is true today. While the basic roles of health sciences librarians remain fairly constant, the tools used to accomplish these tasks have changed.[1] At the same time, the field is always in flux, with "librarians" increasingly called by other titles and moving away from being wedded to a library institution.[2]

In the twenty-first-century information age, information comes at us at astounding rates. Filtering and organizing information for efficacious usage—on personal and professional levels—is a constant challenge. Information must be stored and transformed to create and disseminate new knowledge. Working within information environments requires multidisciplinary and collaborative teamwork that integrates the entirety of the healthcare system, including health librarians. This team is made up of clinicians, researchers, statisticians, and information professionals.[3, 4]

Health sciences librarianship is a dynamic, complex, and multifaceted health information profession. As information and communications technologies usage continues to expand, health sciences librarians are likewise increasingly challenged to redefine their roles as professionals in the information marketplace. The Special Library Association (SLA) defines *information professionals* as those who strategically use information in their jobs to advance the mission of the organization. "The information professional accomplishes this through the development, deployment, and management of information resources and services. The informational professional harnesses technology as a critical tool to accomplish goals."[5] The Special Library Association further defines *information organizations* as "those entities that deliver information-based solutions to a given market."[6] Some commonly used names for these organizations include libraries, information centers, competitive intelligence units, intranet departments, knowledge resource centers, and content management organizations.[7]

Information professionals may have a variety of titles, including health sciences librarian, medical librarian, health information professional, health information specialist, informatician, and informationist (*hereafter called health sciences librarians*).[8] Health sciences librarians work in academia, hospitals, government agencies, corporations, professional organizations, society libraries, and other information-centric environments.

According to the Medical Library Association (MLA), health sciences librarians function in ways shaped by a number of significant factors, including:

- Changing elements and structure of medical knowledge,
- Rapid introduction of new technologies and techniques for information processing and dissemination,
- Altered patterns of institutional organization, management, and governance, and the
- Drive to maintain excellence.[9]

"Health sciences librarianship stands apart" from other information professions "in ensuring that knowledge about advances in the science and technology of healthcare research and practice is readily accessible to healthcare professionals, educators, students, researchers and the public."[10] In short, health sciences librarians create, collect, manage, and distribute health information to support and drive the educational, research, and clinical missions of the organizations they serve. In the twenty-first-century information age, libraries and librarians remain in a unique position to provide information and knowledge management solutions that integrate and make optimal use of resources. Health information professionals not only support their organizations' missions by using new technologies to "organize, synthesize, and filter information for scholarly, clinical, and institutional decision making," but also play a critical role in the "investigation and study of information storage, organization, use, and application in education, patient care and generation of new knowledge."[11] Health sciences librarianship is the one information field that ensures that knowledge in the sciences and technology of healthcare research and practice are accessible to healthcare workers and the public.[12]

Moore's model of health sciences librarianship represents the role of health sciences librarians and libraries in the healthcare culture. This model defines health sciences librarianship in terms of the context in which it operates.[13] Here, the field is defined by the profession (values, education, salaries, nature of the work, etc.), characteristics of libraries (collections, facilities, etc.), the National Library of Medicine (NLM), and trends. Trends in healthcare as varied as evidence-based practice and scholarly communication impact the practice of librarianship. Couching the field in terms of the profession, characteristics of libraries, the NLM, and trends takes into consideration the myriad issues, challenges, and sheer potential work and projects available to health sciences librarians. *We ARE what we DO* emerges as a useful theme when one views the field in terms of the many environments (some competing) in which librarians operate. Awareness of context is a major theme, as librarians operate as partners to many clients in differing environments. Operating successfully in myriad environments requires flexibility, thinking on one's feet, imagination, and proactive services.

Professional Roles, Competencies and Standards

Reviewing our professional competencies and standards is perhaps one of the best ways to understand health sciences librarianship. Professional competencies and standards reveal what health sciences librarians value. Competencies also illustrate the similarities and differences between health sciences and other types of libraries. Core competencies from the American Library Association (ALA), the Special Library Association (SLA), and the Medical Library Association (MLA) combine personal and professional skills, qualifications, characteristics, values, and qualities that are essential in every information professional and information organization. These competencies are useful tools for professional recruitment, growth, and assessment.

The ALA's *Core Competencies of Librarianship* (2009) describes information professionals as those who "understand the value of developing and sharing their knowledge. ... This is accomplished through association networks and by conducting and sharing research. ... Information professionals also acknowledge and adhere to the ethics of the profession."[14] The ALA *Competencies* describe the basic knowledge required of librarians, framed in terms of knowledge possessed by those who graduate from an ALA-accredited master's degree program. All library types are represented in the core competency areas:

1. Foundations of the Profession
2. Information Resources
3. Organization of Recorded Knowledge and Information
4. Technological Knowledge and Skills
5. Reference and User Services
6. Research
7. Continuing Education and Lifelong Learning
8. Administration and Management

Each core area also includes between two and seven specific professional objectives. For example, Competency 2, Information Resources, includes:

2A. Concepts and issues related to the lifecycle or recorded knowledge and information, from creation through various stages of use to disposition.

2B. Concepts, issues and methods related to the acquisition and disposition of resources, including evaluation, selection, purchasing, processing, storing, and deselection.[15]

The Special Library Association's *SLA Competencies for Information Professionals of the 21st Century* are less library-centric. Instead, SLA competencies emphasize the knowledge requirements of information professionals in information organizations. Their scope and coverage are driven more by information management and knowledge management, and they are grounded in the skills required for "specialized information management."[16] The document begins with two core competencies:

1. Information professionals contribute to the knowledge base of the profession by sharing best practices and experiences, and continue to learn about information products, services, and management practices throughout . . . his/her career.

2. Information professionals commit to professional excellence and ethics, and to the values and principles of the profession.[17]

The *SLA Competencies* then move on to specific skills, values, and qualities related to:

• Managing information organizations
• Managing information resources
• Managing information services
• Applying information tools and technologies

Personal competencies—or attitudes, skills, and values for effective practice in information organizations—are also included.

The *Competencies for Lifelong Learning and Professional Success* from the Medical Library Association are the most relevant to health sciences librarianship.[18] These *Competencies* are written for health sciences librarians, other health information professionals, and stakeholders such as health sciences administrators. The MLA *Competencies* are grounded in *Platform for Change*, published in 1991 by the MLA Center for Research and Education (CORE). *Platform for Change* noted that "exponential growth in biomedical knowledge, new information technologies, and upheaval in the health care environment are all driving transformation."[19] This rings true more than 20 years later.

The MLA *Competencies* take a future-oriented, lifelong learning approach to qualifications, skills, values, and qualities required for professional practice. They emphasize the things informationists, librarians, and health information professionals of all kinds will need to know in the future. The MLA asserts that "the management of information and knowledge in the healthcare environment is a national priority with increasing attention paid to evidence-based healthcare, patient safety and privacy, health literacy, and the creation of electronic patient records. Technology has become central to the operation of every library."[20]

The philosophy behind the *Competencies* is that change is constant, knowledge expands exponentially, and technology is the means through which information flows. Lifelong learning is critical to keeping current within the context of this ever-changing environment. Rigorous improvement of one's skills and qualifications are necessary for changing twenty-first-century roles. A regular, systematic, and deliberate program of continuing education (CE) is vital for long-term professional success. It is important to direct one's learning with specific goals and a framework for learning in mind. Mentoring activities and participating in the life of the profession through committee roles are important for lifelong learning as well. These key areas are useful for mapping out longer-term CE and directing one's career development. Important roles include the ability to understand "the health sciences and health care environment and the policies, issues, and trends that impact" it, as well as "the application of leadership, finance, communication, and management theory and techniques," the ability to "manage information sources in broad range of formats," "use technology and systems to manage information," and "understand curricular design and instruction" and "scientific research methods."[21]

The MLA *Competencies* also value personal skills, including problem solving, analytical competence, and interpersonal and organizational skills. They emphasize what librarians do that is unique, including ensuring that "knowledge about advances is accessible."[22] Finally, the *Competencies* provide recommendations for librarians, the MLA, the National Library of Medicine, employers, and related professional organizations.[23] On the individual level, librarians must seek opportunities for CE and an engaged commitment to lifelong learning for the advancement of the individual and field.

EDUCATION FOR HEALTH SCIENCES LIBRARIANSHIP

A *profession* is defined by several factors, including being self-regulating and self-licensing, or self-credentialing. Cleveland defines a profession as a "group of individuals who are recognized by the general public as having special knowledge, competencies, and skills based on an extensive knowledgebase, with extended education and training."[24] Preparation for a career in health sciences librarianship includes a bachelor's degree and then the entry-level credential, an American Library Association–accredited master's degree in the library sciences or information sciences. These degrees are commonly called the MLS (Master of Library Science), MSLS (Master of Science in Library Science), or the related MSIS (Master of Science in Information Science), and other variations. Health sciences librarians come to the profession with backgrounds in the arts, humanities, social sciences, or sciences. As the job market continues to be outpaced by the number of MLS graduates each year, a background in healthcare or the basic sciences gives one a competitive edge.[25] Subject expertise in a discipline other than library science, including a second master's degree, may be preferred, particularly in academic settings where one's clients and colleagues are likely to have multiple degrees, including doctoral-level degrees (M.D., Ph.D.). Practical experience in the field is also crucial. MLS students should take advantage of every opportunity for internships and practical experience in health sciences libraries and information settings during their MLS program, and residencies or fellowships following their program.[26]

Of the 55 or so library schools in the United States, about 25 have full-time faculty in the health sciences, and others have adjuncts teaching healthcare-related courses.[27] In terms of what students are learning at library school, only 10 of the 28 iSchools have "foundations" course requirements. There are no uniform requirement for health sciences librarianship across the library schools.[28, 29] However, library schools can base health sciences curriculum on the *Competencies* from the Medical Library Association. Library schools may also base their curricula on competencies from the ALA.[30]

Continuing Education and Credentialing

Continuing education (CE) is vital for practicing health sciences librarians. To that end, our premier association, the Medical Library Association (MLA), offers a wide variety of CE at each year's annual meeting. The MLA chapters, the National Network of Libraries of Medicine (NNLM), and Regional Medical Libraries (RML) also offer CE opportunities throughout the year.

Additionally, the Academy of Health Information Professionals (AHIP) is the peer-reviewed, professional development credentialing unit of the Medical Library Association. Membership is available at paraprofessional and professional levels, including the provisional, basic, senior, distinguished, and emeritus levels for increasingly higher years of service to the profession. To achieve AHIP status, health sciences librarians must accumulate points for continuing education. Points are also accumulated for publications, conference attendance and presentations, and contributions to the association and profession such as holding positions in the MLA and other professional organizations.

The academy recognizes the time and effort involved in engaging in professional development and contributing to the association and to the profession. The MLA describes the differences between certification, credentialing, and licensing: *Certification* focuses on standards and competencies; *credentialing* on time and effort. *Licensure* is legal; *credentialing* is not. "Members of the academy are credentialed as health information professionals by demonstrating their academic preparation, professional experience and professional accomplishments."[31]

Selected Professional Organizations

Professional organizations are vital to the life of the field and to each individual's professional growth and development. Several organizations of particular relevance to health sciences librarianship are described here in Figure 1.1.

Association of American Medical Colleges (AAMC)	http://www.aamc.org/
American Association of Health Sciences Libraries (AAHSL)	http://www.aahsl.org/
American Medical Informatics Association (AMIA)	http://www.amia.org/
Canadian Health Libraries Association / Association des bibliothèques de la santé du Canada (CHLA/ABSC)	http://www.chla-absc.ca/
International Medical Informatics Association (IMIA)	http://www.imia-medinfo.org/
Medical Library Association (MLA)	http://www.mlanet.org/
Special Libraries Association (SLA)	http://www.sla.org/

Figure 1.1 Professional Organizations and Websites

National Library of Medicine (NLM)

The National Library of Medicine (NLM) is the mother ship of health sciences librarianship. Its reach extends to advocacy, funding, library services and resources, and more. This model is fairly unique: Few fields have a national library, and few national libraries exert such pervasive influence on the activities, funds, and reach of health sciences libraries nationwide and worldwide, as does the NLM. Located on the National Institutes of Health (NIH) campus in Bethesda, Maryland, the NLM serves the faculty, staff, and students of the National Institutes of Health, U.S. Congress, and the nation. The "NLM maintains and makes available a vast print collection and produces electronic information resources on a wide range of topics that are searched billions of times each year by millions of people around the globe."[31]

The NLM archives (digitally or in print) the nation's collections of medical realia, literature, serials, monographs, and other related materials. The NLM also "supports and conducts research, development and training in biomedical informatics and health information technology."[32] Finally, the NLM lobbies the national government and is a major funder of grants and contracts to the National Network of Libraries of Medicine (NNLM), and to libraries, organizations, and individual applicants. The NLM is organized into six large, primary divisions:

- Division of Extramural Programs
- Division of Specialized Information Services (SIS)
- Lister Hill National Center for Biomedical Communications
- National Center for Biotechnology Information (NCBI)
- Office of Computer & Communications Systems (OCCS)
- Division of Library Operations

The NLM is the largest biomedical library in the world, with the Division of Library Operations comprised of multiple subdivisions or departments:

- Bibliographic Services Division
- Index Section
- MEDLARS Management Section (produces MEDLINE, PubMed)
- History of Medicine Division
- Medical Subject Headings (MeSH) Section
- National Information Center on Health Services Research (NICHSR)
- National Network Office (NNO)
- Public Services Division
- Technical Services Division

The National Library of Medicine produces some of the most important resources in the health sciences. The MEDLARS Management Section (Medical Literature Archival and Retrieval System) of the NLM creates and distributes MEDLINE through PubMed and sells the database to OVID and other popular vendors for availability on their systems. PubMed and PubMed Central are the National Library of Medicine's premiere health sciences database and literature search and access systems through which the MEDLINE database and other bibliographic resources are made available. MEDLINE is an umbrella database for the entire healthcare arena, covering the professional journal literature in clinical and research medicine, nursing, dentistry, allied health, pharmacy, and others. MEDLINE indexes 4,000 of the world's leading biomedical journals in dozens of languages, dating originally to 1966 and retrospectively to the mid-1940s (at their time of publication).[33]

ToxTown, Toxline, AIDSInfo, HSRR, the National Center for Biotechnology Information (NCBI) database, and many others are also produced by the National Library of Medicine and are made available via the web on user-friendly platforms. These provide healthcare workers and the public an unprecedented level of access to evidence-based, quality-filtered, organized health information.

MEDLINEPlus, the premiere consumer health webography is also produced under the auspices of the NLM. MEDLINEPlus is an expansive collection of resources for health consumers. It includes an alphabetical topical index, a drug index, easy-to-read and large print materials, and a variety of multimedia formats such as videos. Expanded features include MEDLINEPlus mobile and MEDLI-NEPlus Connect, which links to electronic medical records and patient portals.

Additionally, the National Library of Medicine coordinates the 6,000-member National Network of Libraries of Medicine (NNLM) that "promotes and provides access to health information in communities across the United States."[34] The NNLM and corresponding Regional Medical Libraries (RML) programs are also active in the life of health sciences libraries, extending the NLM's reach more deeply into the community. The NNLM is a nationwide network of library organizations that serve specific geographic areas, the libraries, and the public within those areas. The NNLM serves the information needs of clinicians, librarians, administrators, educators, and consumers. Its services include outreach through network libraries, document delivery (DOCLINE and LoansomeDoc), funding, and information services. The RML program is an arm of the NNLM through which one library in each region wins a contract to act as a primary site for information sources and services to colleagues, libraries, healthcare clinicians and administrators, and consumers in that geographic region.

Medical Library Association (MLA)

The Medical Library Association (MLA), established in 1898, is the premier association for health sciences librarianship. It has approximately 3,600 individual members and 1,100 institutional members. Internally, the MLA operates with an executive director and staff, a board of directors, an elected president and officials, and so forth. Committees, juries, and task forces are responsible for the life of the organization. Members can belong to committees, special interest groups (SIGs), and sections. The 23 sections represent a wide variety of themes ranging from cancer to consumer health, and hospital librarianship to medical informatics to the history of medicine. Fourteen MLA chapters represent geographic areas and include the New England, Upstate New York and Ontario, North Atlantic, New York–New Jersey, Philadelphia, Pittsburgh, Mid-Atlantic, South Central, Southern, Midwest, Midcontinental, Northern California and Nevada, Southern California and Arizona, Pacific Northwest, and the Hawaii-Pacific Chapters. The chapters operate independently of the MLA, with elected officials, annual conferences, continuing education, outreach, and other activities relevant to their membership.

The MLA has broad leadership roles, including defining the profession, setting priorities, and envisioning the "art of the possible."[35] The MLA forms liaisons with other organizations and represents health sciences librarianship to the outside world. The MLA also advocates for the field and lobbies local, state, and federal governments. It establishes and chronologizes trends, gathers and publishes library statistics, and archives the history of the field. Professional associations like the MLA also socialize librarians into the field. To this end, the MLA offers new member events, formal mentoring programs, continuing education, and myriad networking opportunities at regional conferences and the annual meeting.

The MLA is responsible for research and publication through its sponsorship of the *Journal of the Medical Library Association,* which is the leading scholarly research and practical publication advancing health sciences librarianship worldwide. It is rigorously peer reviewed and is operated by an editor along with an editorial board. The goal of the journal is to expand our "knowledgebase through research in the organization, delivery, use, and impact of information on health care, biomedical research, and health professionals' education."[36] The journal began in 1902 as the *Bulletin of the Association of Medical Librarians,* continued as the *Bulletin of the Medical Library Association* in 1911, and became the *Journal of the Medical Library Association* in 2002. It celebrated its 100th issue in October 2012.

American Medical Informatics Association (AMIA)

AMIA, formerly known as the American Medical Informatics Association, is an American organization that fosters the development of biomedical informatics and health informatics in support of patient care, research, administration, and teaching. AMIA's subject focus is more highly technical in nature than that of the MLA, ALA, or SLA. AMIA membership includes individuals, institutions, and corporations. Members are physicians, nurses, dentists, pharmacists, clinicians, health information technology professionals, computer and information scientists, biomedical engineers, consultants and industry representatives, medical librarians, academic researchers, educators, and students. AMIA hosts an annual symposium, summits, and other activities that include continuing education. There are approximately 20 working groups ranging from dental informatics to education, to open source and public health informatics working groups. AMIA is operated by a president and chief executive officer (CEO), several vice presidents, and elected officials.

Association of Academic Health Sciences Libraries (AAHSL)

The Association of Academic Health Sciences Libraries (AAHSL), formerly the Association of Academic Health Sciences Libraries Directors, is the body for health sciences library directors. AAHSL supports the libraries and directors in "advancing the patient care, research, education, and community service missions of academic health centers through visionary executive leadership and expertise in health information, scholarly communication, and knowledge management."[37]

AAHSL offers programming and member services, benchmarking, and "the development of a community of colleagues."[38] It fosters collaboration and networking, and seeks to advance knowledge and research in information management through advocacy and a reframing of health information policy. AAHSL forms liaisons with other organizations. For example, AAHSL is closely linked to and meets with the Association of American Medical Colleges (AAMC). This partnership attaches AAHSL, and ultimately all health sciences libraries, to the educational missions of medical schools nationwide.

AAHSL has a variety of initiatives, including the NLM/AAHSL Leadership Fellows Program and engagement with Libraries in Medical Education (LiME). AAHSL also publishes the *Annual Statistics of Medical School Libraries in the United States and Canada*. Started in 1978 and published yearly thereafter, the *Annual Statistics* include comparative data on the major characteristics of medical school (academic health sciences) libraries, including collections, expenditures, facilities, personnel, and specific service areas such as reference, education, and interlibrary loan.

Association of American Medical Colleges (AAMC)

The Association of American Medical Colleges (AAMC) is the educational organization for medical schools in the United States and Canada. The AAMC operates the American Medical College Application Service, the medical school application program, and the Electronic Residency Application Service, the post–medical school residency application program.

Canadian Health Libraries Association/Association des Bibliothèques de la Santé du Canada (CHLA/ABSC)

The Canadian Health Libraries Association/Association des Bibliothèques de la Santé du Canada (CHLA) has approximately 400 members to whom it provides services such as professional development, networking, and advocacy. The CHLA values informed decision making, leadership, and equitable access.[39] The CHLA has chapters and interest groups that provide conferences, continuing education, and awards. The association's triannual, electronic *Journal of the Canadian Health Sciences Libraries Association* dates from 2004 and is available via Pubmed Central.

International Medical Informatics Association (IMIA)

This organization promotes international cooperation through healthcare informatics. The IMIA's membership includes national, institutional, and affiliated member organizations. The IMIA also attracts an international audience through its affiliation with the World Health Organization. Each year, IMIA hosts the annual World Congress on Medical and Health Informatics.

Special Libraries Association (SLA)

Much larger than the MLA, but with a broader audience, the Special Libraries Association (SLA) is an international organization for all information professionals working in business, government, law, finance, nonprofit, and academic organizations and institutions. The SLA focuses on the business and corporate side of information management. The 9,000 SLA members typically hold master's degrees in library sciences, informatics, or the information sciences. Special librarians include medical, corporate, law, news, museum, transportation, and sports librarians. Typically, the SLA is a good fit for corporate, hospital, and special health sciences librarians. Information professionals who do not work in traditional library settings are also often SLA members.

The Special Libraries Association is organized by geographic chapters and multiple topical divisions. It is operated with a CEO, along with an elected president and officers. Association activities include conferences, professional education, networking, and advocacy. The SLA produces the annual *Salary Survey*, a digital publication that breaks down salaries by 21 job responsibilities, job titles, geographic regions, company sizes, years of experience, and other variables. There are 56 regional chapters, each with elected officials and their own publications, meetings, continuing education, and special projects.

WHAT HEALTH SCIENCES LIBRARIANS KNOW AND DO

Health sciences librarianship is characterized by a strong service orientation in which resources, activities, and services are grounded in the use of cutting-edge information technologies to direct and support the missions of the organizations that libraries serve.[40] Awareness of the context of one's work is critical. Librarians do not just *support* the mission of the organization; they also participate on the teams that *determine* and *direct* the organizational mission.[41] Health sciences libraries provide resources to clients, the public, and peer libraries using the best available formats and methods for information delivery at the point of need.

Special, Hospital, and Academic Health Sciences Libraries

Health sciences libraries typically include special, hospital, and academic health sciences (university). There are also society libraries, organization libraries, independent consultants, information firms, and so on. Their similarities and differences are discussed here, as are the daily activities and responsibilities of health sciences librarians. A *special health sciences library* includes corporate, agency, organization, society, and other settings. Special libraries may be focused on the business-related aspects of healthcare in a way that differs from that of academic libraries. To this end, special librarians must be up to speed on business, management, leadership and economic, and medical trends.[42–45] Another difference between types of libraries is that academic health sciences libraries may emphasize teaching and education in their support of the university, while education may be less important in a special library. Special libraries typically serve professional staff and often support a fees-for-services payback structure whereby individuals and departments pay a la carte for services rendered. In some cases, departments also purchase specific library collections. Special librarians may report to a vice president or CEO/chief operating officer (COO) of information technology or information services.

Hospital libraries are similar to academic health sciences libraries in their subject areas but perhaps more like special libraries in their operational styles. Foci of operations may be on teaching residents and nurses, evidence-based medicine, electronic health records, the business of healthcare, and project-based work. A hospital library may serve a single hospital or a hospital system. Within a hospital system, the clientele could include multiple hospitals and remote clinical sites. Clients are doctors (residents and "attending" physicians), nurses, allied health professionals, administrators, administrative staff, and clinical staff. Hospital libraries may report to a vice president of medical affairs or academic affairs.

Under the auspices of managed care, the trend is moving toward consolidating small and independent community hospitals into larger, more centralized, highly competitive enterprises. These are often affiliated with university medical centers. Hospital consolidations merge the corporate, academic, and research enterprises, sometimes under a single large organizational umbrella or sometimes with multiple lines in a more complex, for-profit organizational hierarchy. In terms of patient care, the trend is toward decentralization. The bulk of care is transferred from inpatient to outpatient settings at neighborhood health clinics or outpatient hospital settings. This impacts library services, requiring more arms extended into more communities.

With hospitals consolidating into large, for-profit, multisite organizations, hospital librarians provide sources and services to larger numbers of remote clients.[46] When hospitals close or consolidate, their hospital libraries likewise close or merge.[47] Library services may then be centralized through a remaining hospital library. In other cases, a regional medical library or local academic health sciences library may absorb the services and collections of closed hospital libraries.

In terms of organizational style, the push and pull are somewhat different in special, hospital, and academic libraries. For example, many special and hospital libraries are one-person shops, while academic health sciences libraries may employ dozens of people. In the hospital or special health sciences environment, a librarian is more likely to be a jack of all trades, participating in a broader range of public, technical, administrative, and knowledge service activities throughout the day.

In hospitals, the nature of patient care dictates that everything is a rush. Additionally, many hospital libraries provide concierge-level information services via which any request is answered immediately. A hospital librarian is also more likely to shift rapidly from activity to activity, or work with more individuals in any given day. In fact, flexibility is required for success in hospital librarianship.[48]

In academic health sciences, the departmental structure may promote specialization. For example, an academic health sciences librarian's work may be limited to reference services, educational services, or technical services. This gives one the luxury of specializing in specific and narrower subject areas, and activities. For example, one librarian interviewed for this chapter works with researchers and clinicians on meta-analysis and systematic reviews, for which she spends weeks extensively searching the biomedical databases.[49]

Academic health sciences libraries serve university schools of the health sciences, including medicine, dentistry, nursing, public health, and pharmacy. Clients include doctors, nurses, allied health professionals, faculty, students, administrative staff, research staff, and clinical staff. Academic health sciences libraries also serve university-affiliated hospitals, clinics, or health centers. An academic health sciences library may be open to consumers (i.e., the public). This can translate to 5,000 to 20,000 potential primary and secondary patrons. Interestingly, however, medical libraries are often *not* part of university library systems.

Staggered service levels for varying fees, and with different delivery timeframes, are a common service model among academic health sciences libraries. Fees and timeframes depend on the nature of the request itself or the affiliation of the requestor. A direct patient care request could take precedence over a research request. Rush services may be more expensive.

There are several tenure models under which university librarians operate: (1) tenure track; (2) faculty status, nontenure track; and (3) nonfaculty (staff, administrative) status. In many cases, university librarians are tenure track. To that end, they are required to achieve tenure status, typically in service, research, or teaching. Achieving tenure for excellence in service is typical for university librarians. Nonlibrarian faculty members typically achieve tenure in teaching or research. Librarians fulfill a variety of promotion and tenure-related activities, ranging from engaging in the life of the university and profession, to teaching, to engaging in professional presentations and publications. A dossier of tenure materials is prepared in the fifth or sixth year of employment. The dossier then undergoes extensive internal and external reviews. Tenured librarian faculty members have the same rights, privileges, and responsibilities as all other tenured faculty across the university system.

Other university librarians are staff, which comes with its own set of pros and cons. Staff librarians do not have the clout of faculty but can often be more closely aligned with administration. Nontenure track faculty status runs parallel to the tenure track system in many universities. Some feel that this option is without long-term security, but it is often a matter of personal choice.

Services and Collections

Health sciences library services and service points include those that would be found in any library, such as administration, reference and educational services, technical services, and outreach. Specialized services may include workshops, digitization, and informatics projects such as product (website) development or database development. These specialized services or activities are often grant related or outreach related, or are available to paying or special-tier clients. Some of the activities associated with each service area are outlined in Figure 1.2.

Also, as in any kind of library, services depend on the nature of the primary and secondary clientele. *Primary* clientele are those who are most active in the life of the library itself or who use library resources most heavily. Primary clientele are also

---

Administration
Strategic planning, environmental scanning, fiscal management, grant and proposal writing, personnel management, promotion and advertising, university or hospital administrative activities, and so on.

Public Services
Reference desk and reference question services, literature searching, education activities, liaison activities, website development, multimedia licensing and contract negotiation, vendor relations, licensing, desktop support, statistics gathering and analysis, metadata activities, education and training, workshop development, testing and evaluation, exhibits, consortia activities, clinical medical library or informationist services, collection development, and so on.

Technical Services
Collection development, select and deselection, acquisitions management, materials processing, development and streaming services, metadata activities, website development, multimedia development, streaming services, and so on.

Outreach
Proposal and grant writing, exhibits, promotion and advertising, program development, product development, educational programming, testing and evaluation, exhibits, and so on.

Knowledge Management
Institutional archives and repositories management, database development and management, scholarly communication, and so on.

Figure 1.2   Library Service Points

more likely to contribute to the bottom line. They may pay direct fees for services. Schools or departments may purchase specific collections or pay fees for access to library bibliographic databases. *Secondary* clientele may use the library less frequently, make up a smaller percentage of the total clientele, or contribute less funding and input into library purchases and collections.

In healthcare, the most current and relevant information is published in the biomedical journals. Thus, the core of any library's collection will be healthcare journals. The average academic health sciences library holds approximately 200,000 monographs and 4,000 electronic serials.[50] Ninety-one percent of academic health sciences libraries' current journal subscriptions and 26 percent of book purchases are electronic formats.[51] Certainly, the National Institutes of Health public access policy eases collection burdens, with larger numbers of articles available online free of charge through PubMed Central.[52, 53]

Health sciences library collections also vary according to the makeup of the primary and secondary clientele. Client categories include administrative personnel (*Hospitals and Health Networks [HHN]*), clinical (*Journal of the American Medical Association [JAMA]*), and basic sciences/research (*Brain*) clients. Hospital and special libraries typically have very small collections of the core clinical journals and core clinical reference texts. Academic health sciences libraries collect more broadly in the clinical and research sciences. They may have specialty collections that represent unique areas of the health center, such as cardiology, genomics, or consumer health.

Academic health sciences libraries often have modest noncirculating reference collections. Reference materials are those that are used most heavily by the library staff, usually for addressing reference questions. Noncirculating or limited-circulation course textbooks and workbook collections may be available. Circulating collections range in size from fewer than 100 books to hundreds of thousands of monographs, depending on the size of the library and of the organization it serves. Remote storage for older materials has been necessary for many academic health sciences libraries that suffered from overcrowding. However, with electronic journals replacing printed collections, more space may now be available on site, easing the need for off-site storage.

Reference and technical services librarians can invest considerable time doing collection development and filtering large numbers of publications to introduce into the library's collection. Collection development also includes negotiating vendor licenses and managing access to electronic collections through the library's website. Collection development is not just about library-based print and electronic resources; it is also about knowledge management and the generation of new knowledge through database development for institutional records and archives management. "The health information professional not only provides specific support to the institution by using new technologies to organize, synthesize, and filter information for scholarly, clinical, and institutional decision making, but also plays a critical role in the investigation and study of information storage, organization, use, and application in education, patient care, and generation of new knowledge."[54]

Health sciences librarians, particularly those in business-savvy libraries, also provide a high level of administrative information services with tools and information that assist administrators in making informed decisions. Benchmarking and competitive intelligence activities provide a level of support that makes the library more valuable to the organization's administration. In these environments, librarians participate in strategic planning committees and activities, and partner deliberately and proactively with the whole realm of administrators.

In the course of any given day, health sciences librarians spend their time teaching, searching MEDLINE, attending meetings or conferences, answering reference questions, troubleshooting computers, maintaining library systems or websites, building tutorials, and so on. Librarians consult with faculty, staff, or students; prepare grants, presentations, or publications; and do administrative work like writing reports, budgets, or evaluations.[55-58] To do this work, librarians must have intimate knowledge of the biomedical literature databases (MEDLINE, PubMed, etc.), knowledge of the literature of the field in which they are working, and knowledge of the issues and trends that impact medicine. They must also possess the administrative and leadership skills that are necessary to function successfully in the healthcare environment.

Teaching Librarians: Educational Programming in Health Sciences Libraries

The educational mission of the organization is served through health sciences library educational programming. This is an important area of library services because information literacy skills are critical to academic success and lifelong learning, and one must teach these skills. This is where librarians come in. Librarians are highly qualified to teach and promote these skills, particularly in the academic setting. Educational service models may look very different in special, hospital library, and academic environments. In hospital libraries, for instance, educational programming typically revolves around nursing and residency (post-M.D.) programs. Hospital librarians teach PubMed and OVID, bibliographic management, electronic mail, or skills for evidence-based practice, literature searching, and so on. Academic health sciences libraries are usually heavily engaged in educational programming with several of the university schools of the health sciences, including the schools of medicine, nursing, or pharmacy. In fact, *AAHSL: Tomorrow's Libraries Today* reported that 96 percent of full-time equivalent (FTE) health sciences librarians were engaged in teaching activities.[59] In both hospitals and academic environments, consumer education is typically grant related or outreach related to very specific, small populations of consumers.

In terms of duties or activities, a teaching librarian schedules workshops, coordinates required facilities, loads required software, and plans, executes, and evaluates library training and educational programming. Annual education statistics—including number of teaching hours, number of hours spent preparing, numbers of orientations, numbers of workshops, numbers of students, and so forth—are collected and published annually through the Association of Academic Health Sciences Libraries.

Health sciences libraries, particularly academic health sciences libraries, may implement a four-pronged approach to their training and educational programming:

1. Curriculum-integrated information retrieval, management, and evaluation skills workshops
2. Stand-alone workshops
3. Distance and web-based tutorials and instructional support
4. Outreach and grant-related training opportunities

A curriculum-integrated educational program is typically the keystone of a teaching library's educational program. Key health sciences courses are strategically targeted for the inclusion of information retrieval and management workshops. Often, the model for curriculum-integrated instruction is through liaison programs in which each member of the reference staff participates as a subject expert for one or several subject areas. Liaisons serve as the primary resources, consultants, and teachers to faculty, staff, and students in those subject areas' schools and departments. Liaisons attend department meetings or work closely with the office of medical education to identify, plan, and evaluate information resources and options for supporting the curriculum. They may also sit on curriculum committees and educational resources committees to coordinate library and information resources with curricular needs. Liaisons may be "embedded" in specific departments and activities. Embedded librarians may work primarily outside of the library setting, engaging in departmental activities as the team's information expert. This model may be expensive to implement, as embedded librarians are highly specialized to one department or subject team.

Library educational programs often combine traditional, resource-based bibliographic instruction with more sophisticated information literacy skills education that includes elements of critical thinking and problem solving.[60] Skills specific to searching, evaluating, and analyzing information resources and formats within a lifelong learning framework are emphasized.

The second prong of academic health sciences libraries' educational programs is the "by request" option, which makes training opportunities available to groups or individuals at their request as stand-alone workshops. The primary goals of this model are (1) scheduling flexibility that allows faculty, staff, and students to participate in training at dates and times that are convenient for them and (2) content flexibility that allows participants to come to a session with specific questions, issues, or problems that will be immediately addressed and resolved. Libraries also offer MEDLINE and information skills training through their collections of web-based instructional tutorials.

Distance and online courses are the third prong of health sciences libraries' educational programs. In environments in which the curriculum is already overloaded and students may be scattered across remote clinical sites, instructors and librarians are continually challenged to take advantage of independent virtual learning opportunities. Librarians develop course websites and tutorials to provide effective and sequential training for information retrieval skills, for problem-based learning, or for evidence-based practice.

Health sciences libraries also participate in grant and outreach-related health education programming through face-to-face workshops, or through subject-specific or project-specific websites. Project websites promote grant activities or supplement library-based instruction by providing a central location for resources, information about the grant, or information about the library and its services, policies, and resources. These tools also provide links to select textbooks, journals, and other web-based materials and educational tools that are appropriate for the specific project.

A Rose by Any Other Name: The Informationist

Lucretia McClure's 2003 *Journal of the Medical Library Association* editorial discussed the changing roles of health sciences librarians in the constantly shifting healthcare market. Yet much of our work had remained constant: "a rose by any other name."[61] This brings to mind the roles of the *research informationist* and *clinical informationist* in today's marketplace. A *research informationist* may be intimately involved in research and publication, including usability, testing, evaluation, statistical analysis, and other activities. Research informationists may conduct meta-analyses, scanning the entirety of the literature for all of the materials published on specific topics.[62] They may also be involved in metadata and knowledge management projects.

Clinical medical librarians (CMLs) were fairly common before and during the era of managed care in the 1990s. However, the twenty-first century saw a drop-off of formal CML programs, largely due to the expense involved in dedicating librarians to specific clinical departments.[63] Although the role of the clinical informationist is reminiscent of that of the clinical medical librarian, these roles differ in several ways.[64, 65] Like CMLs, clinical informationists work primarily in the clinical setting. Clinical informationists attend daily medical rounds and meetings, and provide quality-filtered, evidence-based information to support clinical questions.[66] On average, the typical clinician (doctor) has between four and five clinical questions each day.[67] The role of the informationist is to provide information support with which to address these questions. At the same time, a librarian's role does *not* include translating clinical content or providing direct answers to clinical questions.

Clinical informationists differ from CMLs in other important ways. First, CMLs were based in libraries and were library-centric. Informationists, in contrast, are not necessarily employed by libraries. They are employed by clinical or research departments as members of multidisciplinary teams with expertise within one or across several departments and subject areas. The informationist serves as the conduit to information tools and resources within these teams, conducting research, quality-filtering content, finding evidence-based materials, or conducting meta-analyses. Other activities include data mining, data translation, knowledge management, project development, web management, and myriad other information-centric activities.[68]

Second, there are educational differences between CMLs and informationists. The education required of a health sciences librarian includes a B.A. or B.S. and a master's degree in library science, information science (or an equivalent degree). Health sciences librarians may hold second master's degrees in specific subject areas. Informationists are expected to have a second master's degree in the biomedical sciences, or a doctoral-level degree in the clinical sciences or biomedical sciences. This level of education is expensive and requires a fairly high salary once in the workplace. In the current economy, many libraries are not able to pay these salaries. Therefore, there has not been a significant increase in the numbers of library-employed informationist positions in the past several years.[69]

CONTEXT FOR PRACTICE: THE HEALTHCARE ENVIRONMENT

The healthcare industry is 17 percent of the gross domestic product in the United States.[70] The healthcare system treats millions of patients each year and employs hundreds of thousands of people nationwide. In some regions, healthcare systems are the largest employers in the city or state.[71] Healthcare is changing at an astounding rate, with mergers and consolidations just one factor in an industry whose single constant has been continual organizational upheaval. In the current climate of consumer accountability, public oversight, cost containment, and a focus on health services outcomes and patient safety, healthcare is under constant scrutiny.[72] A goal of managed care services includes assessing and measuring quality of care for continuous improvement that leads to cost containment. Librarians, like all players in healthcare—as in any other industry—must operate more cost effectively to ensure cost containment and positive patient outcomes.

Awareness and understanding of healthcare's "volatile context is a critical prerequisite for health sciences librarians to be able to define and redefine their role."[73] It is within this volatile environment that health sciences librarians explore the potential of new technologies to gather, store, archive, manage, filter, and deliver first information, then knowledge. New technologies are regularly available for gathering, storing, and managing information for delivery to traditional and nontraditional clientele in standard, multimedia, mobile, and new formats.[74] Librarians also use these technologies to streamline our work and that of our colleagues.

Where Information and Technology Converge

Cleveland's model of healthcare (see Figure 1.3) is a useful framework for understanding the influences and trends that drive the healthcare system. It represents healthcare as the intersection of information and technology. *Information* (scholarly communication, open access, digitization, semantic web) and *technology* (mobile, wearable, social media, Internet, cloud computing) form the core components of the healthcare environment. This combination is embedded within a triad of the three keystone elements of healthcare: clinical practice, research, and consumers.

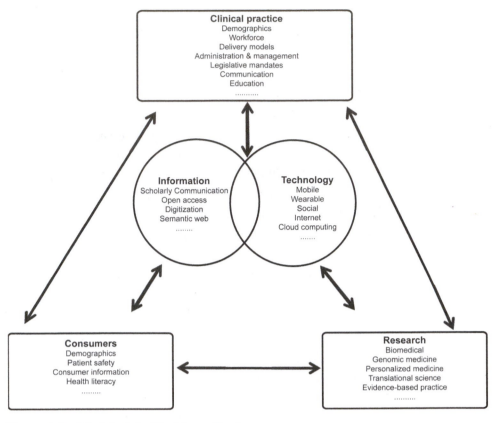

Figure 1.3   Model of the Healthcare Environment

The arrows represent the dynamic nature of healthcare: It is generated by ever-changing interplay between variables within a constantly shifting environment.[75]

Here, health sciences librarians are at the intersection of two major driving forces in healthcare: information and technology. Health sciences librarians "provide specific support to the institution by using new technologies to organize, synthesize, and filter information for scholarly, clinical, and institutional decision making."[76] They also play an important role in the investigation and "study of information storage, organization, use, and application in education, patient care, and generation of new knowledge."[77] The primary areas of healthcare in which librarians serve are clinical practice, research, and consumer health. Within these areas, themes as varied as healthcare education, evidence-based practice, the electronic medical record, patient safety, cost containment, and others are also important to understanding the nature of healthcare and librarianship today. These are discussed here.

Clinical Practice

Clinical practice is the keystone of healthcare. "Clinical practice" and "clinical care" refer to patient care or "direct patient care" activities. Personnel involved in clinical practice are medical doctors as well as practitioners in nursing, the allied health fields (occupational therapy, physical therapy, physician assistants, etc.), dentistry, pharmacy, public health, hospital administrators, and other health workers on all levels. These clinicians work in large and small healthcare teams for patient care, and for the administration and operation of the organization. Clinical healthcare teams are typically headed by medical doctors, followed by the professional-level nursing staff, then support care staff. High-level administrative teams are led by hospital administrators, who are often M.D.s or have health administration and/or public health advanced degrees (MPH).

Hospitals are organized into "units" or "floors" based on disease or treatment types: general surgery, neonatology, pediatrics, oncology, intensive care unit, intensive pulmonary critical care unit, and others. Hospitals are the primary teaching location for most healthcare practitioners. Doctors, nurses, and pharmacists, for instance, are required to work hundreds of hours on site in clinical rotations.

Medical school assumes a bachelor's degree and a high score on the Medical College Admission Test (MCAT). Problem-based learning, team-based learning, and an emphasis on lifelong learning continue to characterize medical education in the early twenty-first century. Healthcare education, specifically medical education, is changing the way in which it recruits and teaches. This is due, in large part, to the ongoing shortage of primary care physicians.[78] Doctors go into higher paid specialties. Like all careers, educational debt is an issue, as is the desire to benefit financially in one's career.

Medical school is four years in length, during which students take the USMLE (United States Medical Licensing) exams in years two and four. The M.D. is earned upon graduation from medical school. At that point, the new medical doctors go into full-time clinical residency programs in specialty accreditation and licensure areas. These could include cosmetic surgery, general surgery, neurosurgery, internal medicine, obstetrics/gynecology, pediatrics, podiatry, and many others. Most residency programs range between three and five years in length, and result in licensure or accreditation in the field of specialty.

Nursing education is more complicated, with degree options ranging from nine-month licensed practical nurse degrees (LPN) to two-year associate degree programs and four-year bachelor's degrees in nursing (BSN). The BSN may be followed by a master degree (MSN) and doctoral degree (Ph.D. or DNS) in specialty areas such as oncology, cardiac nursing, pediatrics, or critical care. Nurses also earn a myriad of certification options, such as a degree in nurse midwifery or the certified registered nurse practitioner (CRNP) degree. In some states, nurse practitioners can write medication prescriptions. In other states, they cannot write prescriptions without M.D. supervision.

Allied health careers also range from nine-month certification programs to doctoral programs, depending on the subject area and level of specialty achieved. Careers could include phlebotomy, X-ray technician, occupational therapy, physical therapy, child health, and more. Doctor extenders are D.O.s and physician assistants. In some states, they can write prescriptions independently of a physician.

Clinical practice is grounded in patient care, which typically assumes that a patient is in the bed waiting for a decision that will impact on his or her life. With this assumption, the clinical practice environment is characterized by its "do it now," fast-paced, and highly technical orientation. Early adopters focus more effectively in this evidence-based, outcomes-focused, cutting-edge environment. In anticipation of and in response to their clientele, health sciences librarians too have also always been early adopters of information technologies.

Librarians' roles in clinical practice are significant and varied. These include heavy information literacy teaching responsibilities in undergraduate and graduate medical education, as well as in nursing education. Librarians provide basic and concierge-level reference and information services, including basic and complex MEDLINE, PubMed, and biomedical journal literature searching. Librarians, clinical informationists, and clinical medical librarians also attend morning report and medical rounds, and participate on patient care teams. Services are often fee-based in health sciences libraries, particularly in academic and corporate environments.

Problem-Based Learning and Team-Based Learning in Medical Education

Another area that has increased academic health sciences librarians' visibility as partners in the educational enterprise of the university is problem-based learning (PBL) in medical education. PBL is a process through which students gather in small teams to study real or fictitious patient cases. They discuss the cases, identify what they do and do not know, go out and find information to address questions that they have, and come back and report to the team. In problem-based learning, faculty members do not direct or lead the process. Instead, the faculty role is to facilitate learning by supporting, guiding, and monitoring the process.[79]

The PBL environment is designed so that specific educational objectives can be met while also providing a forum for students to apply problem-solving skills directly to clinical cases. It is based on the belief that knowledge is remembered and applied more easily if self-directed learning takes place in a setting that allows for immediate application of new concepts. This approach allows for the immediate practical application of acquired skills and knowledge and enables students to learn about scientific decision making, clinical reasoning, and the humanistic approach to patient interaction.[80]

Problem-based learning often includes intensive information requirements. The literature indicates that training in the proper use of information is crucial to successful information seeking and management in PBL.[81] This has offered significant new roles and challenges for libraries, including the opportunity for intensive "point of need," curriculum-integrated instruction. PBL may also necessitate significant and advanced coordination of library tools and resources. Librarians work closely with case coordinators or act as clinical case coordinators to prepare for the information seeking part of the PBL course. Librarians also serve as information consultants to one or several small learning teams, or they participate as small team faculty facilitators.[82]

Team-based learning (TBL), which is similar to PBL, has become popular as an alternative to traditional problem-based learning. Team-based learning is more flexible in terms of methodology and does not require large numbers of small teams (8–25), each with a faculty facilitator. TBL is less tightly structured in terms of resources required and the specifics of the team process.

Evidence-Based Practice

Evidence-based practice (EBP) is another area of healthcare that stands out as having engaged librarians in clinical care. Evidence-based practice (evidence-based medicine, evidence-based nursing, evidence-based librarianship, etc.) is defined as "the conscientious, explicit and judicious use of current best evidence in making decisions about the care of individual patients."[83] Through evidence-based practice, healthcare practitioners find and use the best evidence (e.g., the gold standard literature) to help them make decisions about patient care: treatment, diagnosis, cause and harm, and prognosis (outcome) decisions. The gold standard literature is made up of those journal articles that represent the best available, most rigorous research on the topic. These are typically randomized controlled trials (RCTs).

The five steps in EBP are:

1. Formulate the clinical question.
2. Search for the best evidence.
3. Critically appraise the evidence.
4. Apply the evidence to patient care.
5. Evaluate the use of evidence-based practice on patient outcomes.[84]

Each of these five steps requires a unique approach and a unique set of skills. Therefore, learning how to practice evidence-based medicine requires work, study, and practice. Librarians are heavily involved in EBP because it requires a real understanding of literature searching, through MEDLINE, the Cochrane databases, and other bibliographic resources. EBP requires specific strategies for retrieving RCTs and other gold standard literature on any given topic. Health sciences librarians have taken positive advantage of this market, making a strong niche for themselves in teaching healthcare providers about EBP, specifically the literature searching part of EBP. In hospitals or evidence-heavy academic environments, librarians may spend significant time teaching evidence-based searching methods to medical and nursing students, residents, and medical faculty.

The Electronic Medical Record

The electronic medical record is another important innovation in healthcare that involves librarians at multiple levels. The development of the electronic medical record (EMR) and electronic health records (EHR) was driven by the American Recovery and Reinvestment Act, better known as the Stimulus Act of 2009.[85] The EMR has since attracted the attention of the Institute of Medicine and other national organizations. Policy development and funding for electronic medical records is grounded in developing systems to impact future healthcare quality and costs.[86, 87] However, a disconnect exists between public expectations of the electronic medical record versus what has been delivered to date. Electronic medical records are plagued with problems due to system incompatibility, system glitches, and usability problems. The goal remains to create an electronic medical record that can be easily retrieved and updated at any clinical site in any location nationwide.[88] Librarians are involved in this effort as they seek to integrate targeted and tailored bibliographic information directly into the electronic health record.[89]

Research

The research arena is the second cornerstone of healthcare in which librarians are integral. Biomedical researchers are typically clinical scientists or basic scientists. The education of basic scientists includes bachelor's degrees in a basic science such as biology, biochemistry, chemistry, or another field, followed by master's and doctoral degrees in specialty areas such as biochemistry or cytology. Clinical scientists and research scientists may have an M.D., an M.D./Ph.D. (a seven-year postbachelor degree option), or a Ph.D. These degrees are offered by schools of medicine or, sometimes, schools of public health. Clinical scientists (M.D.s) usually see patients on a regular basis and conduct part-time research in the clinical settings. Research scientists (basic scientists) typically hold a Ph.D. They conduct laboratory-based research in biochemistry, hematology, immunology, and many other areas.

Because researchers are funded in part by grant monies, their work is heavily impacted by U.S. government funding, particularly that of the National Institutes of Health (NIH). In fact, the U.S. government is one of the largest healthcare research funders in the world. Biomedical research remains under high scrutiny due to national attention (politicization) that is focused on cost containment in managed healthcare. The rate of NIH funding has remained stagnant since 2003, at or below the level of inflation.[90] Patients who participate in research are typically recruited into large clinical trials of therapies and drug regimes, often sponsored by government organizations such as the National Cancer Institute (NCI).

Health Services Research

Health services research is another important area. In fact, health services research has gained increased interest from the Agency for Healthcare Research and Quality, and the Institute of Medicine (IOM). Health services research primarily focuses on cost containment, that is, the bottom line. It identifies the most effective ways to organize, manage, finance, and deliver high-quality care; reduce medical errors; and improve patient safety.[91] This research does not focus on therapies, like clinical trials do, but on the efficiencies of the healthcare system itself—everything from whether patients arrive to their appointments on time to the efficiencies of clinical dashboards.[92, 93]

Translational research—that is, research that moves quickly "from bench to bedside"—is desirable in a setting in which one goal of research is to impact clinical practice. Translation research "translates" research findings into clinical practice more quickly and efficiently for the improvement of healthcare and wellness. Research is typically slow to move from bench to bedside. Therefore, a goal of translational research is to speed the process by which research findings are used in practice. Quick publication turnaround, open access, and desktop delivery increase the speed by which the journal literature is available for use.

Librarians may work on research teams as *research informationists*. They draw on experience and expertise in clinical and academic settings to serve the information-based clinical, research, educational, and administration functions of their environments. These environments can be hospital, academic health sciences, corporate, special, or others. In the research environment, health sciences librarians may conduct research and teach, conducting library education programming for students in the basic sciences, toxicology, genetics, and other areas. This role requires deep understanding of the importance of the integration and connection between the basic sciences and clinical aspects of the medical curriculum.

Consumer Health and Patient Self-Management

Another cornerstone of Cleveland's model of the healthcare system is the *consumer*. A health *consumer* is any person who uses health information or is interested in some aspect of healthcare. In contrast, a *patient* is someone who is already part of the healthcare system, already having been diagnosed with a disease or condition and seeing a particular physician or physician extender. With millions of Americans searching the web for healthcare information each year, consumer health is a million-dollar industry.[94] Thousands of health-related resources and websites are available both free of charge and for a fee.

Librarians have been rigorously engaged in consumer health for decades, with significant funding coming from the National Institutes of Health, the National Library of Medicine, the National Network of Libraries of Medicine, and the Regional Medical Libraries program. Outreach includes services, web resources (webographies, tutorials), and online and face-to-face information skills training on a wide variety of topics ranging from PubMed searching skills, to evaluating websites, to clinical trials resources for myriad consumer groups. Librarians partner with multi-institutional, multidisciplinary partners such as public health agencies, hospitals, and hospital systems for the distribution of educational and information outreach.

Consumers are an important part of the healthcare triad. Several of the most significant issues arising out of consumer health are literacy, health literacy, health information literacy, and numeracy issues. "Literacy" refers to a person's ability to read and understand what he or she has read. [95] "Health literacy" is the degree to which individuals have the capacity to obtain, process, and understand basic health information (health information literacy) and services needed to make appropriate health decisions.[96] "Numeracy" is the ability to understand numbers, such as the skills and knowledge required to apply arithmetic operations. These functions include understanding percentages, statistics, tables and charts, and how to use a checkbook. Numeracy impacts patients' understanding of health instructions and information, particularly because health risk and prevention information is often presented in numerical and graphical formats. In addition, the bulk of health-related information on the Internet is written at a college level, while the average American adult reads at or below the ninth-grade level.[97]

Basic literacy (reading levels), health literacy, and health information literacy are barriers to efficacious information seeking and usage.[98, 99] Eleven million U.S. adults are illiterate in English, and 7.8 million senior citizens can perform only the most simple and concrete literacy tasks.[100] These adults cannot read a prescription bottle or prescription insert, or follow simple written directions. Therefore, even if patients receive quality information and education, they may not be equipped to put into practice efficacious self-management activities.[101]

Health literacy, or the skills required to understand and act on health information, is another of the least recognized, yet most widespread, challenges to achieving better health outcomes and lowering healthcare costs in the United States. By some estimates, low health literacy is estimated to cost the U.S. healthcare system more than $58 billion each year, yet many healthcare providers and patients remain largely unaware of the extent of this problem.[102]

Librarians have been heavily involved in health information literacy advocacy. For example, through the Medical Library Association's Health Information Literacy (HIL) project and other initiatives, librarians work with clinicians and consumers to increase their awareness of the impact of literacy issues on healthcare, on their own medical practice, and on their own health.[103] Through HIL, hospital librarians across the country distributed an MLA-produced curriculum for training providers in hospital settings. Providers and nurses can then use this information within their own medical practices. The National Library of Medicine has sponsored health literacy–related funding opportunities for the development and dissemination of strategies, systems, and services for promoting health literacy and health information literacy through primary care, hospital libraries, and other routes. The field's understanding of the issues, and the roles it can play in health literacy and health information literacy, are expanded through practice and research.

Another important trend in consumer health has to do with the increasing interest in *patient self-management* in the primary care setting. Consumer advocacies combined with technology access have created a large empowered pool of health consumers worldwide. No longer is information flow controlled from the top down, or even primarily from provider to patient. Patient self-management is based on the idea that professionals are experts about disease, but patients are experts about their own lives and experiences. Consumers and ePatients use information and communication technologies to share information with providers and one another. Consumerism has changed the patient-doctor relationship. Knowledge makes its way up the chain, changing the ways in which patients are diagnosed and treated.[104, 105] This patient-provider partnership paradigm involves two components: (1) collaborative care, through which patients and providers share mutual responsibility in healthcare decision making and (2) patient self-management education, which promotes self-efficacy by providing patients with problem-solving skills and behavioral management tools. These two components are closely interrelated, as the success of each depends on the implementation of the other.[106]

A goal also remains to integrate best evidence more aggressively into patient practice through the integration of the gold standard materials into clinical care systems.[107] Librarians have myriad opportunities to integrate into patient self-management activities, although one barrier is logistical: There are thousands of primary care settings with which to work. All are remote, however, meaning that streaming services and resources becomes a particular challenge.

TRENDS IN HEALTH SCIENCES LIBRARIANSHIP

In addition to the trends and issues discussed earlier—translational research, medical education, the electronic medical record, health services research, patient self-management, and others—there are a plethora of trends that impact and are impacted by health sciences librarianship. The majority of themes driving healthcare are grounded in informed decision making and shared decision making in outcomes-based, evidence-based environments. These trends are broadly related to healthcare and more specific to librarianship or health sciences libraries. Each trend includes a unique set of opportunities and challenges to librarians and the healthcare industry alike.

The move toward government-sponsored healthcare for all Americans, for example, is a political hotbed in the United States today. It is an open question as to whether this will result in better healthcare for all, but increasing numbers of insured Americans may result in more people seeking care. More patients can have a tremendous impact on consumer health and consumer services in health sciences libraries.

Cost containment is another issue impacting health sciences libraries. We are impacted by higher education economic problems, transformations in medical education, and decreasing levels of NIH funding. Since 2003, there has been a trend of flat or below-inflation funding for the NIH.[108] Reduced and flat funding directly impacts biomedical libraries' abilities to achieve funding of their own and benefit from a trickle-down effect when university or hospital faculty and clinicians achieve NIH funding.

Another important issue impacting our field is the NIH public access policy. Often confused with open access, the NIH public health access policy dictates that the results of NIH-funded research be made freely available via PubMed Central within 12 months of acceptance for publication. In early 2013, the White House Office of Science and Technology Policy issued a policy that applies to federal agencies that spend more than $100 million a year to support research and development. These agencies are likewise called upon to develop plans to make publicly available within a year of publication the results of research they support. The new policy also requires scientific data from unclassified, federally supported research. These policies impact clients' expectations and libraries' abilities to provide access to important and timely evidence. Librarians are also well positioned to clear up confusion and educate clients about the realities of these public access policies.[109, 110]

Librarians are also challenged to continually distinguish themselves from *informatics* professionals, particularly in the research arena. While related, informatics is a unique discipline. Informatics uses technology to solve problems and is technology focused and technology driven.[111] At the same time, informatics researchers now work in domains traditionally associated with libraries and information workers.[112–114] Librarians should be integral leaders in these research and grant seeking efforts.

Other trends and issues central to health sciences librarianship include:

- Scholarly communication
- Metadata (big data)
- Universal integration of the electronic medical record
- ePatients
- Library revenue
- The informationist
- Decision care teams
- And others!

CONCLUSION

This chapter defined and described health sciences librarianship in terms of the field's professional competencies and standards from the ALA, SLA, and MLA. Professional organizations' roles in the life of the field were overviewed, as were the keystone areas in healthcare: clinical practice, research, and consumers. Trends and issues in healthcare and health sciences librarianship were discussed. This chapter also reiterated librarians' role in healthcare: integrating technology tools to store, communicate, and format information and knowledge for the future. "Information and technology are fundamental to health care. Changing health care and the advent of sophisticated information technology are impacting the way health information is generated, published, organized, accessed, communicated, shared, and used. The effect can be felt in clinical, research, and consumerism environments."[115]

The saying "there is nothing new under the sun" seems incompatible with the technological advances in today's libraries. That librarian in ancient Alexandria would certainly not agree if he saw today's marvelous new technologies and the sheer volume of information that is available. The nature of the challenge of information access and use remain the same, however. Where does the customer find information and seek knowledge? Or more to the point, how do we, as librarians, go about keeping it all organized so that it is accessible and useful before it turns into a pile of just so much paper or just so many dots and dashes on an unfocused screen?

As illustrated here, a constant theme in health sciences librarianship is technology-driven or information-driven *change*. Change happens continually—and is an integral part of our professional lives. Being at the forefront of information technologies is a dizzying ride in the twenty-first-century information environment. This is to be expected when one chooses health sciences librarianship and ultimately makes for an exciting career. Health sciences librarians who do it right are never bored and are always intellectually challenged. They enjoy their professional lives.

NOTES

1. Lynch, C. "Medical Libraries, Bioinformatics, and Networked Information: A Coming Convergence?" *Bulletin of the Medical Library Association* 87 (1999 October): 408–414.

2. Starr, Susan. "The Customer versus the Container." *Journal of the Medical Library Association: JMLA* 98 (2010): 95–96.

3. Watson, Linda A. "Health Sciences Environment." In *Health Sciences Environment and Librarianship in Health Sciences Libraries*, 1–21. New York: Forbes Custom Publishing, 1999.

4. Cleveland, Ana D. "Miles to Go before We Sleep: Education, Technology, and the Changing Paradigms in Health Information." *Journal of the Medical Library Association: JMLA* 99 (January 2011): 61–69.

5. Abels, Eileen, Rebecca Jones, John Latham, Dee Magnoni, and Joanne Gard Marshall. "Competencies for Information Professionals of the 21st Century." Special Libraries Association. Last modified June 2003. http://www.sla.org/PDFs/Competencies2003_revised.pdf.

6. Ibid., 1.

7. Ibid.

8. "Competencies for Lifelong Learning and Professional Success: The Educational Policy Statement of the Medical Library Association." Medical Library Association. Last modified May 2007. http://mlanet.org/pdf/ce/200705_edu_policy.pdf.

9. Ibid., 3.

10. Ibid., 7.

11. Ibid.

12. Ibid.

13. Moore, Mary. "Overview of Health Sciences Libraries and Librarianship." In *Introduction to Health Sciences Librarianship*, 3–27. New York: Haworth, 2008.

14. "ALA's Core Competencies of Librarianship." American Library Association. Last modified January 2009. http://www.ala.org/educationcareers/sites/ala.org.educationcareers/files/content/careers/corecomp/corecompetences/finalcorecompstat09.pdf.

15. Ibid.

16. Abels et al., *op cit.*

17. Ibid., 1.

18. "Competencies for Lifelong Learning and Professional Success." Medical Library Association, 3.

19. Ibid., 3.

20. Ibid., 7

21. Ibid., 4–5.

22. Ibid., 3.

23. Ibid., 15–17.

24. Cleveland, Ana D., *op. cit.*, 61–69.

25. Raszewski, Rebecca. "A Survey of Librarians with a Health Sciences Background." *Journal of the Medical Library Association: JMLA* 99 (2011): 304–306.

26. Scherrer, Carol S. "Evaluating a Health Sciences Library Residency Program: What Have We Learned?" *Journal of the Medical Library Association: JMLA* 98 (2010): 300–302.

27. Detlefsen, Ellen G. "What Should We Be Teaching in Library and Information Programs?" *MLA News* 52 (2012): 1, 7.

28. Detlefsen, Ellen G. "A Snapshot of the Health of Medical Library Education and Recognition of Our Educator Colleagues." *MLA News* 50 (2010): 1, 14–15.

29. Ibid., 1.

30. "ALA's Core Competencies of Librarianship." American Library Association, 1–5.

31. "The Academy of Health Information Professionals." Medical Library Association. Last modified May 12, 2012. http://www.mlanet.org/academy/.

32. "National Library of Medicine." National Library of Medicine. Last modified February 12, 2013. http://www.nlm.nih.gov/.

33. "Facts Sheet: MEDLINE." National Library of Medicine. Last modified February 20, 2012. http://www.nlm.nih.gov/pubs/factsheets/medline.html.

34. "National Network of Libraries of Medicine." National Network of Libraries of Medicine. Last modified May 12, 2012. http://nnlm.gov/.

35. "Medical Library Association." Medical Library Association. Last modified February 21, 2013. http://www.mlanet.org/.

36. "Information for JMLA Authors and Reviewers." Medical Library Association. Last modified February 21, 2013. http://www.mlanet.org/publications/jmla/author_reviewer_info.html.

37. "Association of Academic Health Sciences Libraries." Association of Academic Health Sciences Libraries. Last modified February 25, 2013. http://www.aahsl.org/.

38. Ibid.

39. "About the CHLA." Canadian Health Libraries Association / Association des bibliothèques de la santé du Canada. Last modified April 14, 2007. http://www.chla-absc.ca/node/29.

40. Holst, Ruth, Carla J. Funk, Heidi S. Adams, Margaret Bandy, Catherine Mary Boss, Beth Hill, Claire B. Joseph, and Rosalind K. Lett. "Vital Pathways for Hospital Librarians: Present and Future Roles." *Journal of the Medical Library Association: JMLA* 97 (2009): 285–292.

41. Holst, Ruth. "RETHINK Our Value and Our Roles: Presidential Priorities for 2010/11." *MLA News* 50 (2010): 1, 9.

42. Elizabeth Whipple. Interview by Katherine Schilling. Indiana University, October 22, 2012.

43. Chastain-Warheit, Christine, and Barbara Henry. "How Hospital Librarians Can Demonstrate Internal Revenue Service–Mandated 'Community Benefit' for Their Nonprofit Organizations: Reflecting on Value Provided and Connecting the Hospital Library to 'Community Benefit.'" Edited by Claire B. Joseph. *MLA News* 50 (2010): 1, 7.

44. Holst, Ruth, et al., *op. cit.*, 292.

45. Miller, Dick R. "Identities and Relationships: Parallels between Metadata and Professional Relevance." *Journal of the Medical Library Association: JMLA* 100 (2012): 83–86.

46. Tooey, Mary Joan. "A Pathway for Hospital Librarians: Why Is It Vital?" *Journal of the Medical Library Association: JMLA* 97 (2009): 268–272.

47. Thibodeau, Patricia L., and Carla J. Funk. "Trends in Hospital Librarianship and Hospital Library Services, 1989 to 2006." *Journal of the Medical Library Association: JMLA* 97 (2009): 273–279.

48. Elizabeth Whipple. Interview by Katherine Schilling. October 22, 2012.

49. Elaine Skopelja, Interview by Katherine Schilling, October 17, 2012.

50. Association of Research Libraries. "ARL Academic Health Sciences Library Statistics, 2009–2010." Last Modified February 2012. http://www.arl.org/stats/annualsurveys/med/index.shtml.

51. Ibid., 1.

52. McGowan, Julie J. "Tomorrow's Academic Health Sciences Library Today." *Journal of the Medical Library Association: JMLA* 100 (2012): 43–46.

53. Brewer, Michelle Volesko. "Why Shold You Care about the National Institutes of Health Public Access Policy?" *MLA News* 412 (January 2009): 1, 15–16.

54. Medical Library Association, *op. cit.*, 7.

55. Moore, Mary. "Overview of Health Sciences Libraries and Librarianship." In *Introduction to Health Sciences Librarianship*. Philadelphia: Haworth, 2008.

56. Elizabeth Whipple. Interview by Katherine Schilling. Indiana University, October 17, 2012.

57. Elaine Skopelja. Interview by Katherine Schilling. Indiana University, October 21, 2012.

58. Rankin, Jocelyn A., Susan F. Grefsheim, and Candace C. Canto. "The Emerging Informationist Specialty: A Systematic Review of the Literature." *Journal of the Medical Library Association: JMLA* 96 (2008): 194–206.

59. Association of Research Libraries. "ARL Academic Health Sciences Library Statistics, 2009–2010."

60. Schilling, Katherine, David S. Ginn, Patricia Michelson, and Loren H. Roth. "Integration of Information-Seeking Skills and Activities into a Problem-Based Curriculum." *Bulletin of the Medical Library Association* 83 (April 1995): 176–183.

61. McClure, L. W. "A Rose Is a Rose." *Journal of the Medical Library Association: JMLA* 91 (2003): 144–146.

62. Rankin, Jocelyn, et al., *op. cit.*, 194–206.

63. Klein-Fedyshin, Michele. "It Was the Worst of Times, It Was the Best of Times: Positive Trends Influencing Hospital Libraries." *Journal of the Medical Library Association: JMLA* 98 (2010): 196–198.

64. McGowan, Julie J. "Tomorrow's Academic Health Sciences Library Today." *Journal of the Medical Library Association: JMLA* 100 (2012): 43–46.

65. Elizabeth Whipple. Interview by Katherine Schilling. Indiana University, October 18, 2012.

66. Elaine Skopelja. Interview by Katherine Schilling. Indiana University, October 21, 2012.

67. Osheroff, J. A., D. E. Forsythe, B. G. Buchanan, R. A. Bankowitz, B. H. Blumenfeld, and R. A. Miller. "Physicians' Information Needs: Analysis of Questions Posed during Clinical Teaching." *Annals of Internal Medicine* 114 (April 1991): 576–581.

68. Denise Rumschlag. Interview by Katherine Schilling. Indiana University, October 18, 2012.

69. Rankin, J. A., S. F Grefsheim, and C. C. Canto. "The Emerging Informationist Specialty: A Systematic Review of the Literature." *Journal of the Medical Library Association: JMLA* 96 (July 2008): 194–206.

70. World Bank. "Health Expenditure, Total (% of GDP)." Last modified June 2012. http://data.worldbank.org/indicator/SH.XPD.TOTL.ZS.

71. University of Pittsburgh Medical Center. "UPMC Facts & Stats." Last Modified 2013. http://www.upmc.com/about/facts/pages/default.aspx.

72. Cleveland, Ana D., *op. cit.*, 65.

73. Watson, Linda A., *op. cit.*, 2.

74. Cleveland, Ana D., *op. cit.*, 64.

75. Ibid., 65.

76. Ibid., 68.

77. Watson, Linda A., *op. cit.*, 2

78. Moore, Mary. "Overview of Health Sciences Libraries and Librarianship," 3–29.

79. Barrows, Howard S. "A Taxonomy of Problem-Based Learning Methods." *Medical Education* 20 (2009): 481–486.

80. Walton, H. J., and M. B. Matthews "Essentials of Problem-Based Learning." *Medical Education* 23 (1989): 542–558.

81. Vickers, J. D. "Catching Information Technology by the Tail for Problem-Based Learning." *Journal of Dental Education* 54 (1990): 557–559.

82. Rankin, Jocelyn A. "Problem-Based Learning and Libraries: A Survey of the Literature." *Health Libraries Review* 13 (1996): 33–42.

83. Straus, Sharon E., W. Scott Richardson, Paul Glasziou, and R. Brian Haynes. *Evidence-Based Medicine: How to Practice and Teach EBM.* Philadelphia: Elsevier, Churchill, Livingstone, 2005.

84. Sackett, D. L., W. M. Rosenberg, J. A. Gray, R. B. Haynes, and W. S. Richardson. "Evidence Based Medicine: What It Is and What It Isn't" *BMJ: British Medical Journal* 312 (1996): 71–72.

85. Recovery.gov. "The American Recovery and Reinvestment Act." Last modified 2013. http://www.recovery.gov/About/Pages/The_Act.aspx.

86. Curtis, James A. "Introduction: The Association of Academic Health Sciences Libraries Symposium: 'Electronic Health Records and Knowledge-Based Information; State-of-the-Art and Roles for Libraries in Health Information Technology.'" *Journal of the Medical Library Association: JMLA* 98 (2010): 204–206.

87. Guise, Nunzia, B., Annette M. Williams, and Dario A. Guise. "Integrating Best Evidence into Patient Care: A Process Facilitated by a Seamless Integration with Informatics Tools." *Journal of the Medical Library Association: JMLA* 98 (July 2010): 200–222.

88. Menachemi, N., O. Mazurenko, A. S. Kazley, M. L. Diana, and E. W. Ford. "Market Factors and Electronic Medical Record Adoption in Medical Practices. *Health Care Management Review* 37 (2012): 14–22.

89. Curtis, "Introduction."

90. MedCity News. "NIH Budget Cuts Would Decrease Agency's Budget by $1.6 Billion." Last modified March 1, 2011. http://medcitynews.com/2011/03/nih-budget-cuts-would-decrease-agencys-funding-by-1-6-billion/.

91. Pope, Catherine, and Nick Mays. "Reaching the Parts Other Methods Cannot Reach: An Introduction to Qualitative Methods in Health and Health Services Research." *BMJ: British Medical Journal* 311, no. 6996 (1995): 42.

92. University of Washington. School of Public Health. Department of Health Services. "What Is Health Services Research?" Last modified 2011. http://depts.washington.edu/hserv/hs-research-definitions/.

93. Grimshaw, J. M., M. P. Eccles, J. N. Lavis, S. J. Hill, and J. E. Squires. "Knowledge Translation of Research Findings." *Implementation Science* 7 (2012): 50.

94. Berkman, N. D., S. L. Sheridan, K. E. Donahue, D. J. Halpern, A. Viera, K. Crotty, A. Holland, M. Brasure, K. N. Lohr, E. Harden, E. Tant, I. Wallace, and M. Viswanathan. "Health Literacy Interventions and Outcomes: An Updated Systematic Review." *Evidence Report/Technology Assessment* 199 (2011): 1–941.

95. Butson, Linda C. "E-Patients: The Techno-Cultural Revolution of Health Consumers: Report on the Symposium." *MLA News* 50 (August 2010): 1, 14.

96. Kutner, Mark, Elizabeth Greenburg, Ying Jin, and Christine Paulsen. "The Health Literacy of America's Adults: Results from the 2003 National Assessment of Adult Literacy; NCES 2006-483." *National Center for Education Statistics* (2006).

97. Schardt, Connie. "Health Information Literacy Meets Evidence-Based Practice." *Journal of the Medical Library Association: JMLA* 99 (2011): 1–2.

98. Cox, N., C. Bowmer, and A. Ring. "Health Literacy and the Provision of Information to Women with Breast Cancer." *Clinical Oncology (Royal College of Radiologists [Great Britain])* 23 (2011): 223–227.

99. Rust, C., and C. Davis. "Health Literacy and Medication Adherence in Underserved African-American Breast Cancer Survivors: A Qualitative Study." *Social Work in Health Care* 50 (2011): 739–761.

100. "The Health Literacy of American Adults: Results from the 2003 National Assessment of Adult Literacy." National Center for Education Statistics. Last modified 2006. http://nces.ed.gov/naal/health.asp.

101. National Center for Education Statistics. "The Health Literacy of American Adults: Results from the 2003 National Assessment of Adult Literacy."

102. Nielson-Bohlman, Lynn, Allison M. Panzer, and David A. Kindig. *Health Literacy: A Prescription to End Confusion.* Washington, D.C.: National Academies Press, 2004.

103. Bodenheimer, T., K. Lorig, H. Holman, and K. Grumbach. "Patient Self-Management of Chronic Disease in Primary Care." *JAMA: Journal of the American Medical Association* 288 (2002 November): 2469–2475.

104. Butson, "E-Patients."

105. Michie, Susan, Jane Miles, and John Weinman. "Patient-Centredness in Chronic Illness: What Is It and Does It Matter?" *Patient Education and Counseling* 51 (2003): 197–206.

106. Corrigan, Janet. *Priority Areas for National Action: Transforming Health Care Quality.* Washington D.C.: National Academy Press, 2003.

107. Guise et al., *op. cit.*

108. MedCity News. "NIH Budget Cuts Would Decrease Agency's Budget by $1.6 Billion."

109. White House Office of Science and Technology Policy. "OSTP Public Access Policy Forum." Last Modified February 22, 2013. http://www.whitehouse.gov/administration/eop/ostp/library/publicaccesspolicy.

110. Bailey Charles W., Jr. "Open Access and Libraries." *Collection Management* 32 (2008): 351–383.

111. Hackbarth G, T. Cata, and L. Cole. "Developing a Capstone Course within a Health Informatics Program." *Perspectives in Health Information Management* 9 (2012): 1b.

112. Meek, J. A., M. Lee, J. Jones, N. Mutea, and A. Prizevoits. "Using Podcasts to Help Students Apply Health Informatics Concepts: Benefits and Unintended Consequences." *CIN: Computers, Informatics, Nursing* 30 (2012): 426–439.

113. Sahama, T., J. Liang, and R. Iannella "Impact of the Social Networking Applications for Health Information Management for Patients and Physicians." *Studies in Health Technology & Informatics* 180 (2012): 803–807.

114. Bolchini, Davide, and P. Paolini. "Capturing Web Application Requirements through Goal-Oriented Analysis." *Proceedings of the Workshop on Requirements Engineering* (WER 02) (2002): 16–28.

115. Cleveland, Ana D., *op. cit.*, 64.

Chapter 2

OVERVIEW OF THE HEALTHCARE ENVIRONMENT

Fay J. Towell

INTRODUCTION TO THE HEALTHCARE ENVIRONMENT

The operative word now in healthcare is "change." With the total cost of healthcare in 2009 for the United States tipping the scales at $2.5 trillion (17.6 percent of the gross domestic product), U.S. healthcare went on record as being the most expensive system in the world followed by Switzerland, Canada, Germany, and France.[1, 2] In a speech to the American Medical Association in 2009, President Obama stated that ". . . we aren't any healthier. In fact, citizens in some countries that spend substantially less than we do are actually living longer than we do."[3] This escalation was not sustainable, and changes are, thankfully, underway.

Corporations have a vested interest in controlling healthcare costs. Jeff Immelt, CEO of General Electric since 2001, stated that approximately 3 billion company dollars are applied annually to health expenses for employees.[4] Although life expectancy has increased by over 30 years, chronic diseases such as diabetes, heart and vascular disease, and re-emerging infectious diseases require early detection for improved outcomes and reduced hospital stays. Evolving U.S. demographics—including greater racial and ethnic diversity, population growth, and aging—are all factors that affect healthcare; and since informed consumers now participate in their own healthcare choices, they need to be in the forefront of planning, direction, and decisions. With the application of advanced technology, efficiency of healthcare has been greatly enhanced, thereby allowing patients to be the focus.

According to Immelt, "strife in Washington is the new normal."[5] He acknowledged the changes that will be necessary as result of the Patient Protection and Affordable Care Act signed into effect by President Obama on March 23, 2010. This act and the Healthcare and Education Reconciliation Act of 2010 constitute the Affordable Care Act, or the ACA, which created the "most transformational legislation since social security."[6] While creating tax penalties for businesses that fail to comply and protecting patients with pre-existing conditions, this act seeks to inspire providers to increase quality, eliminate waste, and reduce costs through a series of incentives and rewards.

TYPES OF HEALTHCARE SETTINGS

Hospital care for those who are sick or injured has only just developed in the past century. Prior to this, acutely ill patients were cared for and either died or recovered at home. Surgery, most often for gunshot wounds or other trauma, was performed at the place where the accident occurred because there was no anesthesia or awareness of the need for a sterile environment. If physicians had offices, they were usually extensions of their homes. During the Civil War, hospitals became a necessity so that injured soldiers could get treatment, although homes and churches were frequently used for this purpose.

The first hospital in the United States to treat medical conditions is thought to be Pennsylvania Hospital, which opened in 1751 with the assistance of Benjamin Franklin.[7] However, at this time, most of the inpatients were mentally ill, indigent, or in need of isolation or shelter. As medical care became more sophisticated, so did the concept that communities take responsibility for caring and healing. Medical and nursing education was an active part of the many hospitals built by major church denominations as part of their mission. When World War II drove an escalating demand for healthcare, the Hill Burton Act of 1947 provided funds for construction or expansion of hospitals that would in return offer charity or discounted care.[8]

The next major transformation of hospitals took place in 1965 with the enactment of Medicare (healthcare for those over age 65) and Medicaid (healthcare for the poor), which was followed by increased government regulations in the 1980s in the form of DRG's—diagnosis related groups. This prospective payment system gave a set payment for a specific diagnosis. Later, when for-profit hospital networks mushroomed, many smaller hospitals closed, and the 1990s focused on cost containment, culminating in the Balanced Budget Act, which decreased Medicare payments to hospitals.

In response to addressing cost containment and rapid advances in medicine, healthcare settings in the twenty-first century became varied and numerous. Physicians offer diagnosis and treatment in offices staffed with nurses and assistants. Specialists who concentrate on caring for patients with a select disease may sometimes be in the same office, making for easy referral and access. Since 2005, hospitals have often negotiated to acquire personnel, including physicians and sometimes office staff, thus guaranteeing a referral pattern to the hospital.

In the early 1970s, ambulatory surgery centers (http://www.ascassociation.org/) offering simple surgeries with no overnight care began to open throughout the United States. Soon fiscal caps on hospital costs fueled the growth of these services, which included urgent care centers and outpatient clinics. Many hospitals now have an outpatient surgery center, allowing patients without complications to return home the same day. Reimbursement methods have driven healthcare organizations to focus on keeping patients out of the hospital as a cost reduction, marking the rise of outpatient care. The year 2011 found over 5,300 ambulatory surgery centers performing 23 million procedures each year.[9]

For more complex surgeries and to diagnose and treat diseases, hospitals—which can be either acute care or general—provide healthcare services for a relatively short period of time. Several hospitals grouped under the same corporate office make up a "hospital system." With a broader scope wherein health settings include physician practices, clinics, urgent care centers, and specialty hospitals to name a few, the term "health system" may also be appropriate.

Echoing earlier days, home health has gained popularity in the twenty-first century. With infectious diseases and childbirth as the leading cause of death in the nineteenth and early twentieth centuries, doctors and midwives made house calls, which often resulted in families being quarantined to prevent the spread of disease. As early as 1909, Metropolitan Life Insurance Company was offering policies for home healthcare.[10] However, advancements in drugs and medical equipment placed the traveling physician at a disadvantage so much so that it became practical to provide treatment in an office or hospital. When Congress passed Medicare legislation, which included home healthcare, this industry began to expand. Now, home health has become a means of reducing length of hospital stays and readmissions, and it can cover nursing, physical therapy, personal care, and even housekeeping, allowing the patient to enjoy the familiarity of his or her own home. Another option for care is a nursing home or long-term care facility, a choice setting for patients who are expected to return home but need rehabilitation after an injury or illness.

Hospice care, a type of home healthcare provided for terminally ill patients who have a six-month life expectancy, can be provided in a private home, a health center, or a special "hospice house." Patients who are facing a life-threatening condition or who are terminally ill receive palliative care, which offers comfort and support to improve quality of life socially, emotionally, spiritually, and physically with pain management. As early as 1948, Dame Cicely Saunders applied the term "hospice" and, in 1967, she created St. Christopher's Hospice in London.[11] Dame Cicely introduced this concept to the United States during a lecture at Yale University; in 1993, hospice became a nationally guaranteed healthcare benefit.[12] As of 2009, there were a record 550,000 hospice volunteers.[13] Entire families have the ability to be part of a hospice care plan, making it an outstanding example of how healthcare has become more patient- and family-centered.

The trend when designing new healthcare facilities is to spotlight patient, family, and staff needs to yield an increase in patient satisfaction and outcomes, and a decreased length of stay—thereby reducing costs. Plans for a physical environment in any health facility have tended to embrace the idea that "nature will nurture" and may include healing gardens, pet therapy, sunlight, noise reduction, comfortable furniture, and decentralized nursing stations.

Patients and families have become partners in their own healthcare, and knowing their thoughts about this experience is crucial. The need to collect and publically report patient satisfaction data led to HCAPHS—Hospital Consumer Assessment of Healthcare Providers and Systems. This standardized 27-question national survey about the hospital experience is distributed randomly to patients 48 hours to six weeks after discharge, and results are reported quarterly. With this information, hospital consumer satisfaction can be observed, quality of care enhanced, and accountability created.

DISCIPLINES IN HEALTHCARE

In the past, when one thought of healthcare workers, a doctor (who would treat everything) or a nurse came to mind. Today, disciplines in healthcare are numerous.

In the field of medicine, general practitioners focus on care of the family. The premise is to offer patients continuity in healthcare, treating the entire family throughout their life cycle as each family member is born; specialists are called as needed. After World War II, there was an increase in specialists, and later, subspecialists grew in number: Specialists today include those for allergy and immunology, dermatology, emergency medicine, internal medicine, genetics, nuclear medicine, obstetrics and gynecology, ophthalmology, pathology, psychiatry and neurology, radiology, urology, and subspecialists in all types of surgery. Additional subspecialties for both adults and children include adolescent medicine, cardiology, child abuse, critical care, developmental-behavioral pediatrics, gastroenterology, hematology, infectious diseases, medical oncology, nephrology, and rheumatology.

A U.S. physician assistant program began in 1961. With training similar to what was offered as physician education and training during World War II, the goal of this program was to rapidly increase the pool of doctors treating injured soldiers. Nine years later, the American Medical Association established guidelines and certification for this group to practice medicine with a physician or team of physicians or surgeons. Located in all types of healthcare facilities, physician's assistants (known as P.A.s) perform physician exams, order and interpret tests, make diagnostic and treatment decisions, prescribe, and assist with surgery.

The field of nursing has grown exponentially as well, remaining both rewarding and challenging with its long hours and extended physical exertion. The ravages of war (oftentimes a catalyst for events in history) inspired Florence Nightingale to found the first school of nursing, located in London, where students learned the importance of quality patient care and good hygiene. As a result of shortages in medical supplies during the Civil War, Clara Barton founded the American Red Cross, where Walt Whitman, one of America's most famous poets, served for three years as a volunteer nurse.

Today, specialized education, training, and certification are required for nurses, depending on the choice of nondegree, degree, or advanced degree programs. The nondegree categories, which both require certification, include certified nurse's aides (CNAs) and licensed practical nurses (LPNs). Participants in these programs are strongly encouraged to continue into a degree program for broader career opportunities.

Undergraduate nursing programs generally refer to the registered nurses' (RN) degree, which includes either an associate's (two-year) or bachelor's (four-year) degree. Nurses working in specialized areas, such as labor and delivery or the emergency room, must be registered nurses. Nurse practitioners, who manage basic health needs, including chronic conditions or maternal care, can write prescriptions and must complete a master's degree. For those interested in university teaching or research, the doctoral degree in nursing is required. With a shortage of healthcare workers looming in the future, nursing professionals are in demand at all levels; between now and 2020, a 26 percent employment growth in this field is anticipated. The certified registered nurse anesthetist (CRNA) is among the highest paid in the nursing profession, with a median salary of $159,000.[14]

Another discipline in healthcare with a wide range of interests is public health. Whereas the clinical health professions embrace the individual for diagnosis and treatment, public health incorporates larger population groups via the investigation of health promotion and disease prevention. Skills involving epidemiology, biostatistics, science, business, and management are critical in many facets of public health administration, while the development of community-wide prevention programs and new health policies calls for action that is both assertive and legally based.

Environmental issues and emergency preparedness fall under public health, creating an ever-expanding field for research and planning that aims to ultimately improve the health of entire communities. With behavioral change at the forefront of issues such as child abuse, women's health, obesity, and substance abuse, school health has also played a key role, as has the health of minority and disadvantaged populations in which health disparities are rampant. Looking toward future health concerns, experts have placed greater emphasis on health promotion and disease prevention, which will reduce healthcare costs—a major national goal.

Growth and development of the allied health professions has also contributed to healthcare cost reduction. Defined during President Truman's administration, allied health professionals are "personnel, other than physicians, dentists, and nurses, who are engaged in investigation, treatment and prevention of disease and disability, and in the promotion of health by virtue of some special skill."[15] Following World War II, advancements in medicine increased public demand for care and personnel in physicians' offices, clinics, and community health facilities; presently, as much as 60 percent of the healthcare workforce in the United States is composed of allied health practitioners,[16] and their training should be part of the academic medical center.

Depending on their discipline, allied health professionals provide patient care after having received degrees, diplomas, certified credentials, or continuing education, all of which are offered in most postsecondary institutions. In community

colleges throughout the United States, allied health programs have high enroll-
ments, and their graduates have been successful in finding employment. As part of
the comprehensive healthcare team, allied health professionals deliver preventive
or rehabilitative therapy, provide dietary and nutritional services, and conduct diagnostic procedures in clinics, hospitals, rehabilitation centers, laboratories, schools,
long-term care facilities, and home health agencies to name a few. Examples of
categories and positions include:

- Diagnostic: cardiovascular technologist, radiologic technologist
- Direct patient care: respiratory therapist, surgical technologist
- Nondirect care: pharmacy technician, food services
- Rehabilitation: occupational, speech, or physical therapist

Most of these professions are predicted to increase 30 to 40 percent by 2020.

The discipline of healthcare administration also merits mention. An estimated
100,000 health administrators serve in positions from middle management to
CEO in hospitals and health systems, physician group practices, long-term care
facilities, home health agencies, and state or federal agencies. Employment is
offered to administrators with a master's degree, strong communication skills, analytical thinking, and leadership qualities, including the ability to motivate others.
Once employed, their responsibilities are numerous and varied, including budget,
finance, facility expansion or reduction, equipment purchase, strategic planning,
service involvement or collaboration, technology adaptation, regulatory requirements, and overall organizational direction. As healthcare continues to grow, so
does the need for healthcare administrators, who are ever challenged to balance
"the need to put patients first with the financial demands of an industry where up
to 80 percent of costs are labor based."[17]

In many hospitals, medical librarians are part of the healthcare team and may
round with residents and physicians. Here the librarian may be called upon to search
the literature for the most recent articles on a patient's disease, procedure, or recommended treatment. Often the professional library staff teaches classes on the most
effective methods of searching databases or are asked to find a specific article or
book title. If a hospital includes a medical school, the librarian will likely be considered faculty and may interact in the classroom when appropriate.

TRENDS AND ISSUES IN HEALTHCARE

Known as the father of Western medicine, the Greek physician Hippocrates
(460 BCE–320 BCE) noted that the physician "must be able to . . . know the
present, and foretell the future . . . and have two special objects in view with regard
to disease, namely to do good or to do no harm. The art consists in three things—
the disease, the patient, and the physician."[18]

Although the Hippocratic oath is still used today, healthcare issues have become
more complex—or rather, healthcare appears to have been forced into complexity.

Regardless, Hippocrates might be surprised to learn that between 1980 and 2010, Medicare spending went from $37 billion to $533 billion and continues to run a $228 million deficit, representing 3.6 percent of the U.S. gross domestic product.[19] If it continues at this rate, Medicare will not be sustainable. Therefore, ". . . pressure to get a handle on healthcare costs has never been greater."[20]

As suggested by Hippocrates, we may easily know the present, but foretelling the future, as in the long-range effects of the Patient Protection and Affordable Care Act, can be compared to saving for that long-awaited object when the price is unknown. In spite of this, most accept that something must be done to control the escalation of costs that could ultimately contribute to worldwide financial instability.

Before the 1900s, the few existing hospitals were for the poor; the wealthy were cared for at home. As hospitals developed and became attractive to the middle class, medical care became a business. In 1910, William Osler's model of medical education was adopted, and care was organized around the provider and individual patient need. Navigation through the hospital maze by patients was difficult, and billing was complex, with a high cost for inferior-quality care that was often fragmented. Procedures followed intervention for acute illness or injury where value was often lost and care inefficient. Without identifying a method to connect finance with quality, was no means to eliminate waste, making it challenging to save money or improve standards.

According to the results of one Kaiser Health Tracking Poll, healthcare placed third among the top concerns of the American public.[21] Insurance reform, as represented by the Affordable Care Act (ACA) mentioned earlier, marked the first step in seeking to align incentives with quality and value. Passed after close scrutiny, the ACA mandates insurance coverage for all, including those with pre-existing conditions. Providers who decrease costs, eliminate waste, and improve quality are rewarded under the ACA; for example, physicians could be reimbursed for managing patients with diabetes so that hospitalization is not necessary.[22]

Payment methods have begun moving from the old fee-for-service model to a wider range of options such as lump sum payments for services. This change will necessitate a culture shift: Outcomes of various treatment methods will be examined while seamless service will be designed around the patient and community with safety at the forefront. Reduction of errors can be achieved in high-reliability organizations partly by adapting new technologies, such as the electronic medical record, and creating a value-conscious patient and provider. The resulting accountable organization will be required to answer to the patient and provider for the quality, appropriateness, and efficiency of healthcare rendered. An idea represented by a term first used by Elliott Fisher at Dartmouth Medical School in 2006, "accountable care," will lower expenses while enhancing quality, rendering overwhelming potential for cost reduction that includes a strong focus on preventive care.[23] Accomplished with improved communication, incentives for primary care, disease management, patient engagement, and lower utilization, the goals of accountable care will be to monitor and evaluate quality and costs, and merge hospitals with physicians for greater success. The result will be uniform coordination for the patient from all points of care.

A brief look at demographics shows an aging population with a longer life expectancy by at least 30 years. In 2010, over 40 million Americans comprising 13 percent of the population were over 65 years of age and high consumers of healthcare.[24] Nationality, ethnicity, and race were factors in access to care as evidenced in the Institute of Medicine's book *Unequal Treatment*, which documents vast disparities.[25] Chronic diseases such as diabetes and re-emerging infectious diseases have become significant issues. In the United States, unhealthy lifestyles have led to a 34 percent obesity rate versus 24 percent in the United Kingdom and 16 percent in Canada.[26] Anticipated population growth by 2025 is 15 percent, with as much as 40 percent growth by 2050.[27] The need to address the predicted shortage of healthcare professionals that could impact high quality and timely care is urgent. Potential results of such shortages include waiting lists for procedures, traveling long distances for treatment, and overuse of emergency departments, where some patients may elect to leave without receiving care.

The ACA strongly indicates that primary care medicine could be the nation's ticket to implementing lower costs, higher quality, and patient-centered care. Graduate medical education, medical school graduates' continued study in a hospital setting under the supervision of an attending physician, has been included in the ACA under the Teaching Health Center Graduate Medical Education program, which offers funding directly to health centers for new primary care residency programs. After passage of the ACA, a declining 10-year trend of medical students entering primary care saw a 1.8 percent increase between 2009 and 2011.[28] The decision to select a specialty rather than primary care can be strongly influenced by student debt for medical school as well as personal income and lifestyle choices. Historically, hospitals have been strong supporters of specialties.

In this new paradigm, academic medical centers where many of the 32 million new insurance beneficiaries will likely access healthcare must adopt or continue an innovative path. Research that is translational (that is, it shows results at the point of care) is highly desirable, and patient care must be paramount in the process.[29] Whereas the ACA requires reimbursements to be aligned with desired outcomes, no directive exists as to how this should be achieved. One suggestion is for the academic health center to take the lead with personalized health planning, focusing on patient assessment for risks, a plan to track and minimize these risks with physician involvement as needed, and patient participation in his or her own care options. This centralized care facilitates the data collection that is required for reimbursement.[30]

In addition to changes in care models, the financing of graduate medical education—which now receives federal and state funding in excess of $13.3 billion annually—must be carefully examined for potential reallocation.[31] Investment in technology is critical for the success of the ACA. The electronic medical record is one example of technology benefits. The EMR (electronic medical record) contains information on the patient's medical history in digital format from one provider's office; the EMR typically remains within the practice, where it is used to track data, monitor how patients measure up to certain standards, and identify preventive visit dates. The electronic health record (EHR), containing information from each provider that can be shared throughout the organization, is more comprehensive, giving a broader view of the patient. With a personalized electronic health record, the patient finds changes in insurance, employment, or location easy to facilitate because their personal information follows them throughout their testing and treatment. Through automation of the administrative process—including improved ways to store, analyze, and share health information—a reliable exchange is possible that results in clinical registries and linked outcomes research networks. With the electronic patient record, medical errors are reduced or eliminated, and the challenge of reading a physician's handwritten orders or prescriptions can become a thing of the past. Social media and mobile phone apps have a place in healthcare marketing and most importantly, consumers are selecting practices based on the availability of an electronic health system where they can make appointments online, view lab results, refill prescriptions, and email their provider. Some physician practices distribute iPads to patients in the waiting rooms for registration and updates.[32] Healthcare consumers are therefore becoming actively engaged in their own care and desire a certain transparency in price, quality, and safety.

Linking progress in medicine with progress in technology, the medical tricorder used by Captain Kirk and Dr. Spock in *Star Trek* is coming close to being a reality.[33] Mobile phones with special adaptive devices have the capacity to take vital signs, detect ear infections and even heart attacks, monitor glucose, perform ultrasounds and retinal scans, diagnose malaria and TB, and finally transmit these results back to the physician's office for further evaluation—"patient power" for the not-too-distant future.[34]

The shift to patient-centered care requires a change of perception, framework, and process with a careful look not only at the patient and caregiver, but also at care coordination, patient safety, disease prevention, and patients at risk. Uniting the informed consumer with the process and financing of services is critical. Healthcare organizations that are integrated via electronic records, treatment models, improved communications, and follow-up patterns will ultimately reduce healthcare costs and augment the quality of care.

Additional transformations to make healthcare compliant with the ACA are numerous and widespread. One such requirement placed on hospitals is reduced readmission rates, a previous concern but one never before linked to reimbursement. In the past, one in five Medicare patients returned to the hospital within 30 days, costing the government over $12 billion annually.[35] By October 2015, the maximum penalty for returning patients will reach 3 percent, so the pressure is on to partner with community organizations to coordinate home care following hospital discharge.[36] Another agency authorized by the ACA will give special attention to chronically ill Medicare recipients, with multidisciplinary teams coordinating efforts 24/7.[37] Finally, aligning payment with outcome will also play a major role in reducing readmissions.

Since connectivity drives change at a rapid pace, the resulting consensus is that clinical integration becomes the foundation upon which new delivery systems are built. The right care at the right place at the right time coordinates patient care throughout the entire experience, in any location, with any specialist, and in the scheduling and reporting of any diagnostic test. Not only that, but patient care, generally offered in a primary care practice, is available where patients live and work. With providers in the new system being allocated resources based on value, data from electronic medical records must be accurate and of high quality. Wellness programs and incentives will be sought by employers so that comprehensive benefit programs with reduced premiums can present an attractive package to potential employees.

To implement patient-centered care that is interdisciplinary with attention to personalized issues and prevention, most experts agree that the focus needs to be redirected from volume to value, using the past to formulate the future. Value needs to be defined, applied, measured, and reported with use of advanced technology. Enhancing communication and fostering teamwork will assist in identifying barriers and building networks. By reaching across a diverse constituency for solutions, patients, families, and healthcare professionals will become engaged in formulating a clear mission, vision, and strategy for successful implementation of low-cost, high-quality healthcare.

NOTES

1. O'Neil, Ed. "Health Care Environment Drivers." Center for the Health Professions, University of California, 2012. Accessed December 12, 2013. http://futurehealth.ucsf.edu/Public/Publications-and-Resources/Content.aspx?topic=Health_Care_Environment_Drivers.

2. Shedlock, James. "Apocalypse Now: Health Care Financing: an Interview with Jeffrey C. Miller, Part1." Medical Library Association. *MLA News* 52, no. 8 (September 2012): 8.

3. Frech, J. E., III "Is U.S. Health Care Less Efficient Than Other Countries' Systems?" *Regulation* (Summer 2012): 56-59.

4. Immelt, Jeff. "Presentation by Jeff Immelt, CEO of General Electric to Greenville Health System Leadership." Greeneville, SC, January 10, 2013.

5. Ibid.

6. Cherf, John. "Navigating a Changing Healthcare Environment." American Academy of Orthopaedic Surgeons. *AAOS Now*, August 2011. Accessed December 5, 2013. http://www.aaos.org/news/aaosnow/aug11/managing3.asp.

7. Cutter, J. B. "Early Hospital History in the United States." *California State Journal of Medicine* 20, no. 8 (August 1922): 272-274.

8. Wall, Barbra M. "History of Hospitals." *American Statesman*, August 20 1998.

9. Ambulatory Surgery Center Association. "History." Accessed December 5, 2013. http://www.ascaconnect.org/ASCA/AboutUs/WhatisanASC/History/.

10. Moore Health Sciences Library, University of Virginia. "Metropolitan Life Insurance's Health Campaign." Last modified 2007, accessed December 12, 2013. http://exhibits.hsl.virginia.edu/hands/metlife/.

11. National Hospice Foundation. "History of Hospice Care. National Hospice and Palliative Care Organization." Accessed December 5, 2013. http://www.nationalhospicefoundation.org/i4a/pages/index.dfm?pageid=218.

12. Ibid.

13. Ibid.

14. CNNMoney. "Nurse Anesthetist (CRNA) (#41), Best Jobs." Last modified 2012, accessed December 12, 2013. http://money.cnn.com/pf/best-jobs/2012/snapshots/41.html.

15. "Introduction to Allied Health Care." American Institute of Medical Sciences and Education (AIMS), 2013. Accessed December 5, 2013. http://www.aimseducation.edu/blog/introduction-to-allied-health-care.

16. Ibid.

17. AllAlliedHealthSchools. "Health Care Administration Careers." Accessed December 5, 2013. http://www.allalliedhealthschools.com/health-careers/health-care-administrator/health-care-administration-resource-center.

18. Gill, N. S. "Is 'First Do No Harm' from the Hippocratic Oath? Myth vs. Fact." Accessed December 12, 2013. http://ancienthistory.about.com/od/greekmedicine/f/HippocraticOath.htm.

19. Bush, Haydn. "Health Care's Costliest." *Hospitals & Health Networks*, September 2012. Accessed December 5, 2013. http://www.hhnmag.com/hhnmag/features/1Percent/PDFs/No1.pdf.

20. Ibid.

21. Henry J. Kaiser Family Foundation. "Kaiser Health Tracking Poll: November 2012." Last modified November 13, 2012, accessed December 12, 2013. http://kff.org/health-reform/poll-finding/kaiser-health-tracking-poll-november-2012/.

22. Editors of Scientific American. "Science Policy Issues That Matter Most." *Science Agenda* 308, no. 1 (January 10, 2013): 1. Accessed December 12, 2013. http://www.scientificamerican.com/article.cfm?id=science-policy-issues-matter-most.

23. Wikipedia. "Accountable Care Organization." Accessed December 12, 2013. http://en.wikipedia.org/wiki/Health.administration.

24. O'Neil, *op. cit.*

25. Smedley, Brian D., Adrienne Y. Stith, Alan R. Nelson, and Institute of Medicine Committee on Understanding and Eliminating Racial and Ethnic Disparities in Health Care. *Unequal Treatment: Confronting Racial and Ethnic Disparities in Health Care.* Washington, D.C.: National Academy Press, 2003.

26. Frech, *op. cit.*

27. O'Neil, *op. cit.*

28. Sommers, B. D., and A. B. Bindman. "New Physicians, the Affordable Care Act, and the Changing Practice of Medicine." *JAMA: Journal of the American Medical Association* 307, no. 16 (April 25, 2012): 1697-1698.

29. Shomaker, T. S. "Commentary: Preparing for Health Care Reform; Ten Recommendations for Academic Health Centers." *Academic Medicine* 86, no. 5 (May 2011): 555-558.

30. Dinan, M. A., L. A. Simmons, and R. Snyderman. "Commentary: Personalized Health Planning and the Patient Protection and Affordable Care Act; An Opportunity for Academic Medicine to Lead Health Care Reform." *Academic Medicine* 85, no. 11 (November 2010): 1665-1668.

31. Voorhees, K. I., A. Prado-Gutierrez, T. Epperly, and D. Dirkson. "A Proposal for Reform of the Structure and Financing of Primary Care Graduate Medical Education." *Family Medicine* 45, no. 3 (March 2013): 164-170.

32. McBride, M. "Patient Demand Will Ensure Technology Adoption." *Medical Economics* 89, no. 23 (December 10, 2012): 59.

33. "The Dream of the Medical Tricorder." *Economist*, December 1, 2012. Accessed December 5, 2013. http://www.economist.com/news/technology-quarterly/21567208-medical-technology-hand-held-diagnostic-devices-seen-star-trek-are-inspiring.

34. Ibid.

35. HealthAffairs.org. "Medicare Hospital Readmissions Reduction Program." In *Health Policy Briefs*: Project HOPE: The People-to-People Health Foundation, Inc., 2013. Accessed December 12, 2013. http://healthaffairs.org/healthpolicybriefs/brief_pdfs/healthpolicybrief_102.pdf.

36. Kocher, R. P., and E. Y. Adashi. "Commentary: Hospital Readmissions and the Affordable Care Act; Paying for Coordinated Quality Care." *JAMA: Journal of the American Medical Association* 306, no. 16 (October 26, 2011): 1794-1795. Accessed December 12, 2013. http://jama.jamanetwork.com/article.aspx?articleid=1104541.

37. Ibid.

Chapter 3

SITUATING HEALTH LIBRARIANSHIP WITHIN THE HEALTHCARE ENVIRONMENT

Anna Getselman and *Sandra G. Franklin*

INTRODUCTION

A strong relationship between healthcare systems and health sciences librarianship is well established and documented. Notably, in 1971, a team of librarians led by Estelle Brodman identified nine crucial elements they thought would have a major impact on demands for services from the library at Washington University School of Medicine and the ability of the library to meet these demands. The nine elements included medical care delivery systems, medical education, medical research, medical practice, government projects for medical information, general economic situation, medical librarians, and delivery of medical information services.[1] Brodman's diagram further illustrated the close relationship between these elements, which in her own words "must be viewed together if one is to arrive at a concept of the whole wheel."[2]

In 1987, Judith Messerle expanded Brodman's position by stating: "Health sciences libraries are not islands into themselves. They reflect the philosophy, mission, and economy of their parent institution."[3] More recently, a 2009 publication about the MLA's Vital Pathways for Hospital Librarians survey results reaffirmed a strong link between ever-evolving hospital library services and the "dynamic nature of the healthcare and financial environments."[4]

A 2011 summary of twentieth-century trends in health sciences librarianship by Murphy further detailed just how strongly health sciences libraries followed the direction of the healthcare system during the 40 years following Brodman's clinical librarianship model. It started during the golden years in the 1960s—when, encouraged by the rapid growth in the healthcare sector, libraries expanded collections and staff, instituted better training, and formalized continuing education—and continued into the healthcare financial downturn in the 1970s when health sciences libraries had to figure out how to plan, understand user needs, and respond to them in a fiscally responsible way.[5] Mediated searching, information and knowledge management, instruction and education, evidence-based medicine support, management of electronic resources—each of these initiatives started as a response to changes that occurred in the healthcare system over the past few decades.

In 1971, Brodman predicted that with the expansion of library clientele to include paramedical workers, the new biomedical librarian could find herself or himself coming to make value judgments for readers.[6] Indeed, filtering and summarizing information is one of the new roles for informationists. Importantly, Brodman had already recognized in the 1970s that libraries would have to figure out how to serve existing user groups and new ones with the same staffing levels and the same economic challenges. Since then, the clientele of health sciences libraries has grown to include nurses, allied health professionals, pharmacists, researchers, and health administrators to name a few. Health sciences libraries responded by creating liaison programs with specialist librarians such as nursing, research, medical education, and pharmacy informationists.

In 1987, Messerle warned that speed in positioning the library's role would be critical to prevent other "information specialists" from usurping it. She went on to say that the "customary library services will fall far short of satisfying information needs brought on by changes in healthcare delivery."[7] Perhaps one of the least desired statements in Matheson's Delphi study on future perspectives for health sciences libraries was that which predicted that "the rapidity of development in clinical knowledge bases will outstrip the current capacity and training of health sciences librarians to participate in their development and implementation."[8] Indeed, in the late 1990s and early 2000s, new competitive forces such as information technology and bioinformatics professionals have been introduced into what used to be medical information delivery, the domain of health sciences libraries. Medical information itself has undergone a fundamental change, not only in format, but also in content, with the ever-expanding base of primary, secondary, and tertiary sources, along with a variety of methods to deliver information to the user. In the 1997 Leiter Lecture, the associate vice chancellor for health affairs at Vanderbilt University, William W. Stead, stated that "to position the library at the epicenter of the networked biomedical enterprise we must meet three challenges: We must align the library's business strategy with that of the larger enterprise. We must provide services in ways that will scale up to enable new business strategies. We must measure the effectiveness of services in ways that document their role in supporting the enterprise."[9] A position paper by Roderer, Perry, and Assar published in 2005 provided a perspective on medical informatics and health sciences librarianship, noting "overlapping agendas for both disciplines" and the increasingly collaborative nature of discourse between library and informatics professionals, who act as "boundary spanners."[10]

As healthcare delivery in the United States and around the world continues to evolve, so do health sciences libraries. In this chapter, we will describe how the key driving forces behind the changes in healthcare continue to influence the evolution of information services, emerging service models, and new roles for librarians in health sciences libraries.

EVIDENCE-BASED MEDICINE: FROM CLINICAL LIBRARIANSHIP TO INFORMATIONISTS AND EMBEDDED LIBRARIANS

Healthcare delivery is a complex system with complex relationships between healthcare, need, demand, supply, and access.[11] The 1999 Institute of Medicine report "To Err Is Human" started a critical debate in medicine that crossed into the twenty-first century.[12, 13, 14] It brought attention and national awareness to the topic of eradication of medical errors, renewed interest in the evidence-based practice of medicine, and introduced funded initiatives in medical decision making, including technological solutions to document patient care and share it with the team of healthcare providers, as well as ensure the patient's access to reliable information. It led to today's patient-centered care movement and stimulated health professionals to examine topics such as access to information, communication with patients, and professionalism as a set of critical competencies and skills for physicians and nurses.

Librarians, both in academic health sciences and hospital libraries fully embraced the concept of evidence-based medicine (EBM), and they were astute to recognize the opportunity to revitalize clinical librarianship, which had already in practice for almost 30 years. As EBM prompted the proliferation of randomized controlled trials, meta-analyses, systematic reviews, as well as the production of highly advanced point-of-care information tools, librarians followed these developments by expanding their roles from expert searcher into instructor and advisor on how to discriminate information resources and sources of information to locate published evidence efficiently and effectively. Furthermore, as the EBM model matured to become patient-centered and providing information to patients became an integral part of healthcare delivery, clinical librarians took on yet another role and became patient advocates, sharing with physicians their expertise as information providers.

With the spread and maturity of EBM, the exponential growth of published clinical evidence, and a better understanding of the barriers to practicing EBM came questions about the scope, scalability, and effectiveness of the clinical librarianship service model. A 2000 editorial by Davidoff and Florance published in the *Annals of Internal Medicine* started a national debate about how to make clinical evidence retrieval truly a part of clinical practice and how to "establish a national program, modeled on the experience of clinical librarianship."[15] Summarizing the 2001

Medical Library Association symposium on this topic, Homan and McGowan stated, "Quality information will be one of the keys to changing the system and the IOM report, as well as reports by professional societies and accrediting agencies, recommends that the new systems must be knowledge and evidence based."[16] These rigorous discussions resulted in experimental educational programs and new service models at Vanderbilt, John's Hopkins, the NIH, and other libraries. Informationist became a recognizable profession within health sciences libraries and centers. A new set of skills and competencies, including critical appraisal and synthesis of clinical information, was clearly identified and documented.[17, 18] These new health professionals embraced quality assessment, an element vital to healthcare delivery, which started the evidence-based librarianship movement and produced systematic reviews to assess the effectiveness of the newly developed service models. A randomized effectiveness trial of a clinical informatics consult service (CICS) at Vanderbilt confirmed that the primary impact of providing synthesized evidence to clinicians by librarians was on the use of new or different treatment. This trial not only demonstrated that CICS made a statistically significant impact on clinical decision making, but it also supplied data to suggest possible future benefits of this type of library-based program to facilitate "the integration of research evidence into the management of complex patient care and. . . foster clinicians' engagement with the biomedical literature."[20]

Health Information Technology and Librarianship at the Point of Care

In his keynote address to the Association of Academic Health Sciences Libraries, Kenneth Mandl began by asking two questions that were central to his presentation: "How do we get knowledge to the point of care?" and "Where can we insert the knowledge necessary to drive better clinical care and ultimately contribute to health care reform?" Mandl went on to say that while the electronic health record (EHR) is viewed by many as "a piece of technology that is intended to move the country toward the 'holy grail' of data and information exchange, liquidity, and accumulation so that knowledge can be brought to bear on clinical decision making at the point of care to improve health," many barriers are present that thwart successful implementation and—more importantly—utilization of health information technology (HIT) in practice.[20] The Health Information Technology for Economic and Clinical Health (HITECH) Act, signed in 2009, gave new impetus to the development of EHR. HITECH created a mix of incentives and penalties to induce a large percentage of physicians and hospitals to move toward EHR systems by the end of this decade.[21] It is believed EHRs have the potential to enable the level of clinical information exchange and instantaneous continuous quality assessment that are critical to transform healthcare delivery and make it more safe and less costly.[22] As occurred when they first supported evidence-based medicine, health sciences librarians were quick to recognize and welcome the prospect of utilizing EHRs, which they saw as an opportunity to insert information services into clinicians' workflow. The Clinical Consult service at Vanderbilt and the development of InfoButtons pioneered such services.[23] While the promise of EHRs is yet to be realized, a growing belief exists that other HIT applications currently in develop-ment or being explored will be part of the solution as they share and communicate information between healthcare providers and with patients. Ensuring that the right evidence is placed at the physician's fingertips at the right moment—when it is criti-cally needed—is part of the solution and an opportunity for informationists to work with HIT professionals.

DEVELOPING A CULTURE OF RESEARCH IN CLINICAL PRACTICE

In parallel to these developments, prompted by what was perceived as insufficient and slow realization of biomedical discoveries in clinical practice, the National Insti-tutes of Health developed the Roadmap for Medical Research.[24, 25] At the same time, a new program was launched to fund the institutional Clinical and Transla-tional Science Awards (CTSAs). CTSAs started a series of new initiatives, namely in undergraduate medical and graduate biomedical education, with a focus on a new clinician investigator persona; continuing training and retraining for clinicians and scientists; interdisciplinary collaboration; and close tracking, evaluation, and assessment of outcomes for research, clinical care, and education. These develop-ments created an opening for librarians to utilize existing expertise in instruction, EBM, and assessment with a new audience. As researchers seek to collaborate with clinicians and interact with patients and as clinicians seek to collaborate with researchers, librarians can serve as neutral facilitators. Both clinicians and research-ers have to acquire new skills and competencies, and learn to communicate and share knowledge. A new concept of knowledge translation and transfer has emerged, with librarians as active partners in many institutions. Sharing knowledge, resources, and expertise—and working as a team—led to a new concept called team science, and again, in many instances, librarians work hand in hand with adminis-trators of CTSAs and HIT developers to share their knowledge on information seeking behaviors, patterns in knowledge translation and transfer, and other aspects of tracking these and related factors, ultimately influencing the collaborative nature of science.

Diversity and the Interdisciplinary Nature of the Twenty-First-Century Healthcare Workforce

The twenty-first-century healthcare workforce is increasingly diverse and inter-disciplinary. This was predicted by Brodman in the early 1970s and was seen as a possible response to economic pressures and Medicaid. Today, it is generally acknowledged that to be able to receive effective and efficient care, a patient must be treated by a team that includes junior and senior healthcare providers, specialists (if needed), nurses, social workers, pharmacists, and many other professionals. Each healthcare professional may use intensive technologies for information acquisition and knowledge transfer, accessing different techniques and terminologies. In fact, information technologies in healthcare increasingly facilitate more optimal information management practices. However, while technology allows getting more "just-in-time" information faster than ever, filtering and sharing information, data, and knowledge has become a complex endeavor, with privacy restrictions to access, different standards in data acquisition and description, and diverse retrieval approaches all being the compounding factors that make information a critical resource to be considered in any project or endeavor. The complexities of information management and knowledge transfer were especially evident during the many natural and human-made disasters of the past 20 years.[26, 27] The lessons learned point at three factors for successful knowledge integration to ensure that information reaches the primary healthcare providers: efficiency, scope, and flexibility.[28] Health sciences librarians and informationists have become an important part of the solution because they can observe the different information management strategies employed by all healthcare team members in a variety of situations and then proactively model best practices.[29, 30]

Healthcare Costs and Healthcare Delivery Impact on Health Sciences Librarianship

Rising healthcare costs continue to shape the healthcare delivery debate. An expanding population, access to preventive medicine, Medicare and primary care crises, a shortage of physicians in rural areas, and the Patient Protection and Affordable Care Act are but a few of today's key topics. Presently, the realization is growing in the healthcare sector that it is critically important that academic physicians understand healthcare financing so that they can provide leadership in policy discussions and create innovative payment and delivery for healthcare services, allowing future physicians to be competent stewards of our healthcare financing resources.[31] Also, more healthcare professionals are beginning to understand that to transform the healthcare system, need, demand, access, and supply have to be balanced.[32] In fact, two new healthcare delivery models are currently being explored: accountable care organizations and patient-centered medical homes. The Patient-Centered Outcomes Research Institute (PCORI), which was authorized by Congress to conduct research to provide information about the best available evidence to help patients and healthcare providers make more informed decisions, is another important example of developments associated with the Affordable Care Act and trends in healthcare delivery toward utilization of information and HIT to make patient care more effective and efficient.

Healthcare costs and the quality of healthcare are a primary focus of national discourse in the United States, and healthcare providers are largely focused on optimizing healthcare delivery, including personalized medicine, speedy utilization of the latest research discoveries in patient care, optimal use of available diagnostic and treatment options, and predictive health. Each of these areas requires judicious use of quality information and an understanding of the best possible ways to share and track knowledge. Case reports, systematic reviews, and other recent publications provide ample evidence that health sciences libraries have followed these cues and have used them as opportunities to insert themselves into these processes, identify new skills, and develop new services.

EMERGING SERVICE MODELS: LESSONS, CHALLENGES, FUTURE DIRECTION

The 2013 systematic review published in the *Journal of the Medical Library Association* identified more than 10 new roles and titles for health sciences librarians: embedded librarian (such as clinical informationist, bioinformationist, public health informationist, disaster information specialist), systematic review librarian, emerging technologies librarian, continuing medical education librarian, grants development librarian, data management librarian, digital librarian, metadata librarian, scholarly communication librarian, and translational research librarian.[33, 34] According to this review and earlier published reviews of the emerging service models, as well as the few published case reports, informationists are contributing to the quality of healthcare delivery by conducting assessment and evaluation research to measure the success rate of evidence utilization in clinical practices and to assist in identifying barriers to utilizing information resources and evidence as part of healthcare provision. In 2011, Davidoff acknowledged that "since it was proposed more than 10 years ago, the new profession of informationist has reframed and extended clinical librarianship in important ways."[35] Lessons learned from these first experiences point at the following value drivers for the provision of information services within the healthcare enterprise:

- *Proximity and direct access to healthcare providers* were identified early as the critical advantage for clinical librarianship and informationists alike. Today, this success driver is conceptualized by embedded clinical librarians and informationists who are playing a unique role in healthcare delivery in utilizing intensive knowledge and technologies to solve distinctive sets of information problems for healthcare providers. Being close to where the need is allows informationists to observe and collect all the information needed to resolve problems as they arise. Significantly, location enables informationists to develop close relationships with healthcare providers and become part of clinical teams while retaining their unique roles. Proximity to healthcare delivery enables informationists to solve healthcare information issues in a more effective and efficient way, not only saving time for healthcare providers, but also addressing the critical issue of scalability and duplication of effort.

- *Evaluation and assessment* have gradually become staples of health sciences librarianship, just as quality care control has always been an integral part of healthcare delivery. Framed as evidence-based librarianship, it is, in fact, a critical set of learning activities that allow librarians to establish and maintain high-level knowledge competency, share it across and throughout the program, ensure timely responses, and generate a high level of confidence in the reliability, quality, and professionalism of services rendered. Productivity, reduction of errors, accuracy and standardization, trust and attention to detail, service innovation, research, and development—these terms are frequently used to discuss the emerging function of health sciences librarianship.

• *Success* has always been the conventional measure of how well service delivery was performed. In healthcare, success is customarily revealed through lasting relationships that result in recognition and a good reputation. In health science librarianship, successful service results in fewer problems, wider reach, and continuous relationships. The ability to demonstrate the impact of the information-ist program is closely related to its assessment and the ability to document and communicate assessment results to the healthcare establishment. More and more informationist programs recognize that communication is a planned set of activities, and it has to start before the program is in place and continue as it progresses.

It is important to note that over the years, health sciences librarianship has developed a close bond with the healthcare system and an appreciation for the urgency and intensity of the information needs of healthcare providers and patients. In less than 20 years, an entirely new branch of the growing number of embedded informationists has grown and matured, representing the profession envisioned by Davidoff and Florance in 2000. Most importantly, these new professionals are widely accepted by both librarians and healthcare providers. Being on the forefront of healthcare delivery, informationists have had an opportunity to intimately observe healthcare, anticipate changes, and respond to the ever-changing needs in healthcare more rapidly than ever, with greater usefulness and impact. Indeed, health sciences librarianship is at its best when librarians model information delivery services after healthcare delivery. As stated by Brodman in 1971, "the provision of medical information is naturally a parallel operation to the provision of medical care; it takes its raison d'etre from the forms of medical delivery, and it bends and changes as medicine itself changes."[36] Becoming an integral part of the healthcare delivery team proved to be the key to success and sustainability for health sciences libraries, just as the deliberate assessment of information needs, quality of service, and attention to the scope and scalability of service are becoming the norm for the future of health information services.

NOTES

1. Brodman, E. "The Delivery of Medical Information in the 1970s." *Bulletin of the Medical Library Association* 59, no. 4 (1971): 579–584.

2. Ibid.

3. Messerle, J. "Health Sciences Libraries: Strategies in an Era of Changing Economics." *Bulletin of the Medical Library Association* 75, no. 1 (January 1987): 27–33.

4. Thibodeau, P. L., and C. J. Funk. "Trends in Hospital Librarianship and Hospital Library Services, 1989–2006." *Journal of the Medical Library Association: JMLA* 97, no. 4 (October 2009): 273–279.

5. Murphy, J. "Trend Spotting: Whither Health Science Librarianship?" *Health information and libraries journal* 28, no. 4 (December 2011): 321–325.

6. Brodman, *op. cit.*

7. Messerle, *op. cit.*

8. Matheson, N. W. "Perspectives on Academic Health-Sciences Libraries in the 1980s: Indicators from a Delphi Study." *Bulletin of the Medical Library Association* 70, no. 1 (1982): 28–49.

9. Stead, W. W. "Positioning the Library at the Epicenter of the Networked Biomedical Enterprise." *Bulletin of the Medical Library Association* 86, no. 1 (January 1998): 26–30.

10. Perry, G. J., N. K. Roderer, and S. Assar. "A Current Perspective on Medical Informatics and Health Sciences Librarianship." *Journal of the Medical Library Association: JMLA* 93, no. 2 (April 2005): 199–205.

11. Gray, P., O. A. El Sawy, G. Asper, and M. Thordarson. "Realizing Strategic Value through Center-Edge Digital Transformation in Consumer-Centric Industries." *MIS Quarterly Executive* 12, no. 1 (March 2013): 1–17

12. "Keeping Patients Safe: Institute of Medicine Looks at Transforming Nurses' Work Environment." *Quality Letter for Healthcare Leaders* 16, no. 1 (January 2004): 9–11, 1.

13. "The Iom Medical Errors Report: 5 Years Later, the Journey Continues." *Letter for Healthcare Leaders* 17, no. 1 (January 2005): 2–10, 1.

14. Stelfox, H. T., S. Palmisani, C. Scurlock, E. J. Orav, and D. W. Bates. "The 'To Err Is Human' Report and the Patient Safety Literature." *Quality & Safety in Health Care* 15, no. 3 (June 2006): 174–178.

15. Davidoff, F., and V. Florance. "The Informationist: A New Health Profession?" *Annals of Internal Medicine* 132, no. 12 (June 20, 2000): 996–998.

16. Homan, J. M., and J. J. McGowan. "The Medical Library Association: Promoting New Roles for Health Information Professionals." *Journal of the Medical Library Association: JMLA* 90, no. 1 (January 2002): 80–85.

17. Grefsheim, S. F., S. C. Whitmore, B. A. Rapp, J. A. Rankin, R. R. Robison, and C. C. Canto. "The Informationist: Building Evidence for an Emerging Health Profession." *Journal of the Medical Library Association: JMLA* 98, no. 2 (April 2010): 147–156.

18. Rankin, J. A., S. F. Grefsheim, and C. C. Canto. "The Emerging Informationist Specialty: A Systematic Review of the Literature." *Journal of the Medical Library Association: JMLA* 96, no. 3 (July 2008): 194–206.

19. Mulvaney, S. A., L. Bickman, N. B. Giuse, E. W. Lambert, N. A. Sathe, and R. N. Jerome. "A Randomized Effectiveness Trial of a Clinical Informatics Consult Service: Impact on Evidence-Based Decision-Making and Knowledge Implementation." *Journal of the American Medical Informatics Association* 15, no. 2 (March–April 2008): 203–211.

20. Curtis, J. A. "Electronic Health Records, Platforms, Libraries, and Evidence: Report on the Association of Academic Health Sciences Libraries Symposium's Keynote Presentation by Kenneth Mandl." *Journal of the Medical Library Association: JMLA* 98, no. 3 (July 2010): 206–209.

21. Adler-Milstein, J., C. M. DesRoches, and A. K. Jha. "Health Information Exchange among U.S. Hospitals." *American Journal of Managed Care* 17, no. 11 (November 2011): 761–768.

22. Bates, D. W., and A. Bitton. "The Future of Health Information Technology in the Patient-Centered Medical Home." *Health Affairs* 29, no. 4 (April 2010): 614–621.

23. Guse, N. B., S. R. Kafantaris, M. D. Miller, K. S. Wilder, S. L. Martin, N. A. Sathe, and J. D. Campbell. "Clinical Medical Librarianship: The Vanderbilt Experience." *Bulletin of the Medical Library Association* 86, no. 3 (July 1998): 412–416.

24. Zerhouni, E. A. "Translational and Clinical Science: Time for a New Vision." *New England Journal of Medicine* 353, no. 15 (October 13, 2005): 1621–1623.

25. Zerhouni, E. A. "U.S. Biomedical Research: Basic, Translational, and Clinical Sciences." *JAMA: Journal of the American Medical Association* 294, no. 11 (September 21, 2005): 1352–1358.

26. Devadoss, P. R., S. L. Pan, and S. Singh. "Managing Knowledge Integration in a National Health-Care Crisis: Lessons Learned from Combating SARS in Singapore." *IEEE Transactions on Information Technology in Biomedicine* 9, no. 2 (June 2005): 266–275.

27. Sobel, R. S., and P. T. Leeson. "The Use of Knowledge in Natural-Disaster Relief Management." *Independent Review* 11, no. 4 (Spring 2007): 519–532.

28. Devadoss et al., *op. cit.*

29. Gray et al., *op. cit.*

30. Grefsheim et al., *op. cit.*

31. Sklar, D. P. "Financial Incentives, Health Care Delivery, and the Crucial Role of Academic Medicine." *Academic Medicine* 88, no. 3 (March 2013): 293–294.

32. Adler-Milstein et al., *op. cit.*

33. Cooper, I. D., and J. A. Crum. "New Activities and Changing Roles of Health Sciences Librarians: A Systematic Review, 1990–2012." *Journal of the Medical Library Association: JMLA* 101, no. 4 (October 2013): 268–277.

34. Crum, J. A., and I. D. Cooper. "Emerging Roles for Biomedical Librarians: A Survey of Current Practice, Challenges, and Changes." *Journal of the Medical Library Association: JMLA* 101, no. 4 (October 2013): 278–286.

35. Davidoff, F., and J. Miglus. "Delivering Clinical Evidence where It's Needed: Building an Information System Worthy of the Profession." *JAMA: Journal of the American Medical Association* 305, no. 18 (May 11, 2011): 1906–1907.

36. Brodman, *op. cit.*

Chapter 4

EVIDENCE-BASED HEALTHCARE/ EVIDENCE-BASED PRACTICE

Connie Schardt

WHY IS IT IMPORTANT FOR LIBRARIANS TO KNOW ABOUT EVIDENCE-BASED PRACTICE (EBP)?

Evidence-based practice (EBP) is about managing patient care and managing the abundance of information available to healthcare providers and consumers. It is about acknowledging uncertainty and identifying an information gap related to a specific patient problem. It is about finding relevant and specific information and being able to critically evaluate the validity of that information. EBP applies the principles of information management to a specific task (caring for patients) and a specific body of information (the medical literature). The body of medical literature is vast and constantly expanding. PubMed, the primary source for current medical literature, adds over 500,000 new citations to its database every year. Currently, the database contains over 22 million citations. Other sources for the medical literature include other academic databases, hundreds of biomedical journals, and professional associations that provide access to studies, guidelines, editorials, and other content. Managing this information is at the core of the practice of librarianship, which applies knowledge and skills to collect, organize, evaluate, and disseminate information. Understanding the process of EBP helps us identify ways we can use our services of collection development and instruction to help make it easier for clinicians to practice EBP.

WHAT IS EVIDENCE-BASED PRACTICE (EBP)?

Evidence-based medicine (EBM), evidence-based healthcare (EBHC), and evidence-based practice (EBP) are all terms to describe the same process of making clinical decisions about patient care. The movement was started by physicians (and thus was first labeled evidence-based medicine) in the early 1990s and over time has expanded to include nurses, physical therapists, physician assistants, and other allied health professionals. The official definition of EBM is "the conscientious, explicit, and judicious use of current best evidence in making decisions about the care of individual patients."[1]

Sackett further explains that evidence-based practice requires the integration of three sources of information (see Figure 4.1):

- Clinical expertise, which is the education, experience, and judgment of individual practitioners
- Best available external clinical evidence, which is clinically relevant patient-centered published research into the "the accuracy and precision of diagnostic tests (including the clinical examination), the power of prognostic markers, and the efficacy and safety of therapeutic, rehabilitative, and preventive regimens"[2]
- Patient values and preferences, which give the patient equal participation in the clinical decision

All three sources of information need to be part of the decision-making process. While they place a strong emphasis on clinical research and randomized controlled trials, proponents of EBP agree that the evidence alone does not make the decision, but rather contributes to it. To make this a conscientious effort at finding the best available evidence from clinical research, a series of steps was first suggested in 1992[3] and further codified in the Sicily statement on evidence-based practice.[4] The steps offer a framework for dealing with the clinical uncertainty that can arise from caring for patients and the process of identifying additional reliable information. The steps form a cycle (Figure 4.2) and always begin with a patient dilemma.

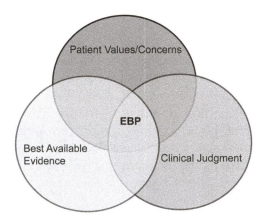

Figure 4.1   The Evidence-Based Practice Triad

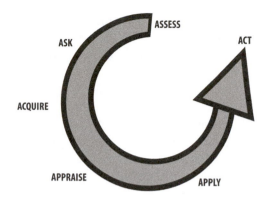

Figure 4.2   The Evidence-Based Practice Cycle

The best way to fully understand the skills, knowledge, and resources needed to practice EBP and the way that librarians can help is to work through the steps with a case example.

The first step (ASK) is recognizing that additional information is needed and translating that information into a well-focused clinical question. Two basic types of questions comprise ASK: Background questions seek general information about a condition or treatment such as "What are the clinical manifestations of a specific disease?" or "How is a specific disease commonly treated?" They are usually answered by textbooks. New learners generally have more background questions as they begin to learn about disease processes. Foreground or clinical questions are more specific and come out of the need for additional information to make good clinical decisions about specific patient problems. This type of question should be directly relevant to the specific patient problem or dilemma and should be phrased in such a way as to facilitate searching the literature. Within the EBP framework, four parts comprise a well-built clinical question, which is often referred to as PICO: the *P*atient problem (the main medical problem), the *I*ntervention (the treatment or test that is being considered for the patient), the *C*omparison (the alternative treatment or test, if any) and the *O*utcome (the expected benefit of the treatment or test). The PICO was developed by a physician,[5] but librarians should recognize this as a framework for the reference interview and a way for clinicians to use their own vocabulary to help clarify their specific information need. The literature reports several variations of the PICO:

PICOT, where the *T* stands for Time, or the duration for the data collection[6, 7]

PICOT, where the *T* stands for Type of question (therapy, diagnosis, prognosis, harm, etc.) or Type of study (randomized controlled trial, cohort study, case control study, etc.)[8]

PICOTS, where the *TS* stands for Timing and Setting[9]

The type of question is important, as it helps focus the query and identifies the best study design appropriate to the type of question being asked. For example, a question about the effectiveness of a treatment would best be answered by a randomized controlled trial or systematic review, but for questions of harm, a case-control or cohort study would be more ethical and appropriate. These variations of the PICO focus on quantitative research that uses objective observations and experiments to test and evaluate treatments, prognostic factors, or diagnostic tools (see Figure 4.3 for a case example). A growing interest exists within medicine for qualitative research focusing on the human experience of healthcare that tries to explain and understand how it affects individuals and groups. This type of research is very different from quantitiative and asks a different type of question using the SPIDER (Sample, Phenomenon of Interest, Design, Evaluation, Research type) neumonic.[10]

The PICOT should include enough information to help answer the question by generating terms for the search query and to identify the relevant articles that match your patient problem and intervention. A single patient encounter may generate more than one question, but each question should have its own PICO or PICOT.

Case Example: ASK

It's Monday morning, and you are a new nurse practitioner at a rural health clinic. Your first patient is Sarah, and poor Sarah has an earache. She is 18 months old, she has a fever and is very irritable, and she continually tugs at her ears. Your physical examination shows a bulging of the tympanic membrane in the left ear. You are fairly confident that she has a case of acute otitis media. You want to help Sarah, but you don't want to expose her unnecessarily to antibiotics that may not make a difference and could cause adverse effects. You are also aware that most of the literature indicates that watchful waiting is just as effective as antibiotics and that most kids will get better without them.

However, this patient is under 2 years of age, and she may be more vulnerable to complications. You have some uncertainty as to how to proceed and recognize that you need additional information specific to this case to help her mother make a good clinical decision. You use the PICOT to focus your clinical question.

Patient problem	Acute otitis media, child under 2 years of age
Intervention	Antibiotics (any type, including Amoxicillin)
Comparison	Watchful waiting or no antibiotics
Outcome	Reduce the pain; reduce the duration of the disease; prevent complications such as hearing loss
Type of question	Therapy or treatment
Type of study	Randomized controlled trial; systematic review
Question:	In infants under the age of 2 years with acute otitis media, are antibiotics more effective than watchful waiting for reducing the duration of pain and disease and preventing complications?

Figure 4.3   ASK: Example of a Clinical Case and Question

The second step (ACQUIRE) is using the information from the clinical question to formulate a search strategy and find relevant and valid information to answer the question. This can often be the most frustrating part of the EBP process. It requires easy access to library or knowledge-based resources as well as the time and skill to search them efficiently and effectively.

Two broad categories exist for resources that are used in answering clinical questions: preappraised and primary resources. Preappraised resources have gone through a vetting process that has identified studies relevant to clinical practice and has appraised the methodology of the studies to determine that they were done properly so that the results reflect the truth of the research. Specific and validated criteria are used in appraising each type of study.[11] Examples of preappraised resources are *ACP Journal Club*, *Evidence-Based Medicine* (BMJ), *Evidence-Based Nursing* (BMJ), *Evidence-Based Mental Health* (BMJ), and Database of Abstracts of Reviews of Effects (DARE). Other resources such as Clinical Evidence, DynaMed, First Consult, Physicians' Information and Education Resources (PIER), and *UpToDate* provide some critical appraisal of the literature, as they provide in-depth summaries or reviews of the management of diseases. These pre-appraised resources are extremely important as their simple search engines and their current and reliable information can save the clinician valuable time.. However, these resources are usually not comprehensive and may not always provide an answer to the question. The other category of resource is the primary literature found in major databases such as Medline or PubMed (22 million indexed records), CINAHL (Cumulative Index to Nursing and Allied Health Literature, with 3.2 million records), and Embase (25 million indexed records). While these databases of original research are much larger and more comprehensive, they do not validate the study methodology, and therefore the clinician must have the time and the skill to critically appraise the study before applying the results to patient care. (It should be noted that the peer-review process can vary widely from journal to journal and cannot always be used to determine the validity of a study.) The trade-off with the primary literature is that the answer may be more likely to be found, but additional time and energy is needed to properly review it.

Once the appropriate resource has been chosen, a search strategy needs to be formulated to find the specific information. The PICOT can facilitate this by identifying the key concepts that need to be in the article that addresses the question. The preappraised resources usually require a simple strategy that might include the main patient problem or intervention, while the primary resources require a much more complex strategy. The PICO or PICOT has the dual purpose of refining the clinical question and helping formulate the search strategy.[12] For our question, *ACP Journal Club* did not have a study that included children under two years, and *UpToDate* recommended following the American Academy of Family Physicians (AAFP) guidelines, which were written in 2004. Our clinician was concerned about any additional new information, so an answer was sought in PubMed (all resources were searched on December 12, 2012).

Case Example: ACQUIRE	
Patient problem	Acute otitis media, child under 2 years of age
Intervention	Antibiotics (any type, including Amoxicillin)
Comparison	Watchful waiting or no antibiotics
Outcome	Reduce the pain; reduce the duration of the disease; prevent complications such as hearing loss
Type of question	Therapy or treatment
Type of study	Randomized controlled trial; systematic review
Question:	In infants under the age of 2 years with acute otitis media, are antibiotics more effective than watchful waiting for reducing the duration of pain and disease and preventing complications?
Article: Hoberman A. Treatment of acute otitis media in children under 2 years of age. N Engl J Med. 2011 Jan 13;364(2):105-15. doi:10.1056/NEJMoa0912254. PubMed PMID: 21226576;	

Figure 4.4   Example of PICO and Search Strategy for PubMed

Note: The terms highlighted in the PICO were used to formulate the search strategy in PubMed. While the search retrieved 222 randomized controlled trials, the fifth citation on the list appeared to be relevant and specific to our population.

The third step (APPRAISE) is critically appraising the methodology of the study to determine that it was done properly, that it eliminated potential bias or improper influence, and that it therefore validates credible results. Bias can affect the outcome of a study in many ways. For example, selection bias can occur if the researcher is allowed to pick and choose the patients that are assigned to the treatment and control groups. Either consciously or subconsciously, they may pick healthier patients for the treatment group if they think that will work better. Assessment bias can be a problem if the researchers know what treatment their patient received. They may look harder for outcomes that show a benefit or adverse event, depending on their perceptions of the treatment. The critical appraisal process helps determine if the researchers took the necessary steps to eliminate these and other types of potential bias. Clinicians need to understand study design and the criteria used to judge the methodology of specific studies. (See Figure 4.5 for an example of validity criteria for a randomized controlled trial.) As mentioned previously, the preappraised resources conduct this critical appraisal and facilitate evidence-based practice. However, as we saw from our example, many clinical questions are answered by studies found in PubMed, and these require some critical appraisal. Once the study has been validated, the clinician should review the results for their clinical significance and potential impact on the patient.

The last step (APPLY) in the EBP process is to take the information obtained from the best available external clinical evidence and integrate it with the clinical expertise and patient preferences and values to reach a shared decision with the patient. It is also important to understand the statistical terminology used to report

Validity Criteria for Randomized Controlled Trial	Hoberman A. Treatment of acute otitis media in children under 2 years. N Engl J Med. 2011 Jan 13;364(2):105-15.
Randomization and concealed allocation Were patients assigned to the interventions by a randomization process, which gave each participant an equal chance of getting into either group of the study? Was the randomization scheme concealed from the researcher who was enrolling patients into the study?	Stratified (history & exposure; block randomization for 2 sites; concealed allocation – not mentioned
Baseline characteristics After randomization, are the groups similar in terms of demographics and factors that could affect the outcome?	Table 1; no significant differences
Blinding Are the key participants in the study (patients, caregivers, researchers, data analysts, and adjudicators) aware of what treatment each group received?	Patients (placebo), parents, research personnel; and care givers unaware of assignments
Equal treatment Were groups treated equally except for the interventions?	All patients given same dosage; all patients allowed rescue meds; telephone interviews
Follow-up Were all patients follow-up and accounted for at the end of the study? And was the study long enough to have the outcomes of interest occur?	96% completed all scheduled visits
Intention to treat Were groups analyzed according to their original randomized assignments, regardless of what they ended up actually taking?	Patients analyzed within original randomized groups
Results for Resolution by Day 2	
Absolute risk reduction The absolute mathematical difference between the event rate in the experimental group and the control group	35% – 28% = 7% (favors antibiotics)
Relative risk reduction The proportional difference between the event rate in the experimental group and the control group	7% / 28% = 25% (favors antibiotics)
Number needed to treat The number of patients that need to be treated with the intervention to have one good outcome	1 /7 = 14 (14 patients under the age of 2 years with acute otitis media need to be treated with antibiotics to have 1 good outcome)

Figure 4.5 Example of a Critical Appraisal of the Study by Hoberman

Note: After reviewing the validity criteria for this article, it appears to have a strong methodology, which reduced potential biases, and therefore the results are valid.

Case Example: APPLY

You return to the patient to discuss the physical exam, the adverse effects of antibiotics, the controversy surrounding overuse of antibiotics, the evidence from the NEJM article, the potential side effects of antibiotics, and what is important for the child and the child's mother. Together you make an informed decision about whether to prescribe antibiotics for Sarah.

Figure 4.6   Example of Applying Evidence to a Clinical Decision

the results so that magnitude of effect is not misleading. In the example in Figure 4.6, the absolute risk reduction shows the mathematical difference between the two interventions, and the relative risk reduction shows the difference as a percentage of change from the base or control group. The relative number often looks larger and can make small differences look much bigger than they really are.

This process of EBP can take as little as a few minutes, depending on the availability of library resources and the knowledge and skill level of the practitioner. Practicing EBP can also take more time than allocated for a patient visit and thus might be done after regular office hours or sometimes not at all. The literature tells us that healthcare practitioners have many questions, as many as two questions per three patients, during the course of a busy clinical day.[13, 14, 15, 16]

The literature also reports that when clinicians find answers to their clinical questions, it changes their management decisions as much as half the time. In 1992, the Rochester Study asked clinicians to request information from the library related to a specific patient case and then evaluate its impact on care for that patient. Eighty percent of the 208 physicians who returned the questionnaires reported that the information changed the diagnosis (29 percent), the choice of tests (51 percent), the choice of drugs (45 percent), the length of stay (19 percent), or the advice given to the patient (72 percent).[17] Sackett used an "evidence cart" with core textbooks and a computer that was pushed along with the rounding team so that clinical questions could be answered in real time. He found that of the 71 successful searches, 37 (52 percent) confirmed the team's current or tentative diagnosis or treatment plan, 18 (25 percent) led to a new diagnostic test or management decision, and 16 (23 percent) corrected a previous test or treatment. Sadly, when the study ended and the cart was removed, the perceived need for evidence rose sharply, but a search for it was carried out only 12 percent of the time.[18] Crowley created a database of clinical questions generated at sign-outs by general medicine residents. The residents were then asked to search the literature to answer their question and self-report any changes in decisions related to the management of their patients. They reported that obtaining useful information altered patient management decisions 47 percent of the time.[19] Clearly, finding answers to clinical questions can affect clinical decisions made when caring for patients. However, we also know that many of these questions go unanswered.[20, 21, 22] The most commonly reported barriers to practicing EBP include not having enough time, not having ready access to the resources, not having the skills to search efficiently, and not having an efficient tracking system to manage the questions that do arise.[23, 24]

WHAT ROLES DO MEDICAL LIBRARIANS PLAY IN THE PRACTICE OF EBP?

Medical librarians can play a vital role in eliminating some of these barriers to practicing EBP. Supporting the practice of EBP leverages the core competencies of medical librarians by providing easy access to relevant resources and by educating patrons on information management skills.[25, 26]

Making Relevant Collections Easily Accessible

EBP requires a collection of medical and health-related resources (electronic books, journals, and databases) that are up to date, accurate, and comprehensive. We know two basic types of resources to support EBP: preappraised resources and the primary literature. Preappraised resources are more efficient because they contain information that has gone through an appraisal process, meaning that the included studies have been evaluated for the quality of their methodology. Haynes has suggested a hierarchy of preappraised resources based on level of evidence synthesis and synopsis.[27, 28] The higher levels of the table in Figure 4.7 provide synopses of valid studies that make it easy for clinicians to quickly find and utilize current and relevant information. The lower levels represent the primary literature, which is also useful but requires additional time and work on the part of the clinician.

While this hierarchy can be useful in making final decisions about which resources to purchase, librarians should consult with practitioners to verify that the resources will meet their information needs.

However, having a relevant collection is not enough. Clinicians must have reliable network connectivity and be able to quickly find the important resources. A comprehensive, alphabetical list of all available resources, while impressive, can be overwhelming and frustrating to a busy clinician. A better strategy is to create a single web page or portal that identifies the key clinical resources used most often. The clinician then has one site from which to find most of the information he or she needs. Taking the access issue one step further, librarians can use this as an opportunity to be creative and innovative. Developing a portal to make finding key resources is helpful, but developing federated search engines can save the clinician additional time. A federated search allows for the simultaneous search of multiple databases or resources. A clinician can make a single query and get results from a variety of resources. This is especially helpful when the databases are small and do not require a controlled vocabulary. Federated searches vary in sophistication, and they can be developed in-house or purchased from commercial vendors.

Customizing PubMed

The EBP preappraised resources are often small databases that may require only one or two concepts in the search query to identify relevant information. PubMed, with its 22 million citations, usually requires a more complicated strategy and a thorough understanding of the various methods of limiting search results. Because the limits are not always intuitive, clinicians who do not search often may find it hard to remember these special features of PubMed. However, PubMed has customizable

Systems: Include clinical pathways or textbook summaries that integrate evidence-based information about specific clinical problems, provide regular updating, and automatically link (through an electronic medical record) a specific patient's circumstances to the relevant information

Computerized decision support systems

Summaries: Include clinical pathways or textbook summaries that integrate evidence-based information about specific clinical problems and provide regular updating

Clinical Evidence, http://clinicalevidence.bmj.com/x/index.html
DynaMed, https://dynamed.ebscohost.com/
First Consult, http://www.mdconsult.com/php/390137092-2/home.html
National Guideline Clearinghouse, http://www.guidelines.gov/
Physicians' Information and Education Resources (PIER), http://pier.acponline.org/index.html
UpToDate, http://www.uptodate.com/

Syntheses: Systematic reviews

Cochrane Library, http://www.thecochranelibrary.com/
Evidence Updates, http://plus.mcmaster.ca/evidenceupdates/

Synopses of studies: A brief, but often sufficiently detailed, summary of a high-quality study that can inform clinical practice

ACP Journal Club, http://acpjc.acponline.org/
Evidence-based Medicine (BMJ), http://ebm.bmj.com/
Evidence-Based Nursing (BMJ), http://ebn.bmj.com/
Evidence-Based Mental Health (BMJ), http://ebmh.bmj.com/

Studies: Single original study

PubMed, http://www.ncbi.nlm.nih.gov/pubmed/
Medline, (Ovid) http://www.ovid.com/
CINAHL (Cumulative Index to Nursing and Allied Health Literature), http://www.ebscohost.com/biomedical-libraries/the-cinahl-database
Embase, http://www.embase.com

Figure 4.7   Hierarchy of Preappraised Evidence Based on Haynes 6S

features that make it easier to refine large search results. For example, the Clinical Queries (Table 4.1) are short strategies that can filter citations to a specific type of clinical question (Therapy, Diagnosis, Etiology or Harm) and scope (Narrow or Broad). The search strategies behind the Clinical Queries were developed by Haynes and his research team at McMaster University to improve the efficacy of PubMed for retrieving scientifically strong studies on treatment and other types of questions.

The link to the Clinical Queries is currently on the front page of PubMed and not very accessible when reviewing results in the database. Placing the Clinical Queries on the results page as a customized search filter through MyShare and MyNCBI make it easier to find and use them.

The ultimate goal for collection access should be to embed links to knowledge-based resources directly within the electronic medical record (EMR). Most clinicians work in environments where patient care is carefully documented in electronic medical records. Medical librarians should collaborate with information technology

Table 4.1   Clinical Query Search Strategies in PubMed

Category	Optimized For	PubMed Equivalent
Therapy	Sensitive/broad	((clinical[Title/Abstract] AND trial[Title/Abstract]) OR clinical trials[MeSH Terms] OR clinical trial[Publication Type] OR random*[Title/Abstract] OR random allocation [MeSH Terms] OR therapeutic use[MeSH Subheading])
	Specific/narrow	(randomized controlled trial[Publication Type] OR (randomized[Title/Abstract] AND controlled[Title/Abstract] AND trial[Title/Abstract]))
Diagnosis	Sensitive/broad	(sensitiv*[Title/Abstract] OR sensitivity and specificity[MeSH Terms] OR diagnos*[Title/Abstract] OR diagnosis[MeSH: noexp] OR diagnostic*[MeSH:noexp] OR diagnosis, differential[MeSH:noexp] OR diagnosis[Subheading:noexp])
	Specific/narrow	(specificity[Title/Abstract])
Etiology	Sensitive/broad	(risk*[Title/Abstract] OR risk*[MeSH:noexp] OR risk* [MeSH:noexp] OR cohort studies[MeSH Terms] OR group* [Text Word])
	Specific/narrow	((relative[Title/Abstract] AND risk*[Title/Abstract]) OR (relative risk[Text Word]) OR risks[Text Word] OR cohort studies[MeSH:noexp] OR (cohort[Title/Abstract] AND stud* [Title/Abstract]))
Prognosis	Sensitive/broad	(incidence[MeSH:noexp] OR mortality[MeSH Terms] OR follow up studies[MeSH:noexp] OR prognos*[Text Word] OR predict*[Text Word] OR course*[Text Word])
	Specific/narrow	(prognos*[Title/Abstract] OR (first[Title/Abstract] AND episode[Title/Abstract]) OR cohort[Title/Abstract])
Clinical prediction guides	Sensitive/broad	(predict*[tiab] OR predictive value of tests[mh] OR scor*[tiab] OR observ*[tiab] OR observer variation[mh])
	Specific/narrow	(validation[tiab] OR validate[tiab])

departments to investigate ways to integrate library resources into the medical record and therefore into the workflow of busy clinicians. This can be as simple as a hyperlink in the medical record to the web portal of key resources or implementing the OpenInfobutton protocol. The OpenInfobutton protocol allows for the creation of context-sensitive links that automatically extract data from the medical record to generate and send a search query to a knowledge-based resource, pulling the answer to the question directly to the clinician.[29] An electronic medical record with an OpenInfobutton link will take the clinician to a library resource for more information on the specific disease. The OpenInfobutton is open source and is one example of how library resources can be integrated into the electronic medical record. Vendors of products such as *UpToDate* and DynaMed provide their own application interface to integrate into the electronic medical record.

Teaching Efficient Search Skills

The first two steps (ASK and ACQUIRE) in the EBP process require that clinicians be skilled and comfortable forming good clinical questions and searching the literature. Understanding how to ask a question and how to efficiently and effectively search the literature are core competencies for medical librarians and the focus of much of the educational activities of the library. For in-library classes and instruction, class content should be organized around the tenants of EBP—starting with a case scenario, getting the learner to work through the focused question using the PICO or PICOT framework, and then applying that to an efficient and effective search strategy. This models and reinforces the EBP process and gives learners the opportunity to actively practice these skills. The challenge is to find the right balance in teaching clinicians to be successful in their searching but not making it so complicated that they easily become discouraged.

Medical librarians can partner with clinical faculty who are teaching their own EBP courses. Librarians can teach question formation and searching while clinical faculty focuses on critical appraisal and applying information to patient care. Most faculty members will welcome the opportunity to share teaching responsibilities and collaborate with the library. A variety of venues and opportunities (e.g., journal clubs, morning reports, noon conferences) for the library to participate in the education and training of students and clinicians in evidence-based practice are currently available. Supporting instruction in EBP does not always have to involve direct face-to-face teaching. Since the core curriculum of asking, acquiring, and appraising is common across most disciplines, librarians should consider ways to support education with core materials that can then be customized to specific learners or disciplines:

- Develop online modules that cover key components of EBP
- Create library portals that provide access to key resources and teaching tools for instructors of EBP
- Create wikis or blogs that provide course content and resources for the students of EBP courses
- Help identify key articles to use as class examples for critical appraisal
- Identify EBP assessment tools that support research into the effectiveness of EBP instruction

Other examples of library support include a web-based consult service, a customizable search engine, and development of an evidence-based practice curriculum.[30, 31, 32]

Supporting the Development of Systematic Reviews

Well-done systematic reviews and meta-analysis can be extremely important in helping clinicians answer clinical questions. A systematic review addresses a well-focused question, often following the PICO framework; conducts a thorough and systematic search of the literature (both published and unpublished); conducts a critical appraisal of included studies; and provides an analysis and summary of the results of the included studies. A meta-analysis includes the mathematical pooling of the results of the included studies to show an overall effect. The advantage to a systematic review of the literature is that all relevant studies are reviewed and the conclusions summarized, thus saving the busy clinician from the task of reading each individual study.

The Cochrane Collaboration is an international network of healthcare providers and researchers who prepare, update, and promote the Cochrane Systematic Reviews as part of the Cochrane Library. The *Cochrane Handbook for Systematic Reviews of Interventions* provides detailed documentation on the process of preparing and updating a systematic review.[33] In the *Medicare Improvement for Patients and Providers Act of 2008*, Congress directed the Institute of Medicine (IOM) to develop standards for conducting systematic reviews. These standards, *Finding What Works in Health Care: Standards for Systematic Review*, were published in 2011 and state that the team should "work with a librarian or other information specialist trained in performing systematic reviews to plan the search strategy."[34]

Therefore, librarians are an essential part of the systematic review process. They work with the team to develop comprehensive search strategies that are designed to retrieve all the literature for each key research question. The strategies are broad in scope and include indexing terms as well as natural language, related terms, and synonyms. The searches are conducted in the major bibliographic databases such as PubMed, Embase and the Cochrane Library, as well as other databases appropriate to the topic. To address the issue of publication bias, that is, the tendency to publish positive studies rather than negative studies, the unpublished or "grey literature" also needs to be searched. Sources of unpublished studies include conference proceedings, pharmaceutical and regulatory agency websites, as well as subject experts. The librarian contributes to the publication of the systematic review by providing detailed documentation of the search strategy in each database searched. Often this is summarized in the methods section of the manuscript, with the complete strategies included as an appendix.

ARE LIBRARIANS SUPPORTING EBP WITHIN THEIR INSTITUTION?

In 2007, Li and Wu explored how practicing medical librarians were playing a role in supporting and enhancing EBP within their institutions. Their data is based on 596 completed questionnaires from libraries in the United States and other countries.[35] Respondents were asked to identify their EBP-related responsibilities within broad categories. The results were tabulated for type of library and showed that libraries *are* involved in EBP activities, especially those with librarians working in hospital environments. Most of the EBM responsibilities are related to one of the core competencies of librarians: expertise with resources and database searching. (When librarians say they "teach EBM," this usually means that they teach database searching within the broader context of EBM.) Table 4.2 shows the reported EBM activity for academic, hospital, and special libraries.

Li and Wu conclude that "US medical librarians are taking the EBM challenge and have been playing an active role in supporting and enhancing EBM practice. Supporting EBM practice requires not only knowledge of EBM resources and skills

Table 4.2   EBM Responsibility and Involvement Reported by Type of Library

EBM Responsibility	Academic Library	Hosiptal Library	Special Library
Expertise with EBM resources	197 (88%)	252 (94%)	33 (89%)
Providing EBM research	189 (85%)	256 (96%)	28 (74%)
Contributing to EBM initiatives	135 (61%)	163 (61%)	17 (45%)
Attending morning report	28 (13%)	27 (11%)	1 (3%)
Attending medical round	23 (11%)	25 (10%)	1 (3%)
Attending journal club	30 (14%)	34 (13%)	3 (8%)
Teaching EBM	179 (80%)	132 (50%)	13 (34%)

in information searching and retrieving, but also an understanding of what health-care professionals need to practice EBM. Medical librarians, especially those who provide services directly to healthcare professionals, are in need of training to acquire and update their EBM related skills."[36]

EBP TRAINING FOR LIBRARIANS

Many opportunities exist for librarians to learn about evidence-based practice. The Medical Library Association (MLA) maintains the Educational Clearinghouse (http://cech.mlanet.org/), which lists CE courses covering EBM or EBP topics. The courses offered include distance education as well as traditional face-to-face courses. Supporting Clinical Care: An Institute in Evidence-Based Practice for Medical Librarians is an intensive introductory three-day workshop designed and taught by medical librarians. (From 2008 to 2012, it was held at Dartmouth College. It continues with rotating venues. In 2013, it was held in Calgary, Canada, and in 2014 it is scheduled for Denver, Colorado.) The workshop includes large group inter-active lectures followed by small group sessions where the new skills can be practiced and improved. The curriculum is based on the EBP workshops designed for clinicians and covers study design, focusing clinical questions, searching for the evidence, and critically appraising therapy and diagnostic testing studies, as well as systematic reviews and qualitative research. A similar workshop, the Australian Evidence Based Practice Librarian's Institute, was developed to help meet the growing need for EBP training in Australia. In addition, librarians have been invited to participate as tutors at several workshops designed for practicing clinicians:

- Teaching and Leading EBM: A Workshop for Educators and Champions of Evidence-Based Medicine at the Duke University campus in Durham, North Carolina (http://sites.duke.edu/ebmworkshop/)
- Rocky Mountain Workshop on How to Practice Evidence-Based Healthcare, directed by the Colorado School of Public Health (http://www.ucdenver.edu/academics/colleges/PublicHealth/community/ebhc/Pages/default.aspx)
- EBCP Workshop: Improving Your Practice/Teaching through Evidence-Based Clinical Practice, held at McMaster University, in Hamilton, California (http://ebm.mcmaster.ca/)

- Oxford Workshop in Teaching Evidence-Based Practice at St. Hugh's College, in Oxford, United Kingdom (http://www.cebm.net/index.aspx?o=5920)

Participating in these workshops not only exposes librarians to the curriculum of EBP, but also provides an opportunity to work one-on-one with clinicians and gain a better understanding of how they use library resources to answer clinical questions.[37]

EPB AND ACCREDITATION

The major accrediting bodies for medical schools and graduate medical education have recognized the important role that evidence-based practice plays in training and educating new physicians. Medical schools and teaching hospitals must document how they are meeting these accreditation requirements. Medical librarians should become familiar with the requirements and find ways to collaborate with educators and clinicians to help develop a plan for meeting the objectives or milestones.

The Association of American Medical Colleges (AAMC) developed learning objectives for the medical school curriculum based on attributes that students should possess at the time of graduation. Under the heading of "Physicians must be dutiful," they state that physicians in the care of patients must "apply the principles of evidence-based medicine and cost effectiveness in making decisions about the utilization of limited medical resources."[38] The document goes on to state that the medical school must ensure that before graduation, students are able to demonstrate "The ability to retrieve (from electronic databases and other resources), manage, and utilize biomedical information for solving problems and making decisions that are relevant to the care of individuals and populations."[39] Many of these information management skills can be taught by medical librarians in partnership with clinicians. The skills can be taught at various times during medical school, starting with the basics of searching the major databases such as PubMed and Medline and later incorporating EBP principles when the students begin to experience patients on the clinical rotations. A review of the medical literature provides interesting and useful examples and experiences of medical librarians involved in teaching some of the components of EBP in medical schools.[40–46]

The Accreditation Council for Graduate Medical Education (ACGME), the accrediting body for residency training, began implementing its Next Accreditation System (NAS) in July 2013. This restructuring of the accreditation system will be based on educational outcomes of the six domains of clinical competency: patient care, practice-based learning and improvement, medical knowledge, interpersonal and communication skills, professionalism, and systems-based practice.[47] Educational milestones are being developed to describe in behavioral terms the learning and performance levels expected of residents at various levels of their training. Some of the suggested milestones are:

- Medical students: Understand basic terminology of clinical epidemiology and bio-statistics and be able to identify the study design of a research study
- Residents: Formulate a searchable question, understand potential sources of bias within research studies, and be able to apply critical appraisal criteria to different types of research studies
- Graduating resident: Model clinical practice that incorporates the basic concepts of evidence-based practice
- Advanced, specialist residents or practicing physicians: Teach new learners the basic concepts of evidence-based practice[48]

Evidence-based practice is about managing patient care and managing the abundance of information available to healthcare providers. It is about applying the principles of information management to the world of clinical medicine. It is clear that evidence-based practice is now an essential part of practicing healthcare and therefore an essential part of the education and training of physicians and other healthcare providers. Librarians understand these principles and should take advantage of the opportunities to play a major role in supporting EBP education and training within their institutions.

NOTES

1. Sackett, D. L., W. M. Rosenberg, J. A. Gray, R. B. Haynes, and W. S. Richardson. "Evidence Based Medicine: What It Is and What It Isn't." *British Medical Journal* 312, no. 7023 (January 13, 1996): 71–72.
2. Ibid.
3. Cook, D. J., R. Jaeschke, and G. H. Guyatt. "Critical Appraisal of Therapeutic Interventions in the Intensive Care Unit: Human Monoclonal Antibody Treatment in Sepsis; Journal Club of the Hamilton Regional Critical Care Group." *Journal of Intensive Care Medicine* 7, no. 6 (November–December 1992): 275–282.
4. Dawes, M., W. Summerskill, P. Glasziou, A. Cartabellotta, J. Martin, K. Hopayian, F. Porzsolt, A. Burls, and J. Osborne. "Sicily Statement on Evidence-Based Practice." *BMC Medical Education* 5, no. 1 (January 5, 2005): 1.
5. Richardson, W. S., M. C. Wilson, J. Nishikawa, and R. S. Hayward. "The Well-Built Clinical Question: A Key to Evidence-Based Decisions." *ACP Journal Club* 123, no. 3 (November–December 1995): A12-3.
6. Lorena, P. Rios, Ye Chenglin, and Thabane Lehana. "Association between Framing of the Research Question Using the PICOTFormat and Reporting Quality of Randomized Controlled Trials." *BMC Medical Research Methodology* 10, no. 1 (2010): 11.
7. Thabane, L., T. Thomas, C. Ye, and J. Paul. "Posing the Research Question: Not So Simple." *Canadian Journal of Anesthesia [Journal canadien d'anesthésie]* 56, no. 1 (2009): 71-9.
8. Krupski, Tracey L., Philipp Dahm, Susan F. Fesperman, and Connie M. Schardt. "How to Perform a Literature Search." *Journal of Urology* 179, no. 4 (2008): 1264–1270.
9. Thompson, M. M.; US Agency for Healthcare Research and Quality; and Pacific Northwest Evidence-Based Practice Center, Oregon Health & Science University. *A Framework to Facilitate the Use of Systematic Reviews and Meta-Analyses in the Design of Primary Research Studies.* [Web Document.] Rockville, MD: Agency for Healthcare Research and Quality, 2012. http://www.ncbi.nlm.nih.gov/books/NBK83621/.

10. Booth, A., A. J. O'Rourke, and N. J. Ford. "Structuring the Pre-Search Reference Interview: A Useful Technique for Handling Clinical Questions." *Bulletin of the Medical Library Association* 88, no. 3 (July 2000): 239–246.

11. Guyatt, Gordon , Drummond Rennie, Evidence-Based Medicine Working Group, and American Medical Association. *Users' Guide to the Medical Literature: Essentials of Evidence-Based Clinical Practice*. Chicago: AMA Press, 2008.

12. Booth et al., *op. cit.*

13. Allan, G. M., V. Ma, S. Aaron, B. Vandermeer, D. Manca, and C. Korownyk. "Residents' Clinical Questions: How Are They Answered and Are the Answers Helpful?" *Canadian Family Physician [Médecin de famille canadien]* 58, no. 6 (June 2012): e344–e351.

14. Covell, D. G., G. C. Uman, and P. R. Manning. "Information Needs in Office Practice: Are They Being Met?" *Annals of Internal Medicine* 103, no. 4 (October 1985): 596–599.

15. Green, M. L., M. A. Ciampi, and P. J. Ellis. "Residents' Medical Information Needs in Clinic: Are They Being Met?" *American Journal of Medicine* 109, no. 3 (August 15, 2000): 218–223.

16. Osheroff, J. A., D. E. Forsythe, B. G. Buchanan, R. A. Bankowitz, B. H. Blumenfeld, and R. A. Miller. "Physicians' Information Needs: Analysis of Questions Posed During Clinical Teaching." *Annals of Internal Medicine* 114, no. 7 (April 1, 1991): 576–581.

17. Marshall, J. G. "The Impact of the Hospital Library on Clinical Decision Making: The Rochester Study." *Bulletin of the Medical Library Association* 80, no. 2 (April 1992): 169–178.

18. Sackett, D. L., and S. E. Straus. "Finding and Applying Evidence during Clinical Rounds: The 'Evidence Cart.'" *JAMA: Journal of the American Medical Association* 280, no. 15 (October 21, 1998): 1336–1338.

19. Crowley, S. D., T. A. Owens, C. M. Schardt, S. I. Wardell, J. Peterson, S. Garrison, and S. A. Keitz. "A Web-Based Compendium of Clinical Questions and Medical Evidence to Educate Internal Medicine Residents." *Academic Medicine: Journal of the Association of American Medical Colleges* 78, no. 3 (March 2003): 270–274.

20. Ely, J. W., J. A. Osheroff, S. M. Maviglia, and M. E. Rosenbaum. "Patient-Care Questions That Physicians Are Unable to Answer." *Journal of the American Medical Information Association* 14, no. 4 (July–August 2007): 407–414.

21. Green, M. L., and T. R. Ruff. "Why Do Residents Fail to Answer Their Clinical Questions? A Qualitative Study of Barriers to Practicing Evidence-Based Medicine." *Academic Medicine: Journal of the Association of American Medical Colleges* 80, no. 2 (February 2005): 176–182.

22. McCord, G., W. D. Smucker, B. A. Selius, S. Hannan, E. Davidson, S. L. Schrop, V. Rao, and P. Albrecht. "Answering Questions at the Point of Care: Do Residents Practice EBM or Manage Information Sources?" *Academic Medicine: Journal of the Association of American Medical Colleges* 82, no. 3 (March 2007): 298–303.

23. Green and Ruff, *op. cit.*

24. van Dijk, N., L. Hooft, and M. Wieringa-de Waard. "What Are the Barriers to Residents' Practicing Evidence-Based Medicine? A Systematic Review." *Academic Medicine: Journal of the Association of American Medical Colleges* 85, no. 7 (July 2010): 1163–1170.

25. Perry, G. J., and M. R. Kronenfeld. "Evidence-Based Practice: A New Paradigm Brings New Opportunities for Health Sciences Librarians." *Medical Reference Services Quarterly* 24, no. 4 (Winter 2005): 1–16.

26. Scherrer, C. S., and J. L. Dorsch. "The Evolving Role of the Librarian in Evidence-Based Medicine." *Bulletin of the Medical Library Association* 87, no. 3 (July 1999): 322–328.

27. DiCenso, A., L. Bayley, and R. B. Haynes. "ACP Journal Club: Editorial; Accessing Preappraised Evidence. Fine-Tuning the 5s Model into a 6s Model." *Annals of Internal Medicine* 151, no. 6 (September 15, 2009): JC3-2, JC3-3.

28. Haynes, R. B. "Of Studies, Syntheses, Synopses, Summaries, and Systems: The '5s' Evolution of Information Services for Evidence-Based Health Care Decisions." *ACP Journal Club* 145, no. 3 (November–December 2006): A8.

29. Del Fiol, G., R. A. Rocha, and P. D. Clayton. "Infobuttons at Intermountain Healthcare: Utilization and Infrastructure." *AMIA . . . Annual Symposium Proceedings/AMIA Symposium. AMIA Symposium* (2006): 180–184.

30. Bracke, P. J., D. K. Howse, and S. M. Keim. "Evidence-Based Medicine Search: A Customizable Federated Search Engine." *Journal of the Medical Library Association: JMLA* 96, no. 2 (April 2008): 108–113.

31. Klem, M. L., and P. M. Weiss. "Evidence-Based Resources and the Role of Librarians in Developing Evidence-Based Practice Curricula." *Journal of Professional Nursing: Official Journal of the American Association of Colleges of Nursing* 21, no. 6 (November–December 2005): 380–387.

32. Schwartz, A., and G. Millam. "A Web-Based Library Consult Service for Evidence-Based Medicine: Technical Development." *BMC Medical Informatics and Decision Making* 6 (2006): 16.

33. "Cochrane Handbook for Systematic Reviews of Interventions." Cochrane Collaboration, 2011. Accessed February 22, 2013. http://handbook.cochrane.org/.

34. *Finding What Works in Health Care: Standards for Systematic Review.* Institute of Medicine, 2011. http://www.iom.edu/Reports/2011/Finding-What-Works-in-Health-Care-Standards-for-Systematic-Reviews.aspx.

35. Li, P., and L. Wu. "Supporting Evidence-Based Medicine: A Survey of U.S. Medical Librarians." *Medical Reference Services Quarterly* 30, no. 4 (2011): 365–381.

36. Ibid.

37. Traditi, L. K., J. M. Le Ber, M. Beattie, and S. E. Meadows. "From Both Sides Now: Librarians' Experiences at the Rocky Mountain Evidence-Based Health Care Workshop." *Journal of the Medical Library Association: JMLA* 92, no. 1 (January 2004): 72–77.

38. AAMC Medical School Objectives Project Advisory Group. *Learning Objectives for Medical Student Education: Guidelines for Medical Schools.* Washington D.C.: Association of American Medical Colleges (AAMC), 1998.

39. Ibid.

40. Bradley, D. R., G. K. Rana, M. L. Lypson, and S. J. Hamstra. "A Centralized Practice-Based Learning and Improvement Curriculum for Residents and Fellows: A Collaboration of Health Sciences Librarians and Graduate Medical Education Administration." *Journal of the Medical Library Association: JMLA* 98, no. 2 (April 2010): 175–178.

41. Brown, J. F., and J. L. Nelson. "Integration of Information Literacy into a Revised Medical School Curriculum." *Medical Reference Services Quarterly* 22, no. 3 (Fall 2003): 63–74.

42. Innes, G. "Faculty-Librarian Collaboration: An Online Information Literacy Tutorial for Students." *Nurse Educator* 33, no. 4 (July-August 2008): 145–146.

43. Jeffery, K. M., L. Maggio, and M. Blanchard. "Making Generic Tutorials Content Specific: Recycling Evidence-Based Practice (EBP) Tutorials for Two Disciplines." *Medical Reference Services Quarterly* 28, no. 1 (Spring 2009): 1–9.

44. Kealey, S. "Continual Evolution: The Experience over Three Semesters of a Librarian Embedded in an Online Evidence-Based Medicine Course for Physician Assistant Students." *Medical Reference Services Quarterly* 30, no. 4 (2011): 411–425.

45. Moore, M. "Teaching Physicians to Make Informed Decisions in the Face of Uncertainty: Librarians and Informaticians on the Health Care Team." *Academic Medicine: Journal of the Association of American Medical Colleges* 86, no. 11 (November 2011): 1345.

46. O'Dwyer, L., and S. C. Kerns. "Evolution of an Information Literacy Curriculum for Third-Year Medical Students." *Medical Reference Services Quarterly* 30, no. 3 (2011): 221–232.

47. Swing, S. R., S. G. Clyman, E. S. Holmboe, and R. G. Williams. "Advancing Resident Assessment in Graduate Medical Education." *Journal of Graduate Medical Education* 1, no. 2 (December 2009): 278–286.

48. Nasca, T. J., I. Philibert, T. Brigham, and T. C. Flynn. "The Next GME Accreditation System: Rationale and Benefits." *New England Journal of Medicine* 366, no. 11 (March 15, 2012): 1051–1056.

Chapter 5

GOVERNMENT AGENCY AND PROFESSIONAL ASSOCIATION RESOURCES AND SERVICES

Keith Cogdill

Health sciences librarians in the United States should be aware of the major federal and international nongovernmental libraries and the professional associations influencing our field. A handful of previous publications have considered some of these organizations from an historical perspective, but the emphasis of this chapter is on the resources and services they currently provide.[1, 2]

NATIONAL LIBRARY OF MEDICINE

Overview and History

The National Library of Medicine (NLM) is one of the 27 institutes and centers comprising the National Institutes of Health (NIH). Now occupying two buildings at the NIH's main campus in Bethesda, Maryland, NLM has the largest collection of biomedical literature in the world, with approximately 19 million physical items in its collection. The history of NLM can be traced to 1836, when it began as a small collection of books in the office of the surgeon general of the army. It continued under the auspices of the military until 1956, when it was transferred to the Public Health Service and began operating as part of NIH in Bethesda in 1962.

Information Resources

NLM has made significant progress in making digital versions of historical material in its collection available online through its website (http:// www.nlm.nih.gov). Primarily the work of the NLM's History of Medicine Division, reproductions of many items have also been displayed as part of exhibits at NLM in Bethesda and through traveling exhibits hosted at libraries across the United States. Past exhibits have explored medicine in the Civil War era, women physicians, African American surgeons, and Native American concepts of wellness and disease.[3]

In addition to its extensive collection, NLM has developed an impressive array of valuable information resources for health professionals, consumers, and health sciences librarians. These are accessible from NLM's website, and many are compatible with mobile devices. Chief among these is the MEDLINE database, now most commonly accessed through NLM's PubMed search interface (http:// www.ncbi.nlm.nih.gov/pubmed). Beginning in the 1960s, NLM leveraged emerging computer technologies to increase the efficiency of its production of the printed Index Medicus. Computer files with these records were made available for remote searches in the early 1970s, and now over 2 billion searches are performed in PubMed each year. Indexing journal articles for MEDLINE is one of the responsibilities of NLM's Division of Library Operations, and the PubMed search system is maintained by NLM's National Center for Biotechnology Information (NCBI).

PubMed Central (PMC, http://www.ncbi.nlm.nih.gov/pmc/) is an online archive of journal literature in the health sciences. Begun in 2000, PMC now provides access to the full text of more than 2.5 million articles. Approximately 1,200 journals participate in PMC fully by contributing their complete content. Many of the participating journals make the full text of their articles available only after an embargo period. Like the PubMed search system, PMC is maintained by NLM's NCBI.

In addition to PubMed/MEDLINE and PMC, NLM has developed and maintains a number of other information resources, including an international registry of clinical trials. Developed by NLM's Lister Hill Center for Biomedical Communications, the ClinicalTrials.gov database began in response to the Food and Drug Administration Modernization Act of 1997. Now, records of over 137,000 clinical trials are available, with approximately 37,000 of these currently recruiting participants. Almost half of the records in ClinicalTrials.gov represent research being conducted outside of the United States. In addition to patients and families interested in participating in a clinical trial, ClinicalTrials.gov may be helpful for health sciences librarians looking for information about research in advance of published reports.

Building on its heritage of providing resources and services in support of health professionals, in 1998, NLM launched MedlinePlus.gov, a site focused on the health information needs of consumers. Originally launched with content on 22 topics, MedlinePlus now provides access to carefully reviewed content on over 900 health topics in both English and Spanish. NLM also licenses a health encyclopedia, a collection of surgical videos, and a medical dictionary that it makes available from MedlinePlus.

NN/LM and Health Information Outreach

The National Network of Libraries of Medicine (NN/LM) operates with NLM's financial support in the form of contracts awarded to libraries across the United States that serve as regional medical libraries (RMLs). While the number of RMLs has fluctuated since the NN/LM program began in the late 1960s, the NN/LM has operated with eight regions for several of the past five-year contract cycles. One of the primary reasons for NLM's creation of the RMLs and the NN/LM was to distribute the effort of providing copies of health sciences journal articles through interlibrary loan. Rather than having most interlibrary loan requests filled from NLM's collection, the RMLs promote the exchange of materials among libraries at academic health sciences centers and hospitals in their regions, with requests that cannot otherwise be filled going to NLM. The system for managing interlibrary loan requests among NN/LM members is DOCLINE (https://docline.gov/).

In 1989, a report from an NLM Board of Regents committee chaired by Michael DeBakey outlined a vision for NLM to leverage the NN/LM infrastructure in order to sponsor community health information outreach projects.[4] These projects initially focused on the information needs of health professionals who did not have an affiliation with a library at a hospital or academic health sciences center. Awarded through the RMLs, these projects have since enabled health sciences libraries across the United States to address a wide range of community health information issues, often in partnership with public libraries and other community-based organizations.[5] Chapter 14 provides additional information about health information outreach projects and funding opportunities. On a national level, NLM collaborates with the Centers for Disease Control and Prevention (CDC), the American Public Health Association, and several other organizations to enhance access to information for members of the public health workforce. This collaboration has resulted in the PHPartners.org website, with news and links to a wide range of public health content.

NLM-Sponsored Research, Education and Training

In addition to sponsoring outreach projects and other awards through the NN/LM, NLM also maintains an active grants program through its Division of Extramural Programs. Since 1972, NLM's informatics training grants have supported the education of informaticists at many universities across the United States.[6] The majority of students in these programs are physicians, but the range of trainees receiving fellowships from NLM also includes other clinicians, basic scientists, and librarians. NLM's grants program also supports a wide range of other efforts, including investigator-initiated research on topics related to biomedical information and informatics.

Another opportunity for informatics training from NLM is the weeklong program held on the campus of the Marine Biological Laboratory in Massachusetts (http://hermes.mbl.edu/education/courses/special_topics/med.html). Begun in 1992, this program is now offered twice a year. Participants include clinicians, biomedical researchers, and librarians.

For librarians who have recently completed their master's in information/library science, NLM's associate fellowship program (http://www.nlm.nih.gov/about/training/associate/) is an opportunity to spend one year at NLM and an optional second year at another health sciences library. The associate fellowship program began in 1957and now has typically four to six associate fellows each year.

For more experienced librarians in academic settings, NLM has partnered with the Association of Academic Health Sciences Libraries (AAHSL) to offer opportunities for leadership development. For more than a decade, NLM and AAHSL have offered a yearlong fellowship program aimed at librarians preparing to serve as library directors in academic health sciences settings (http://www.aahsl.org/leadershipfellows). This program includes mentorship with an experienced director as well as in-person and teleconference gatherings throughout the year.

NIH LIBRARY

Located in the National Institutes of Health (NIH) Clinical Center (Building 10) on the main NIH campus in Bethesda, the NIH Library operates as a division of the Office of Research Services within NIH's Office of the Director. The NIH Library's collection and services support the programs and research conducted across the 27 NIH institutes and centers, including the National Library of Medicine. While open to the public, the NIH Library focuses on the needs of the NIH staff who are intramural researchers and extramural grant administrators. Through interagency agreements, the NIH Library also serves federal employees at 18 other agencies and offices across the Department of Health and Human Services, including the Agency for Healthcare Research and Quality, the Health Resources and Services Administration, the Centers for Medicare and Medicaid Services, the Office of the National Coordinator for Health Information Technology, and the Indian Health Service.

The NIH Library was established in 1901 with funds appropriated for the library by Congress as part of its support for a new building for the Hygienic Laboratory, as NIH was known until 1930. Throughout its first 100 years, the NIH Library focused on collecting and organizing print materials and providing assistance in response to questions received from library patrons. In 2001, the NIH Library began an informationist program with the aim of embedding information professionals as part of the workflow of NIH research and clinical teams. NIH's informationist program now includes 14 individuals who each spend approximately three-quarters of their time working outside the library with clinical researchers and basic scientists. The program also includes support for bioinformatics research across NIH, with two Ph.D.-level biologists among the NIH Library's 14 informationists. The services most commonly provided by informationists include training and consultation on information resources and applications, literature searching, manuscript editing, and database development.[7]

CDC PUBLIC HEALTH LIBRARY AND INFORMATION CENTER (PHLIC)

In addition to its main library in Atlanta, the Centers for Disease Control and Prevention (CDC) also has a number of branch libraries across the United States. The scope of CDC's collection covers all major areas of public health, including materials on the history of public health practice. CDC's librarians maintain a current literature alert service known as CDC Science Clips (http://www.cdc.gov/phlic/sciclips/). CDC is also an active member in the Partners in Information Access for Public Health Workforce collaboration (http://phpartners.org). CDC leads the development of many recommendations in support of evidence-based public health practice, compiled in the Community Guide (http://www.thecommunityguide.org). CDC's National Center for Health Statistics also collects and disseminates a wide range of epidemiological data (http://www.cdc.gov/nchs/). CDC's FastStats site is especially helpful as a compilation of recent data (http://www.cdc.gov/nchs/fastats/). The Morbidity and Mortality Weekly Report series (MMWR, http://www.cdc.gov/mmwr/) is the CDC's principal vehicle for communicating public health information and recommendations. Much of the data in the MMWR is based on weekly reports to the CDC from state health departments.

FDA BIOSCIENCES LIBRARY

Located in the Food and Drug Administration's White Oak Campus in Silver Spring, Maryland, the FDA Biosciences Library focuses on meeting the information needs of FDA staff, although it is open to members of the public by appointment. The FDA maintains several information resources that are helpful for health sciences librarians, including information on approved drug products (the Orange Book, http://www.accessdata.fda.gov/scripts/cder/ob/). The FDA is also responsible for collecting reports of adverse events through its MedWatch system (http://www.fda.gov/Safety/MedWatch).

NATIONAL AGRICULTURAL LIBRARY

Established by Congress in 1862, the National Agricultural Library (NAL, http://www.nal.usda.gov) is one of the four national libraries in the United States. Located in Beltsville, Maryland, NAL serves the staff of the U.S. Department of Agriculture and is also charged with being the principal agricultural information resource for the country. Health sciences librarians should be aware of NAL's collection and its flagship database, AGRICOLA (http://agricola.nal.usda.gov/), especially for questions related to nutrition, veterinary medicine, or zoonotic diseases.

WORLD HEALTH ORGANIZATION AND PAN AMERICAN HEALTH ORGANIZATION LIBRARIES

Based in Geneva and open to the public, the World Health Organization (WHO) Library is an essential resource for global public health information.

The WHO Library's Institutional Repository for Information Sharing (IRIS, http://apps.who.int/iris/) is a collection of reports and other materials published by WHO over the past 60 years. Primary publications by WHO include the World Health Report (http://www.who.int/whr/en) and World Health Statistics (http://www.who.int/gho/publications/world_health_statistics/en/).

Begun by WHO in 2002, the HINARI program (http://www.who.int/hinari/en/) is a collaboration with many major publishers that provides free and low-cost access to health-related online journals and electronic books in developing countries. Currently, over 150 publishers participate in this program, making more than 11,000 journals and 18,000 eBooks available.

With its headquarters in Washington, D.C., the Pan American Health Organization (PAHO) serves as the regional office for the Americas for WHO. The PAHO Library limits its services to PAHO staff as well as staff from other international and diplomatic agencies. However, PAHO also maintains the Virtual Health Library (http://regional.bvsalud.org/) with access to a number of resources related to public health in the Americas. Among these is LILACS, a bibliographic database of health sciences literature from Latin America and the Caribbean. PAHO's Virtual Health Library also makes the Cochrane Library available to clinical and public health personnel in many countries.

MEDICAL LIBRARY ASSOCIATION

Formed in 1898 by four librarians and four physicians, the Medical Library Association's (MLA, http://mlanet.org) membership now includes approximately 3,600 librarians. MLA currently has 23 topical sections, including sections devoted to informatics, international cooperation, education, public health, federal libraries, nursing and allied health, and hospital libraries. Thirteen geographic chapters affiliated with MLA are also present. For most health sciences librarians, active membership in MLA and its chapters is a primary method of professional development.

The *Journal of the Medical Library Association* is the oldest peer-reviewed publication in the field of health sciences librarianship, with its first volume appearing in 1898. The title of the journal changed a number of times over its first several years of publication, but since 2002, it has been the *Journal of the Medical Library Association*. The founding editor, Dr. Charles Spivak, was a Russian immigrant trained as a physician at Jefferson Medical College in Philadelphia. In addition to his service to the Medical Library Association in its earliest years, Dr. Spivak was also a leader in the management of tuberculosis in the United States.[8]

Now published 10 times a year, *MLA News* is the association's primary newsletter, providing important updates about developments in the field as well as profiles of colleagues. MLA also publishes book titles on a regular basis, including *Introduction to Reference Sources in the Health Sciences*, now in its sixth edition. Other MLA-sponsored book titles cover topics such as health informatics, consumer health information, and drug information.

MLA began a credentialing program for health sciences librarians in 1949, and in 1974, this initiative led to the formation of the Academy of Health Information

Professionals (AHIP) as the association's professional development and career recognition program. More than 1,100 health sciences librarians are now members of AHIP. Five levels of AHIP membership are possible, ranging from "provisional" to "distinguished."[9]

Each year, several health sciences librarians are honored as recipients of awards, grants, and scholarships from MLA. The Ida and George Eliot Prize recognizes health sciences librarians who have published a seminal work, and the Janet Doe Lectureship recognizes a health sciences librarian for his or her broad perspective on the field. Janet Doe lectures are delivered at MLA's annual meetings and subsequently published in the *Journal of the Medical Library Association*. First awarded in 1949, the Marcia C. Noyes Award represents MLA's highest distinction and recognizes individuals whose career has had a lasting impact on the profession. MLA's grants program includes support for research as well as a traveling fellowship. The association also provides scholarships for students in master's and doctoral degree programs. In addition, MLA's Public Health/Health Administration Section administers a stipend established by Win Sewell that reimburses members for attending a meeting of the American Public Health Association.

ASSOCIATION OF ACADEMIC HEALTH SCIENCES LIBRARIES

The Association of Academic Health Sciences Library Directors was formed in 1978, with a change of names in 1996 to the Association of Academic Health Sciences Libraries (AAHSL, http://www.aahsl.org).[10] In 1989, AAHSL was granted membership in the Council of Academic Societies (CAS) by the Association of American Medical Colleges (AAMC) General Assembly.[11] Held in conjunction with AAMC's annual meetings, AAHSL's annual gatherings now typically include a half-day plenary educational event as well as additional presentations by members on a wide range of topics of interest to academic health sciences librarians. Often in collaboration with MLA, AAHSL is active in governmental relations on matters pertaining to scholarly communication and information management in the health sciences. A key resource from AAHSL is its annual compilation of benchmarking data, the Annual Statistics of Medical School Libraries in the United States and Canada, more commonly referred to as the AAHSL Annual Statistics. Begun in 1978, this annual data compilation covers library collections, budgets, personnel, and services. AAHSL's leadership development programs include funding for academic health sciences librarians to participate in a variety of established leadership development programs. As noted earlier in this discussion, AAHSL has also received support from NLM since 2002 to provide a yearlong leadership program for individuals who aspire to serve as director for an academic health sciences library.

SPECIAL LIBRARIES ASSOCIATION

Founded in 1909, the Special Libraries Association (SLA, http://www.sla.org) now has more than 9,000 members, many of whom are from libraries serving corporations and nonprofit organizations. Many SLA members also work independently as consultants. In 1935, SLA formed its Biomedical and Life Sciences Division, a valuable professional network for a number of health sciences librarians. SLA's Pharmaceutical Section was originally formed in 1947 and became the Pharmaceutical and Health Technology Division in 1966. SLA's third health-focused division, the Food, Agriculture and Nutrition Division, was formally recognized in 1974. The regional chapters of SLA provide members with many opportunities for professional development and collaboration, complementing SLA's annual conference.

AMERICAN MEDICAL INFORMATICS ASSOCIATION

Originally focused on computer applications in medicine, the 4,000 members of the American Medical Informatics Association (AMIA, http://www.amia.org) now represent many more professional perspectives, including a broad range of clinicians, biomedical researchers, public health personnel, social scientists with an interest in healthcare, and health sciences librarians. The five domains AMIA formally sponsors are translational bioinformatics, clinical research informatics, clinical informatics, consumer health informatics, and public health informatics. Begun in 1994, the *Journal of the American Medical Informatics Association* (JAMIA) is the association's peer-reviewed journal. AMIA's annual symposia and summit meetings provide many opportunities for continuing education opportunities, especially on topics related to clinical decision support, human-computer interaction, clinical ontologies, and data mining.

AMERICAN LIBRARY ASSOCIATION

Founded in 1876, the American Library Association (ALA, http://www.ala.org) is now librarianship's largest association, with more than 62,000 members. While many health sciences librarians focus on MLA, SLA, AMIA, and AAHSL, involvement with ALA can provide valuable opportunities for collaboration with public and general academic librarians. Membership and participation in ALA also promotes an understanding of broad issues in the field. ALA maintains an extensive publication program, including many standard texts on the practice of librarianship. Since 2002, ALA has recognized over 550 librarians as "movers and shakers."[12] Many of the individuals selected for this honor have been health sciences librarians.

AMERICAN SOCIETY FOR INFORMATION SCIENCE AND TECHNOLOGY

The American Society for Information Science and Technology (ASIST, http://www.asist.org), formed in 1937, focuses on research in the field of information and library science, with many of its members from the faculty of graduate programs in library and information science. ASIST's members also include many general academic librarians with an interest in research. Its peer-reviewed journal, the *Journal of the American Society of Information Science and Technology*, is published monthly. Recent articles have addressed topics such as bibliometrics, social tagging, latent semantic indexing, and virtual reference service.

INTERNATIONAL FEDERATION OF LIBRARY ASSOCIATIONS AND INSTITUTIONS

The International Federation of Library Associations and Institutions (IFLA, http://www.ifla.org/) was established in 1927 in Edinburgh and now has approximately 1,500 members from 150 countries. Since 1971, IFLA has maintained its headquarters in The Hague at the Royal Library, the national library of the Netherlands. Among IFLA's 43 sections, the Health and Biosciences Section focuses on coordination among health sciences libraries and library associations across the world. Among its major activities is planning the International Congress on Medical Librarianship (ICML), begun in 1953 and now held every four to five years.

EUROPEAN ASSOCIATION FOR HEALTH INFORMATION AND LIBRARIES

During the Fifth International Congress on Medical Librarianship (ICML) in Tokyo in 1985, a group of European attendees met to begin planning a future meeting for European health sciences librarians. This meeting was held a year later in Brussels with approximately 300 participants. In 1987, the European Association for Health Information and Libraries (EAHIL, http://www.eahil.net) was formally established and now has more than 1,400 members. EAHIL began publishing the *Newsletter to European Health Librarians* in 1987, and in 2005, this became the *Journal of the European Association for Health Information and Libraries* (JEAHIL).

CONCLUSION

A host of government agencies and professional associations provide resources and services in support of libraries and librarians. The 14 highlighted in this chapter are among those that may be most helpful for health sciences librarians. Awareness of the overall mission of these organizations as well as the specific services and resources they provide is valuable for any librarian practicing in a health sciences setting. While the National Library of Medicine's services and resources for the health sciences library community are unparalleled, it can be helpful to understand the scope and responsibilities of other federal and international nongovernmental libraries that have a health-related mission. Similarly, the Medical Library Association may be the most common choice for health sciences librarians pursuing involvement in a professional association, but many others can be valuable in terms of providing relevant continuing education and connections to colleagues with related interests.

NOTES

1. Humphreys, Betsy L. "Adjusting to Progress: Interactions between the National Library of Medicine and Health Sciences Librarians, 1961–2001." *Journal of the Medical Library Association: JMLA* 90, no. 1 (January 2002): 4–20.

2. Cogdill, Keith W. "Progress in Health Sciences Librarianship, 1970–2005." In *Advances in Librarianship*, volume 30, edited by Danuta Nitecki and Eileen Abels, 145–177. New York: Academic Press, 2006.

3. National Library of Medicine. "Exhibition Program Previous Displays at the National Library of Medicine." Last updated April 8, 2013, accessed April 8, 2013. http://www.nlm.nih.gov/hmd/about/exhibition/exhibitions-previous.html.

4. U.S. Department of Health and Human Services, National Institutes of Health, National Library of Medicine, Board of Regents. *Improving Health Professionals' Access to Information: Report of the Board of Regents*. Bethesda, MD: U.S. Dept. of Health and Human Services, Public Health Service, National Institutes of Health, 1989. Accessed April 4, 2013. http://www.nlm.nih.gov/archive/20040721/pubs/plan/ih/contents.html.

5. Ruffin, Angela B., Keith W. Cogdill, Lalitha Kutty, and Michelle Ochillo. "Access to Electronic Health Information for the Public: Analysis of Fifty-Three Funded Projects." *Library Trends* 53, no. 3 (Winter 2005): 434–452.

6. Braude, Robert M. "A Descriptive Analysis of NLM-Funded Medical Informatics Training Programs and the Career Choice of Their Graduates." *Proceedings of the Annual Symposium on Computer Applications in Medical Care* (November 4–7, 1990): 504–508.

7. Whitmore, Susan C., Suzanne F. Grefsheim, and Jocelyn A. Rankin. "Informationist Programme in Support of Biomedical Research: A Programme Description and Preliminary Findings of an Evaluation." *Health Information and Libraries Journal* 25, no. 2 (June 2008): 135–141.

8. Abrams, Jeanne E. *Dr. Charles David Spivak: A Jewish immigrant and the American Tuberculosis Movement*. Boulder: University Press of Colorado, 2009.

9. Academy of Academic Health Professionals, Medical Library Association. "Requirements for AHIP Membership Levels (Initial Application) | MLANET." Last updated May 2, 2014, accessed May 2, 2014. http://www.mlanet.org/academy/summ.html.

10. Jacobson, Susan, and Gary D. Byrd. "The Association of Academic Health Sciences Libraries: Twenty-Five Years of Excellence." *Journal of the Medical Library Association: JMLA* 91, no. 2 (April 2003): 148.

11. Jenkins, Carol G., and Shelley Bader. "The Association of Academic Health Sciences Libraries' Collaboration with the Association of American Medical Colleges, Medical Library Association, and Other Organizations." *Journal of the Medical Library Association: JMLA* 91, no. 2 (April 2003): 161–167.

12. Library Journal. "Movers on the Map, 2002–2013." Accessed April 8, 2013. http://lj.libraryjournal.com/movers-on-the-map-2002-2013/.

Chapter 6

HEALTH LIBRARIANSHIP: MANAGEMENT AND ADMINISTRATION

Gerald Perry

PROLOGUE: FOCUSING OUR LENS ON THE IMPORTANT

In 2005, I was asked by the Medical Library Association's[1] (MLA) Mid-Continental Chapter Region[2] to develop a course on the many professional roles played by the contemporary health sciences librarian with a focus on management. The result was the somewhat awkwardly titled "The Librarian as Professional, or How I Learned to Stop Worrying and Love Complexity." It was a highly interactive, hands-on class focusing on practical and metaphoric tools for excelling in the current health sciences library work environment.

Course takers had homework; I asked registrants to consider some compelling models of interactive social behaviors drawn from the cinema. In essence, they were asked to consider the films as work environments, in a metaphorical sense. We started with *Dr. Strangelove*,[3] a "surreal" and paranoid film that comes to us from the 1960s and that decade's conflicted perspective on authority. We then advanced to *Crouching Tiger, Hidden Dragon*,[4] with a consideration of ethics and the moral response, which we applied to some typical challenges in the workplace.

Perhaps most troubling in terms of symbolism, the film *Mystic River*[5] was looked at as a contemporary example of tragedy in a format akin to the dramas of ancient Greece, where personality defined early and reinforced by seemingly random events provides a context for the expression of one's fate and how that limits or affords opportunity. Have any of us worked in environments where we seem to be playing out our destined role: visionary, questioner or peacemaker?

The final film we considered was the charming animated feature *The Triplets of Belleville*,[6] the antithesis of *Mystic River*, being an exemplar of the power of positivity in the face of formidable odds and the joy of creative teamwork.

In each instance, we looked at the paths taken by the protagonists in the film and considered their active choices. The point of the exercise was to disrupt the course takers' normative thinking process, as we do not usually attempt to think of films as exemplars of workplaces. The exercise encouraged course attendees and me as the facilitator to step back and establish a new frame of reference for our discussions, forcing us to approach the class from a big picture, "what really matters here" perspective. The course was a chance for attendees to stop and reflect, and to consider the important over the immediate. That, in a nutshell, is the challenge of leadership for the contemporary health library manager and administrator.

In our technology-enabled, resources-challenged, and highly disrupted work environments, it is the norm for most everyone to be in reaction mode, responding to the day's crisis or the most pressing demands and deadlines. Health libraries are no exception. It is the role of the leader to consider strategy and to recognize opportunities. Like a film director, the effective library administrator must coordinate and align the "blockbuster" themes of budgeting, staffing, personnel management, delivering effective and efficient information services, marketing and advocacy, space and facilities planning, and keeping current and managing change in order to meaningfully flourish. These core areas are thus the focus of this chapter.

The goal of "The Librarian as Professional" was to create an active and adaptive learning context where course takers could literally act their way through scenarios intended to prepare them to address these blockbuster themes, leveraging practical tools and resources such that participants would hopefully leave with a clearer sense of their vision and values for the library services they provide. With you the reader, hopefully in this chapter, we will collaboratively achieve the same end.

CONTEXT FOR HEALTH SCIENCES LIBRARIES TODAY

Members of the community of practice that is health librarianship are truly blessed, despite the many and seeming endless challenges that we face in our day-to-day work lives, in that there is a rich and deep corpus of literature upon which to derive practical advice and perspective. For those interested in health library management and administration, MLA with Neal-Schuman Publishers has produced two editions of the essential *The Medical Library Association Guide to Managing Health Care Libraries*, the second edition of which was published in 2011.[7] Both editions, but in particular the second, take an almost encyclopedic approach to the management of health libraries. For the second, editors Margaret Bandy and Rosalind Dudden across 16 comprehensive chapters and with a stellar cast of authors consider the healthcare environment, financial management, human resources management, evaluation and improvement, collection planning, space management, onsite versus virtual services provision, the teaching/learning mission, information services, services for healthcare provider stakeholders as well as health consumers, and the specialized practice of solo librarians, among many, many other topics.

MLA has also published, with Scarecrow Press, the *Current Practice in Health Sciences Librarianship* series, Volume 8 of which was dedicated to administration and management in health sciences libraries and was published in 2000.[8] Lest we imagine that the current health librarian is uniquely challenged by change, the lead chapter in this well-crafted book edited by Rick Forsman is titled "Management Challenges in an Era of Change." Other chapters address fiscal management, human resources management, marketing, technology transformations, and facilities planning.

Volume 3 of MLA's *Handbook of Medical Library Practice, 4th edition*, published in 1988 under the editorship of perhaps one of the most renowned health sciences librarians of the modern era, Louise Darling, was dedicated entirely to health sciences librarianship and administration.[9] The contributing authors, luminaries of the profession, included Lois Ann Colianni, who provided an overview; Robert Mehnert and Joseph Leiter, who contributed a chapter dedicated entirely to the U.S. National Library of Medicine; Robert (Bob) Braude on general principles of administration; Samuel Hitt on personnel; Nelson Gilman on library promotion; and Nancy Whitten Zinn on special collections.

Dating some 20 years later, M. Sandra Wood in 2008 edited *Introduction to Health Sciences Librarianship*, which features a section on administration and three outstanding overviews of library management, including academic health sciences libraries (Francesca Allegri and Martha Bedard), management and special concerns for hospital libraries (Dixie Jones), and space planning (Elizabeth Connor).[10]

While the particulars vary and are largely determined by the era and the interests of the editors, common themes and key areas of focus are detailed in all of these eminently practical titles: budgeting, staffing and personnel management, delivering effective and efficient information services, marketing and advocacy, library space planning, and keeping current and managing change. However, the emphasis of health librarianship has decidedly changed over the years, with increasing attention on the quality of the library user experience,[11] alignment of the library's goals and objectives with the various missions of the parent institution,[12] and enhanced attention to advocacy and demonstrating the "value proposition" of the library.[13]

AN EXERCISE IN WHAT MATTERS

A critical summative exercise conducted near the end of the "Librarian as Professional" course had attendees considering nearly 50 services and/or areas of staff activity and focus provided by the contemporary academic health sciences library, recognizing that hospital, clinical, or highly specialized health libraries typically will offer fewer. Among the services were the traditional, including staffing a service desk, cataloging, circulating materials, reserves, interlibrary lending and document copy services, archives, user orientations and instructional programming, literature search services, managing and developing collections, marketing and outreach, budgeting, and gathering resource usage data.

Less traditional but well-established areas of activity were also featured, such as services to consumers and patients; managing and offering web-based access to resources and services; electronic resources licensing, linking, and troubleshooting; liaison outreach services to key stakeholder groups; research consultations; citation and personal database management assistance; providing information commons areas for user computing; copyright support; and remote storage access.

Emerging areas of engagement were also included for consideration by the course takers and included managing curricular software; informatics services support[14]; assistance with mobile computing and telecommunications devices; social media engagement via syndication services, wiki blogs, and social presence sites such as Facebook[15]; video streaming support; linking of licensed information resources into institutionally supported electronic medical record systems[16]; and embedded clinical librarian services.[17]

Course takers were given a total of 10 "ballots" and asked to distribute them to those services or areas of engagement that they felt were *most essential to the provision of library services*. I facilitated the course from 2005 until 2011, and over that six-year period anecdotally noted the dramatic decline in emphasis on circulation, cataloging, and collections and the emergence of emphasis on consulting, liaising, connecting with users wherever they are, outreach, and the teaching mission. By the last time I taught the class, not a single vote was awarded to cataloging, circulation, or managing (print) collections.

While the areas of emphasis for health libraries are clearly keeping pace with the changing needs of our technologically sophisticated users and their expectations of ubiquitous and ready access to information resources and services, the administration of library services continues to depend on a fundamental core set of managerial activities: budgeting; staffing, and personnel management; delivering effective and efficient information services; marketing and advocacy; space planning; and keeping current and managing change.

BUDGETING: OUTCOMES AND KEY PERFORMANCE INDICATORS

Providing an exceptional customer experience for the library user, whether she or he interfaces with the library in person or virtually, is dependent on the ability to access and leverage financial resources. The budget is the essential building block for the administration of library services, and how funds are used serves as shorthand for how success is defined by the library's administration. Fundamental to effectively deploying fiscal assets is an understanding of the mission, vision, and values of the parent institution. The effective library manager will understand intuitively these elements and will know the areas of strategic emphasis and priority for the parent organization. In turn, the library manager will coordinate the deployment of financial resources in alignment with the priorities of the parent, ever mindful of the need to assess how that deployment contributes to advancing the mission.

For the novice library manager, a good overview of the typical health library budgeting process is included in Lynn Kasner Morgan's chapter "Fiscal Management in

Health Sciences Libraries," in *Administration and Management in Health Sciences Libraries*. Sharon Phillips provides a more in-depth review that is particularly useful to the new manager in "Financial Management," in *MLA Guide to Managing Health Care Libraries*.[18] Phillips includes useful charts and tables with examples of budgets and budget analysis tools. More granular articles that may be of interest include "Holistic Budgeting: A Process" by Asantewa D'Llle, where the author offers a budgeting viewpoint from a Special Library Association perspective, noting that it is always useful to see how "for profits" do things.[19]

David Osborne and Peter Hutchinson provide an excellent primer on the concept of outcomes-based budgeting in "Budgeting for Outcomes: Delivering Results Citizens Value at a Price They Are Willing to Pay."[20] The public sector is undergoing a revolution in terms of perspectives on value for money. Whether the library manager works for a nonprofit, for-profit, private, or state-run enterprise, this revolution is catching.

A contrarian perspective on the very need for budgeting in provided by David Parmeter in "Annual Budget: Time to Throw It Away?" While a move away from budgeting is unlikely in our lifetimes, this assessment offers an interesting perspective on the need to link expenditures to "key performance indicators," that is, the outcomes that customers/patrons/users care most about and that are absolutely integral to the library's raison d'etre.[21]

Purposes of Budgets

Budgets can be used to satisfy entirely basic needs through to very high levels of outcomes expectations (See Figure 6.1):

At the least sophisticated end, a budget can be used to describe expenses and revenues. A budget can also be used as an "argument" through which the library manager has the opportunity to make a case for enhancing revenue and thereby uses the budget request as an opportunity to explain where the manager plans to spend and why. A more challenging approach to budgeting, but one that is increasingly critical for cash-strapped organizations, is the alignment of spending with desired

Basic Needs	• Identify expenses and revenues • Monitor the same • Communicate the value of the service • Communicate and demonstrate priorities • Serve as a fiscal argument • Match spending to goals and objectives • Align spending priorities with desired outcomes
High-Level Outcomes	• Prove value for money invested • Prove degree of accomplishment towards mission and vision, the strategic plan • Demonstrate best evidence of programmatic, outcomes-based successes

Figure 6.1 Basic Needs and High Level Outcomes for Budgets

goals and outcomes, where the manager describes through the budget where funds will be dedicated according to her or his understanding of the parent institution's strategic priorities. An outcomes-oriented budget is perhaps the most sophisticated expression of this alignment, where measures that are meaningful to the parent organizations are demonstrated in the spending plan.

Types of Budgets

- Operating budgets: All that is needed to manage the day-to-day operations (supplies, minor equipment, telecommunications devices and services, contractual expenses, photocopiers, etc.). Collection resources can be considered operating expenses, or they can be broken out into a separate budget.
- Personnel budgets: Salaries, including costs of benefits, overtime if permitted, and shift differential. Typically expressed as full-time equivalent (FTE); for example, 1 FTE = the typical 40-hour-per-week employee, 0.25 FTE = "quarter-time" person.
- Capital equipment: "Big ticket" purchases, usually defined by the parent institution. Typically $500 or more.

Budgeting Approaches

- Line item: Most common; featuring expenses grouped into broad categories with an allotment typically assigned for each "line," or category. May be very granular or not, depending on local culture. It is easy to track line item budgets longitudinally and therefore identify cost trends. It can be a challenge to readily see how specific line item costs impact or relate to specific library programs or strategic goals. Line item amounts are typically based on previous years' allotments, with a pinch added for inflation.
- Lump sum: Where the department (library) receives a single total sum that it may spend; usually requires the library staff to in turn develop a local, more granular budget.
- Zero based: Budgeting from the ground up; each line item is afforded zero dollars and then, through the budget process, costs are justified and summed.
- Program: An accounting of all individual expenses/funding needs for each program or service provided by the library, for example, Reference Services, Circulation, Interlibrary Loan, Collections, Cataloging. This type of budget approach is helpful when considering the total costs of individual programs and links easily with strategic plans, where those plans are specific about programs and services.
- Outcome: Where the library first identifies what outcomes it wishes to achieve and then costs out what it will require to attain success. Newly popular among public service agencies, this sort of budgeting process allows the library manager to prioritize among a number of competing desired outcomes and focus on what matters most to customers and/or the parent organization. Typically, this approach requires that the manager identify alternative routes to success.
- Performance-based: Not unlike outcome-oriented budgets; the library identifies what constitutes key performance indicators (those outcomes that define unequivocal success) and then costs out what is required to deliver those successes.

STAFFING: LINE OF REPORT, DISTRIBUTION OF AUTHORITY, AND ORGANIZATION OF PERSONNEL

Providing an exceptional customer or library user experience, no matter how the library manager aligns spending, is entirely dependent on the deployment of an effective team of staff. Personnel are the library's most critical and often most expensive asset. They are the key individuals who deliver on the "promises" made by the budget; they are the ones who "make or break" a library's attempts to achieve key performance goals. In a nutshell, the quality of their performance can ultimately ensure the library's fate!

Organizing human resources in the health library, along with assigning leadership roles and reporting responsibilities, is critical to defining and managing decision-making authority. Most academic health libraries have a designated leader (director or dean, if the enterprise is academic and the faculty staff members have tenure). Lines of reporting up the chain of command vary based to a great degree on legacy and local managerial culture; the academic health library leader may report to the leadership of a school (often medicine), the chief academic officer (provost) or her or his delegate, health affairs leadership, or other executive office. In a hospital, clinical, or specialized library setting, the library manager may report to the leadership of information technology, educational resources, nursing or medical staff, or others.

In larger health library operations, there is often a "second in command" (a deputy or assistant/associate director[s]), and unit or department heads with oversight over specific areas of service deployment or resources management (e.g., access services, management of patron affiliations, circulation of materials, and inventory; and reference and education, responsible for responding to customers'/users' information requirements and learning needs). Hospital, clinical, and specialized libraries, with fewer staff than the typical academic health sciences library, will have fewer levels of administration and subsequently fewer organizational departments.

The manner in which decision making is coordinated and conducted bears careful consideration. It is typically most effective and efficient to delegate decision-making authority as close as possible to the locus of activity. Budget and strategic decisions of direction and mission are best aligned with the library's top leadership, as she or he bears responsibility for leading the library, and these functions define the role of the director. Departmental contributions to the overall priorities of the library are best assigned to the unit or department head that will have responsibility for ensuring the fulfillment of those priorities.

Most libraries coordinate decision-making authority and formal unit communications through leadership team meetings, where the leaders represent units, departments, or project leads. While meetings may often be monopolized by operational issues, it is generally a good rule of thumb to make sure that strategic issues of priority are routinely discussed and monitored when the leadership team gathers.

However the staff is organized, a key first human resources step for the library manager is to determine staffing needs. Following are steps for the manager to consider in the process of assessing needs, with related questions that should be

• Review the library's strategic plan…	• What personnel assets are already on hand? • Which skills are present? Which are lacking, in terms of desired outcomes? • If one can hire, what would one like the new employee to do?
• Lacking a plan, consider key performance indicators or desired outcomes…	• If one cannot hire, what would one like present employee(s) to do? • Draft a job description to describe the new role imagined. • Compare that with something similar from peer libraries.
• Get familiar with parent institution personnel policies…	• What is the local comparable salary? • Can one afford to hire? Alternatively, can one afford staff development? • If one can hire, what are the local human resources hiring policies?
• How will staff be evaluated? How will they be rewarded for excellence? Challenged to achieve?	• If one cannot hire, what staff development options are at hand? • How will the manager advertise to a diverse pool of candidates? • How will one vet candidates? • What matters most—flexibility and ability to learn and adapt, or evident skills?
• How will the manager develop a learning culture for continual staff development?	• How will one introduce the new hire to the present work culture? • If one cannot hire, how will the manager prepare staff for new roles?

Figure 6.2   Questions for Managers Assessing Needs

addressed in each context. These are equally applicable for health libraries in academic, hospital, clinical, or specialized settings (See Figure 6.2).

WORKING WITH A POINT OF VIEW

Administering the contemporary health library places a burden of leadership on the manager, whether that role is entrusted to an individual or in a matrix organization to a team.

At the heart of leadership is caring along with demonstrating and modeling commitment to the mission of the library and the parent organization. Without caring, leadership has no purpose. And without showing others that one cares and what one cares about, other people in the organization will not care about what the manager says or what the manager knows. Leadership is an ongoing relationship and requires a living connection between leaders and their constituents.

Healthy work relationships can and should be managed to achieve desired outcomes and to create positive and attractive work experiences that can be used to define the success of a library or other organization. It is therefore useful for the

At the University of Colorado Health Sciences Library, the management philosophy is an "organic blend" of appreciative inquiry[24] with "co-leadership." Library leadership works with individual staff members to assess strengths and areas of professional interest. Work performance plans are crafted to leverage areas of interest and address skills enhancement. Leadership opportunities are subsequently identified collaboratively with individual staff to leverage strengths and provide opportunities for professional growth. Leadership is subsequently vested in staff according to their commitment to and passion for a topic, service, or resource, rather than necessarily in individuals with seniority or status. This approach allows for co-leadership to occur throughout the organization and enhances the commitment of individuals to their performance plans, their unit, the library, and the parent institution.

Figure 6.3 Who Leads?

library manager to actively research and define a philosophy of management that informs her or his practice and that can be readily articulated.

There remains and probably always will be a never-ending supply of managerial "self-help" books available to the library manager, far too many for consideration in this chapter. However, in defining one's own personal philosophy, a few key considerations and actions are recommended:

- Define one's communications approach. The Myers-Briggs[22] and DISC[23] personality assessment tools are particularly helpful.

- Research and assess the normative communications patterns of parent institution leadership. How are key messages articulated and delivered?

- Assess the workplace "culture" and discern the communications approaches and learning styles of the cohort. Human resources personnel typically are well versed at performing such assessments and may be valuable assets for the library manger to know and with whom to work.

- Identify one's need for control versus one's ability to share in decision-making processes. The contemporary work environment is increasingly dynamic, interdisciplinary, and collaborative, with a growing emphasis on shared and collective decision making necessitated by the sheer complexity of our parent organizations and the many competing agendas of the workplace.

Leadership in organizations is not limited to those with the official title of manager or director. Organizations have "thought leaders" as well as influencers who contribute to the culture of an organization and help establish its tone. It is essential for the titular leader to assess and identify who the thought leaders are in the parent organization and the library, and to understand their values and communication styles. If one is going to exercise influence and provide leadership, it is important to know what is valued in a work environment and how that environment is described. Thought leaders provide that knowledge. To adjust, change, or "reinvent" an organization requires knowledge of the culture and what is meaningful to its practitioners (See Figure 6.3).

SERVICES: THE RAISON D'ETRE

Reference . . . circulation . . . collection development . . . electronic journals . . . databases . . . document delivery/interlibrary loan . . . literature searching . . . research consultations . . . remote access troubleshooting . . . website design . . . reserves (print and electronic) . . . consumer health . . . clinical librarianship . . .

Libraries are about services, and most health libraries offer one or more of the previously mentioned services, plus perhaps a legion of others! Note the Librarian as Professional service prioritization exercise previously described.

Ideally, the library manager will have assessed each service, understand the level of demand and interest from customers being helped by that service, and have deployed both funding within the context of the budget and personnel assets according to the needs of the service and the value in which it is held by the organization. By example, a contemporary library that is heavily invested in electronic resources and that has assigned the majority of its technical services assets to print materials is out of alignment with its mission and that of its parent if the parent organization values access to eResources. Similarly, a library that values deep integration of its information resources into the electronic medical record of the clinical enterprise with which it is affiliated will find the wherewithal for its staff to work with those in the parent organization that are implementing that system.

Essential to the provision of meaningful services is discerning what is valued by the users of the service (both potential and current), assessing utility, and changing (perhaps discontinuing) services to stay current and evolve with the parent organization. Does the library offer a wiki? Do staff blog the latest news about new resources or services? Do staff members use texting to answer questions or assist users? The answers to these questions hopefully are not about being current or offering the latest flavor of service, but rather knowing what is needed by the user, what will be embraced, and what is materially helpful to that individual in achieving her or his own success.

A key question that is often overlooked by the library manager is "How will the library maintain the quality of services offered while adding new ones?" Ancillary to that question is knowing when it is time to terminate a service. Fundamental to knowing is assessing the library's users' needs and satisfaction. Needs, however, do not equate with satisfaction; users may be perfectly happy with a service that is of little or no significant utility.

Reconnaissance, Resolve, and Reflection

It is almost universally understood that there is little time anymore for reflection—that is, unless as a library manager you are facing a budget cut or need to justify a service. One way to prevent the budget axe is to have a clear idea of what customers want and need, and to be proactive about delivering it, with bells and whistles.

A common problem for librarians—and thus libraries—is making assumptions that we know what customers want because it is what we have always done, it is what the budget indicates we are supposed to do, or because we are trapped in the cycle of the "tyranny" of the emergent over the important. Do one's customers really want print journals? Do they necessarily prefer one database over another? Do they really want to come to the library to attend a class, or would they rather you went to them? Or, would they *really* prefer that the library provide shorthand assistance through brief video tutorials? Maybe what we think is true really is not.

One way to find out what customers want is to conduct a needs assessment. Health libraries—big and small, academic, hospital, and specialized—do them, and while the initial effort may seem burdensome, the benefits can last years and move the service forward in terms of investment in continuous quality improvement.

Many examples of successful needs assessment instruments deployed by libraries are available on the Internet. Popular proactive outreach-oriented techniques include conducting user surveys (print and online), assembling focus groups, and using a combination of sampling and strategic interviewing. Popular passive systems include hits on library webpages, downloads of licensed content, and assessments of numbers and types of queries addressed through virtual communications systems.

MARKETING AND ADVOCACY

In the contemporary health library, the role of advocacy on behalf of the library and its contributions to the mission of the parent institution rests with every staff member. Necessarily, the lead and coordinating role for advocacy sits with the top leader, however the library is functionally organized. That noted, given the increasingly complex and interdisciplinary nature of library work, nearly every staff member will have contact with constituents and therefore an opportunity to make a positive or negative impression of the library and its capacity to serve the parent institution.

The goal of advocacy on behalf of the library is to highlight and advance persuasive messaging throughout the organization, within and externally to the library, as to the contribution made by the library to the achievement of key performance indicators or other metrics of success as embraced by the parent institution. Quantitative and qualitative assessment data are critical to making the case, and it is ethically essential for the library that teaches evidence-based practice to embrace the same in the administration of its responsibilities. The Association of Academic Health Sciences Libraries (AAHSL) with its annual statistic program,[25] the Association of Research Libraries with its LibQual and LibQual+ initiatives,[26] the Association of College and Research Libraries' significant work in the area of information literacy,[27] and the National Network of Libraries of Medicine advocacy initiatives[28] are eminently helpful resources to consult when crafting local metrics to be used in making the case for the library's value proposition.

Advocacy is advanced through engagement with the library's customers/users. For the library manager, that engagement should be strategic and focused on meaningful outreach to and offers of collaboration and assistance to leadership throughout the parent institution. Examples of such engagement in the academic setting include service on accreditation and regulatory compliance committees, participation in overarching strategic planning initiatives, and membership on teams exercising authority over curricular activities. In the hospital, clinical, or specialized library context, advocacy engagement may take the form of membership on patient safety assurance committees, participation in magnet status efforts, emergency and disaster planning, and involvement in efforts to integrate information resources into electronic medical record systems, among others.

Advocacy is *not* marketing. Marketing of the library at its core is focused on raising awareness and hopefully appreciation, and subsequently affiliation, with the services and resources offered. Through marketing, a relationship is ideally established whereby the customer/user recognizes the utility of a service or resource and assigns the sourcing of that service or resource to the library. Meaningful metrics of successful marketing include demonstrably increased usage and, where feasible, clear indications of the utility of a resource or service by the library's customers/users.

SPACE PLANNING

Nearly every recent publication on health library management and administration has included a section and/or chapter on space planning, and for very good reason. Long referred to as the "heart of the campus," the academic library often must contend with the somewhat romantic legacy that may accompany traditional notions of the library. Hospital, clinical, and specialized libraries typically do not operate with the same attendant cultural freight, since such libraries operate within the health economy sphere where financially productive clinical space is always at a premium.

Given the often strategic placement of the library on the academic campus (and if one is lucky, within the hospital), special attention must be paid to the most effective and efficient use of space. Library managers are well advised to consider the publications of Elizabeth Connor, associate professor of library science and science liaison at the Daniel Library of the Citadel, the Military College of South Carolina in Charleston, who has made a career in recent years of tracking and reporting on space planning issues. Her 2005 publication, *Planning, Renovating, Expanding, and Constructing Library Facilities in Hospitals, Academic Medical Centers, and Health Organizations*[29] is an essential reference source.

Just as with budgets, allocation of space should be aligned with the mission of the parent institution (See Figure 6.4).

Space needs are not immutable; they change as the mission of the parent institution evolves, expands, or contracts. Further, space needs are highly specific, reflecting the local priorities of the parent institution and library. In most health libraries,

---

Key space planning question to be considered:

- Who are the principle users of library physical space?
- What are their space-related needs?
- What is the volume of activity to be expected in the library space (frequency and duration of visits)?
- What technologies must be accessible in the spaces that are to be provided? Who is to support that technology, and how will support be delivered?
- Are their institutional, system, local, state, or regional approval, accreditation, or oversight requisites for the nature and accessibility of space?
- What are the intended (and likely unintended) uses of space? How might those intentions change over time?
- Who will exercise authority over space and its use? Will spaces be accessible for scheduling?

Figure 6.4   Space Planning

space is usually afforded to customers/users for study, group activities, and computing; to staff for performing the work of the library and accomplishing day-to-day tasks; to technological infrastructure (servers and workstation deployment); and to collections.

With the dramatic shift to digital collection formats, the need for space to house and maintain collections is radically decreasing. Collaborative print preservation schemes such as those supported by the U.S. National Library of Medicine,[30] the California Digital Library's WEST: Western Regional Storage Trust initiative,[31] and others are likely to have a significant impact on the retention of localized print assets, where sharing access to legacy print resources is an increasingly viable and affordable option. How many back copies of *JAMA* in print does a city, let alone a state, region, or nation really need to ensure access and preservation of that intellectual content?

Just as no two academic health or clinical practice sites are identical, no two libraries' space needs are identical. Libraries with a mission to support student academic life and with an emphasis on the customer experience will have dramatically different space needs from the library supporting a research-intensive, highly distributed commuter campus (see Figure 6.5).

In October 2007, the University of Colorado Health Sciences Library on the Anschutz Medical Campus in Aurora, Colorado, opened, with then–state-of-the-art features. This $35-million, 113,000-square-foot facility provides:

• 30 group study rooms
• Ubiquitous wireless connectivity
• Over 40 open-access computer workstations
• Four large group conferencing and meeting areas
• Art gallery
• Dedicated reading room
• Three teaching labs
• 24,000 linear feet of shelving (second and third floors)
• Five outdoor patios
• Library Cafe
• Special Collections Room (History of Health Sciences, Rare Book, and three endowed collections)
• Capacity for 215,000 volumes

Planning for the facility was a comprehensive and inclusive process that began with orchestrated conversions led by the architectural design firm in concert with the library's leadership. The process also included key stakeholders such as campus faculty, staff and students, library donors and supporters, and campus leadership, among others. The planning process was effective; in the five years since opening, there have been only minor structural changes to the facility. One significant challenge for the library that was not anticipated in planning was just how rapid the decline would be in the use of print collections. As of late 2012, the library's leaders were engaged in reimagining the use of stacks space, with the intent of placing nearly all print collections in high-density storage and repurposing former collections areas for teaching/learning programming, possibly to include a large active teaching laboratory and additional solo study "pods."

Figure 6.5 A Twenty-First Century Library for Twenty-First Century Healthcare

STAYING CURRENT

Whether one stays current and up-to-date with trends through "friending" colleagues via a social media platform, reading—or better, authoring—the wikis and blogs of thought leaders, surveying the electronic tables of contents of favorite professional journals, or networking at professional meetings and conferences, arguably the best and most rewarding means of engagement with what is new and emerging is through membership in the professional association of one's choice. A community of practice as defined by society membership provides a ready-made context for the consideration of issues of common interest.

Key organizations for the library manager include the Association of Academic Health Sciences Libraries, the Medical Library Association and in particular the association's Leadership and Management section, the American Medical Informatics Association, the American Library Association's affiliated Library and Information Technology Association (LITA), and the local and regional chapters and sections of these organizations.

Key Trends

Forecasting the future is a dubious proposition, even for the stoutest of heart! Five years ago, we did not have the Apple iPad. Five years ago, who would have imagined the present ubiquity of that technology? Nonetheless, reliable and typically thought-provoking resources to which to turn for prognostication *do* exist. The Pew Internet and American Life Project[32] is a trusted and typically unbiased resource for learning about and putting into context key developments in the broader culture and involving the adoption of technologies and innovations. LITA's "Top Technology Trends"[33] and EDUCASE's[34] "Current Issues Surveys" are trustworthy turn-to resources (See Figure 6.6).

- Changing demographics of the healthcare delivery and health education workforces
- Changing demographics within the health library community of practice
- Emerging solutions to the health insurance and healthcare delivery funding crises in the United States
- The impact of open access publishing and the ongoing "crisis" in scholarly communications[35]
- Consolidation in the publishing marketplace
- Evolution of priorities and the availability of research funding from federal agencies such as the National Institutes of Health
- Developments in online teaching and learning, and where information resources and services "fit" in these digital environments
- The state of funding for higher education
- The adoption of eBbook platforms and attendant business models
- The future of the subscription model for access to journal content versus pay per view[36]
- Evolving metrics for assessing the contribution of the health library to the success of the parent institution

---

Figure 6.6   Key Trends of Which to Be Aware for Library Managers (2012)

Managing Change

Our work lives are complicated. The expectations placed on us, and those which we choose to place on ourselves, are complex and demanding. But every library manager has options—which are exercised each instance she or he says *yes* and each instance he or she says *no*.

Three options for managing change to consider as a librarian and administrator include choosing to be optimistic, responding positively to and getting comfortable with the inevitable ambiguity surrounding us, and being mindfully creative, that is, being explicitly and knowingly creative in response to a challenge. All are powerful, empowering choices explicitly linked to becoming familiar with and aware of one's personal philosophy of management and with one's communications approach. Leveraging these options also enhances one's ability to stay current and ahead of the change curve. It is easy to become overwhelmed by the burdens of leadership, ambiguity in the work and political environments, and rapidly changing developments in the scholarly publishing and healthcare economies. Knowing one's self and making intentional choices to address challenges with an open mind and decision to be creative allows one to refocus and take control when control seems most out of reach.

The library manager who embraces challenges and acts with compassion toward oneself, one's coworkers, and one's customers is well on the way to ensuring the right sort of leadership legacy to impart.

NOTES

1. Medical Library Association. "Medical Library Association/MLANET: MLANET Home." Last modified January 13, 2013. http://mlanet.org/.

2. National Library of Medicine. "National Network of Libraries of Medicine (NN/LM) Home Page." Last modified May 12, 2012. http://nnlm.gov/.

3. Kubrick, Stanley. *Dr. Strangelove, or How I Learned to Stop Worrying and Love the Bomb.* Columbia Pictures Corporation, 1964.

4. Lee, Ang. *Crouching Tiger, Hidden Dragon.* Columbia Pictures Film Production Asia, 2000.

5. Eastwood, Clint. *Mystic River.* Warner Bros. Pictures, 2003.

6. Chomet, Sylvain. *Les Triplettes De Belleville.* Les Armateurs, 2003.

7. Bandy, Margaret. *The Medical Library Association Guide to Managing Health Care Libraries.* New York: Neal-Schuman, 2011.

8. Ibid.

9. Forsman, Rick B., and Alison Bunting. *Current Practice in Health Sciences Librarianship.* Lanham, MD: Medical Library Association, 2000.

10. Darling, Louise, David Bishop, Lois Ann Colaianni, and Association Medical Library. *Handbook of Medical Library Practice.* Chicago: Medical Library Association, 1988.

11. Wood, M. Sandra. *Introduction to Health Sciences Librarianship.* Binghamton, NY: Haworth Information, 2008.

12. Shi, Xi, Patricia J. Holahan, and M. Peter Jurkat. "Satisfaction Formation Processes in Library Users: Understanding Multisource Effects." *Journal of Academic Librarianship* 30, no. 2 (2004): 122-131.

13. Davis, Hiram L, and Mary M. Somerville. "Learning Our Way to Change: Improved Institutional Alignment." *New World Library* 107 , no. 3/4 (2006): 127-140.

14. Warnaby, Gary, and Jill Finney. "Creating Customer Value in the Not-for-Profit Sector: A Case Study of the British Library." *International Journal of Nonprofit and Voluntary Sector Marketing* 10, no. 3 (August 2005): 183-195.

15. Yarfitz, Stuart, and Debra S. Ketchell. "A Library-Based Bioinformatics Service Program." *Bulletin of the Medical Library Association* 88, no. 1 (January 2000): 36-48.

16. Hendrix, D., D. Chiarella, L. Hasman, S. Murphy, and M. L. Zafron. "Use of Facebook in Academic Health Sciences Libraries." *Journal of the Medical Library Association: JMLA* 97, no. 1 (2009): 44-47.

17. Epstein, B. A., N. H. Tannery, C. B. Wessel, F. Yarger, J. LaDue, and A. B. Fiorillo. "Development of a Clinical Information Tool for the Electronic Medical Record: A Case Study." *Journal of the Medical Library Association: JMLA* 98, no. 3 (2010): 223-227.

18. Rankin, Jocelyn A, Susan F. Grefsheim, and Candace C. Canto. "The Emerging Informationist Specialty: A Systematic Review of the Literature." *Journal of the Medical Library Association: JMLA* 96, no. 3 (July 2008): 194-206.

19. Phillips, Sharon A. "Financial Management." In *The Medical Library Association Guide to Managing Health Care Libraries,* edited by Ruth Holst. New York: Neal-Schuman, 2000.

20. Asantewa, D'Llle. "Holistic Budgeting: A Process." *Information Outlook* 7, no. 8 (2003): 14-18.

21. Osborne, David, and Peter Hutchinson. "Budgeting for Outcomes: Delivering Results Citizens Value at a Price They Are Willing to Pay." *Government Finance Review* 20, no. 5 (2004): 10-15.

22. Parmenter, David. "Annual Budget: Time to Throw It Away?" *Accountancy Ireland* 36, no. 4 (August 2004): 27-29.

23. Myers & Briggs Foundation. "The Myers & Briggs Foundation." http://www.myersbriggs.org/.

24. Wikipedia. "Disc Assessment." Last modified January 28, 2013. http://en.wikipedia.org/wiki/DISC_assessment.

25. Weatherhead School of Management, and Case Western Reserve University. "What Is Appreciative Inquiry? The Appreciative Inquiry Commons." Accessed February 2013. http://appreciativeinquiry.case.edu/intro/whatisai.cfm.

26. Association of Academic Health Sciences Libraries (AAHSL). "Annual Statistics: AAHSL." Last modified 2012. http://www.aahsl.org/annual-statistics.

27. American Library Association, Association of College and Research Libraries. "Information Literacy Resources/Association of College and Research Libraries (ACRL)." Last modified 2013. http://www.ala.org/acrl/issues/infolit.

28. National Network of Libraries of Medicine. "Valuing Library Services Calculator." Last modified December 2, 2011. http://nnlm.gov/mcr/evaluation/calculator.html.

29. Connor, Elizabeth. *Planning, Renovating, Expanding, and Constructing Library Facilities in Hospitals, Academic Medical Centers, and Health Organizations.* Binghamton, NY: Haworth Information, 2005.

30. U.S. National Library of Medicine. "MedPrint: Medical Serials Print Preservation Program." Last modified December 21, 2012. http://www.nlm.nih.gov/psd/printretention main.html.

31. Stambaugh, Emily, and California Digital Library. "WEST: Western Regional Storage Trust." Last modified December 14, 2012. http://www.cdlib.org/west/.

32. Pew Internet and American Life Project. "Pew Research Center's Internet & American Life Project." Last modified February 5, 2013. http://www.pewinternet.org/.

33. Library and Information Technology Association. "LITA Blog: Top Technology Trends Archive." Last modified January 27, 2013. http://litablog.org/category/top -technology-trends/.

34. EDUCAUSE. "EDUCAUSE Homepage." Last modified 2013. http://www .educause.edu/.

35. Wikipedia. "Scholarly Communication." Last modified January 29, 2013. http:// en.wikipedia.org/wiki/Scholarly_communication.

36. Sammonds, Laurel Ivy. "Sustainable Collections: The Pay-per-View Model." *Serials Librarian* 63, no. 2 (2012): 173-177.

Chapter 7

TECHNICAL SERVICES IN HEALTH SCIENCES LIBRARIES

Susan Swogger

When most people picture a librarian, they likely think of someone who provides research assistance or helps them use library materials. They might picture someone putting books on a shelf in a physical library or the person who helps them with the latest changes to their favorite online resources—the sort of activities usually described as "public services." They rarely think of the invisible infrastructure that supports the visible resources that their libraries provide. "Technical services" include the activities that make up most of that hidden infrastructure.

WHAT ARE TECHNICAL SERVICES?

The term "technical services" typically refers to library collections management and organization tasks such as resource selection, resource acquisition, cataloging and metadata, physical and digital preservation, electronic resources and serials management, and the management of library discovery tools. It can also include interlibrary loan and document delivery. Most facets of technical services are experiencing a period of rapid change as libraries collect new types of materials and begin to explore new activities. This chapter will discuss technical services in general, special qualities in respect to health sciences libraries, and some current industry trends and shifts.

Most technical services fall roughly into three categories: development or creation of a library collection, maintenance of physical or digital materials of the library collection, and provision of avenues of access to the collection. The ultimate ambition supporting each and every one of these activities is to facilitate user access to information and knowledge, just as it is in public services. This aim is the underlying foundation for every aspect of technical services rather than the methods used. As such, methods and specializations change very rapidly to support the changing environment of information resource form and use. Adaptability to change is a critical necessity for any technical services position, as the skills needed to support changing library materials, activities, and budgets are in continual flux.

WHO DOES IT? IN THE ORGANIZATIONAL STRUCTURE

As many different structures for technical services exist as do libraries. Depending on the library, these activities may all be undertaken by one librarian, some or all may be outsourced to a contractual service, or each functional area may have several staff at different levels specializing in different tasks. Some libraries may have several different departments devoted to aspects of technical services, while others may have one formal technical services department with some responsibilities distributed to other departments. Increasingly, technical services librarianship includes the management and supervision of skilled support staff, who are handling tasks and activities once undertaken by librarians but now routinized.

Examples of Technical Services Organization

Academic health sciences library: Orange University has a school of nursing, a medical school, and a large teaching hospital, all of which are served by a subject library focused on the health sciences. It has 32 staff, with five librarians and five support staff devoted to technical services. Some of the physical processing is outsourced to the library's book jobber, or supplier, and some of the electronic resources management is shared with the academic library on campus.

Public library: Purple Branch Public Library has a large consumer health collection. Most technical services activities are performed by a large staff at the central office in the Rainbow Public Library District, but the health sciences collection development and selection is performed by a librarian at the Purple Branch, who also answers health-related questions in the Reference Department of Public Services.

Hospital library: Green Hospital serves a large rural county and has 75 beds. It has one librarian who maintains an entirely electronic collection of resources to support clinical staff and a small print consumer health collection for patients. The librarian fulfills every function of the library, including all technical services activities, and also spends considerable time organizing continuing medical education resources for the hospital's physicians.

Regardless of the organizational structure, technical services activities are focused on building, maintaining, and providing access to information resources and library collections.

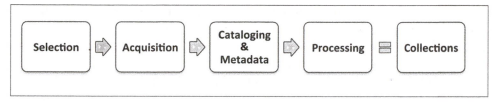

Figure 7.1 The Collections Development Process

THE CREATION OF A LIBRARY COLLECTION: COLLECTION DEVELOPMENT

The development of a library collection involves a range of activities, most of which fall into a predictable pattern. Figure 7.1 shows the path followed by each new library item as it joins the library collection.

Selection and Acquisitions

One of the most valuable functions of libraries and librarians is as a filter between library users and the exponentially exploding accumulation of information and texts. Librarians are experts at evaluating the undifferentiated mass of materials to choose the best resources available to serve the needs of their user populations. These best resources become a library collection, which may be hundreds of thousands of books, journals, and other resources or may simply be access to the free medical database PubMed plus a few core medical references.

The selection of new library materials and the details of acquiring them are two separate but intertwined technical services areas. Often, multiple options exist for acquiring the same selected resource—different formats, vendors, and thus contractual details; different pricing for different levels of access; and so on—that mean acquisitions considerations must be part of selection. However, auditing requirements sometimes mandate that the selector and the purchaser be separate individuals, and in libraries with a solo librarian, some acquisitions tasks may be performed by someone outside of the library in another department. Even setting aside this requirement, the processes of collections development and acquisitions each require considerable specialized knowledge and skills, meaning that it is typical for the areas to be split between multiple positions. The intertwined nature of selection and acquisitions means that said positions work very closely together and will be discussed together in this section.

The first task for selection of new library materials is to know the library's users, and therefore their needs and interests. An effective selector will develop strong relationships with the library's user community and be aware of changes in activities and focus. Regular communication and collaborative relations with this community are vital to successful collection development. A close connection enables the library to respond quickly to new needs and requests as well as to continue broad support for longer-established aims of the institution.

In many academic libraries, individual librarians have responsibility for both research support and selection for specific subjects, facilitating this necessary connection. In others, collection development and selection is a specialized position that allows little time for other responsibilities. In such situations, it is critical for a selector to seek out contact and communication with library users, in and outside of the library. Most institutions, whether universities or hospitals, offer numerous opportunities for connection outside of the library—committee service, volunteer work, service on the institutional review board, involvement in professional organizations, and so on.

Knowledge of and involvement with the institution beyond the library allows librarians to make good decisions about changes to the collections, including keeping the collections development policy living and current, balancing the types and formats of resources in the collections, adding the most useful new items, and, later, making them most accessible via relevant cataloging and description.

Collection Development Policy

To support the mission of the institution and maintain long-term consistency, every library should have a collection development policy. This document codifies exactly which subjects and resources will be collected by a library and by what qualifications. When kept current to reflect the changing needs of the library's users, it provides a blueprint for adding new materials and withdrawing old ones. Common elements include the mission of the library, a description of the community and users served, subjects collected and to what degree, types and formats collected, geographical and chronological limits, and criteria for withdrawal or cancellation.

In addition to serving as an institutional record of the library's focuses and content choices, the collection development policy can help ensure that the collection is least affected by the unconscious biases and interests of selectors. Clear guidelines can help selectors discover neglected or oversubscribed subject areas, explain or defend collections choices to others, avoid investment in unneeded areas, and so on. Collection development policies are invaluable for communicating the bounds of a collection to new selectors, other library staff, and the community served by the library.

The Shift to Online Collections

Most libraries collect multiple types of information resources, each with different management requirements. Ever-more rapid changes are occurring in available forms and types of materials, patterns of use, and sources, requiring an effective selector to be both flexible and exploratory. A library that 30 years before purchased only print journals, print books and monographs, and paper government documents might now purchase entirely electronic journal subscriptions, eBook collections, aggregator database access, and large online data collections with comparatively few new print books.

One of the most impactful changes in formats in recent years has been the shift to online resources. Online journals have been available for decades, and health sciences libraries and library users have been enthusiastic adopters. Online journals require far less valuable library or hospital space to house than their equivalent print editions, and can be searched both in concert and much more quickly. Clinical and research information needs tend to be much more time-critical in nature than those of other disciplines—a classics scholar will likely be able to wait to visit a physical library without harm, while a critical care specialist suddenly presented with unusual findings typically cannot and is better served by immediate online access.

As increasing numbers of journals are available online as well as in print, or even only online, more and more libraries are choosing to subscribe only to the online editions of new or renewed journals. The PCG Library Budget Survey showed that top academic libraries subscribed to 73 percent of journals as online only in 2011— and only 16 percent as print only.[1] There has been a flood of discussion on professional electronic discussion lists and blogs as well as of articles discussing academic and medical libraries reallocating space from storage of print journal collections to use for study or teaching or even additional hospital needs. However, some journals are still available only in print or have prohibitive licensing terms for libraries. If the journal is critical to a particular user need for the library, it should be retained if possible, as reflected in PCG's subscription statistics—the user's needs are more important than the desire to have a single format or policy for the library. This sort of decision requires the journal selector to be knowledgeable of specific library user needs, publishing options, and the management of print as well as online journals.

While the online journal has become the default selection for many libraries, the choice between an online book and a print book is not yet as clear. Online or eBooks are currently in the position that online journals once were—publishers and vendors have not yet settled into standard formats or licensing models, as they largely have with online journals. Many or even most eBooks are essentially identical to their print editions, as are the vast majority of online journals, but there is an increasing exploitation by publishers of the opportunity to add additional media content and functionality, especially among scientific, technical and medical (STM) publishers. Most academic eBook platforms offer at a minimum the ability to save bookmarks, notes, highlighting, built-in citations, search the full text of each book, and more.

Unfortunately, the eBook for libraries has numerous complications. eBooks are widely available to individual users in a format that is not yet easily available to academic or health sciences libraries, as academic libraries typically cannot offer downloadable eBooks such as Kindle books due to licensing complications. Many academic libraries have large collections of monographic eBooks that can be accessed on a variety of platforms but typically only while the user is online. They are often usable by only one person at a time, leading to frustration when multiple users attempt to access a book at once, frustration that is usually directed at the library rather than the eBook vendor. Occasionally, eBooks are unable to include all of the text or images that would be found in a print edition due to copyright issues. eBook publishers often limit printing or copying due to restrictive digital rights management (DRM) strictures that make the books less usable for study than a print book would typically be. However, growing numbers of eBooks are available in downloadable formats or with much more sensible DRM, and with time, publishers and libraries will work out mutually agreeable formats and licensing.

Health sciences publishers were some of the earliest producers of eBooks and offer a number of innovative options. Many if not most of the major health sciences references and textbooks are available as eBooks. Though many of these are available only as simple reproductions of print text, as is most common with eBooks, more and more publishers are taking advantage of the opportunities offered by the online world to include video and extensive images that can be hugely valuable. Most of the major publishers also offer their books on their own platforms, usually permitting multiple users to access them simultaneously and taking advantage of the opportunity to include medical calculators, dictionaries, image banks, large data files, and more. Increasingly, the major medical references are also available on either mobile optimized websites or as downloadable apps, supporting their use even in the sometimes poorly connected environment of the hospital or on clinical rotations away from the campus.

The growth of online collections has added new layers of complexity to library acquisitions. Online resources of every variety require licenses as part of their subscription or purchase process, and each has strictly defined limits on how libraries may offer access, to whom they may offer access, and what can be done with online content. Libraries must negotiate such varied details as number of users able to concurrently access content; archival rights to older content after the end of a subscription; the ability of users to print, save, or download; the definition of legitimate library users; the rights to reproduce online content for interlibrary loans or even faculty presentations; and so on. Many libraries have an electronic resources librarian position to manage these critical details, while others fold this responsibility into the general acquisitions or collection development positions.

JOURNALS AND SERIALS

Journals in any format are both the core of any academic or clinical health sciences library collection and the greatest occupation of any technical services department. Journals are widely considered to be the preferred information resource for health sciences library users. They not uncommonly consume 76 percent or more of the average academic medical library's annual collections budget. In comparison, they made up about 68 percent of the equivalent academic library collections budget in 2011.[2,3] That 76 percent does not even include the additional 17 percent of the typical health sciences library budget devoted to database subscriptions, databases which are largely made up of *more* journals.[4] Perhaps due to this preference, thousands of medical journals are available—no library could afford to subscribe to them all or would attempt to.

The selection of a new journal requires considerable thought and care. The long-term trend in journal subscription costs is that of continual increases ranging between 3 and 10 percent annually. Despite considerable negative discussion of this situation among librarians over recent decades, this trend shows no sign of stopping, and any new journal subscription will very likely encumber an ever-increasing percentage of a library's annual budget. As such, new journals should meet a higher standard for selection than one-time purchases such as monographs or similar materials.

Discovery and Evaluation of Potential New Journals

Several common avenues provide possibilities for discovering the need for a new journal. Most new journals meet explicitly expressed library user needs. Users may directly request a new journal, and methods of communication for doing so should be made easy to find. The institution may launch a new academic or clinical program that requires new support resources. High interlibrary loan activity for an unsubscribed journal may indicate that library users need more direct access. More rarely, library selectors may desire to subscribe to a new journal in speculation that library users will then find and use it.

The librarian in charge of collections development for journals or serials—sometimes a specific position, sometimes a responsibility undertaken as one among many—should investigate the journal carefully before subscribing to it, using criteria standard to the library.

Individual Journal Evaluation Criteria

Journal quality can be evaluated by examining a number of details about the title, some of which may or may not be relevant to an individual selection decision:

Quality

- Is the publisher known and respected?
  - While new publishers can certainly produce good journals, a respected publisher can provide a certain amount of security regarding the quality of the journal.
- Who are the editorial staff, and what are their professional qualifications? Do they fit the journal scope?
  - The editorial staff should have an appropriate level of education and expertise to support the journal's scope. Look carefully for a good balance of academic, research, and possibly corporate affiliation.
- Has any of the institution's faculty or staff published there?
  - If the library's user group is interested enough in the journal to publish in it, it is very likely that it will be used if subscribed.
- Is it a society publication?
  - Sometimes a journal is widely used because everyone who joins the society receives a subscription. If all of the likely users of a journal at an institution are members of this society, it is unlikely to be used.
- Is the journal scholarly—is it peer reviewed? Or is it a trade journal with relevance to the library's users?
  - The journal should fit the need described in the request and be likely to be of use to more than just the requestor. If the journal is an esoteric scholarly publication and the library serves a small regional hospital without researchers, it may not be the best choice for the library's limited budget.

- Does the journal have a high impact factor? Does this matter for the specific library?
  - Journals are considered high impact if they have a sufficiently high rating on Thomson Reuter's Journal Citation Index in comparison to similar journals on the same subject. This rating is established by an algorithm that determines frequency of citation of "average articles" from a journal during a particular time period.[5]
  - The impact factor was originally developed to help libraries decide which journals to subscribe but was then adopted by faculty and has been heavily influential in deciding tenure and promotion.[6] This is both controversial among researchers and becoming less important for some fields with the rise of new publishing avenues and rating sources, but it is still very widespread. Other means of determining impact and evaluating the effects of research are being explored, but the Journal Citation Index is the most established.[7]

Subject

- Is the journal on a subject core to the library, or is it of secondary interest?
  - This information will assist in deciding the appropriate level of access necessary, for example, does the library need full access, or will free but limited access do?
- Does the library have many other journals on the subject, or few? If it has other journals, do they have high or low usage in the library, as reported by the online journal publishers?
  - If the library has other journals and all are used, it is highly likely that the new one will be as well. If the library has no other journals on the subject, is it very unique, or is it not very relevant for the library?

Usability

- Where is the journal indexed? Is it included in PubMed?
  - Journals will be used only if they are included in a bibliographic database that the library's users can access. The NIH-produced PubMed database is freely available and indexes most prominent medical journals, though not all, and medical researchers are taught to use it with every search.
- Is the journal on an acceptable platform?
  - If the journal is online, it must be on a platform that meets the standards of the library for good use.
- Does the journal provide backfile access?
  - Most online journal subscriptions provide some years of older content with new subscriptions, that is, a backfile. This additional content makes the journal more useful to the library's users, though it is not always available.

Cost

- Can the library budget afford it this year *and* next year?
  - Journals are continuing expenses and should be factored into ongoing budget planning.

License and Access

- Are the terms of the license acceptable to the library?
  - Universities, hospitals, and other large institutions have legal departments that will determine what is acceptable in a contract and license. Acquisitions or electronic resource librarians work with them to review and approve all licenses before subscribing to or purchasing any new serial or other resource.
- What are the terms of access?
  - If the journal is an online journal, it may be available either by password and login, by IP range, or even only by email. If available only by password and login, that single password and login must be shared with every library user—a time-consuming and insecure method of access for most libraries. Much preferable in most situations is access by IP range, which will allow all within a specific IP range to use the journal.
- How many users can access the content at once?
  - Some publishers offer a variety of levels of concurrency, or numbers of simultaneous "user seats," each with different pricing. Too low, and an unacceptable numbers of students will be turned away from the resource, but too high, and capacity and money are wasted.
- Does the subscription include perpetual access?
  - Journal subscriptions should include perpetual access to years subscribed, even if the subscription is ended or the journal ceases publication.
- Does the publisher participate in CLOCKSS or Portico to safeguard perpetual access?
  - CLOCKSS (Controlled Lots of Copies Keep Stuff Safe) is a dark archive joint venture between publishers and libraries that attempts to make sure that scholarly content available only online is not lost if a publisher goes out of business or ceases to support a journal. Multiple libraries store files of journal content offline, never making it available unless and until certain trigger events occur. This is hoped to ensure that content is never lost, despite any inability on the part of the publisher to continue to provide access.[8]
  - Portico is another major dark archive with the same purpose as CLOCKSS—to forever preserve digital scholarly content. Its mission is to work with libraries, publishers, and funders to "preserve e-journals, e-books, and other electronic scholarly content to ensure researchers and students will have access to it in the future."[9]

Journal Acquisitions Options

Once the library selects a journal, a number of decisions must be made about how to acquire it.

Electronic versus Print Journals

Academic library users prefer to access journals online, as shown in numerous studies over the past decade.[10, 11, 12] As such, this chapter assumes that the default decision for a journal will always be an online subscription.

Despite this preference, a library may have many reasons to continue to subscribe to an individual journal in print—lower subscription costs, user preferences, online access limitations, unacceptable online licensing, lack of availability, and so on. In those cases, the technical services department will be responsible for arranging to bind each volume of issues to preserve it on the library shelves or discard it at a specific date if not desired for long-term preservation.

Ownership versus Access versus Open Access versus Pay per View

Subscription decisions were simpler before the advent of online journals—the library either *did* subscribe to a print journal and *did* have access to all of its content, or it did *not* subscribe and did *not* have access. This is not necessarily the case with on-line journals, where there can be several different levels of access and archival rights.

Traditional subscriptions to online journals are very similar to print subscriptions, and many in fact include both online access and a print copy of the journal. Libraries subscribe to the journal and are presumed to own perpetual archival access to the years for which they subscribe, even if they cease the subscription or the publisher goes out of business catastrophically. The subscription terms may promise that if the publisher fails, it will opt into a preservation program such as CLOCKSS that will maintain access to the content for all subscribers, or it may promise that an electronic file of the lost content will be given to the library. Other than some details of access provision, there is relatively little difference between traditional print and online journal acquisitions activities.

Increasingly, however, traditional subscriptions of any kind are not the only choice for journal access. Nearly all academic libraries subscribe to aggregator databases, large collections of journal articles and other materials that may include thousands of journals—each of which can also be subscribed to individually. Aggregator database collections of journals have several advantages, the major ones being a single subscription payment, far lower costs than individual subscriptions to each journal, the ability to search hundreds of journals from different publishers together, and additional nonjournal content and research management tools.

The disadvantages are that there is no guarantee that journals that are included in the database on Monday will be there Tuesday, there is no perpetual archival access to older content if the library drops the database subscription, and there are frequent embargos of recent issues. This means that the journal will lack the most recent six, 12, or 18 months of content—typically the most desirable content, especially for any scientific researcher. Despite these flaws, the library may already have access to a journal at this level without need of any additional subscriptions, which may be acceptable if its subject is noncore and the cost per use is expected to be high.

The rapidly increasing field of open access journals consists of journals that are freely available to all users online, and libraries may include them in their collections without paying any subscription fees. Many more—but not all—journals offer some open access content, and these hybrid journals may offer open research articles but not editorial and trade articles, articles that the authors have paid fees to make open access, or articles past a certain date. This mixed access, like aggregator access, may or may not be sufficient to meet an individual library's needs—this decision will require the selector's close knowledge of the library users. It is also sometimes possible to secure reduced open access publication fees for authors from an institution with a paid library subscription, which may be a deciding factor in the decision to subscribe.

Open access journals are becoming a strong and respected presence in the academic and research community in part in response to a growing belief that publicly funded research should be available to the public—and the vast majority of research *is* government grant–funded. A movement now exists that is seeking a requirement that all publications arising from government-funded research be deposited in open repository archives, typically with a delay or embargo.

This is of particularly vital importance for health sciences and biomedical researchers in the United States, as all National Institutes of Health–funded research articles must be deposited in the open PubMed Central (PMC) repository. Journals included in PMC therefore offer open access to at least some of their research content, though not necessarily all content, which may be sufficient for a particular library. As of this date, more than 2.5 million biomedical research articles are publicly available in PMC, and its mission is to provide permanent and free access to biomedical and life sciences literature.[13]

As publishers have from the first proposal and inception of this project viewed it as a direct competition for paid subscriptions, there is ongoing conflict about its justification and whether it should continue in its present repository delivery–based form or shift to other implementations. The coming years will see yet more discussion and controversy about the best ways to ensure fairness to researchers, taxpayer-funders, and publishers. Despite the controversies, other large national research funders—in the United States, the United Kingdom and beyond—are following, and more large repositories are likely to come online.[14]

An additional method of access that has been available for a number of years but is growing in prominence is known as pay per view. This can mean that users pay for an individual journal article, downloading it from a publisher's website without any connection to a library. This option is available from most publishers with well-established online platforms and can be quite expensive, with most articles ranging in price from $25 to $65 per download. In critical cases where an article is needed immediately (as may happen in hospital libraries) but the journal is neither subscribed nor available freely, this may be the best option.

More commonly in the library context, it can mean that the library budgets to pay this price for its users, which can be done via a deposit account at a publisher, an annual library purchase of a certain number of "tokens" that can be exchanged by users for articles, or some similar method.[15] For some libraries, this cost can be far lower than subscriptions to all of the journals, while for others, it might be far higher. Additional concerns are the lack of perpetual access to purchased articles, the additional work required by the library to carefully manage the necessary usage review, and the constraining effect on library users, who will typically use far fewer journal articles than with other methods of access. Conversely, users will quickly run through the account by unconsidered downloads.[16] As with every choice involved in acquisitions, knowledge of the library's users and their needs and activities is key to making wise decisions.

Direct Subscription versus Subscription Agents

Libraries may subscribe to journals by direct contract with a publisher or through a subscription agent that can easily handle multiple subscriptions and packages with different publishers, typically for a percentage of the total subscription costs. Dealing with a subscription agent has a number of advantages—one searchable database of information about journals from multiple sources, management of currency exchanges and other payment details, different renewal dates, contact and address changes, missing issue claims, and increasingly, provision of cataloging records and online journal usage statistics consolidation. The disadvantage, of course, is that that small percentage of the subscription cost can add up to a considerable amount. Individual publishers may also offer more opportunity for customization of any subscribed package with direct subscription, but most provide equal service regardless of whether a customer pays directly or through an agent. The advantages are great enough that most libraries with more than a few subscriptions work with one or more subscription agents, possibly combined with a few individual subscriptions not available through a particular agent.

Individual versus Package Subscriptions

Journals are often available individually or as part of a discounted package. Individual journal subscriptions are just that—a library subscribes to one journal title, and it is handled independently for renewal decisions. Package subscriptions include multiple journals from the same publisher and can be for a subset of journals or for the publisher's entire title list. Individual journal costs in a package are often very heavily discounted in comparison to a single journal subscription, but packages cost more overall. Renewal of the package renews all or most of the titles together or not at all, regardless of whether a particular journal title is desired by the library.

Big Deals

A special kind of package is a "big deal," that is, a library commitment to subscribe to the entirety of a publisher's title list for multiple years in exchange for a large discount in comparison to individual purchase of selected titles. Big deals are typically available only when all or most members of a library consortium, or group of libraries clubbing together on purchases and other projects, agree to participate in them. As nearly all academic and medical libraries belong to consortia—the Publishers Communications Group's Library Budget Survey showed 98 percent of top academic libraries worldwide as consortia members—this type of deal is usually available from at least some publishers.[17]

Most academic libraries are party to numerous big deals, as they allow the library to offer far more content than would otherwise generally be possible. Quite frequently, a library would pay nearly as much for its desired journal titles at list price as it does for a big deal consisting of all of the wanted journals *and* hundreds of additional titles, some of which may then be used more than the selected core titles. The major disadvantages of a big deal are the overall high costs and the reduction in discretion about journal retention or additions, as a library may be obligated under its contract to keep journals with limited usage while being forced to cancel better-used journals from other publishers to pay for them.

Despite this flaw, big deals have become increasingly common over the past two decades, and many academic libraries have a very high percentage of their annual journal and serials budgets tied into them. The recent recession and consequent massive cuts or slowing in library budgets nationwide has led to unprecedented numbers of libraries discussing cancelling big deals and then relying on aggregator databases, pay per view (which allows articles to be purchased on an individual basis), or interlibrary loans to supply the lost content. In response, publishers are beginning to offer smaller packages of content that are subject specific under similar terms, which may allow some compromise between the publisher's desire for maximum profit and the library's desire for maximum useful content.[18] Regardless of some discontent among librarians, big deals seem likely to continue as a dominant subscription and pricing model.

BOOKS AND MONOGRAPHS

The selection and acquisition of an individual book is simpler than that of a journal, as it usually represents a single, much smaller, nonrecurring expense, with the exception of some very few subscription-based eBooks. That said, though journal subscriptions consume the majority of any library's budget, they generally require subscription and renewal actions during only part of the year. Books are usually purchased throughout the year and thus require regular selection and acquisitions attention.

Librarians can and do find out about new health sciences books from a number of the same places that library users do—word of mouth from colleagues, publisher advertisements or blogs, book reviews in journals, professional listservs, and publisher booths at conferences—and also from librarian-specific sources such as special review services and library book jobber (specialized wholesale booksellers) notifications. They may select them individually or in collections, receive them automatically, or purchase them on request.

Health Sciences Book Types

Health sciences books differ in type, and some may be more appropriate for a particular library than others.

Medical Textbooks

- Many medical textbooks also serve as core reference books.
- Most print editions come with DVDs, which may or may not be licensed for library use, and/or online content, which is almost never licensed for library use. Some

publishers offer this supplementary content with eBooks purchased or subscribed from their own platforms, but not all do, and almost none offer it if eBooks are accessed through an aggregator site with books from multiple publishers.

Academic Books

- Academic monographs or edited collections on medical and health sciences subjects are common.

Medical Handbooks

- Handbooks are basic references intended for either laypeople or clinical staff, and they generally include brief information, charts, reviews, algorithms, and so on.
- They are not often purchased by academic libraries—due to insufficient depth of content—but may be held in hospital libraries as review resources.
- Increasingly, this type of book is available in a mobile format for use in the clinical setting. Some are so established in this format that users may not even realize that it is also or was once available as a print book.

Encyclopedias and Pharmacopeia

- Numerous encyclopedias serve as core references for the health sciences. A pharmacopeia is a special encyclopedia focused on drug listing and description. This type of book is most frequently purchased or subscribed to as an eBook when available in that format due to the increased ease of searching.

Medical and Surgical Atlases

- These are reference collections of detailed images and illustrations of human anatomy and physiology, whether normal, diseased, or as seen during surgical procedures. Increasingly, they include significant online video content.

Consumer Health Books

- These are intended for a lay audience and tend to focus on coping with disease or disability, or on various aspects of health and wellness.

Exam Preparation Books

- These are review and practice books for the various medical and health sciences board and licensing examinations.
- They are often of intense but fleeting interest to library users—they are both quickly outdated and frequently damaged or stolen. Most libraries do not carry them in print for these reasons, but many do offer them as eBooks. This type of book is well suited to an eBook subscription model rather than a purchase model due to the rapid release of new editions, but only if they are available for multiple simultaneous users.

eBooks: A or B?

As discussed earlier in this chapter, a rapidly increasing number of books are available as either print or eBooks. eBooks may be purchased or subscribed, selected individually or as part of a collection, selected by librarians or by library users directly, owned by one library or shared by several, or accessed online or via a mobile app. Whatever the case, one user or many, change is occurring very rapidly, and many options are available. Most libraries choose a mix of options to offer to users. The following are some current options that may apply.

Purchase versus Subscription

Libraries may purchase perpetual access to one edition of an eBook or subscribe, which typically provides access only for the term of the subscription but usually automatically updates with any new editions without additional charges. Some eBook subscriptions may even update in real time rather than waiting for a new edition.

Unlimited versus Few Simultaneous or Concurrent Users

The number of library users permitted to access an eBook at once varies by publisher and even by book title. Many eBook aggregators offer the option to pay more to allow more users to use an individual book title, which is often desirable if a book is likely to be frequently used or assigned as a textbook.

If a book is likely to be used in a clinical setting, it must be purchased with multiple users permitted if at all possible.

Individual Book versus Book Collection

Some publishers allow libraries to purchase their entire yearly output at a discounted price, rather than the more typical individual selection and payment.

Librarian versus Patron-Driven Acquisition

While most eBooks are selected by librarians individually or as part of a collection, many libraries have large or small patron-driven acquisition (PDA) programs that allow users to select eBooks for the library to instantly purchase through the library catalog itself, often without even realizing that the library did not own it.

Consortial versus Library Ownership

A new and experimental model has some library consortia subscribing or purchasing eBook collections to be shared. They may pay more for the individual books or allow only one user throughout the system to use each at once.

Online versus Mobile App versus Download

Most library eBooks are accessed online, and users must use them while logged on via a website. Some eBooks may be downloaded to a Kindle or other eReader, though this is currently less common for academic books than it is for popular works.

Increasing numbers of eBooks accessed via the web also offer the option of mobile optimization, recognizing that the user is accessing the content via a mobile device and reformatting to suit it. A few publishers and vendors are beginning to offer apps that a library might pay for the right for its users to download, which then allow them to access particular eBooks via the app. This important new trend seems likely to be of great interest to libraries serving users in a clinical setting, who may have both poor online access and urgent, immediate need for information resources.

Book Jobbers and Approval Plans

Libraries may purchase print and eBooks directly from publishers, from physical or online bookstores, or most commonly for academic libraries, from a book jobber. Book jobbers are wholesale booksellers who sell directly to libraries, schools, or bookstores. They provide a single point of contact for buyers for books from numerous publishers or eBook aggregators, large discounts off of list prices, and a useful filtering function in the form of an approval plan. Libraries work with book jobbers to develop an approval plan based on their collection development policy that tells the jobber which new book notices the library would like to receive—they can be limited by subject, reading level, audience, publisher, format, and so on. An approval plan may also tell the jobber to send certain new books automatically based on these criteria, most of which are accepted and paid for without the need for a librarian to individually select them. This automatic shipping feature can be turned on or off based on the library's preferences and budgetary needs, and it is a great time-saver for libraries that purchase large numbers of books.

Selection by Librarians

Librarian selectors also choose books to support the aims in the collection development policy or identified user needs. As with journals, potential library books should be reviewed for appropriate quality and content level, subject, utility, costs, type, and (if online) license terms.

In support of the existing collection, librarians will select books discovered by some combination of book reviews, publisher websites or catalogs, peer communications, other library catalogs, and jobber information. Medical and medical librarian trade journals offer numerous reviews of books, as do various services. Book jobbers, in addition to sending books based on preset parameters, will provide notification slips for new books that may be, but are not assumed to be, of interest to the library and can provide most other books as desired.

New or changing programs, courses, or clinical specialties should also trigger collection reviews and growth. Existing collections should be considered in light of changes, and then any needed books or other resources should be sought for acquisition. The collections development librarian should work with the people involved with the new program or specialty and the public services librarians to discover what new books are needed.

Health Sciences Book News and Review Sources

The available professional review services deliver news and reviews about new books to librarians. The most prominent of these for health sciences librarians is

Doody's Book Reviews, which publishes some 2,000 new reviews annually about healthcare publications. It also maintains a core title list for a wide range of clinical and nursing specialty areas.[19] Doody's ratings have become familiar to most health sciences librarians and can be a useful tool for finding well-established and reviewed titles for specific subject areas.

Selection by Library Users

Users also often request that libraries purchase books. If the book is suitable for the library collection and funds are available, user-requested books should always be purchased. In many libraries, if multiple library users request the same book via interlibrary loan, it is treated as a purchase request and added to the library collection.

Selection Using Patron-Driven Acquisition

A trend in user requests that has been growing and is beginning to pick up steam is patron-driven acquisitions for books (PDA)—the "automated practice of allowing patrons to select books for their library, most often through clicking on records that have been added to their library's catalog."[20] This could have a large impact on both library collections development and library relationships with users. Unlike traditional models where librarians select books preuse based on their knowledge of the field and of their library community, the library's users select the books they need. Libraries retain control over the development of their collections by designating eBook purchase triggers, parameters of available eBooks for PDA selection, whether the plan applies only to eBooks or also to print books, available funds, and so on. The aim of PDA is to provide immediate access to desired books at the time of need, hence the typical though not universal focus on eBooks.[21] In most current libraries that have or are using PDA, it serves as an additional selection technique directed at just-in-time acquisition of resources, in combination with the traditional just-in-case preservation of resources rather than a replacement, but this may change.

DATABASES AND OTHER ELECTRONIC RESOURCES

The selection of and acquisition of a new online database subscription is similar to the process for a new online journal, as each requires a large financial commitment that demands careful consideration, each requires the same care with licenses, and each undergoes a similar acquisitions process. Additionally—due to the expense—it is typically a good idea to offer library users a trial of a database before subscribing, along with a burst of publicity about the new resources after.

A wide range of specialized online research, education, and clinical support resources are available, and most health sciences libraries have a mix of the following types.

One-Time Purchase of Databases

Some databases do not require continuing budgetary support, other than that required for staff time devoted to maintenance activities—journal backfiles, archives, eBook or video collections, or other similar items. These are typically very large one-time expenses. This sort of choice is generally made to purchase many years of older content, most often of a publisher's entire title list. Such purchases are usually necessary only to support researchers who need access to older materials in the most useful medium. They occasionally require the commitment of an annual hosting fee. These hosting fees typically include a commitment to perpetual access by the vendor but sometimes may consist of a purchase of access for a period of three to five years, which may or may not be renewed.

Subscription Databases

Much more commonly, a library will subscribe to one or several databases on an annual basis from a vendor. While databases offer far more variability in content types and formats than journal subscriptions, they tend to consist of several common types.

Bibliographic/Citation Databases

These databases index and abstract articles from a variety of journals and other items, and can be broad in coverage or subject specific. Increasingly, they offer the capability to link to outside full-text content, either of open access or library-subscribed journal or database titles. PubMed, freely available from the United States' National Institutes of Health and the first and most critical step for biomedical and life sciences research, is one such, though it may appear otherwise to the user because many health sciences libraries set it to link to their subscribed full-text content when within their institutional IP ranges, and it can link to other outside content. It also integrates fully with the full-text PubMed Central database, which though similar in name is separate.

Full-Text Content Database

These databases include the full text of either or both journals and books. Aggregator databases include content from a multitude of publishers, often with a delay or embargo between actual publication and appearance in the databases. Other full-text databases offer content from a single publisher, usually without the delay. For example, the National Institutes of Health's other database, PubMed Central (PMC), is a true full-text database focused on archiving scientific literature in biomedical and life sciences. It hosts and provides the full text of its included content.

Teaching Databases

Usually full-text databases including content from one publisher, these are special resources intended for teaching support. They often include large image banks, quizzing capability, and academic management features available to faculty. They are always specific to one subject area. Some, such as the various board exam preparation resources of interest to the health sciences, require considerable administrative responsibility for tracking student activities and progress. Typically, this is set up to be managed both by faculty and by the site administrator, who is usually the technical services librarian responsible for dealing with electronic resources.

Clinical Decision Support and Point of Care Resources

Libraries serving hospitals and other settings often also subscribe to point of care resources, that is, resources intended to help physicians and other practitioners on the front line of practice. These are used by physicians, pharmacists, nurses, and others to quickly find the information necessary to make clinical decisions. They are often more similar to print handbooks, pharmacopeia, and atlases than to more research-oriented journal databases. They are based on research and may include references and links to it but are typically summaries, treatment algorithms, charts, collections of example images, and so on, rather than articles. Increasingly, they are available both online and as mobile apps. They can be broad in coverage and include resources for many specialties, or they can be very narrow with a focus on one field of practice or type of information.

CATALOGING AND METADATA

The technical services department also performs the next steps for adding a new item—its formal addition to the library's collections via a process known as cataloging. Catalogers create new or adapt existing bibliographic records about library materials to add to the library catalog using traditional library standardized rules, classification systems, and vocabularies. In most libraries, they also work with other newer systems of metadata standards, meaning standards about the use of data to describe data, to describe and organize objects both physical and digital. The ultimate aim of any library catalog or metadata librarian is to promote resource discovery through effective and standardized resource description.

While at one time most cataloging librarians may have created original catalog records for each item in a library collection, catalog records now come to the library in a variety of ways. They may indeed be created as original cataloging and then possibly shared with other libraries via Online Computer Library Center, Inc. (OCLC), the world's largest library cooperative and the producer of WorldCat. WorldCat is "a global network of library-management and user-facing services built upon cooperatively-maintained databases of bibliographic and institutional metadata." It is a shared online public access catalog that includes records from most libraries in the United States and Canada, and many beyond.[22] This shared catalog is the discovery and communication method used in much of the interlibrary lending process in North America. It is also publicly accessible and included in Google Scholar.

In most libraries, librarians or cataloging staff do a mix of original and copy cataloging, acquiring an externally authored record and then changing it to fit the needs of the library. Very commonly, catalogers engaged in copy cataloging may download records contributed by other library staff from OCLC, which will also automatically list the library's holdings in WorldCat. Libraries may also subscribe to a commercial cataloging service that sells bibliographic records or pay to receive them with purchases from a book jobber. Many publishers also provide bibliographic records for their books or journals, especially if the library buys an online collection rather than a single item. All of these externally acquired records usually require some adjustment by the catalogers to best facilitate access for a particular library's population of users.

Cataloging Standards: The Transition to RDA

English-language libraries use one dominant set of cataloging rules, but this is currently undergoing a transition from one long-established standard to a very different new one. Most existing English-language library catalog records as of 2012 were created using the AACR2 (Anglo-American Cataloging Rules, Second Edition) rules, which were first released in 1978 and then refreshed with periodic updates. AACR2 is the standard for what content is *included* in cataloging records, while the standard for how it is *represented* and *communicated* when used in an electronic catalog is the MARC, or MAchine-Readable Cataloging format.[23] The MARC standard most widely used in North America is MARC 21, which is maintained by the Library of Congress.[24] AACR2 was developed before the explosion of digital formats and opportunities of the past few decades and is very much print oriented. As described elsewhere in this chapter, this focus on print no longer reflects modern libraries, and a change was needed.

Over the past decade, the American Library Association, the Canadian Library Association, and the Chartered Institute of Library and Information Professionals (CILIP) in the United Kingdom worked together to create a new system of rules designed to be inclusive of print materials, legacy formats such as microfiche, and common digital library materials such as eJournals and eBooks—*and* be flexible enough to adapt to and include all other types of digital materials and communications formats.[25] RDA, or Resource Description and Access, also works with metadata term sets other than the aging MARC21 standard, such as the very widely used Dublin Core, and is expected to eventually provide a much greater capacity for interoperability between different systems of cataloging.[26] It was first released in 2010 and fully implemented in 2013 by the three national libraries of the United States—the National Library of Medicine, the National Library of Agriculture, and the Library of Congress—as well as a number of international libraries.[27]

Library of Congress versus National Library of Medicine

Regardless of whether they are using AACR2 or RDA, catalogers assign controlled vocabulary subject headings as well as classification numbers to records. The most common authoritative list of subject headings in the United States, the Library of Congress Subject Headings (LCSH), has been maintained by its namesake since 1898 and is used in most academic libraries.[28] As LCSH is not sufficiently detailed or flexible enough for medical topics to meet many researchers' needs, most medical libraries use the Medical Subject Heading (MeSH) vocabulary from the National Library of Medicine, often in combination with LCSH. MeSH is also used to provide entry terms to assist users in searching the very widely used PubMed database, making it quite familiar to most medical researchers.[29]

Health sciences libraries also use a different classification scheme than is common in most academic or public libraries, which use the Library of Congress (academic libraries) or Dewey decimal classification systems (public libraries), respectively. Classification or call numbers describe where an item should be placed on the shelf relative to similar items, and as with the use of MeSH, the biomedical NLM classification scheme allows for much greater granularity. It is common for academic health sciences libraries to have monographic and journal holdings with a mix of LC and NLM classification, as NLM classification can be used only for biomedical subjects, and most libraries also include a range of other subjects.

Management of the Catalog and Other Discovery Tools

Catalogers may also manage the library's catalog and any other discovery tools, usually in close cooperation with the information technology (IT) or library systems staff. While the IT or systems staff will likely maintain the structure and stability of any electronic catalog or other metadata storage database, the catalogers will control and create the metadata for said databases. Increasingly, academic libraries are creating and using non-MARC metadata to manage some types of resources in their digital collections. While a library catalog stores metadata about traditional library resources, many libraries also maintain additional databases for other types of information resources or to offer additional access to traditional resources that cannot be provided using AACR2 and/or MARC21. These may include digital collections of images, datasets, or other information created and/or managed by proprietary digital collection management software such as ContentDM or SimpleDL; A-to-Z access lists for electronic journals or databases; institutional data or article repositories built using protocols such as DSpace; information discovery tools that can cross-search multiple databases, including the catalog; and more.

PHYSICAL PROCESSING

Many people immediately picture the next technical services activity when they try to picture a technical services department—processing, the physical transformation of new books or journal issues into library materials. Traditionally, technical services staff put labels, barcodes, tattle or RFID tags that alert when the material is removed from the building, and so forth on new items after they have been cataloged. If a book is purchased from a library book jobber and the library intends to use provided MARC records for cataloging, the book may arrive with labels and barcodes already affixed and require just delivery to the circulation department. However, many book jobbers do not offer the option of NLM call numbers, so this option is less common in health sciences libraries. In larger libraries, processing materials is usually performed by staff members rather than librarians.

COLLECTIONS MANAGEMENT AND MAINTENANCE

New materials are not abandoned after they are purchased and processed. The various routines of collection management are also part of technical services.

Electronic Resources Management

The technical services department also manages online resources after subscribing to or purchasing them. On the surface, it might seem that online resources would require less care than print—they require no space, they need not be checked out or in, they cannot be destroyed or stolen ... But this is decidedly *not* the case. In many libraries, there is enough activity involved in supporting online resources to require a dedicated position or positions, and individual online resources are often more time consuming for technical services than print ones. Print books and journals usually become at least in part the responsibility of public services and the circulation departments, but not so for online resources.

Electronic resources require frequent updating and checking of links, which requires fairly frequent cataloging changes. They also are prone to becoming unavailable whenever their hosting website has problems, which is outside of the library's control. This is inevitably the cause of problems and distress for library users and must be dealt with quickly. Electronic resources require regular contact with vendors to ensure that changes on either the vendor or library end are properly managed and communicated to users.

Health sciences libraries have a special responsibility to make sure that any outage or problem with point of care or clinical decision support resources are dealt with appropriately, as lives could conceivably be at risk. The library should work with vendors and the hospital to ensure that any necessary outages are at the least troublesome time for the hospital if possible, and well publicized if not. Sometimes, alternate resources or services must be provided for those hours. It is imperative to ensure that any supported hospital does not lack clinical information.

As most electronic resources are renewed annually, they should be evaluated annually to ensure that they still meet the needs of the library. Electronic resources should be evaluated for cost per use, low or high usage, relevance to institutional programs, stability of access, and other factors before renewal. Much of this is knowable by close connection and communication with the institution served by the library, as previously mentioned. The vast majority of electronic resource vendors will provide usage statistics that can give much more detailed information than is available for print resources, which will provide much of the rest of what is needed. Most English-language electronic resource vendors use the international COUNTER (Counting Online Usage of Networked Electronic Resources) standard to format and provide usage statistics for journals, databases, and increasingly, eBooks.[30] COUNTER allows librarians to compare like to like usage information for different journals or databases from different publishers.

Library Electronic Resources and the Electronic Health Record

In hospital settings, point of care databases and resources may be integrated into the electronic health record (EHR) system to improve clinical practice and reduce errors. An EHR is a standardized, systematic digital collection of information and records about a patient that is intended to be shared across a variety of clinical settings and maintained over time. The meaningful use component of the 2009 Health Information Technology for Economic and Clinical Health Act, or HITECH Act, which is part of the American Recovery and Reinvestment Act of 2009 (ARRA), requires that hospital EHRs include "clinical decision support systems."[31] It does not define what these might be or require them to be based on the biomedical literature.[32]

Regardless, library databases and resources can fulfill this requirement for the hospital and add a great deal of value to an EHR system. Health sciences librarians have been working with hospital IT staff and EHR vendors to integrate subscribed resources since before the passage of the act.[33, 34, 35] Librarian expertise and experience with the management and use of electronic information resources can be hugely valuable to the most useful implementation of an EHR. Not all hospitals currently have EHR systems, but most will implement them to comply with the 2015 deadline of the act and avoid Medicare and Medicaid payment penalties.

PRESERVATION OF PRINT AND DIGITAL MATERIALS

Technical services also includes any activities undertaken toward the preservation of materials of every variety. "Preservation" in this context refers to activities intended to save library materials for long-term access, whether digital or physical. This area of technical services has become both increasingly specialized and increasingly rare over recent years, as the easy availability of digital resources both adds to the variety of materials to be preserved and allows libraries to discard older materials yet still maintain access to their content electronically. The shift to electronic resources has changed the focus of library preservation in many libraries from maintenance of the media storing information to the information itself—print resources are still preserved when appropriate as they have always been, but the existence of continually changing and expanding forms of new digital media and information is driving innovative new practice.

Print Preservation

Library books and journals are in print and available for only a short period of time, and they are easily damaged—especially the most desirable and thus most heavily used materials. As such, preservation and maintenance of the fragile has long been a library preoccupation. According to Pillette, physical preservation can be said to include "good house-keeping, controlled environment and relative humidity, instructions on care and handling, an emergency response plan, and collection security, as well as more traditional activities of reformatting, repair and binding."[36]

Technical services librarians may be involved in management or policy making for any or all of these activities, as well as the day-to-day tasks involved.

Any library with a circulating print book collection is likely to use a mix of outsourcing and in-house activities for the "traditional" technical services tasks of reformatting, repairing, and binding. It is common for a book or bound journal volume to need repairs after many years of use, and in most academic and public libraries, the technical services department will make minor repairs in-house or send them to another library within the system that specializes in repairs. Most such minor repairs are aimed primarily at keeping the book usable and not at maintaining its original state, and books needing more involved repairs are often withdrawn, with or without replacement. In most hospital libraries, there is typically almost no concern for preservation beyond the current edition of a book, as superseded materials are withdraw at once, and damaged books are discarded without replacement unless they are of critical importance.

Most libraries that still receive print journals will collect the new issues over a year, send them to be bound into serials volumes, and then put them on the shelf. Many libraries also send fragile paperbacks to be bound to extend the usable life of the book. Before the large-scale move to digital collections, most academic libraries had several support staff devoted to binding, but this is increasingly uncommon.

Retention of older print materials is increasingly relegated to academic research libraries, as others shift to a reliance on electronic backfile collections. This is especially true of health sciences libraries focused on clinical support, where currency is critical to the value of information. As such, there is far less focus on widespread preservation of physical materials than might have once been the case, with the exception of the rare and unique.

Rare Book Conservation

As discussed elsewhere in this volume, academic and research libraries often have collections of rare books and historical materials, which require special handling and conditions. Libraries without rare books conservators will typically send such materials to special consultants for any needed attention. A conservator is a professional who specializes in "the preservation of cultural property for the future," according to the American Institute for Conservation of Historic and Artistic Works.[37] Conservators use a variety of well-researched techniques to maintain materials in their original state and minimize any further damage. Conservation typically requires a much higher investment of resources than can be afforded to every book, so it is reserved for books judged to be of special enduring value.

Digital Preservation

Digital preservation refers to the activities necessary to maintain access to information created and stored online or in other digital formats. Many people do not realize that most electronic storage media and formats are extremely fragile, in addition to being dependent on rapidly obsolescing technology for access. If information resides on a CD-ROM, DVD, zip disk, floppy disk, VHS cassette, flash drive, server, or any other digital storage material, it must periodically be migrated to newer formats or storage to retain access to it. DVDs, CD-ROMs, and VHS films rot; flash drives become corrupted; servers fail; online files are corrupted; and zip and floppy disk readers are dependent on obsolete technology. All of these occurances affect preservation of material. Even if the file survives storage and transfer, it may be of such an obsolete file type that no software or online framework exists that is capable of reading it. Digital preservation involves continual attempts to meet these challenges and meet them again with each new change in technology and standards.

There is a broad recognition of the difficulties and necessity of the preservation of access to digital information, especially amongst the sciences. Librarians, other information specialists, scientists, government agencies, and others are involved in numerous attempts to standardize avenues for digital preservation.

Digitization of Print Collections

Even as researchers experiment with different means of preserving digital information and data for the long term, many libraries are already using digital preservation software, both commercial and open source, to open access to their collections. In an attempt to broaden access to information, some academic libraries are digitizing their older archival collections of historical journals and documents to make them available online. Technical services librarians are often at the forefront of digitization projects, often working with archivists, special collections librarians, and IT staff.

Digital Data Curation and Data Management

Digital data curation is a special aspect of digital preservation—the management and preservation of data, usually meaning large-scale research data. Science and social science research studies often result in very large datasets that are left confined and abandoned on one laboratory server at the close of a project, at risk of destruction and without ever meeting the potential for wider usage. There is an increasing recognition that the loss of access to this "big data" is a major problem, and numerous options for archiving such data are being explored. Librarians have a definite opportunity to partner with researchers and faculty in building best practices for data management and preservation. While this is commonly the province of an informatics librarian, cataloging and metadata librarians can contribute much valuable expertise.

INTERLIBRARY LOAN/DOCUMENT DELIVERY

No matter how well preserved or well organized, no library collection will ever answer every need for a library's users. Interlibrary loan or document delivery activities also often reside within technical services and serve to provide swift access to resources not owned by the library.

Libraries belong to various resource sharing networks that allow one library to borrow books or articles from another on behalf of users. The interlibrary loan transaction follows these steps: library users request their desired materials; the interlibrary loan librarian or staffer searches for libraries that own the materials; requests them on behalf of the user; and then manages their arrival, loan to the requester, and return to the lender. This system has been in existence in the United States since 1894 in one form or another and is currently widespread and heavily used. The growth of available information resources has vastly outpaced the purchasing ability of most libraries, leading to an increase in the need to rely on interlibrary borrowing even for the largest of academic medical libraries.[38]

The two major interlibrary lending networks used by most libraries in the United States and Canada are OCLC (the Online Computer Library Center) and DOCLINE, which is provided by the National Library of Medicine. Each provides a service to manage lending relationships between libraries and a massive shared catalog consisting of all materials available to borrow for all member libraries, while the member libraries set any prices or limits on borrowing individually. Many libraries also belong to smaller networks that agree to provide loans to each other at lower or standardized fees, preferentially, and so on.

OCLC's resource sharing network is used by nearly all public and academic libraries, and makes its shared catalog available as WorldCat. WorldCat is even included in Google as part of Google Books and Google Scholar, and is thus easily available to any interested party, whether a member of the network or not. Though it is not a specialized medical catalog, academic health sciences libraries are usually very active users of OCLC.

DOCLINE, supported by the National Library of Medicine, is entirely focused on sharing health sciences and medical resources. While OCLC includes both books and journals in its catalog, DOCLINE is primarily focused on the journals indexed in NLM's SERHOLD, a database of holdings from approximately 2,600 medical libraries in the United States, Canada, and Mexico.[39] NLM also provides the service Loansome Doc, which allows individual users to make DOCLINE requests for articles found in PubMed through a special interface rather than going through their home library site.[40] This service can serve in place of a specific interlibrary loan interface for smaller libraries and/or permit larger ones to offer services to otherwise unaffiliated users.

CONCLUSION

This chapter has discussed the rapidly changing domains of technical services, and it is likely that they will have changed further by the time this volume is published. As is clear from the descriptions of a few of the many new trends and changes affecting the resources and activities that form the core of technical services, good practice requires constant learning and growth in skills. As discussed elsewhere in this volume, professional memberships provide vital resources for this necessary awareness of current and innovative practice. The two major professional organizations in the United States and Canada each have special sections and divisions specific to technical services—the Association for Library Collections & Technical Services (ALCTS) division of the American Library Association

(ALA), and the Collection Development Section and Technical Services Section of the Medical Library Association. Conferences and associations are also commonly built around specific areas of interest, and new ones appear and change or fade with changes in practice. Some examples are the Electronic Resources & Libraries Conference, the North American Serials Interest Group (NASIG) annual conference, and the Charleston Conference for acquisitions. The branches of technical services provide the structure and foundation for the information resources that the library makes accessible via public services, and it is to be hoped that this chapter will provide readers with a good understanding of their changing scope, and of the consequent need for continual new knowledge.

NOTES

1. Publishers Communications Group, Inc. "Library Budget Predictions for 2012." Last modified 2012. http://www.pcgplus.com/.

2. Association of Academic Health Sciences Libraries (AHSL). *Annual Statistics of Medical School Libraries in the United States and Canada, 2010–2011*, edited by Gary Byrd. Seattle, WA: Association of Academic Health Science Libraries, 2011.

3. Publishers Communications Group, Inc., *op. cit.*

4. AHSL, *op. cit.*

5. Thomson Reuters. "The Thomson Reuters Impact Factor." Last modified June 20, 1994. http://thomsonreuters.com/products_services/science/free/essays/impact_factor/.

6. Walker, R. L., L. Sykes, B. R. Hemmelgarn, and H. Quan. "Authors' Opinions on Publication in Relation to Annual Performance Assessment." *BMC Medical Education* 10 (2010): 21.

7. Lane, J. "Let's Make Science Metrics More Scientific." *Nature* 464, no. 7288 (2010): 488–489.

8. CLOCKSS. "How CLOCKSS Works." Last modified 2012. http://www.clockss.org/clockss/How_CLOCKSS_Works.

9. ITHAKA. "Portico. About Us." Portico, 2012. http://www.portico.org/digital-preservation/about-us.

10. Hemminger, Bradley M., Dihui Lu, K. T. L. Vaughan, and Stephanie J. Adams. "Information Seeking Behavior of Academic Scientists." *Journal of the American Society for Information Science and Technology: JASIST* 58, no. 14 (2007): 2205.

11. Higher Education Funding Council for England. "Researchers' Use of Libraries and Other Information Sources: Current Patterns and Future Trends." Education for Change Ltd., Social Informatics Research Unit (SIRU): U of Brighton, 2002. Last modified June 20, 2002. http://www.rslg.ac.uk/research/libuse/.

12. De Groote, S. L., and J. L. Dorsch. "Online Journals: Impact on Print Journal Usage." *Bulletin of the Medical Library Association* 89, no. 4 (2001): 372–378.

13. National Center for Biotechnology Information. "PMC Overview." Last modified November 14, 2011. http://www.ncbi.nlm.nih.gov/pmc/about/intro/.

14. Suber, P. "Ensuring Open Access for Publicly Funded Research." *British Medical Journal (Clinical research ed.)* 345:e5184 (2012): 1–2. http://www.bmj.com/content/345/bmj.e5184.

15. Carr, Patrick L., and Maria Collins. "Acquiring Articles through Unmediated, User-Initiated Pay-per-View Transactions: An Assessment of Current Practices." *Serials Review* 35, no. 4 (2009): 272–277.

16. Ibid.

17. Publishers Communications Group, Inc., *op. cit.*

18. Bosch, S., and Henderson, K. S. "Seeking the New Normal: Budget Strains Force Radical Change." *Library Journal* 135, no. 7 (April 15, 2010): 36+.

19. Doody Enterprises, Inc. "About Doody's Book Reviews." Last modified 2008. http://www.doody.com/corp/DoodysBookReviews/AboutDoodysBookReviews/tabid/62/Default.aspx.

20. Dahl, Candice. "Primed for Patron-Driven Acquisition: A Look at the Big Picture." *Journal of Electronic Resources Librarianship* 24, no. 2 (2012): 119–126.

21. Ibid.

22. Online Computer Library Center, Inc. (OCLC). "WorldCat at a Glance." OCLC, 2012. http://www.oclc.org/worldcat/about/default.htm.

23. American Library Association and Library of Congress. "The MARC 21 Formats: Background and Principles." Last modified November 1996. http://www.loc.gov/marc/96principl.html.

24. Furrie, B. "Understanding MARC Bibliographic: Machine-Readable Cataloging." Washington D.C.: Library of Congress, 2009. http://www.loc.gov/marc/umb/.

25. Moore, Julie Renee. "RDA: New Cataloging Rules, Coming Soon to a Library near You!" *Library Hi Tech News* 23, no. 9 (2006): 12–17.

26. Tolkoff, Ilana. "The Path toward Global Interoperability in Cataloging." *Information Technology and Libraries* 29, no. 1 (2010): 30.

27. Library of Congress. "RDA Training Plan for 2012–March 30, 2013." Washington D.C.: Library of Congress, 2012. http://www.loc.gov/aba/rda/pdf/RDA_Long-Range_Training_Plan.pdf.

28. Library of Congress. "Library of Congress Subject Headings." Washington D.C.: Library of Congress, 2011. http://id.loc.gov/authorities/subjects.html.

29. U.S. National Library of Medicine (NLM). "Fact Sheet: Medical Subject Headings (MeSH)." NLM, 2012. http://www.nlm.nih.gov/pubs/factsheets/mesh.html.

30. COUNTER. "About COUNTER." Project COUNTER, 2012. http://www.projectcounter.org/about.html.

31. American Recovery Reinvestment Act of 2009. Pub. L. 111-5. HR1 (February 17, 2009).

32. Ibid.

33. Epstein, B. A., N. H. Tannery, C. B. Wessel, F. Yarger, J. LaDue, and A. B. Fiorillo. "Development of a Clinical Information Tool for the Electronic Medical Record: A Case Study." *Journal of the Medical Library Association: JMLA* 98, no. 3 (2010): 223–227.

34. Welton, Nanette J. "The University of Washington Electronic Medical Record Experience." *Journal of the Medical Library Association: JMLA* 98, no. 3 (2010): 217–219. doi: 10.3163/1536-5050.98.3.008.

35. Giuse, N. B., A. M. Williams, and D. A. Giuse. "Integrating Best Evidence into Patient Care: A Process Facilitated by a Seamless Integration with Informatics Tools." *Journal of the Medical Library Association: JMLA* 98, no. 3 (2010): 220–222.

36. Pilette, Roberta. "Book Conservation within Library Preservation." *Collection Management* 31, no. 1/2 (2007): 213–225.

37. American Institute for Conservation of Historic and Artistic Works. "About AIC: Definitions of Conservation Terminology." Last modified 2012. http://www.conservation-us.org/index.cfm?fuseaction=Page.ViewPage&PageID=620.

38. Byrd, G. D., and J. Shedlock. "The Association of Academic Health Sciences Libraries Annual Statistics: An Exploratory Twenty-Five-Year Trend Analysis." *Journal of the Medical Library Association: JMLA* 91, no. 2 (2003): 186–202.

39. U.S. National Library of Medicine (NLM). "Fact Sheet: SERHOLD." NLM, 2012. http://www.nlm.nih.gov/pubs/factsheets/serhold.html.

40. U.S. National Library of Medicine (NLM). "Fact Sheet: Loansome Doc." NLM, December 2011. http://www.nlm.nih.gov/pubs/factsheets/loansome_doc.html.

Chapter 8

PUBLIC SERVICES IN HEALTH SCIENCES LIBRARIES

Melissa De Santis

WHAT ARE PUBLIC SERVICES?

Broadly defined, public services comprise any of the services or functions that involve direct contact with library users. Because of that broad definition, a large variety of services or functions could be considered to fall under public services. However, the services that fall under the umbrella of public services will vary from library to library. The differences will be based on some combination of historical circumstances, institutional culture, differences in personnel, or differences in funding.

The most common public services are:

- Reference services
- Research services
- Education services
- Liaison programs
- Outreach
- Access services
- Course reserves
- Interlibrary loan (ILL)/document delivery (doc del)
- Media resource center

- Space planning
- Programming

HOW ARE PUBLIC SERVICES DIFFERENT IN HEALTH SCIENCES LIBRARIES?

Before discussing how public services are different in health sciences libraries, it is helpful to be reminded of some of the unique characteristics of the health sciences environment. These topics were discussed in Chapters 1 and 2, so please refer to those chapters for more in-depth information. A brief summary includes:

- Emphasis on speed and timeliness. Most obviously driven by the clinical care side of health sciences, there is urgency on gathering information when people's lives are involved. This also means that not only is information wanted quickly, but that the most recent information is highly preferred.
- Emphasis on research. Health sciences environments are heavily centered on scientific experiments and theories, which means these environments are very research intensive.
- Focus on privacy. Due to the presence of patients as well as experiments with human subjects, greater awareness of topics related to privacy and security exists.

As a result of these unique factors in health sciences environments, health sciences libraries carry a number of special characteristics:

- A much higher level of importance is placed on *journal articles* than other types of information sources. This is because journal articles can be produced and the information shared so much more quickly than information in monographs.
- *Recent information* is in higher demand than historical information. Users of health sciences libraries will be primarily interested in information that has been published within the last five years.
- *Electronic information resources* are in higher demand. Users are always pressed for time, so they want to be able to access information wherever they may be. This means they do not have time to physically visit a library but instead prefer to access library resources from their own computer—which is more often than not a smartphone or tablet device. In 2010–2011, the Association of Academic Health Sciences Libraries' (AAHSL) statistics show that 91.6 percent of health sciences libraries collections were electronic.[1]
- Resources that will *summarize* information to help healthcare providers quickly answer questions and refresh their memory have garnered attention. Likewise, resources and services that *simplify* workflows are also of interest.

HOW PUBLIC SERVICES MIGHT BE DIFFERENT IN HEALTH SCIENCES ENVIRONMENTS

Reference Services

Reference transactions are defined by ALA's Reference and User Services Association (RUSA) as information consultations in which library staff recommend, interpret, evaluate, and/or use information resources to help others meet particular information needs.[2] The goal of reference services is to assist users with their information needs. These services are usually provided "on the fly," meaning that users ask questions as they have them.

Historically, reference work was performed at a reference desk located within a library. Users would walk up to the reference desk, or call the desk on the phone, and ask their questions. However, over the past 15 years, advances in technology have created new means of communication that have been incorporated into reference services. In addition to the in-person and telephone questions that librarians have always answered, they now also answer questions via email, chat and texting.

Partly due to advances in technology, the physical reference desk is being removed in many libraries. As library collections become primarily electronic, most users now access library resources through the library's website. This means that the vast majority of times, users do not need to be physically present in the library building to use library resources. Fewer people are going inside the physical building and asking questions at a reference desk. Instead, more questions are coming from users who are located outside the building. This means that librarians can provide reference service from their offices, so they do not need to be sitting at a desk waiting for users to come inside the building. Additionally, librarians are more likely to be able to leave the library building and have face-to-face interactions with their users if they are not trapped at a reference desk. This has encouraged many libraries to remove desks for specific services such as reference or circulation and instead have one single service desk. This one desk can answer most basic questions and triage higher-level questions. This change also makes library services simpler for users, as they do not have to differentiate between multiple desks.

The trend of replacing standalone reference desks with single service desks can be seen in health sciences libraries. This is partly based on the fact that fewer people are entering library buildings now that the vast majority of resources can be accessed electronically.[3] This is particularly evident in academic health sciences libraries, where healthcare providers and researchers are often located in busy clinics and labs that are in a physically separate building than the building where health sciences library is located. For this reason, chat, email, and phone reference can be more heavily used in health sciences libraries, as these are methods by which users of health sciences libraries already communicate.

Text (SMS; short message service) reference does not appear to be as heavily utilized in health sciences libraries as it is in other types of libraries. One possible reason for the low use of this type of service could be that the questions asked by health sciences library users are too long for a text message. It is also possible that health sciences library users might not be as inclined to communicate via text messaging for their research and clinical work.

Research Services

These services include what are usually considered to be higher-level, specialized assistance. They typically involve research-related questions from users such as faculty or healthcare providers that are conducting research experiments or students doing research for an assignment. Services usually include consultations and mediated searching.

During consultations, a librarian meets with a user to find out more about his or her information needs. Users might need help formulating a search strategy, using a specific database, or learning how to use a tool like EndNote to organize their resources. What is unique about these services is that they are customized to the needs of the user. They are usually set up in advance as an appointment instead of being done on the fly, as reference services usually are. Consultations can take place in the library or at the user's office or lab.

Mediated searching occurs when librarians conduct searches, usually of the journal literature, to find information for users. However, the searches can encompass more than just journal articles, depending on the needs of the user. Mediated searching is particularly helpful when healthcare professionals do not have the time to conduct their own searches. Some health sciences libraries charge a fee to their users to conduct a mediated search, while others will offer this as a free service. Related to mediated searching, librarians also assist users with creating SDI (Selective Dissemination of Information) services or "auto alerts." These are saved searches that are run every time a database is updated. If any new articles are found, the citations are emailed to the user. This helps a researcher stay current on publications in their field of study.

In health sciences information environments, research services are highly regarded. Many times, these services include teaching an individual user how to use an information resource or tool. Library users at academic health sciences campuses often want to do their own research. The ability to have a librarian educate and assist via a consultation at a time and location selected by the user is very helpful.

However, consultations might not be popular in all health sciences library settings. For example, in a hospital setting, services such as mediated literature searches are more likely to be appreciated. Hospital workers are less likely to have time to do their own literature searching. They appreciate being able to rely on librarians to do their literature searching for them and send them current articles.

Education Services

Also known as instructional services, these are services that libraries provide to help teach users how to meet their information needs. Libraries provide a wide variety of instructional services, including in-person classes, online classes, one-on-one consultations, classes integrated into curricula, tipsheets, tutorials, orientations, and tours. Usually libraries will offer a few standard classes that occur on a regular basis that users can just drop in for as well as on-demand and customized learning experiences.

The topic of literacy is part of education and instructional services. Two related terms—"transliteracy"[4] and "metaliteracy"[5]—encompass the idea of being literate across multiple forms of media, specifically Web 2.0 media. This is pertinent to libraries because increasingly, information—specifically research information—is being shared in digital environments such as blogs, wikis, and Twitter. Librarians will instruct users on the various nontraditional sources that faculty and students can use when they are searching for information.

In health sciences libraries, many educational resources will be presented in such a way that users can take advantage of them when it is convenient for them. For example, Yale's Harvey Cushing/John Hay Whitney Medical Library offers a series of tutorials as podcasts or as an iPhone/iPad app.[6] This allows users to get help whenever they need it. Since many library users are accessing the library remotely, a number of health sciences libraries take advantage of a service called LibGuides.[7] LibGuides allows libraries to easily create online tipsheets. Online tipsheets are quickly replacing traditional printed tipsheets because they can be updated quicker, and users can access them without coming to the library.

Academic health sciences libraries in particular are likely to have classes and other means of instruction integrated into the curricula of the various academic programs at their institution. The curricula for professional programs are tightly packed, so it is challenging to find time for library instruction. For that reason, libraries are more likely to be inserted into the curriculum at a specific point when instructors know their students will need assistance. For example, in a pharmacy program, the librarian might participate in a lecture about drug resources and how to use them. The librarian would go to the classroom and participate in one of the regular class sessions. Another example might be a librarian going to a session of a nursing research course and giving an overview of searching CINAHL right before the students start a research assignment. A library orientation for new students, faculty, or staff is not guaranteed, so librarians focus on where in the curriculum it makes the most sense to include library resources.

In hospital libraries, where library staff is very small and library users are extremely busy, education services might be minimal. Hospital librarians might choose to spend less time offering these services and more time offering reference and research services that will be more useful to their users. Additionally, in hospital libraries, it is more common to find librarians coordinating or participating in continuing medical education (CME) programs. Licensure requirements frequently stipulate that doctors acquire a minimum number of hours of CME to keep them current on medical practices. Librarians can assist with CME by assisting with tasks like creating bibliographies, tracking current trends as possible topics for CME sessions, and vetting content for CMS sessions.[8]

Liaison Services

Particularly in academic libraries, as institutions have continued to grow, it has become more difficult for users to know who they should contact when they have a question. In an effort to solve this problem, many libraries have created programs where a specific librarian is paired with a program, school, or department. This gives the library a personal face. Liaisons will often serve as the main point of contact to a program, school, or department. They will advertise events, classes, resources, and services the library is offering. By having one point of contact, the members of the program or school find it easier to interact with the library, and the librarian can focus on the specific information needs of the program, school, or department he or she is liaising to, and therefore provide better and more targeted assistance.

The liaison may not be able to provide all of the services a program or school needs, and many libraries create different tiers of service.[9] However, the goal of a liaison service is to help make connections and facilitate communication. Liaisons are often willing to try to find answers to any questions that their programs, schools, or departments might have, even if they are not questions that fall under the purview of the library. The goal is to form a personal connection so that the user will receive better service and the library will be better informed of user needs.

The services that liaisons provide vary from institution to institution. Sometimes, the liaison will simply forward email news items to the appropriate person at a program, school, or department. Sometimes, the work of a liaison includes helping with collection development or selecting resources for the library to purchase. Since a liaison will usually have constant contact with the users in the program, school, or department they serve, he or she will know the group's areas of interest and can likely make recommendations on items to add to the collection. Likewise, if the library tries a product, the liaison can alert users who have a specific interest in the product.

In the health sciences environment, an example of a liaison service that continues to gain popularity is the embedded librarian. These are librarians that have been situated in the department that they liaise to. This could mean that they spend the majority of their time within the department and not the library building. One form of embedded librarianship is clinical librarianship. These librarians are embedded in the clinical setting. They work as part of the healthcare team and assist with treating patients.

An example of embedded librarians can be found at the Welch Medical Library, which services the Johns Hopkins Medical Institutions. This health sciences library made news in 2011 when it was announced that it would be closing the physical building and focusing on embedded services.[10] For a variety of reasons, the physical library is remaining open, but the embedded librarian program, whose librarians are called informationists, is large and thriving.[11]

Outreach Services

Greater detail about outreach services can be found in Chapter 14. In general, outreach services are those services that are targeted to users outside of the library's primary clientele. The term refers to services that reach outside of one's institution.

Access Services

These are services that relate to providing access—both physical and electronic—to library resources. The services most often associated with access services are circulation, shelving, stacks maintenance, interlibrary loan, document delivery, course reserves, remote storage, and maintenance of the physical building. Staff that work in access services are the frontline staff. They are the staff most likely to be working the single service point as well as the staff working nights and weekends. Student workers often work in the access services department of a library.

Stacks maintenance is the work that is done to keep the physical items in the library organized. It involves processes like shifting, where sections of shelved items are adjusted to compress items or redistribute items on a shelf. It includes keeping the labels on the end caps updated so that they accurately reflect the call number range of each row of shelving. It also involves tasks like shelf reading to make sure that items are arranged in call number order on the shelves.

Remote storage operations often fall under access services duties too, as an extension of the work that staff do for items on the shelves within the library. Remote storage facilities usually house items that are used infrequently so that the prime space within the library building can be used for the popular items that circulate frequently. Remote storage facilities might be located on the institution's central campus or some distance away. They usually include a regular service for retrieving items from the storage facility as users need them.

As recently as 15 years ago, access services was often the busiest department within a library, especially in regards to physical work. At that time, access services staff would have been checking items out, checking items back in, and then reshelving them. However, as libraries have evolved, more and more of a library's collection is available electronically. Electronic resources dramatically decreased circulation rates and reshelving counts.[12] Access services staff are still busy, but their work has dramatically changed. Their tasks are no longer primarily physical but instead are more analytical as they deal primarily with electronic resources.

The services performed in access services exhibit some unique differences in health sciences libraries. Access services staff in health sciences libraries started working with electronic resources sooner because of the quicker transition from print to electronic that has occurred in that subject area. Their workflows were affected sooner than similar staff in general academic and public libraries. The amount of physical circulation tasks that take place at health sciences libraries remains low, and access services staff in health sciences libraries spend much more time assisting users with accessing electronic resources than they spend shelving or checking out physical items.

Defining the users of a health sciences library has become increasingly complicated because the institutions in which health sciences libraries exist have many affiliations with other institutions. There are good reasons for these affiliations, especially in terms of patient care. However, the number of users served usually impacts a library's budget because fees for electronic resources are frequently based on the number of users per resource the library serves. For example, when a university health system and a hospital become affiliated, it is often not clear whom the library is licensing access to resources for. When two institutions merge, the assumption is often that the libraries will serve everyone from both institutions. Economically, this is usually not feasible, and the result is that libraries have to work with administration and vendors to figure out a solution. As consolidation continues in the healthcare industry, these access issues will continue to come up. A standard way of serving users in these types of situations must be developed.

Course Reserves

These are items that instructors make available to students in the courses they teach. This is primarily a service found in academic libraries. The items placed on course reserves can be journal articles, books, book chapters, slide sets, DVDs, or other forms of media. Sometimes, instructors will bring their own personal copies to be placed on course reserves; other times, they will ask for copies to be made and placed on course reserves. Course reserves are usually listed in a separate section of the library's catalog and are organized by course.

The move from print to electronic resources has greatly affected how course reserves are managed. As the items that instructors want to place onto course reserves have become available electronically, there has been a transition to "eReserves" where students access items for their classes online and never interact with library staff to get access. Additionally, as more institutions utilize learning management systems like Blackboard, some instructors will use features within those systems and manage course reserves materials on their own without interacting with the library.

Interlibrary Loan (ILL)/Document Delivery (Doc Del)

These are two similar services frequently found in libraries. Interlibrary loan (ILL) is a service through which libraries will lend items to other libraries for their users. ILL has two sides:

- *Borrowing.* When a library user needs an item that his or her library does not own, the library will ask other libraries to loan the item.
- *Lending.* Loaning items from a library's collection to other libraries.

ILL services have been around for a very long time, and libraries have formed a number of networks to help support the process. Two well-known examples are OCLC[13] and DOCLINE.[14]

Document delivery is a related but slightly different service. It involves making copies of materials a library already owns. At some libraries, this is a service reserved for primary users. This type of service has been popular in health sciences libraries because journal articles are in such high demand, and users sometimes do not have time to come to the library and photocopy articles. As journal collections have moved online, some of this demand for document delivery has diminished. However, these services still exist for two main reasons:

1. Online articles are usually recent, so if an older article is needed, there can be demand for a service to copy or scan the article to save the user a trip to the library.
2. eJournals are not always easy to navigate. Some users prefer to pay to have someone else gather all their articles for them rather than spend time navigating a myriad of eJournal interfaces.

Libraries strive to collect materials that will be useful to their users. However, users will from time to time need items that fall outside of the primary scope of their library's collection. ILL services are not free, so a library would not want to rely on ILL for titles that are in high demand by their users.

Most health sciences libraries that provide ILL services will participate in DOCLINE, the National Library of Medicine's automated interlibrary loan (ILL) request routing and referral system. In addition, most health sciences libraries are likely to also participate in ILL via OCLC. They participate in both systems because while DOCLINE is heavily focused on health sciences materials, OCLC covers the wider range of topics that users might be interested in.

In hospital libraries, which typically have much smaller collections, ILL is a heavily used and highly valued service. In addition, health sciences libraries users expect that material requested via ILL will be received extremely quickly. Obviously, all library users would like their ILL requests to be filled quickly, but the expectation is especially high for health sciences library users because of the fast-paced environment of health sciences institutions.

Media Resource Center

This is a general term used to describe resources that are in a format other than print. This would include items like slides, audiotapes, DVDs, and computer software. Some libraries have separated these collections because using them requires additional equipment or assistance. The shift to electronic resources has affected this area of the library too. Because more of these resources are available online, they no longer require special hardware.

These types of centers are less prevalent in health sciences libraries. For the most part, health sciences libraries are heavily focused on the journal literature and databases, so that is where the majority of the funds for collection resources will be directed. Because users of health sciences libraries are heavily focused on journal literature, they do not express a high need for other media types. Some subject areas lend themselves well to video format, such as anatomy, physical diagnosis, and procedures. But the majority of users are interested in journal articles.

Health sciences libraries are more likely than other types of libraries to be responsible for maintaining a computer lab of some fashion. In hospitals and academic health sciences institutions, there might not be another entity that is willing, or able, to take on management of such a space. Sensing an unfulfilled need, libraries often jump in and help fill the void.

Space Planning

This topic encompasses the ideas that go into planning how to utilize space within the library, primarily public space. Even as library resources convert to an electronic format that no longer requires users to come to the building to access information, demand for library spaces has not disappeared. One of the public service aspects that libraries provide is a physical space for users to study, perform research, collaborate with others, and relax.

Spaces within libraries need planning so that they will be useful and attractive to library users. As time passes, spaces within libraries need to be updated or changed, so space planning is never completed. Some of the items to consider in space planning are location of computers, types of furniture, lighting, and location of electrical outlets. Users often request amenities such as food and drink options. Some areas within a library will need to be set aside for specific uses such as group study rooms, teaching labs, or meeting rooms. This can also create a need to develop policies and procedures for these spaces that serve specific purposes.

Although one could debate how much space libraries need when their collections are primarily electronic, users do regard the library as a physical place. Lindberg and Humphreys expressed this in the *New England Journal of Medicine* when they wrote that as long as the library facility is not decrepit, outmoded, or inconveniently located, it will be used.[15] When the Welch Medical Library at John Hopkins began making plans to close its physical space, there was an outcry from users. Plans to update and otherwise renovate spaces at Welch Medical Library are now in place.[16]

That being said, it is equally true that many libraries have been asked to relinquish stack space for other space needs of the institution. Space is often in short supply, which makes removing library stacks an attractive solution. Stack space in a library can be converted for uses such as small group meeting rooms, classrooms, offices, or labs.

A request to give up a portion of the library's space can be viewed positively or negatively. It is easy to see this as a negative event and a signal that the library is not valued by the institution. However, if the functions that are moving into the library match the library's mission, it could be a good undertaking. Collaborating with tenants in the revised space can be good for the library. Listservs and webinars continue to discuss how libraries are being innovative with renovations and new tenants within their buildings.

Programming

Libraries provide a variety of programming to their users. Examples include symposia, guest lectures, workshops, and exhibits. The main purpose for the majority of programming is to increase user awareness on issues, expose users to different points of view, and open a route for communication. The library is often well suited to perform these services because it is seen as a neutral, unbiased entity with an organization.

Even small libraries with few staff can obtain traveling exhibits that cost very little or nothing and display them for a limited time period. The Public Programming Office (PPO) of the American Library Association[17] provides examples, ideas, and support for programming events such as discussions and exhibits. Health sciences libraries would likely also be interested in the Exhibition Program from the National Library of Medicine (NLM), which features traveling exhibits related to the NLM's resources.[18]

Health sciences libraries do less programming than other types of libraries, especially public libraries. In smaller health sciences libraries, such as hospital libraries, the staff is small, and programming might not always get as much attention. However, health sciences libraries could do more, and doing more could assist them with forming relationships within their institution.

CURRENT TRENDS AND ISSUES

Building Relationships with Virtual Users

As health sciences libraries continue to provide primarily e-only resources, there is no longer a guarantee that users will come to the library's physical building. This means that libraries need to find new ways to reach their users. At the same time, library users are being overwhelmed with email and other electronic advertising. This makes it difficult for libraries to get the attention of their users. Many libraries are trying to figure out the best way to connect with their users in this electronic world.

New Medical Schools

According to the Liaison Committee on Medical Education (LCME), there are currently 10 medical schools with preliminary accreditation and five medical schools with provisional accreditation.[19] This is a large number of new medical schools that will be, or have already, started accepting students. Some of these new schools are connected to a campus with a previously accredited program and will likely utilize services from already-established libraries. However, some of the medical schools are completely new. These schools will likely be starting new libraries. These new libraries are likely to be physically smaller and contain very few or no print collections. It is highly possible that these libraries may create new models to fulfill user demands and service standards.

Support for Researchers

Health sciences libraries continue to work on serving the information needs of the researchers in their institutions. Researchers are often a challenging group for libraries to access. However, when the NIH introduced the Clinical & Translational Science Awards (CTSAs) in 2006, interest in bioinformatics increased, as did the opportunity for librarians to get involved. Libraries could offer services that help with the work of CTSAs. Libraries helped organize profiles of researchers on campuses and assisted with bioinformatics education. Health sciences libraries had always offered these services, but the CTSAs helped get them more involved. Initial CTSA awardees have started the renewal process, and the CTSA awards have changed over the past six years. Libraries are working to determine how they will fit into the CTSA renewals on their campuses.

A related area of interest is assisting researchers with data management. Many grants require the researcher to have a data management plan that would include letting others gain access to the data used in research. Some believe that there is going to be a move away from journals as the major output of research to all types of data being considered outputs.[20] Libraries can help manage these large data sets, preserve them, and provide access. The curation that librarians can do includes creating metadata and digital object identifiers (DOIs) to make the data citable by others. This is a growing area of interest to libraries, and it is similar to the work that librarians have always done to organize, preserve, and provide access to information.

Another trend in health sciences libraries is hiring professionals with science or research backgrounds instead of traditionally trained librarians. The idea is that by hiring someone that has research experience, the library will have staff who can talk with the researchers and provide services to them. It remains to be seen how this will work out. Some libraries, like Becker Medical Library at Washington University and the NIH Library, have very successful bioinformatics support program.[21, 22] However, creating these types of services is challenging. When a library hires researchers, there can be tension between the researchers and the librarians, especially if a researcher is not familiar with librarianship. Additionally, few people with the skill set for this type of position exist, which makes these positions challenging to fill.

Embedded Librarianship

Although embedded librarianship is not a new concept, it is a topic that is getting a lot of attention. As public services are focused on the user, it makes sense that librarians should be located where their users are. The concept of an embedded librarian is identified by a variety of names, but they all focus on the idea of getting librarians out of the physical library building and into environments where their users are located.

The Medical Library Association (MLA) has gathered and organized information on this topic. It has chosen to use the term "informationist," but the concept remains the same.[23] The MLA was partially influenced by an editorial in the *Annals of Internal Medicine* that called for the creation of a new professional—the informationist—that would be part of the clinical team.[24] As part of the clinical team, the informationist would help fill the information needs of the clinical team. He or she would do this by searching the medical literature, reading relevant articles, and extracting information for the clinical team. One of the ideas Davidoff and Florance proposed that was different from traditional librarian duties is that informationists would synthesize the information they located. Informationists would have specialized clinical training so that they could understand both information science and clinical work.

Although the terminology may vary, there are libraries that are trying to develop and expand their embedded librarian programs. The Eskind Biomedical Library at Vanderbilt University Medical Center has developed the Clinical Informatics Consult Service, which functions very much like the informationist described by Davidoff and Florance.[25] Additionally, the information synthesized by the clinical informationists at Vanderbilt is linked to the electronic medical record (EMR) and inpatient care practices.[26]

Space Planning

As libraries continue to field questions about the physical space in their buildings, space planning remains a hot topic. There has always been interest in libraries to remodel spaces and provide services that users are requesting. Sometimes, these services might seem outside the mission of the library; for example, the University of Alabama (UAB) at Birmingham's Lister Hill Library has made a Keurig coffee-maker available to library users.[27] Users have to bring their own coffee, but everyone can use the coffeemaker. It could be argued that providing a coffeemaker is outside the scope of the library. However, from a public services point of view, if this is a service that users are requesting and if it can be fulfilled fairly easily, then it is something that should be done.

Sometimes, the services that users request might seem outdated, such as requests for whiteboards in this highly digital world. And yet the Briscoe Library at the University of Texas Health Sciences Center San Antonio mentioned in their Renovations blog on September 14, 2012, that their remodeling will include painting select walls with whiteboard paint to increase the whiteboard space available in the building.

Another trend in space planning is collaborating with related departments that will be beneficial to the library. Working with an entity that has similar interests usually ensures success for both groups. At the Health Sciences Library on the University of Colorado Anschutz Medical Campus, a group study room was converted to space for a branch of the Writing Center.[28] The Writing Center provides services to students, and because students are the heaviest users of the library building, this was a good fit. Additionally, the mission of the Writing Center falls in line with the mission of the library.

Another example of space collaboration is the Edge of Chaos space in the Lister Hill Library at UAB, the result of a collaboration between the library and the School of Public Health.[29] The space is meant allow people from campus to gather and discuss ideas. It includes conference rooms, media rooms, sofas, desks, glassed-in offices, and chalkboard walls. The Edge of Chaos space is not what one traditionally thinks of in a library space. However, the idea of collaboration fits well with the library, and sharing space within a library for a service like the Edge of Chaos is a good way to utilize space that had previously been used for print collections.

Scholarly Publishing

Helping users navigate scholarly publishing is a popular topic in libraries, especially health sciences libraries. Part of that popularity is based on the increased interest in open access publications as a way to counteract the high cost of scholarly publications. Educating users about open access publications increases the chances that users will publish in these formats. On a broader level, librarians have been educating users about their rights and options as copyright holders for articles they produce. The hope is that if an author chooses to publish in a traditional journal, he or she can still negotiate to retain author rights.

Assisting authors with adhering to the NIH Public Access policy is another area of scholarly publishing where health sciences libraries are providing assistance. This was chiefly the case in 2008 when the Public Access policy was new. In the past few years, the emphasis of NIH has shifted to compliance. Starting in the spring of 2013, the NIH will delay processing of noncompeting continuation grant awards if publications arising from a particular award are not in compliance with the NIH public access policy.[30] Health sciences libraries are now educating and assisting authors with the steps they need to take to demonstrate compliance.

CONCLUSION

Public services are those services in a library that involve direct contact with library users. The contact with users can happen in person or through any number of virtual communication methods. A variety of services are included in public services, and the exact services will vary between libraries. Due to some of the unique character-istics of health sciences library users, public services in health sciences libraries can vary from similar services at other types of libraries. Most of these differences stem from the emphasis on digital resources and timeliness in health sciences environ-ments. Public services trends and current issues in health sciences libraries are also influenced by these two factors as well as changes in the healthcare industry.

Challenges that librarians have in providing high-quality public services to users are often related to timeliness and funding. Users of health sciences libraries are very busy, whether they are students, clinicians, or researchers. They are often geographi-cally distant from the library and access resources electronically. This makes it chal-lenging for librarians to reach their users. In regards to funding, many resources that health sciences libraries would like to access are expensive. It is not always financially possible to access all the high-quality resources a librarian would like. And particu-larly in hospital libraries, librarian positions are being eliminated when budget cuts occur. There can be a perception that as long as institutions subscribe to databases and journals, a librarian is not needed. However, the public services that a knowl-edgeable health sciences librarian can provide are far more than just access to infor-mation resources.

NOTES

1. Association of Academic Health Sciences Libraries (AAHSL) (ed.). *Annual Statistics of Medical School Libraries in the United States and Canada, 2010–2011*, 34th ed. Houston: Houston Academy of Medicine–Texas Medical Center Library, 2012.

2. ALA's Reference & User Services Association (RUSA). "Definitions of Reference, Reference & User Services Association (RUSA)." Accessed April 9, 2013. http://www.ala.org/rusa/resources/guidelines/definitionsreference.

3. AAHSL, *op. cit.*

4. Ipri, T. "Introducing Transliteracy: What Does It Mean to Academic Libraries?" *College and Research Libraries News* 71, no. 10 (2010): 532–533.

5. Mackey, T. P., and T. E. Jacobson. "Reframing Information Literacy as a Metaliteracy." *College and Research Libraries* 72, no. 1 (2011): 62–78.

6. Yale University. 2013. "Guides and Tutorials, Medical Library." Accessed April 4, 2013. http://library.medicine.yale.edu/tutorials/.

7. Springshare. "LibGuides by Springshare: Knowledge and Content Sharing," 2012. Accessed April 4, 2013. http://springshare.com/libguides/.

8. Leman, Hope, Donna Bales, Daniel Sokolow, Alison Aldrich, and Marlene Englander. "Associated Services." In *The Medical Library Association Guide to Managing*

Health Care Libraries, edited by Margaret Bandy, Rosalind F. Dudden, and Association Medical Library. New York: Neal-Schuman, 2011.

9. Ferree, N., N. Schaefer, L. C. Butson, and M. R. Tennant. "Liaison Librarian Tiers: Levels of Service." *Journal of the Medical Library Association: JMLA* 97, no. 2 (2009): 145–148.

10. Roderer, Nancy, Alonzo Lamont, Blair Anton, and Oliver Obst. "The Closing of the Welch Library Building: Interview with the Director, Nancy Roderer." *Journal of the European Association for Health Information and Libraries* 7, no. 4 (2011): 7–10.

11. William H. Welch Medical Library, Johns Hopkins University School of Medicine. "Informationist Program." Accessed April 9, 2013. http://www.welch.jhmi.edu/welchone/node/19.

12. AAHSL, *op. cit.*

13. Online Computer Library Center, Inc. (OCLC). "Worldshare Interlibrary Loan Migration." Accessed April 9, 2013. https://www.oclc.org/migrate-worldshare-ill.en.html.

14. National Library of Medicine (NLM), National Institutes of Health (NIH). "Docline® System." Accessed April 9, 2013. http://www.nlm.nih.gov/docline/.

15. Lindberg, Donald A. B., and Betsy L. Humphreys. "2015: The Future of Medical Libraries." *New England Journal of Medicine* 352, no. 11 (2005): 1067–1070.

16. William H. Welch Medical Library, John Hopkins University School of Medicine. "Deans Letter for 21st-Century Welch Library (August 17, 2012)." Accessed December 26, 2012. http://162.129.243.233/newlibrary/pdf/DeansLetterFor21Welch.pdf.

17. American Library Association (ALA). "Public Programs Office (PPO), American Library Association." Accessed April 9, 2013. http://www.ala.org/offices/ppo.

18. National Library of Medicine (NLM), National Institutes of Health (NIH). "Exhibition Program Homepage." Accessed April 9, 2013. http://www.nlm.nih.gov/hmd/about/exhibition/index.html.

19. Liaison Committee on Medical Education (LCME). "Directory of LCME-Accredited M.D. Programs in the U.S. and Canada, Showing Dates of Last and Next Full Surveys." Last modified 2013, http://www.lcme.org/directory.htm.

20. Monastersky, R. "Publishing Frontiers: The Library Reboot." *Nature* 495, no. 7442 (2013): 430–432.

21. Becker Medical Library, Washington University School of Medicine. "Bioinformatics@Becker." Accessed April 9, 2013. https://becker.wustl.edu/services/bioinformatics.

22. NIH Library. "Bioinformatics Support Program." Accessed April 9, 2013. http://nihlibrary.nih.gov/Services/Bioinformatics/Pages/default.aspx.

23. Medical Library Association (MLA). "Research: Informationist/Information Specialist in Context Concept." Accessed April 9, 2013. http://www.mlanet.org/research/informationist/.

24. Davidoff, F., and V. Florance. "The Informationist: A New Health Profession?" *Annals of Internal Medicine* 132, no. 12 (2000): 996–998.

25. Vanderbilt University. "Knowledge Management: Clinical Informatics Consult Service," 2013. Accessed April 5, 2013. http://www.mc.vanderbilt.edu/km/ebm/cics.html.

26. Giuse, N. B., T. Y. Koonce, R. N. Jerome, M. Cahall, N. A. Sathe, and A. Williams. "Evolution of a Mature Clinical Informationist Model." *Journal of the American Medical Informatics Association: JAMIA* 12, no. 3 (2005): 249–255.

27. Lister Hill Library, University of Alabama at Birmingham. "Keurig Coffeemaker for Patron Use Now Available," 2012. Last updated January 18, 2012. http://www.uab.edu/lister/news/images/EEP_How2ReReg2008.pdf?newsID=1&ID=1186.

28. Writing Center at the Anschutz Medical Campus, University of Colorado Denver. "The Writing Center at the Anschutz Medical Campus," 2012. Accessed January 9, 2013. http://www.ucdenver.edu/academics/colleges/CLAS/Centers/writing/InfoforStudents/Pages/AMCinfo.aspx.

29. School of Public Health, University of Alabama Birmingham. "Lister Hill Library: Edge of Chaos." Accessed April 9, 2013. http://www.soph.uab.edu/news/edgeofchaos.

30. National Institutes of Health (NIH). "Public Access Homepage." Accessed April 9, 2013. http://publicaccess.nih.gov/.

Chapter 9

INFORMATION RETRIEVAL

James E. Andrews and *Denise Shereff*

INTRODUCTION

Information retrieval (IR) is a multifaceted field that, in one form or another, constitutes the majority of work for most information professionals. Contributions to the evolution of IR primarily have come from information science and computer science but more recently have come from a number of other disciplines, including cognitive science, interdisciplinary fields focused on human factors and interaction design, and behavioral and social science. Librarians have a central focus on identifying, accessing, and evaluating information in myriad forms to meet our users' needs as we understand them. Many of the chapters in this book examine the processes related to these and contributing functions. Our focus in this chapter is the underlying concepts and processes of modern IR, which usually involve digital information stored and accessed through computing hardware and software collectively identified as information storage and retrieval systems (ISARs). IR models and algorithms have grown increasingly complex to take advantage of enhanced computing and networking capabilities as well as evolving user information behaviors. In the context of health sciences librarianship, we are overwhelmingly considering knowledge-based IR and the systems, models, and concepts related to effective access to these in support of a variety of users in the biomedical community.

An appreciation of the core components of IR is important to becoming an effective health sciences librarian or any other information professional. As those charged with supporting a host of users within the biomedical community, it is incumbent on the professional health sciences librarian to understand these core constructs of

IR, including the structure of the various databases and information sources, methods of representation, metadata and related standards, and the behaviors of user communities. Although this chapter is not intended to provide a highly detailed, exhaustive, and technical treatment of IR, it does provide a practical introduction that can be used as a foundation for further investigations.

BASIC CONCEPTS AND MODELS

Definitions

In its simplest sense, IR refers to finding, retrieving, and presenting information relevant to a user's expressed need.[1] The universal goal, perhaps stated too simply, is to get the right information, to the right person, in the right form, at the right time. This has been a cornerstone of librarianship for some time, even during the print-only era, and the centrality of this goal has not decreased despite an information environment that has changed dramatically.

A more accurate focus is seen in information science or related information professions; that is, we are largely dealing with textual information representing some area of knowledge. Hersh provides another basic definition for IR that reflects this: "the retrieval of information from databases that predominantly contain textual information."[2] Moreover, IR involves the representation and storage of such information, its presentation, and a variety of approaches for determining relevant results vis-à-vis a user's expressed need and for other forms of manipulation of searches, results, and the information objects or their representations.

The preceding definitions, and similar ones, are necessarily broad, yet they beg the question of "how." While it is outside the purview of this chapter and book to get deep into the algorithms and specific technologies driving IR and ISARs, we can explore some of the basic concepts and models as a means of introduction and for a richer understanding of how today's most used systems work. There are many books and publications on IR that one should refer to for much deeper explorations such as *Modern Information Retrieval*, by Baeza-Yates and Neto (2011). For coverage of IR in the context of biomedicine and healthcare, though somewhat less technical, Hersh's text is also widely regarded as an excellent resource.

Basic Models

Information retrieval involves several core elements that serve as the basis for any IR model or system. Each area has developed a large body of research that has furthered the design, implementation, and evaluation of IR systems. As a starting point, we present in Figure 9.1 a simple model of IR, partially derived from Salton, with refinements that better reflect the discussions in this chapter.[3]

Like many illustrations, the relative simplicity belies many underlying complexities. Briefly represented in the figure's outer ring are the creators, consumers, and organizers involved in the broader information infrastructure or cycle, which include publishers, grant-funding organizations, researchers reporting their results or knowledge, librarians, database vendors, patients, and practitioners. These groups

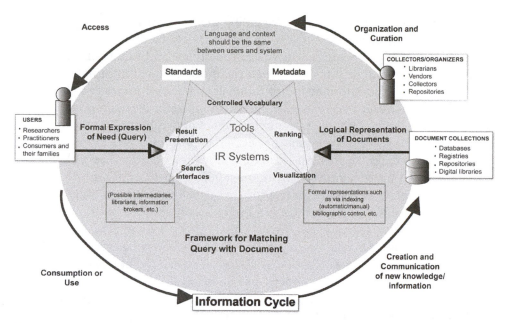

Figure 9.1 Simple IR Model

drive the information lifecycle. While alluded to briefly these groups are primarily outside the scope of our discussion or are discussed in other chapters of this book. Shown on the right in Figure 9.1 are document collections, broadly conceived, which include whatever information objects might be stored in a system, such as textual documents or images. On the left side of Figure 9.1 are the users who have needs that presumably can be met by the information recorded in the documents. The center part of the model in this figure represents the IR system, particularly the manifestation of efforts to match requests from the users (articulated in whatever manner is afforded by the system) with the surrogates of the document collection. A critical part of the success for this part of the model comes from the effective use of metadata standards as well as controlled vocabularies or other tools for ensuring semantic consistency.

Under each element are multiple issues to consider that have been the focus of research leading to new knowledge and improved system design. Here, we briefly cover these key concepts at a basic level to set the context for later discussions.

Information Objects and their Representation

Looking at the basic model presented earlier in this chapter, the "Documents" part refers to information resources and their various attributes. These include the range of objects collected and organized for access and use by users, including journal articles, monographs, indexes, factual databases of various sorts, and ready reference materials. Traditionally, librarians have played a major role in the selection, acquisition, and organization of these information objects. A defining feature of the information revolution has been an explosion of sources. Unfortunately, with this increase, significant questions surrounding the authority and quality of many of these resources must be asked. From websites, to specific datasets, to technology tools that are used by biological researchers, the scope and variety of information sources can confound or overwhelm even the most seasoned information professional or user. Skilled information professionals utilize best practices to help users of every ilk search and retrieve needed information, select the appropriate sources, and determine their authority or credibility. Still, a noticeable trend in many health sciences libraries is the near or total absence of all print materials from the library. As a result, a shift is occurring in the interactions the librarian has with the user community and his or her involvement in shaping a given set of resources. While content distributors have made great strides in search interfaces and other improvements to searchability and use, there has been a steady increase in the cost of electronic subscriptions, which is sometimes a result of the ways sources are "bundled" by publishers. This is in contrast to the days when the library had control over what to select for inclusion in its collection as well as a certain level of bibliographic control. Now, a valuable resource to users may be made accessible to all but could be controlled by the creators of the source without bibliographic standards being applied. As discussed in Chapter 7 ("Technical Services") and Chapter 8 ("Public Services"), managing collections and access in the current environment can be a dynamic function that requires understanding the implications of today's information world.

The host of materials in digital form and the ease in which many people are accustomed to searching the Internet (e.g., via a Google search box or similarly using other search engines) also can mislead the uninformed into assuming they are (1) searching all available information in one fell swoop and (2) searching each document's entire content. For the first point, fee-based information resources might allow some searching via open web access, but access to the actual information object requires purchase (through either a contract with the publisher via the library or purchasing items individually). This "deeper" web generally is not available to the general public without such access, but it can hold more valuable information (e.g., from the most prestigious journals). Regarding the second point, that information objects themselves are thought to be queried with each search, this is not exactly the case. In reality, every information object is represented by a surrogate, or some searchable collection of their attributes, or their metadata. The importance of such indexing requires some additional discussion.

Indexing and Subject Access

Indexing refers to the processes of creating records that describe information objects in a manner that can enhance retrieval. Indexing can also refer to less formalized and equally important forms of describing documents based on their content, where they are located, and factors such as what other sources link to them or how many times they are visited by users. This occurs more in the domain of web search engines like Google, Bing, and Yahoo. For web pages and similar forms of information, "web bots" use complex algorithms that collect various kinds of information to enhance the search experience and success of users. This is relevant to all kinds of IR, including health sciences–related retrieval, because lay individuals, healthcare professionals, and information professionals alike must utilize search engines for different kinds of searches. While search engine algorithms are trade secrets protected to give each company an edge in a highly competitive area, they do provide guidance for advanced users to enhance searching. Help features on the most popular search engines range from assisting users in focusing their searches within domains, to providing enhanced searching of various kinds of media, to creating dynamic tables of integrated datasets. A more technical review of web retrieval is covered in Baeza-Yates's *Modern Information Retrieval*. A more popular coverage geared toward librarians and information professionals is *Semantic Web Technologies and Social Searching for Librarians*.[4]

In the deeper, less public web are more traditional approaches to indexing that should be understood by librarians. Here, we are generally discussing knowledge-based bibliographic resources from content providers, such as publishers of journals, or aggregators of other scholarly information objects. Some of these are covered later in this chapter and in the appendix.

Journal articles remain a key resource for many in the biomedical community as the primary way to communicate study results, new theories and models, and other forms of knowledge across the biomedical community. Millions of articles are published and indexed annually across the globe. To maintain bibliographic control and enhance searching, formal records are created based on a set of standards. For instance, a journal article available via PubMed is indexed according to NLM's indexing rules (partially available to the public at http://www.nlm.nih.gov/bsd/indexing/index.html).

Figure 9.2 is an example MEDLINE record.

By and large, the goal of indexing is to create bibliographic records that describe the item as completely as possible to distinguish records from one another and also to enhance searching. Bibliographic records contain, at one level, information such as author(s), title, journal information (name, issue, number, page, etc.), and other descriptive information. The other critical aspect of indexing involves representing the subjects covered by the article. For this, indexers are compelled to seek both sensitivity (or breadth) and specificity (depth) in their selection of terms. While terms themselves may be gathered from the article's abstract, title, and so on, the content of the article is best described using a "controlled terminology."

Controlled terminologies, also known as controlled vocabularies or thesauri, are collections of terms that represent the concepts within a domain and that show the relationships of these terms to one another. The purpose is to disambiguate or standardize language and give guidance to both indexers assigning terms to a given article and users seeking to achieve more reliable retrieval results.

The most salient example for health sciences librarians is the Medical Subject Headings (MeSH) created by the National Library of Medicine (NLM). Actually, MeSH is an exemplar for domain-specific controlled terminologies given its scope,

```
PMID- 23611924
OWN - NLM
STAT- PubMed-not-MEDLINE
DA  - 20130424
DCOM- 20130425
LR  - 20130429
IS  - 1929-073X (Electronic)
IS  - 1929-073X (Linking)
VI  - 1
IP  - 2
DP  - 2012
TI  - Standardization of Questions in Rare Disease Registries: The PRISM Library
      Project.
PG  - e10
LID - 10.2196/ijmr.2107 [doi]
AB  - BACKGROUND: Patient registries are often a helpful first step in estimating the
      impact and understanding the etiology of rare diseases - both requisites for the
      development of new diagnostics and therapeutics. The value and utility of patient
      registries rely on the use of both well-constructed structured research questions
      and relevant answer sets accompanying them. There are currently no clear
      standards or specifications for developing registry questions, and there are no
      banks of existing questions to support registry developers. OBJECTIVE: This paper
      introduces the [Rare Disease] PRISM (Patient Registry Item Specifications and
      Metadata for Rare Disease) project, a library of standardized questions covering
      a broad spectrum of rare diseases that can be used to support the development of
      new registries, including Internet-based registries. METHODS: A convenience
      sample of questions was identified from well-established (>5 years) natural
      history studies in various diseases and from several existing registries. Face
      validity of the questions was determined by review by many experts (both
      terminology experts at the College of American Pathologists (CAP) and research
      and informatics experts at the University of South Florida (USF)) for
      commonality, clarity, and organization. Questions were re-worded slightly, as
      needed, to make the full semantics of the question clear and to make the
      questions generalizable to multiple diseases where possible. Questions were
      indexed with metadata (structured and descriptive information) using a standard
      metadata framework to record such information as context, format, question asker
      and responder, and data standards information. RESULTS: At present, PRISM
      contains over 2,200 questions, with content of PRISM relevant to virtually all
      rare diseases. While the inclusion of disease-specific questions for thousands of
      rare disease organizations seeking to develop registries would present a
      challenge for traditional standards development organizations, the PRISM library
      could serve as a platform to liaison between rare disease communities and
      existing standardized controlled terminologies, item banks, and coding systems.
      CONCLUSIONS: If widely used, PRISM will enable the re-use of questions across
      registries, reduce variation in registry data collection, and facilitate a
      bottom-up standardization of patient registries. Although it was initially
      developed to fulfill an urgent need in the rare disease community for shared
      resources, the PRISM library of patient-directed registry questions can be a
      valuable resource for registries in any disease - whether common or rare. TRIAL
      REGISTRATION: N/A.
FAU - Richesson, Rachel Lynn
AD  - Richesson RL
AD  - Duke University School of Nursing, Durham, NC, United States.
      rachel.richesson@dm.duke.edu.
FAU - Shereff, Denise
AU  - Shereff D
FAU - Andrews, James Everett
AU  - Andrews JE
LA  - eng
PT  - Journal Article
DEP - 20121010
PL  - Canada
TA  - Interact J Med Res
JT  - Interactive journal of medical research
JID - 101598421
PMC - PMC3626121
OID - NLM: PMC3626121
OTO - NOTNLM
OT  - Patient registries
OT  - data standards
OT  - metadata
OT  - rare diseases
EDAT- 2012/01/01 00:00
MHDA- 2012/01/01 00:01
CRDT- 2013/04/25 06:00
PHST- 2012/03/15 [received]
PHST- 2012/08/30 [accepted]
PHST- 2012/07/02 [revised]
AID - v1i2e10 [pii]
AID - 10.2196/ijmr.2107 [doi]
PST - epublish
SO  - Interact J Med Res. 2012 Oct 10;1(2):e10. doi: 10.2196/ijmr.2107.
```

Figure 9.2 Example of a MEDLINE Record

semantic (syndetic) structure, and use. It is the standard for subject indexing of all
the articles in MEDLINE (and many other NLM-controlled databases) and was
used in MEDLINE's print predecessor, *Index Medicus*. Although one finds legitimate issues with its interindexer consistency (whether MeSH is or can be used consistently across indexers) and with its use in automated indexing (roughly half of
MEDLINE articles are indexed automatically), it remains a critical tool for professional searchers of the biomedical literature. For in-depth details on the structure
and use of MeSH, see the NLM web page on it (http://www.nlm.nih.gov/mesh/
mbinfo.html). Figure 9.3, however, gives an example of the "classification" aspects,
hierarchical structure, and other important features.

USERS AND THEIR INFORMATION NEEDS

Going back to the model shown in Figure 9.1, on the left side, we see that the
users, or those that are seeking information from some collection of resources relevant to their needs, are represented. A health sciences librarian will encounter a

Figure 9.3 Excerpt from C08 Tree, *Respiratory Tract Diseases*

wide range of potential users. In an academic setting, these can be people engaged in any of several health-related educational programs (e.g., medicine, nursing, allied health, pharmacy, and health services administration); people conducting biomedical research, or faculty teaching in programs and—often—practicing in a clinic or hospital. In addition, the academic medical library will provide services outside the institution where it is housed, perhaps to regional hospitals, Area Health Education Centers (AHECs), or other organizations. In a hospital setting, the medical librarian may serve administrators, healthcare providers, and patients and their families.

Matching Information with User Needs

Given the information objects, how they are represented and their overall accessibility, and the users we are trying to serve, we see the overarching

challenge in IR of matching the correct information resource with those who
need it to satisfy a need. In a perfect world, a user could state that she needs
specific information about topic X, enter terms related to this in a system, and
the system would return exactly the correct amount, type, and formatted information about X. Sadly, issues of semantics, limitations of system design, and
even lack of clarity of what one actually needs (let alone how to express it in a
format acceptable to a particular system) are among the confounding variables
that can impede successful searching. The center part of our basic IR model represents this matching of query and document representations, and is where so
much of the efforts from previous decades in IR design and research have been
placed. To illustrate how these efforts have affected the evolution of IR models,
we provide the following walk-through of IR history.

IR MODELS

A basic way to look at how an ISAR might work could be as follows. A document
collection is converted into some searchable file, or index, in a computer system.
The most basic would simply be a listing of all the terms contained in the documents, with pointers to where each term occurs, in an index not unlike a back of
the book index. A user could enter a search term—"dog," for example—the system
would match that with any instance of "dog" in the index, and it would retrieve the
information objects that contain that term. How the results are presented to the user
would vary by system. Clearly, this is an inefficient and inaccurate way to search
compared to what is available today. First, in this example, the index itself is merely
a listing of terms without any indication as to their importance to any given document (that is, how well the system describes the *aboutness* of a document in comparison to others); it would include a host of terms that are not descriptive at all, such as
"a," "the," and "it"; and this basic kind of system may not allow for term variations
including plurals, different tenses, and so on. Moreover, early systems like this
lacked the kind of computing memory and processing power to efficiently search
through long indexes.

Early on, such issues were identified and addressed given the available technology
and the types of records usually being searched, such as index records for journal
articles or bibliographic catalog records that eventually evolved into the MARC
record standard. Commonly occurring but nondescriptive words, referred to as "stop
words," were removed so that only terms that presumably had meaning would comprise the index. Moreover, stemming algorithms were developed to normalize terms
so that spelling and tense variations could be handled. To ensure more accurate
matching, the same algorithm was applied to terms entered by users. The indexes
created were actually document/term matrices. One can imagine this as having rows
representing each unique document in a collection (Dn) and columns consisting of
every term in the collection (Tn). The cells of the matrix indicate whether each term
is present in each document. Thus, documents are represented by the terms that are
present in them, or D1 = {T1, T2, . . .Tn}.

While still limited, these advances allowed for Boolean searching of a collection. This provided users the ability to search for more than a single term, with Boolean operators (AND, OR, NOT) to further qualify the searches. For example, a search for "cats AND dogs" would search the document/term matrix, and even a computer with relatively low processing power could easily extract all documents in which both terms were present. Using the OR operator, then, allowed users to expand searches (e.g., all documents with EITHER cats OR dogs as terms present in them). Finally, "cats NOT dogs" could be used, keeping with our simplified example, to retrieve documents only with cats in them, but NOT dogs. Depending on the system, some more advanced queries were possible so long as the order of precedence was understood by the user. For instance, simply entering "A OR B AND C" could be interpreted differently by different systems, unless it was understood which operator and pair would be processed first.

In addition to Boolean searching, there were refinements to querying that helped users retrieve a more relevant result set. For instance, truncation was a common function that would allow users to enter part of a term and then a symbol to signify to the system to retrieve any variation of that term. So, "infect*" might be entered to return documents with terms including "infection," "infectious," "infected," and so on. Also, systems such as the older command-based Dialog™ had powerful tools for fine-tuning searches. These included the ability to search within specific fields (e.g., author, title, year) and to apply restrictions (e.g., children only, journal articles, years). Additional refinement features include proximity searching, which lets the user specify the relative position of the search terms. The assumption is that terms occurring closer to one another, such as "benign nerve root tumor," are more related than if they are scattered and possibly referring to other topics within a given paper. That is, if these terms occur individually and relatively far apart in a body of text, they will likely have a different meaning than if they are simply multiple parts of a single concept. The example is illustrated in the abstract of the article by Adamson and colleagues that is shown in Figure 9.4.[5]

Proximity operators, truncation, and other functions still exist in the bibliographic database systems of today; however, many non–information professionals do not understand the implications of their use.

Another facet of information retrieval that merits discussion in this chapter is full-text searching. The full-text search is a technique for searching a single resource (e.g., a document or collection of documents) in a *full-text database*. The full-text search is different from searches based on the *metadata* or the portion of the original item (such as its title, abstract, or citation) that is represented in a database. In a metadata search, the IR system examines only the metadata or the other information describing the item in the database, whereas in a full-text search, the system examines each word in the complete document in the database and attempts to match the search terms supplied by the searcher. While inefficient in today's vast network of resources (that, as stated, are processed to enable efficient searching that is still rather close to full-text level searching, at least in

Abstract

We report the development of a malignant peripheral *nerve* sheath *tumor* (MPNST) in 2 patients after irradiation for Hodgkin's lymphoma. Clinicians should be aware of this uncommon, but important fatal complication of radiation therapy. The first case is a 37-year-old man who was diagnosed with nodular sclerosing (NS) Hodgkin's lymphoma and underwent successful mantle radiation. He presented to our neurosurgery service with a left C6 radiculopathy 6 years later. The second case is a 30-year-old female diagnosed with NS Hodgkin's lymphoma. She did well with extensive radiotherapy until 5 years later when she developed severe right arm and chest pain secondary to recurrent lymphoma. After aggressive radio- and chemotherapy, she presented to the neurosurgery service with a right Horner's syndrome, right C6 radiculopathy, and weakness of her right triceps and wrist extensors. Both patients obtained magnetic resonance imaging revealing intradural extramedullary cervical nerve *root* associated mass lesions. Two years after radiation therapy for his Hodgkin's lymphoma, the first patient underwent a C6 laminectomy at an outside institution for resection of a *benign* neurofibroma. Four years later, he underwent a posterior C5-7 laminectomy with lateral mass plate fusion and partial excision of a recurrent mass diagnosed as a MPNST. The second patient underwent a C5-6 hemilaminectomy and partial resection of a *tumor* also pathologically consistent with MPNST. We present 2 case reports of patients who developed neurofibrosarcomatous tumors with malignant transformation after undergoing radiation therapy for Hodgkin's lymphoma. Despite prompt surgical resection, these tumors exhibited aggressive behavior. Numerous cases of soft tissue tumors have been described to arise in areas of prior radiation therapy; however, there have been rare reports of de novo MPNST after radiation therapy, especially in the setting of Hodgkin's lymphoma. Postirradiation MPNST should be considered in the differential diagnosis of a painful, enlarging mass in a previously irradiated area.

Figure 9.4   Abstract Showing Proximity Searches

Source: D.C. Anderson, T.J. Cummings and A.H. Friedman, "Malingnant peripheral nerve sheath tumor of the spine after radiation therapy for Hodgkin's lymphoma," Clinical Neuropathology, vol. 23, No. 5/2004, pp. 245–255. Used with permission.

the case of websites), there are a number of contexts where this might be a preferred approach, for example, online textbooks, specific collections of documents (e.g., legal compliance), digitized collections of clinical narratives, or any instance where such a level of granularity is required. For an excellent introduction to full-text information retrieval, see Sievert.[6]

At this point in our discussion, it is worth briefly noting that a key measure of IR system performance comes from attempting to measure the *relevance* of a retrieval set to a given query. Relevance is a tricky concept, however. First, it is relative to an individual is and highly subjective, thereby making it difficult to test in experimental settings. Second, what might be relevant to an individual at the beginning of a search could easily change as the search gets deeper. That is, the learner may learn more as he or she peruses citations and get a better feeling for what is available in a given context. The earliest Cranfield experiments established the standards of *recall* and *precision*, and these are still used in some form today when attempting to determine the effectiveness of ISARs.[7] Basically, the idea is to have a system help users retrieve items relevant to a query and *not* retrieve those that are nonrelevant. Recall means retrieving all relevant items, regardless of how many nonrelevant items are retrieved. This method is used by those seeking all the information they can retrieve on a topic. A more refined measure is that of precision, or retrieving a high proportion of relevant items with very low (or, ideally, no) nonrelevant ones. The critical reader will quickly notice a key flaw in attempting to measure these; to wit, it is difficult or impossible to truly know how many *relevant* items are in a real-world database, and so some subset of agreed-upon relevant items (given a test query) is necessarily an acknowledged limitation of any study.

Given the limited computing technology and the cost of searching online (before the ubiquity of the Internet and WWW), the tools of several decades ago were rather powerful. Professional searchers (librarians and other experts) could get excellent results once they mastered the system and understood the structure, scope, and limitations of the files they were seeking information from. Nevertheless, serious challenges related to determining meaning, an explosion of accessibility to sources exacerbated by the advent of the Internet, and a proliferation of digital information remained.

One of the most significant advances came when IR models could better analyze term occurrence and importance within a document or collection. Gerard Salton is regarded as one of the pioneers of what Hersh calls "lexical-statistical" approaches to IR.[8] Salton's *vector space method* involved a series of techniques that greatly advanced what we know about the discriminatory value of terms, or how well a term can help discriminate between relevant and nonrelevant documents. A good discriminatory term would occur frequently in a small number of documents and infrequently in the rest of the collection. His approach is given full treatment in his book *Introduction to Modern Information Retrieval* (1983), which has, along with his other scholarly work, been cited by IR researchers in the literature for decades.[9] This chapter is concerned with a few key concepts that, in our opinion, marked a significant advance in IR approaches that have been the basis of the highly complex approaches in use in today's wildly complex IR environment, discussed in technical detail in Baeza-Yates. Considering these central ideas is valuable for future investigations by readers and in understanding the underlying issues of IR in health sciences librarianship.

One of the key ideas in more modern IR systems is that of term weighting. The idea of a term's weight relates to the notion of discriminatory value discussed previously. Terms have more weight in determining relevance, vis-à-vis a query term(s) and their occurrence in a document as compared to other documents in the collection. Although a number of weighting formulae exist, one of the first, and one used as the basis for others, is the *IDF * TF*, where term frequency (*TF*) refers to the frequency that a term occurs in every document, and inverse document frequency (*IDF*) is the logarithm of the ratio of the total number of documents to the number of documents in which the term occurs. IDF is assigned once for each term in the database. So, the weighting formula is, *Weight (term, document) = TF (term, document) x IDF (term)*.[10]

The idea of term weighting was important in refining systems so as to better identify relevant documents. A number of modern variations on this exist (see Baeza-Yates), but this was a departure from more binary treatments of IR. In fact, a version of the IDF*TF weight is used by PubMed's "related articles" function (http://www.nlm.nih.gov/bsd/disted/pubmedtutorial/020_190.html), where the weighted terms from the record identified by the user as being relevant—and so he or she would like to see "related documents"—is used as a query. Thus, users are basically saying, "Yes, I like this, find more please" without having to figure out how to represent that in a new query.

Salton and others recognized limitations of raw IDF*TF weighting. One problem was that longer documents (i.e., ones with abstracts or if the full text is used in the calculation) could skew the weight (longer documents have a greater chance for higher occurrence rates, making them seem more important). Salton addressed this in his vector space method, wherein he used a cosine normalization to account for document length.[11]

In addition, this allowed for better "relevance feedback" mechanisms. Systems using this method could identify more relevant items and so let the system give more weight to terms in those and less weight to those in nonrelevant items.

The groundwork from term weighting and refinements of understanding the discriminatory value of terms has inspired other IR models. Briefly, fuzzy retrieval uses fuzzy set theory to attempt a better representation of information needs. Basically, rather than an element either being part of a set or not, fuzzy theory allows for degrees of membership in a set. Probabilistic IR has seen more success than fuzzy retrieval in IR systems. This is based on Bayes's theorem, with the idea that more weight should be given to terms that have a greater probability of occurring in relevant documents and that are less likely to occur in nonrelevant ones. Both fuzzy and probabilistic retrieval models are meant to give a greater ability to match queries and documents. However, they each have formula requirements that must be met to be successful.

Web search engines are now the cutting edge in IR, and it seems improvements occur weekly to help individuals retrieve relevant information from a bewildering amount of information. As noted earlier, the details of these search engines are trade secrets that are highly protected to help companies maintain or seek a competitive edge. Again, readers interested in a deeper treatment of web retrieval are encouraged to consult one of the cited sources.

TYPES AND EXAMPLES OF HEALTH INFORMATION SOURCES

Health sciences libraries typically provide access to hundreds of electronic resources. An examination of the resources provided in several health and biomedical libraries reveal some overlap in content. It would be impractical in this chapter to review every information retrieval system. Several of the most widely used resources are described in this section, however, with a more exhaustive list in the appendix.

First, we provide the following as a modification of Hersh's classification of sources. This is meant to offer a broad-level categorization of the most often used resources. Key examples follow the list.

1. Bibliographic (articles, user-generated content [blogs, microblogs], registries)
2. Ready Reference for Clinical Decision Support (medical dictionaries, normal lab values, images, drug interactions, etc.)
3. Evidence-Based Medicine—Resources to help to resolve clinical questions, standard of care, and so on.
4. Educational Support—CMEs, patient education

The biomedical community consumes and creates a daunting amount of information. This expanse includes traditional research articles and monographs, factual databases, and clinical trials registries. The types and formats of information within the healthcare environment are as varied in form and purpose as the individual needs of those seeking them. The following provides some major examples of information resources that range in content, organization, and accessibility. The reader may consult excellent resources for deeper explanations, such as *Introduction to Reference Sources in the Health Sciences.*[12]

Perhaps the largest percentage of information needed and used by individuals throughout the biomedical community comes from knowledge-based, bibliographic resources that generally communicate the breadth of knowledge across the health sciences. Such sources include journal and periodical articles, books and monographs, and knowledge that is communicated via other formats or that involves special treatment of other sources. The reward structure within health sciences research still places great value on traditional scholarly communication outlets such as journals. Monographs, periodicals, government documents and reports, conference abstracts and proceedings, and new knowledge created by researchers and practitioners is generally reported through these outlets for consumption, knowledge transfer, and education, among other purposes. A web of knowledge is spun, so to speak, in that literatures from different fields are connected through citations to other work, collaborative connections among researchers, and the content of the articles themselves and their ultimate role in the knowledge creation cycle. It should go without saying that the librarian will continue to play a major role in providing access to these through professional search assistance, new technologies to help users link to needed sources, and input in the design of new systems.

Literature Databases

MEDLINE

The National Library of Medicine's premier bibliographic database MEDLINE contains over 19 million references to biomedical literature, with coverage generally from 1946 to the present. References in MEDLINE are collected from approximately 5,600 journals in 39 languages (in 60 languages for older journals). The Literature Selection Technical Review Committee, an NIH-chartered advisory committee of external experts, makes recommendations regarding most MED-LINE content. Citations for MEDLINE are created by the NLM, international partners, and collaborating organizations and are indexed using the Medical Subject Headings (MeSH) controlled vocabulary (http://www.nlm.nih.gov/pubs/factsheets/medline.html).

Health science libraries offer multiple methods for accessing MEDLINE content. The two most popular methods are PubMed and Ovid MEDLINE

PubMed. In many ways, PubMed is such an important resource, involving such a variety of resources in a host of formats and for such a breadth of purposes, that it merits its own category. PubMed is a free research tool developed and maintained by the National Center for Biotechnology Information (NCBI) at the U.S. National Library of Medicine, an institute of the National Institutes of Health (NIH). PubMed is made up of more than 22 million citations for biomedical literature from MEDLINE, life science journals, and online books. From a particular citation, users may access full-text content through PubMed's Link Out service, which allows users to link directly from PubMed and other NCBI databases to information and services beyond the NCBI systems. A typical PubMed citation provides access to full text either through PubMed Central, an NIH-supported free archive of biomedical and life sciences journal literature at the U.S. National Institutes of Health's National Library of Medicine (NIH/NLM), or through Link Out, to external publisher web sites. Frequently asked questions (FAQs) are also available (http://www.ncbi.nlm.nih.gov/books/NBK3827/#pubmedhelp).

PubMed's strength lies in its automatic term mapping, which attempts to match unqualified terms that are entered into the query box. When a user enters search terms without tagging or other qualification, the terms are matched against subjects in the MeSH translation table, journals in the Journals translation table, and proper names, in the Full Author translation table, Author index, Full Investigator translation table, and Investigator index. Once a match is found in any of these translation tables, the mapping stops. When subject or journal matches are found, query and individual terms are also searched in All Fields. If no match is found in any tables, terms are searched in All Fields and together.[13]

Ovid (MEDLINE). MEDLINE on OvidSP is a commercially supported product that offers an alternative method for searching for MEDLINE content. While it is not in the scope of this chapter to offer a full-scale comparison of the two interfaces, users familiar with a database vendor's interface may prefer the value-added services that a commercial product has to offer.[14]

CINAHL

CINAHL (Cumulative Index to Nursing and Allied Health Literature, http://www.ebscohost.com/biomedical-libraries/the-cinahl-database) indexes nursing and allied health literature from such nursing journals and publications as those of the National League for Nursing and the American Nurses' Association. Content spans a wide range of topics, including nursing, biomedicine, health sciences librarianship, alternative and complementary medicine, consumer health, and numerous allied health disciplines, with records dating back to 1981.

CINAHL also provides access to nursing books, dissertations, selected conference proceedings, standards of practice, and audiovisuals. Full-text access is provided for journal articles, legal cases, clinical innovations, critical paths, research instruments, and clinical trials. CINAHL Subject Headings, based on MeSH, are used to index content and refine searching.

PsycINFO

PsycINFO (http://www.apa.org/pubs/databases/psycinfo/index.aspx) indexes citations for content devoted to peer-reviewed journals, books, and dissertations in the behavioral sciences and mental health. In addition to psychology, PsycINFO covers related disciplines such as medicine, law, social work, neuroscience, business, nursing, forensics, and engineering. Indexing of records is provided by subject experts from the American Psychological Association (APA) using the *Thesaurus of Psychological Index Terms* (http://www.apa.org/pubs/databases/training/thesaurus.aspx).

Publications indexed in PsycINFO are vetted by a team of experts for relevance, with direction advised by scholars, scientists within the APA's membership, and experts from the library and information science community. Of the more than 57 million cited references in PsycINFO, almost 3 million date from the period between 1920 and 1999. Of particular interest is the Tests and Measures field, which enables users to locate specific tests. A coverage list is available also (http://www.apa.org/pubs/databases/psycinfo/coverage.aspx).

Clinical Decision Support

MD Consult. MD Consult aims to be a one-stop shop for clinicians. MD Consult assists with diagnostic support by providing easy access to relevant journal articles, medical images, and evidence-based summaries. In addition to clinical support information, the database offers access to medical textbooks, practice guidelines, new treatment options and medical news, patient information resources, and clinician education resources, including continuing medical education (CME) opportunities.

MD Consult attempts to facilitate the search process for clinicians in multiple ways, and a synonym database of over 2.5 million medical terms serves as the controlled vocabulary for the resource. Recommended resource pages highlight current opinions on major medical topics (http://www.mdconsult.com/about/410003109-46/AboutMDC.html?ws=true&am=true).

CONCLUSION AND FUTURE DIRECTIONS

In many ways, information retrieval involves all that is the core of being a librarian or other information professional. IR includes identifying information objects and understanding how they are created, represented, and stored for the purpose of retrieval and use. It requires recognizing the diversity among users and their information behaviors. Ultimately, IR is the matching of users with information objects using information technology with an understanding of the ever-changing information environment and the tools information professionals use to harness as much of this as we can for our users.

Health sciences librarians have traditionally been on the forefront of new advances in IR. In fact, the first "online" searches were done by health sciences librarians using the MEDLARS system.[15] While all types of librarians have demonstrated a certain level of critical analysis of new technologies, sources, and services, in regards to how these impact their users, the health sciences librarian has unique challenges related to the fact that providing highly effective services to his or her clientele can greatly impact health outcomes and affect peoples' lives directly or indirectly.

The information environment, particularly in the biomedical community, is rapidly expanding and evolving. However, understanding the basics of the core constructs of IR better enables health sciences librarians to negotiate this otherwise daunting world. Health sciences librarians need to keep abreast of current and relevant research on user information behaviors (including the social world of health information), seek out which new technologies are emerging and determine whether these will be useful to their user communities, and continue to thoughtfully implement sources, services, and systems that support the particular mission of their organization.

NOTES

1. Korfhage, Robert R. *Information Storage and Retrieval*. New York: Wiley Computer, 1997.

2. Hersh, William R. *Information Retrieval: A Health and Biomedical Perspective*. New York: Springer, 2009.

3. Salton, Gerard, and Michael J. McGill. *Introduction to Modern Information Retrieval*. New York: McGraw-Hill, 1983.

4. Fay, Robin M., Michael P. Sauers, and the Library and Information Technology Association. *Semantic Web Technologies and Social Searching for Librarians*. Chicago, IL: ALATechSource, 2012.

5. Adamson, D. C., T. J. Cummings, and A. H. Friedman. "Malignant Peripheral Nerve Sheath Tumor of the Spine after Radiation Therapy for Hodgkin's Lymphoma." *Clinical Neuropathology* 23, no. 5 (2004): 245–255.

6. Sievert, MaryEllen C. "Full-Text Information Retrieval: Introduction." *Journal of the American Society for Information Science* 47, no. 4 (1996): 261.

7. Cleverdon, C. W., J. Mills, and E. M. Keen. *Factors Determining the Performance of Indexing Systems*, Vol. 1, *Design*; Vol. 2, *Results*. Cranfield, UK: Aslib Cranfield Research Project, College of Aeronautics, 1996.

8. Hersh, William R. *Information Retrieval: A Health and Biomedical Perspective*, 2nd ed. New York: Springer, 2003.

9. Salton, *op. cit.*

10. Hersh 2009, *op. cit.*

11. Salton, *op. cit.*, p. 121.

12. Huber, Jeffrey T. and Susan Swogger. *Introduction to Reference Sources in the Health Sciences*, 6th ed. Chicago, IL: ALA Neal-Schuman, 2014.

13. "PubMed Tutorial." National Library of Medicine. Last modified February 26, 2014, http://www.nlm.nih.gov/bsd/disted/pubmedtutorial/cover.html.

14. "Ovid MEDLINE." Ovid Technologies, Inc. http://www.ovid.com/webapp/wcs/stores/servlet/ProductDisplay?storeId=13051&catalogId=13151&langId=-1&partNumber=Prod-901).

15. Dee, C. R. "The development of the Medical Literature Analysis and Retrieval System (MEDLARS)." *Journal of the Medical Library Association: JMLA* 95, no. 4 (2007): 416–425.

APPENDIX 9.1: HEALTH INFORMATION SOURCES

Name of Resource	Category	Scope	Search Assistance	Contains	For More Information
Academic Search Premier	Article database (subscription)	• Biology • Chemistry • Engineering • Physics • Psychology • Religion and philosophy • Science and technology • Veterinary science • And more fields	• Visual search • Search modes and expanders • Subject thesaurus terms	• More than 13,600 indexed and abstracted journals • Full text for over 4,700 journals • More than 4,000 peer-reviewed, full-text journals • PDF backfiles to 1975 or further for over 100 journals • Searchable cited references for more than 1,050 titles	http://www.ebscohost.com/academic/academic-search-premier
AccessMedicine	Integrated medical information system (subscription)	Medicine	Keyword	More than 65 clinical and educational resources: • *Harrison's Principles of Internal Medicine* • *Current Medical Diagnosis & Treatment* • LANGE Basic Science and Clinical Libraries • 35,000 images for educational use • Custom curriculum • 1,000 differential diagnoses • Procedural videos and animations, grand rounds lectures	http://accessmedicine.com
Dissertations and Theses	Citation database (subscription)	Dissertations and theses by title words or author	Keyword search	Offers full text for most of the dissertations added since 1997 and strong retrospective full-text coverage for older graduate works. • Coverage: 1637–present • Nearly 3 million sources covered • Full text includes nearly 3 million searchable citations to dissertations and theses from around the world from 1743 to the present. • Over 1 million full-text dissertations available for download in PDF format • Over 2 million titles are available for purchase as printed copies	http://www.umi.com/en-US/catalogs/databases/detail/pqdt.shtml

Web of Science	Citation database (subscription)	Offers access to six comprehensive citation databases: • Science Citation Index Expanded: Over 8,300 major journals across 150 disciplines • Social Sciences Citation Index: Over 4,500 journals across 50 social science disciplines, as well as 3,500 of the world's leading scientific and technical journals • Arts & Humanities Citation Index: Over 2,300 arts and humanities journals, as well as selected items from over 6,000 scientific and social sciences journals • Conference Proceedings Citation Index: Over 148,000 journals and book-based proceedings in two editions, "Science" and "Social Science and Humanities," across 256 disciplines. • Index Chemicus: Over 2.6 million compounds • Current Chemical Reactions: Over 1 million reactions	Uses ranking – weighting impact factor	• Content covers over 12,000 of the highest impact journals worldwide, including open access journals and over 150,000 conference proceedings • Current and retrospective coverage in the sciences, social sciences, arts, and humanities, with coverage to 1900 in many cases	http://thomsonreuters.com/products_services/science/science_products/a–z/web_of_science/
Google Scholar	Web browser/citation database (free to search)	Many disciplines and sources: articles, theses, books, abstracts and court opinions, from academic publishers, professional societies, online repositories, universities and other websites	Ranking – weighting impact factor	• Links to scholarly literature • Related works linking for similar citations, authors, and publications • Location matching to facilitate accessing documents through the local library or on the web • Alerts to allow users to keep up with recent developments in any area of research • Author profiles provide notification when others cite a particular publication	http://scholar.google.com/

APPENDIX 9.1: (Continued)

Name of Resource	Category	Scope	Search Assistance	Contains	For More Information
LexisNexis Academic	Citation database (subscription)	Information for professionals in legal, risk management, corporate, government, law enforcement, accounting, and academic markets	SmartIndexing technology applies controlled vocabulary terms for several different taxonomies to all LexisNexis news and business content (legal content is also indexed but by a different set of taxonomies developed specifically for legal researchers)	Billions of searchable documents and records from more than 45,000 legal, news, and business sources	http://www .lexisnexis.com Continued
TOXNET (TOXicology Data NETwork)	Integrated database system (free to use)	Chemicals and drugs, diseases and the environment, environmental health, occupational safety and health, poisoning, risk assessment and regulations, and toxicology	TOXNET Literature Files • MeSH term searching available • CAS registry numbers • Automatic term mapping	• Specific chemicals, mixtures, and products • Chemical nomenclature • Unknown chemicals • Special toxic effects of chemicals in humans and/or animals • Citations from the scientific literature	http://toxnet .nlm.nih.gov/

Chapter 10

HISTORICAL COLLECTIONS IN HEALTH SCIENCES LIBRARIES

Michael A. Flannery

BACKGROUND

Historical collections in health sciences libraries are best understood in the larger historical context in which they emerged. Here may be seen the broader professional concerns and interests along with the resources upon which these specialized collections were built.

Early medical libraries reflected the general condition of libraries throughout the early Republic; their management was as haphazard as the collections themselves, and there was little institutional interest in either their support or their maintenance. There was little association of research with the classroom throughout the antebellum period in America. Medical education was highly didactic, stressing textbook recitation and memorization of "facts" and "procedures" as given by the instructor. For most medical schools, collections of books were simply seen as largely superfluous to their educational goals and missions. Modern, research-based medicine did not even begin to take shape until the last quarter of the nineteenth century, and it is no accident that real progress was not made in medical libraries or librarianship until then.

The establishment of Pasteur's germ theory of disease and Koch's Postulates, which confirmed it in the laboratory, along with the establishment in 1893 of Johns Hopkins University, the first American institution of higher learning based upon the German graduate research model, revolutionized medical education. Indeed, just four years before, healthcare itself was placed upon a much firmer footing with the creation of Johns Hopkins Hospital. This represented the first in what would be a dramatic expansion of urban hospitals not only as centers for state-of-the-art healthcare, but for clinical research as well. All of this brought about changes in the information needed to support and drive this new research-based education and clinical care.

Historical collections in the healthcare sciences in the United States may be said to have achieved national attention under John Shaw Billings. Billings is most noteworthy for his work in organizing and cataloging the medical collection of the surgeon general's office. Until he was assigned the duty of supervising the Surgeon-General's Library in 1865, this collection, which would evolve into what we know today as the National Library of Medicine, was little more than a small collection of medical books first assembled by Surgeon General Thomas Lawson in 1836. But Billings, also a physician, had the heart of a bibliophile, the soul of a historian, and the mind of a librarian and immediately saw the potential of the collection he was charged to manage. Under his direction, the collection grew to 10,000 volumes by 1870.[1] The fact that this became the largest single medical collection in the country (much of it was historical in nature) reveals much about the state of libraries in the field of medicine. One year later, Billings engaged the surgeon general's office, a position then held by Joseph K. Barnes, in a discussion about the mission of the library. It was during those deliberations that a momentous decision was made: The library of the surgeon general's office would become the National Medical Library, a new vision that became Billings's singular passion. By 1895, Billings had managed to collect some 34,300 journals and more than 117,000 volumes, not to mention large vertical files of theses and pamphlets, clearly the largest single collection of its kind in the world.[2]

Billings provided his most outstanding contribution to medical libraries and librarianship with his *Index-Catalogue* and *Index Medicus*. The *Index-Catalogue of the Library of the Surgeon-General's Office, U.S. Army* (1880) listed books by author and subject and sought to encompass "all important original articles in medical periodicals and transactions of all countries."[3] *Index Medicus* was an idea that struck Billings during his work on the catalogue, namely, to provide a current list of all titles in medicine. It came out one year before his catalogue. Today, of course, it indexes only journal literature (nearly 4,000 titles), and in Lucretia McClure's words, "adds more citations each month than the total for the first year [in 1879]."[4] Thus, it is safe to say that the *Index-Catalogue* is exactly that: a catalog of those items in the surgeon general's office (today the NLM) retrospectively listing all "important" original articles and books in its collection. *Index Medicus*, on the other hand, was intended to be an up-to-date, "complete" listing of "current medical literature." As such, the *Index-Catalogue* remains an important checklist of titles for current special collections librarians.

The *Index-Catalogue* was completed in its first series (i.e., the initial retrospective compilation) in 16 volumes in 1895. But the library's continued acquisitions forced

Billings's successors to issue further series. The *Index-Catalogue* ceased publication with series five in 1961. Because of its retrospective nature, the *Index-Catalogue* remains the most comprehensive bibliographic guide in the history of medicine. Its significance is underscored by the fact that it is digitized. The *Index-Catalogue* is available fully searchable online (http://indexcat.nlm.nih.gov/).

The only other bibliography of comparable use to the history of medicine librarian is *Morton's Medical Bibliography* (originally based upon Fielding Garrison's checklist of 1933 and often referred to even today simply as Garrison & Morton's bibliography), edited by Jeremy Norman.[5] This invaluable resource provides an annotated listing of all major and significant publications in the field, nearly 9,000 in all. The importance of any given title can often be determined by its listing in this volume, and antiquarian dealers will often note it in their catalogs (e.g., Thomas Sydenham, *Observations medicæ circa morborum acutorum historiam et curationem*, Londini: G. Kettilby, 1676. Garrison & Morton listing #2198). Even with its multiple editions and continued expansion, however, the initial 1910 listing of historical items first compiled by Garrison and initially published in the *Index-Catalogue* was the seed from which Garrison & Morton sprang.

Despite Billings's substantial contributions to the field, he was not the only person diligently at work making medical libraries the research centers they are today, nor was he the only figure helping to establish medical librarianship as a profession in its own right. For that we go to three individuals who figured prominently in the founding of the Medical Library Association (hereafter MLA): George M. Gould, Margaret Charlton, and William Osler. It is no mistake that interest in medical libraries came principally from physicians: Billings (whom we have already discussed), Gould (who struck upon an elaborate network of resource sharing among medical center libraries, basically an exchange system whereby duplicates could be freely transferred among participating libraries), and Osler (the paterfamilias of the profession who envisioned, and indeed championed, the medical library as a repository of historically significant volumes necessary for the cultivation of a broad-ranging medical humanities he felt was essential to the well-rounded practitioner).

But it was Margaret Charlton, who along with Dr. F. G. Finley served as librarian at Osler's McGill Library, who actually suggested the formation of an independent association of medical libraries to Gould. It was an idea that Gould embraced with some enthusiasm. When eight people convened in Gould's Philadelphia office on May 2, 1898, the MLA (originally called the Association of Medical Librarians) was born. Gould, editor of the *Philadelphia Medical Journal*, was made the organization's first president. His immediate constituents were a modest but powerful group: there were, besides himself and co-founder Charlton, Dr. William Browning of King's County Medical Society (Brooklyn); Dr. Edwin H. Brigham of the Boston Medical Library; Dr. J. L. Rothrock of the Ramsey County Medical Society, St. Paul; Elisabeth Thies, librarian at Johns Hopkins Hospital; Charles Fisher of the College of Physicians of Philadelphia; and Marcia Noyes, representing the Medical and Chirurgical Faculty of Maryland, Baltimore.

But beyond the immediate founders, the role of Osler was key. Osler's constant support and advice made him a central figure in this seminal movement. As historian Jennifer Connor has observed[6]:

> In general, where Gould—a self-consciously cultured man himself—had pushed scientific communications as the means to transform moribund collections into active workshops, medical leaders afterward reclaimed the notion of humanism in medicine to breathe life into collections of classical books as well. . . . The objective of these later leaders was to use the association to elevate and cultivate the medical profession, in part through reading and celebrating their medical heritage. They were deeply influenced in this respect by the association's second president, William Osler. Prominent participants in the society formed an intricate network of the medical elite through their relationships with Osler, their connections to the Association of American Physicians, and their roles as directors of medical libraries.

Indeed, it was Osler who steered the newly formed association toward historical studies. The first periodical devoted to the history of medicine was also the official publication of the Association of Medical Librarians. The *Medical Library and Historical Journal*, begun in 1903, made the connection between medical libraries and history explicit. The early list of MLA officials reads like a who's who of American medical historians: MLA's fifth president, Dr. George Dock, also edited the *Annals of Medical History* (a journal established in 1917). Later, John F. Fulton, another MLA official, became the first editor of the *Journal of the History of Medicine & Allied Sciences*, which was started in 1946. Other prominent MLA officials like Francis Packard, J. George Adami, Fielding H. Garrison, and Abraham Jacobi were important leaders in the history of medicine.

Together they helped create a culture of professionalism as well as scholarship in an emerging field that distinguished itself from other library professionals emerging collaterally from the work of Melvil Dewey, William Frederick Poole, and Justin Winsor. Along with it came a general elevation in the caliber of medical libraries, from those who staffed them to the collection development resources that filled them.

More than any other event or single year in the history of the MLA, 1946 stands out as pivotal. Where William Osler had addressed Yale students in 1913 with a sweeping historical survey of medicine, Mary Louise Marshall addressed MLA members at Yale in 1946 with an agenda for training in medical librarianship. Just the previous year, a survey conducted by the editors of the *Bulletin of the Medical Library Association* revealed that most of the 97 respondents wished to continue the tradition of publishing half its articles on the history of medicine. Yet with the founding of a new journal for the study of the history of medicine, the *Journal of the History of Medicine* mentioned earlier, under MLA vice president John Fulton, medical history increasingly went its own way. Even the venue for this 1946 meeting signaled change. Organized by Fulton, the meeting celebrated the new Yale University medical library, which had been built during the war. The library formed a Y shape, not because it belonged to Yale as commonly supposed, but because it followed Harvey Cushing's plan, which stipulated that there be two separate divisions for "old" and "modern" books. This design was thus followed despite wartime exigencies which made the historical section appear, according to Fulton, "as an unnecessary luxury."[7] Although the design of the Yale medical library was intended to enhance functionality, ultimately it symbolizes the divergent paths medical history and medical information were to pursue in the postwar period.

By the mid-twentieth century, medical libraries had come of age, and storage and retrieval were performed through cataloging and classification, maintenance of the shelf list, and author/title and subject catalogs. Pencils and manual work-forms ruled the day *without* a central cataloging agency like OCLC (*Index Medicus* and the *National Union Catalog* were medical librarians' mainstays), and a cadre of talented, well-trained women had come to replace the male-dominated scholar/custodians of the clubbish collections of yesteryear. Obviously, libraries at this time were dominated by one thing: namely, The Book. While there may have been some fiche or film in this period, and perhaps even some disc recordings of shellac and vinyl, the book ruled as the principal medium in most libraries. The motto here, "To study the phenomena of disease without books is to sail an uncharted sea," is today (like Osler himself who said it) a modern-day anachronism.[8]

So when we think of modern medical libraries and special collections, three things need to be kept in mind: (1) the development of medical librarianship as a distinct profession and the shift from a custodial role to one of proactive collecting, organizing, disseminating, and maintaining allowed for the further development of specialized collections particularly in medical history and the humanities; (2) the concomitant shift from the administration of book collections to one of managing a virtual explosion of clinical records in a growing number of formats (implicit here too is the transformation of the medical library from a place of quiet study to one of curricular and clinical support)—and even here, as will be seen, historical collections have a part to play; and finally if not somewhat ironically, (3) the contribution of medical library development in its institutional and professional setting toward a wholly distinct specialty with the history of medicine as a recognized academic discipline in its own right.

What Do Historical Collections Include?

Historical collections (sometimes also referred to by the broader designation of special collections) can be made up of any or all of the following: published print material, unpublished material, or physical artifacts. These typically correspond to library, archival, and museum collections respectively. Aggregate data on history of medicine collections in the United States and other select countries such as the United Kingdom, Germany, France, Italy, South Africa, Israel, India, and many others is available at NLM's online Directory of History of Medicine Collections (http://wwwcf.nlm.nih.gov/hmddirectory/index.cfm). The directory offers a robust search engine that allows for comprehensive subject searches and areas of collection strength.

It is also worth mentioning that historical collections in medical libraries may include much more than strictly medical topics. Historically relevant social, economic, cultural, literary, and artistic aspects of healthcare are often included as well. Such a broad contextualizing of the past can have positive impacts upon students and faculty. As such, Megan Curran of the Norris Medical Library at the University of Southern California has called for increased support of medical humanities. "A focus on the medical humanities need not be limited to bolstering student art shows and poetry. It can foster an environment of palpable scientific discovery."[9] Here historical materials play an integral role and serve as an important adjunct to any medical humanities program.

Practical answers for what to include in any given historical collection must be flexible, but efforts should be made to tie the collection either to an internal logic based upon the interests and needs of the holding institution or upon some broader aspect of the history to which the collection is devoted. These should be outlined clearly in a manual or some official policy document. Such a document should ideally be developed in collaboration with those who are going to be most affected by it, including professional and paraprofessional staff. Once a draft is developed, it should also be approved by the library director or another chief institutional executive responsible for library services. An example of such a document from the Historical Collections of Lister Hill Library of the Health Sciences at the University of Alabama at Birmingham should give an idea of the kinds of considerations to be included in a complete policy statement:

> The mission of the Historical Collections unit (hereafter referred to as HC) is to promote the history of the health sciences on the campus of the University of Alabama at Birmingham, in the state of Alabama, and in the nation as a whole. It seeks to do this through the collection and preservation of books, papers, and artifacts relative to the history of medicine and its allied sciences. In addition, it seeks to actively encourage and contribute to historical scholarship through lectures, fellowships, publications, and teaching activities when and where appropriate.
>
> Collection Development Policy:
>
> It is the policy of Historical Collections (hereafter HC) to collect any materials deemed pertinent to history of the health sciences. While the unit is well aware of its holdings in the great classics of medicine, it is also sensitive to the need for a targeted collection development policy. Bearing this in mind, it is the goal of HC to collect materials relating to Southern medicine specifically and medicine of the American antebellum period generally. Of particular interest are materials related to Civil War medicine and healthcare (both Union and Confederate). Additionally, HC is interested in collecting any materials of significance to the development of medicine and its allied health professions at the local, state, and national levels, especially but not exclusively those pre-dating 1910. Areas of interest may also include historical materials relating to one or more medical specialty or fields of growing importance such as human genetics, bio-ethics, etc. These collection areas may always be broadened and amended as new subject areas configure HC in such a way as to present additional areas of interest and opportunity.

In terms of collection inclusion, a general distinction is made between published print materials such as books, journals, and pamphlets and non-published materials such as letters, memos, typescripts, and similar matter. In cases of the former, materials would normally be accessioned into the Reynolds Historical Library; in cases of the latter, such materials would ordinarily go into UAB Archives. For materials such as physical artifacts, apparatus, instruments, uniforms, etc., such items would typically be accessioned into the Alabama Museum of the Health Sciences.

Decisions about what to accession into any one or more of these collections reside with the HC Unit of the University of Alabama at Birmingham. Unless otherwise arranged and spelled out in writing, all materials accessioned into the unit will be considered as gifts and the sole property of the University of Alabama at Birmingham.

Because of legal restrictions mandated by the IRS, no faculty or staff may appraise or otherwise estimate the monetary value of any donation for tax purposes. The IRS does not accept appraisals by the recipients of gifts received. Those wanting such an appraisal are encouraged to have a professional appraisal done prior to donating the materials. HC is aware of the importance of these donations, however, and will provide to all donors upon request a listing and description of all materials given to the unit.

This policy statement outlines the key features of collection development from a conceptual to a procedural basis. While details are dependent upon the specific interests and needs of the institution, every effort should be made to provide clarity and flexibility in collection development scope, content, and processes. All donations should be accompanied by a deed of gift. The legal office of the parent institution can often assist with developing an appropriate deed of gift document. Typically, a deed of gift includes at minimum the name and address of the donor, a list of items donated, and a statement that the donor is the owner of items being donated free of any legal encumbrances.

In collections comprising a variety of material types, a collection allocation statement should be included. For example:

Historical Collections, established in 1996, is comprised of three units at the University of Alabama at Birmingham: the Alabama Museum of the Health Sciences, the Reynolds Historical Library and the UAB Archives. The Historical Collections unit is a component of the Lister Hill Library and reports to its director.

While each unit is distinct, overlap inevitably occurs in the disposition of collections. This policy statement is designed to mitigate confusion as to where various materials should be located within the organization.

The Alabama Museum of the Health Sciences is dedicated to the preservation and display of equipment, instruments and objects that represent the history and development of the health sciences in the areas of education, research and practice in the United States with special emphasis on the state of Alabama and its contributors to the practice of medicine. The scope of the collection includes, but is not limited to the following fields: medicine, nursing, ophthalmology, dentistry, public health and allied health.

The Reynolds Historical Library is devoted to the acquisition, organization, preservation and accessibility of published primary resource materials that document the history of the health sciences. The scope of the collection is broadly based with an emphasis on the development of healthcare in Western Europe and the United States. Currently, collection development is focused on, but not limited to the following fields: Southern medicine, Civil War medicine, 19th century diagnosis and therapeutics, botanical medicine, electrotherapeutics, anatomy, surgery, cardiology, genetics, and transplantation. Items published prior to 1910 receive top priority, although exceptions are made. Occasionally and when deemed appropriate, secondary works that enhance the interpretive and educational value of the collection's primary resources are added to the library.

The function of the UAB Archives is the appraisal, collection, organization, description and reference use of UAB's official records of enduring historical value. The UAB Archives is the repository for the institution and seeks to advance knowledge concerning the origins, mission, and programs of UAB and their historical development. The Archives also seeks to encourage efficient records management, which ensures UAB records of enduring historical value will be identified for inclusion in the Archives. Personal papers and corporate collections, those materials that are not university records, are also collected to document UAB's role in the city, the state, and in the health sciences environment.

In terms of collection inclusion, a general distinction is made between published print materials such as books, journals and pamphlets and non-published materials such as letters, memos, typescripts and similar matter. In cases of the former, materials would normally be accessioned into the Reynolds Historical Library; in cases of the latter, such materials would ordinarily go into the UAB Archives. For materials such as physical artifacts, apparatus, instruments, uniforms, etc., such items would typically be accessioned into the Alabama Museum of the Health Sciences.

Items will be placed in the following locations as listed:

Museum = artifacts (e.g., surgical/medical instruments; laboratory apparatus; pathological specimens; models and figurines; prosthetic devices; medicines, medicine bottles, medical trade cards, and advertisements; all promotional material that was originally designed to supplement and inform the three-dimensional object or objects for which they were created)

Library = books, journals, pamphlets, or other published/printed material

Archives = manuscripts, letters, memos, photographs, scrapbooks, original institutional records, ledgers, audio/visuals, university publications, ephemera and realia

While these distinctions constitute the normal separation of materials, it is recognized that exceptions may be made. This is particularly the case where the physical material, document or publication may appreciably enhance and/or inform a larger collection in another component of the Historical Collections unit and it is considered best to locate the material with the larger collection. Decisions to locate an item or items other than in its normally designated repository will be made on a case-by-case basis by the associate director in consultation with the museum archivist, library collections specialist, or university archivist as appropriate.

Beyond these collection management tools, patrons should be monitored when using materials. Typically, users are restricted to working with paper and pencil (no pens) or (more commonly today) a laptop computer to take notes. Each patron should be asked to fill out a registration form listing his or her name, address, phone number/email address, and research interest. This last item can be useful in compiling collection usage trends.

Finally, copying/scanning policies and related fees should be plainly stated and provided to all patrons. Patrons requesting copies or scans should do so with the understanding that they are requesting the reproductions under "fair use" provisions of copyright law. Patrons are often asked to fill out a copy request agreement form listing the titles and pages to be copied/scanned and confirming that the reproductions are requested under the lawful provisions described earlier. Copyright law can be extremely complex, but a useful guide is available at the Cornell University Copyright Information Center (see the "Copyright Term and the Public Domain in the United States" chart at http://copyright.cornell.edu/resources/publicdomain.cfm). Questions or ambiguities regarding fair use or public domain should always be referred to a legal professional; errors after the fact can pose serious problems and risk of lawsuit.

In summary, historical collections can comprise a wide range of material types. To coordinate each aspect into a coherent whole, policies should be developed and spelled out in the following documents:

- Collection development policy statement
- Collection allocation statement
- Deed of gift
- Patron registration form
- Copy/scan request form

These are basic organizational tools. Additional ones may be added to address special circumstances, institutional needs, or administrative concerns. It needs to be emphasized, however, that whatever policies and procedures are established, they should *be written down.* Anything less will create ambiguities and uncertainties, and will jeopardize consistency in and support for decisions made down the road.

But why do historical collections matter in the first place? It is a fair question and one amenable to multiple answers.

WHY ARE HISTORICAL COLLECTIONS RELEVANT?

The short answer is threefold: first, they have intrinsic monetary value; second, they can provide important curricular support and educational services; and third, they can have significant clinical consequences.

Unlike a general collection, historical materials have value as items in themselves. Determining the value of any given item can be difficult. While high-profile items such as Andreas Vesalius's *De humani corporis fabrica libri septem* (1543) are easily found (e.g., auctioned at Christie's in November 2011 for $412,994),[10] less prominent titles that are scarce may never have been publicly sold. Professional estimators can be employed for such purposes but can be costly. Determining value is generally much more than just age. Place, publisher, edition, author, audience, and provenance all play an important part in determining the value of a given title, document, or object. For example, Nicholas Culpeper's *English Physician*, published in London by Peter Cole in 1652, sold several years ago for $19,125, but a different edition of that same title published by Nicholas Boone in Boston in 1708 would likely go for perhaps twice that amount or more. Why? Because the Boston edition is extremely rare (only five are known to exist), and it is widely regarded as the first stand-alone general medical text printed in the British North American colonies. The point is that place and publisher in this case outweigh age in considering the value of an item.

A large or well-focused historical collection has a monetary value far exceeding most any other aspect of a library's holdings. Even high-tech equipment, while quite valuable in its own right, pales in comparison; high-tech equipment depreciates, often quite rapidly, while rare books, archival materials, and historical objects generally appreciate in value. Most institutions are therefore willing to spend additional financial resources in the preservation (often special humidity and temperate controls are devoted to these areas) and protection (alarm systems and motion detectors are often installed in highly sensitive areas) of rare books, manuscripts, and museum objects.

Curricular support is another way historical collections can make themselves relevant to the constituents they serve. It is not enough to have a premier collection or even a fancy website full of bells and whistles; managers of these collections must engage with the communities they serve, whether area schools off campus or departments and divisions on campus. The most obvious key constituencies are history and literature departments, but others are possible. For example, Vesalius's *De fabrica*, mentioned earlier, was used as a teaching tool by a faculty instructor of gross anatomy at the University of Alabama School of Medicine. The instructor literally pointed out to students why *De fabrica* was important, what Vesalius got right, and what he got wrong. Students were then required to write a paper based upon the experience.[11, 12] This type of teaching innovation engages students with the past in an immediate and very relevant way.

But beyond monetary value and curricular support and education, a third area of relevance for historical collections is in clinical care and research. In some measure, things have moved full circle. Healthcare delivery is again returning to the home and office. The average hospital stay of 18 days in 1946 dropped to less than 12 days in 1963, and by 1995, the average hospital stay was reduced to five or six days.[13] And the number of hospitals is declining as well. According to the American Hospital Association, the number of hospitals in the United States has dropped 14 percent since the mid-1980s, and the number of beds has fallen 18 percent since then.[14] As more and more tests and procedures are performed on an outpatient basis, diagnosis and recovery become less medical center based and more community based, which will undoubtedly impact libraries and their staff as on-site information needs become decentralized and increasingly global. Thus, the virtual presence afforded the doctor and patient via web-based information is necessary, and yet for those charged with providing that information, it presents unprecedented challenges. It is, in fact, this dramatically transformed research and clinical environment that can speak to the relevance of historical literature. A brief but most unfortunate case study will make the point.

Consider the hexamethonium tragedy that occurred in the spring of 2001. Ellen Roche, a 24-year-old lab tech, volunteered for a study at Johns Hopkins Asthma and Allergy Center directed by Dr. Alkis Togias. On May 4, Roche inhaled hexamethonium (a drug used to treat hypertension in the 1950s) to research the neural mechanisms that help keep airways open even when subjected to allergens and irritants. Togias performed a standard PubMed search for possible toxicity of hexamethonium, consulted standard textbooks from the 1980s and later in pharmacology and pulmonary medicine, and concluded that hexamethonium was safe.[15, 16]

What Togias did *not* uncover was the print literature of the 1950s, in particular the following: J. D. Morrow, H. A. Schroeder, H. M. Perry, "Studies on the control of hypertension by hyphex. II. Toxic reactions and side effects"[17]; I. Doniach, Brenda Morrison, R. E. Steiner, "Lung changes during hexamethonium therapy for hypertension"[18]; and H. Mitchell Perry, Robert M. O'Neal, Wilbur A. Thomas, "Pulmonary disease following chronic chemical ganglionic blockade."[19] The serious untoward effects of hexamethonium were described in each of these sources. It was not just a matter of missing a few obscure journal articles; if he had gone to the second edition of the Goodman and Gillman standard textbook in pharmacology, *The Pharmacological Basis of Therapeutics*, he would have discovered the following about hexamethonium: "More severe reactions include marked hypotension, obstipation, paralytic ileus, and urinary retention. Anginal pain may be precipitated in patients with angina pectoris if the hypotension is excessive. Syncope may occur without warning and hypotension and collapse may be profound. Deaths have occurred from therapy with hexamethonium alone and from its use in combination with hydrazinophthalazine."[20] On May 9, Ellen Roche was admitted to the Johns Hopkins Bayview Medical Center complaining of shortness of breath, cough, flu-like symptoms, a progressive decline in pulmonary function, and a lung infiltrate. Indeed, all the things reported in the literature just cited. Ellen Roche died on June 2, 2001. The family settled out of court for an undisclosed amount.

This incident highlights the dangers of easy access, unmediated end-user online searches, and an increasingly presentist notion among clinicians that only the latest information is the relevant information and that if it is not online, it simply must not be important. In the words of librarian Danielle Bodrero Hoggan, "The Johns Hopkins clinical trial . . . drives home the need to thoroughly search the literature, including the older resources. Many of today's popular databases do not cover literature before the 1970s."[21] Although the situation has changed somewhat since Hoggan's article, the dangers of simplistic, presentist thinking remain ominously pertinent, particularly where lives are involved. With a librarian's assistance, scientists can complement their usual web-based searches with databases and print indexes that cover earlier literature, and moreover, the assistance of knowledgeable historical collections librarians can be invaluable in ferreting out older material.

The entire incident should give more than momentary pause to the researcher. It should also force some examination of the training and role of librarians in the institutional review board (IRB) process, an issue that launched an MLA Task Force on Expert Searching chaired by Ruth Holst.[22] The real-life scenario here underscores both the implicit dangers of unfettered access to the mirage of so-called complete online information gathering and the continued importance of material not represented in virtual collections lacking historical depth. The fact that the librarian or library staff was conspicuously absent from the research process is telling.

In a broader sense, this incident underscores the importance of medical libraries that contain not only the latest and best array of online utilities conveniently made available through campus-wide site licensing agreements, but also the remaining importance of collections manifesting historical continuity and disciplinary depth. Hoggan concludes, "Web-based resources present possibilities as well as problems. However, with the right strategies and tools, scientists and librarians can make the most of web-based information."[23] Part of that "right strategy" may indeed include the consultation of historical collections librarians and staff.

CURRENT TRENDS AND ISSUES

Of course today, the library scene has changed drastically. Although computers and other forms of digital communications and social media play an increasingly vital role in libraries today, we would do well to be reminded they are still to some extent paper and print collections, and this is especially true of historical collections. Nevertheless, it goes without saying that sweeping and rapid transformations have characterized the current library environment. Indeed, these very dramatic changes in libraries as they move from the book to the computer age have caused tremendous challenges for library staff. How do we balance our collections during these pivotal changes? How do we preserve and archive an ever-growing array of information media that exist only in virtual form? How do we promote the library as an intellectual entity devoted to the dissemination and exchange of information while at the same time maintaining its traditional role as a place to learn? These are difficult questions.

While most written historical collections material remains paper based, an increasing portion of these history-based collections are becoming electronic. This is especially true of institutional archives where administrative correspondence, minutes, reports, executive summaries, reviews, and related communications are initiated and retained electronically. This raises extremely important challenges for storage and retrieval of data and in maintaining files that are highly techno-dependent. The latest innovation, like the digital DVD, is yesterday's betamax. Consider for a moment the difficulty of finding hardware on which to access data stored on a 3.5-inch floppy disk; how much more difficult still to access data on a 5.25-inch floppy disk. Even if you have the hardware, is the software needed to access and read the data still available? These kinds of issues have caused some archival units to retain hardware with older software applications or to immediately create surrogate copies of electronic media in current formats. Still, the rapidly changing technological environment is creating challenges for special collections managers who have limited budgets and staff at their disposal to keep up. Also, what exactly needs to be retained? Does every common textbook in multiple editions need to take up shelf space? Do titles outside the strengths and research interests of the holding library need to be kept in every case? One way of intelligently answering these questions is to share knowledge about who holds what and in what collections are certain subject strengths.

There has been an ongoing initiative sponsored by the History of Medicine Division of the National Library of Medicine (NLM) to establish an up-to-date Finding Aids Consortium. The consortium (available at http://www.nlm.nih.gov/hmd/con-sortium/index.html) now indexes over 3,600 finding aids from 35 institutions. The consortium, described on its website, is:

> The History of Medicine Finding Aids Consortium is a pilot project to explore the feasibility of crawling, indexing, and delivering web accessible content from external institutions in a union catalog format. The site leverages NLM's enterprise search engine Vivisimo. Using a variety of crawl protocols that are target-site specific, we are able to crawl, index, and provide access to finding aids that exist in a variety of data formats such as xml, html, or pdf. By crawling and indexing content locally with referring links back to an owning repository, NLM can offer a multi-institutional discovery service, but is relieved of the burden of managing external data. Crawls are currently performed on a monthly basis. Our method and tools allow for a widely-inclusive harvesting and search, but at the expense of advance-level services such as author or subject-based browsing or searching.[24]

While sharing collection information among and between historical collections remains a high priority, perhaps the single greatest initiative for nearly *all* such entities is the digitizing of selected portions of materials through scanning projects. To some extent, what is prioritized to scan mirrors what historical collections librarians now buy. Large digitizing projects such as Project Gutenberg (http://www.guten berg.org/), the California Digital Library (http://www.cdlib.org/), and Google Books (http://books.google.com/) have caused many librarians to rethink spending hundreds or thousands of dollars for published items that may be readily accessible in full text through one of these eBook aggregators, or might be in the near future. Still, printed monographs, pamphlets, and the like might warrant such a purchase if it is a unique fit within existing collection strengths, it is relatively scarce, or its topic or place of publication represents a regional fit within the collection's focus. Instead of purchasing previously published items, however, collection development in historical collections is increasingly directed toward one-of-a-kind materials such as journals, casebooks, diaries, and unpublished manuscripts. While such items are often quite expensive, their unique nature warrants both their expense and their acquisition.

These materials can become excellent candidates for scanning and loading into an institutional repository with digital management software like ContentDM (http://www.contentdm.org/). Historical materials that are prime candidates for digitization are items that showcase unique aspects or strengths of a collection. These could be regional or subject based. Important features of scanning projects include proper item selection, care of the physical items during the scanning process, and providing value-added virtual "packaging" of discrete collection groups. An example is the Florence Nightingale letters held at the Lister Hill Library of the Health Sciences at the University of Alabama at Birmingham (http://www.uab.edu/reynolds/exhibits/nightingale). "The Life and Letters of Florence Nightingale" provides much more than the letters themselves. Historical content giving context to the letters, plus an online exhibit, lecture, and other related items have been added. This value-added service provided through the time and expertise of the historical collections staff enhances the overall educational value of the items and, equally important, offers an opportunity for campus outreach and collaboration, in this case with the UAB School of Nursing. In effect, the Nightingale letters now have more educational value than simply a group of stand-alone scans. "Pellagra in Alabama" offered a similar opportunity to partner with the UAB School of Public Health (http://www.uab.edu/reynolds/exhibits/pellagra). Yet another example can be found at the Omohundro Institute of Early American History & Culture: "Exploring Therapeutic Resources in Colonial North America," featuring the manuscripts of George de Benneville and Abraham Wagner (http://oieahc.wm.edu/uncommon/123/therapeutic.cfm). Finally, scanning can be a good means of preservation for materials that might otherwise become compromised with repeated use or that are so extremely rare and valuable that use of the original copy is discouraged. If the original condition allows, the creation of a scanned surrogate copy not only protects the original from further damage, but enhances its research value through its increased searchability.

A couple of developments will round out the discussion of current trends and issues in historical collections. First is the relatively recent development of history-related mobile apps.[25, 26, 27] Of these, the most interesting is that produced by the National Library of Medicine, Turning the Pages (TTP), which is viewable in iPad and iTunes applications (for more information, visit http://www.nlm.nih.gov/news/app_turn_pages.html). The introduction of medical history–related apps is still very much a work in progress, but surely the next few years will see further development of this online utility with more varied and robust features. The second is the use of Facebook and Twitter accounts to help promote awareness of special collections and related activities. These popular social media can be helpful in raising awareness of collections and programming. They can be particularly good at creating "buzz" among constituent groups for highlights of a featured collection group or upcoming events. As useful as social media can be, however, it should not serve as a head count for historical collections effectiveness at providing services to the community it serves. Tabulating tweets and tallying likes and high Facebook activity should be used as a barometer of outreach with extreme caution. These hits do not reflect use of collections or effectiveness of programming. They are tools for increasing the public awareness of special collections, but they are not substitutes for traditional patron use and public programming initiatives.

CONCLUSION

Historical collections exist in the dynamic environment of change that all libraries are currently experiencing. Yet these collections themselves have deep roots in the past. In many cases, these collections—like the profession itself—emerged out of the historical interests of pioneers like John Shaw Billings, William Osler, Francis Packard, John F. Fulton, and Fielding H. Garrison. Their composition is as varied as the interests of those who founded them and the institutions that house them.

Ensuring the continued integrity of these rich emblems of our professional heritage necessitates practical considerations. From a collections management standpoint, it is critical to establish thorough written policies and procedures in terms of acquisition scope and focus and unambiguous material allocation processes. This, plus a structured process for managing patron access and services, is essential to the smooth operations of any special collections unit. Finally, with many historically significant volumes now available in electronic form, special collections librarians are increasingly changing their focus from the purchase of published titles to original holographic items such as journals, diaries, and manuscripts. As more and more titles become electronically available, this trend will likely continue. Of greatest importance for historical collections departments today is scanning selected portions or discrete segments of their collections and loading them into institutional repositories. Scanning projects offer new and unprecedented ways for special collections units to engage with the research community and collaborate with other departments and schools.

An important resource in establishing relevant programs and initiatives to promote historical collections is the white paper titled "Advocating for History of Health Sciences Libraries and Librarians," available at the Medical Library Association's History of the Health Sciences Section website (see the conclusion).[28] This useful document compiled by an ad hoc committee of the section includes information on the historical collection librarian's professional purpose, means of engaging the larger body of medical librarians, and practical advice on how the value of these collections and their managers' expertise can be demonstrated to faculty and students through special programs, friends groups, workshops, lectureships, newsletters, and classroom support.

Keeping up with the changing field of special collections librarianship is best achieved by networking with one's colleagues. Two organizations serve that purpose admirably: first, the Archivists and Librarians in the History of the Health Sciences meet once a year as a constituent society with the American Association for the History of Medicine (http://www.alhhs.org/); the other, mentioned earlier in this chapter, is the History of the Health Sciences Section of MLA (http://www.mla-hhss.org/). The section meets during the annual MLA conference.

Membership in the section is open to any member of MLA for a nominal fee. Both groups maintain an active listserv for members to facilitate ongoing discussions of interest to the profession.

NOTES

1. Miles, Wyndham D. National Library of Medicine. *A History of the National Library of Medicine: The Nation's Treasury of Medical Knowledge.* Bethesda, MD: U.S. Department of Health and Human Services, Public Health Service, National Institutes of Health, National Library of Medicine, 1982.

2. Ibid., 177.

3. Billings, John S., and Robert Fletcher. *Index Medicus.* New York: F. Leypoldt, 1879.

4. McClure, L. W. "A Tribute to Knowledge." *Bulletin of the Medical Library Association* 89, no. 1 (2001): 81–82.

5. Morton, Leslie T., and Jeremy M. Norman. *Morton's Medical Bibliography: An Annotated Check-List of Texts Illustrating the History of Medicine (Garrison and Morton).* Aldershot, Hants, England; Brookfield, VT: Scolar; Gower, 1991.

6. Connor, Jennifer. *Guardians of Medical Knowledge: The Genesis of the Medical Library Association.* Chicago; Lanham, MD: Medical Library Association; Scarecrow Press, 2000.

7. Ibid., 144–145.

8. Bliss, Michael. *William Osler: A Life in Medicine.* Oxford; New York: Oxford University Press, 1999.

9. Curran, M. "A Call for Increased Librarian Support for the Medical Humanities." *Journal of the Medical Library Association: JMLA* 100, no. 3 (2012): 153–155.

10. Christie's. *Vesalius, Andreas (1514–1564). De humani corporis fabrica libri septem. Basel: Johannes Oporinus, June 1543, Books & Manuscripts Auction, Books & Manuscripts, printed books, Christie's,* November 2011. Available from http://www.christies.com/lotfinder/books-manuscripts/vesalius-andreas-de-humani-corporis-fabrica-5495312-details.aspx.

11. Connor, *op. cit.*

12. Flannery, M. A. "Introduction: Librarians Recovering Our Professional Memory: Enriching the Past, Present, and Future." *Journal of the Medical Library Association: JMLA* 99, no. 1 (2011): 5–7.

13. Ludmerer, Kenneth M. *Time to Heal: American Medical Education from the Turn of the Century to the Era of Managed Care.* Oxford; New York: Oxford University Press, 1999.

14. American Hospital Association. "Redefining Hospital Capacity." *AHA Trend Watch* 3, no. 2 (2000). Available from http://www.aha.org/research/reports/tw/twsept2000.pdf.

15. Hoggan, Danielle Bodrero. "Challenges, Strategies, and Tools for Research Scientists: Using Web-Based Information Resources."*Electronic Journal of Academic and Special Librarianship* 3, no. 3 (2002).

16. Holst, R. "Introduction: Expert Searching." *Journal of the Medical Library Association: JMLA* 93, no. 1 (2005): 41.

17. Morrow, J. D., H. A. Schroeder, and H. M. Perry. "Studies on the Control of Hypertension by Hyphex. II. Toxic Reactions and Side Effects." *Circulation* 8, no. 6 (1953): 829–839.

18. Doniach, I., B. Morrison, and R. E. Steiner. "Lung Changes during Hexamethonium Therapy for Hypertension." *British Heart Journal* 16, no. 1 (1954): 101–108.

19. Perry, H. Mitchell, Robert M. O'Neal, and Wilbur A. Thomas. "Pulmonary Disease following Chronic Chemical Ganglionic Blockade." *American Journal of Medicine* 22, no. 1 (1957): 37–50.

20. Goodman, Louis S., and Alfred Gilman. *The Pharmacological Basis of Therapeutics: A Textbook of Pharmacology, Toxicology, and Therapeutics for Physicians and Medical Students.* New York: Macmillan, 1956.

21. Hoggan, *op.cit.*

22. Holst, *op. cit.*

23. Hoggan, *op. cit.*

24. National Library of Medicine. *History of Medicine Finding Aids Consortium.* Last modified 2013. http://www.nlm.nih.gov/hmd/consortium/index.html.

25. BiblioBoard. *History of Medicine.* Last modified 2013. http://www.biblioboard.com/curation/category/history-of-medicine/.

26. iTunes. *Turning The Pages (TTP) for iPad on the iTunes App.* Last modified 2013. https:/itunes.apple.com/us/app/turning-the-pages-ttp/id423830194?mt=8.

27. Top Mobile Apps. *History of Medicine Study Guide.* Last modified 2013. http://www.topmobileapps.com/application/history-medicine-study-guide.

28. Flannery, M. A., E. Holtum, S. Porter, and L. W. McClure. "Advocating for History of the Health Sciences Libraries and Librarians: A Position Paper by the History of the Health Sciences Section, Medical Library Association." *Journal of the Medical Library Association: JMLA* 98, no. 1 (2010): 9–11.

Chapter 11

INTERPERSONAL SKILLS TO THE FORE: CONSUMER HEALTH LIBRARIANSHIP

Mary L. Gillaspy

Petite, erect, elegant, yet hesitant, the elderly woman walked in to the library. She stood uncertainly just inside the door, looking around. A volunteer went to her to ascertain her need.

The woman held up a sheaf of papers and tearfully said, "I don't know what to do!"

The volunteer invited her in, directed her to a comfortable seating area, and called a librarian. The librarian determined that the woman had been referred to the library by her physician, who had printed orders for a sleep study. The woman had no idea what that meant, could not remember what the doctor had told her, and said only that the nurse explained that she could find help in the library.

This brief vignette isa true story (all scenarios/vignettes included in this chapter are drawn from actual experiences with patients and the author or her colleagues. Minor details have been changed to protect the privacy of the individuals involved). It represents a fairly typical event in a large consumer health library located in a big-city teaching hospital. Up to this point, everything happened just the way it should have: The patient received basic information in the busy medical practice and was referred to the library, where trained staff had the time to sit with the patient, reassure her, and direct her appropriately to next steps. Once she arrived at the library, she was met at the door by a trained volunteer, who assessed her state of mind; accompanied her to a comfortable, semiprivate sitting area; and bumped the request up to a librarian. What happened next?

The librarian established rapport with the patient, M, who by this time was identified as suffering some level of dementia. Once the patient was comfortable with the situation, the librarian filled out the sleep study forms as the patient answered the questions. (She stated that she was no longer able to write.) The librarian encouraged the patient to seek assistance from a family member or friend to accompany her to medical appointments, but the patient indicated that she was unwilling to do this, since she liked to handle these things for herself.

The librarian signaled service desk staff to place a page to a social worker in the cognitive neurology clinic; the social worker quickly called back, indicated that the woman was a patient in that clinic, and said that she would call her daughter. The daughter arranged for her mother to be picked up and transported to her home. A volunteer accompanied the patient to the arrival court to meet her ride. The librarian called the nurse manager of the sleep study clinic, informed her of the referral, and faxed her a copy of the completed forms. The sleep study was completed the next week, with extra staff on hand to handle the special needs of this elderly patient.

The outcomes of this patient interaction, coordinated through the library, were positive.

- The patient was supported and reassured throughout the process.
- The physician received the information needed to see to the medical needs of the patient.
- The staff of the sleep study clinic had a heads-up from their manager about the extra care this patient required and were able to plan ahead to deliver it.
- The cognitive neurology social worker was alerted to deterioration in the patient's mental acuity and reported it to the neurologist, and that team increased the care they were providing to the patient and family, which included recommendations for increased supervision.
- The hospital and the associated outpatient services received expressions of gratitude from both the patient and her family, increasing satisfaction with the care provided to the family.
- The library's importance to the larger goals of the organization was reinforced at both operational and executive levels, since the daughter wrote a letter of thanks to the chief executive officer (CEO) of the hospital.

As a side note, this patient in her youth had lived in the Soviet Union, where she danced in the corps de ballet of the Bolshoi. She and her husband, also a dancer, had defected to the West during the 1970s and made a life for themselves and their children in the United States.

This illustration highlights a few of the joys and complexities of providing consumer health information in a clinical setting. This chapter will introduce you to some of the basics of this type of health sciences librarianship, methodologies for delivery of the information, specifics about how to build a program, and some personal and professional attributes required for success in a consumer health setting.

WHAT, WHERE, WHY?

Definitions

All areas of librarianship require intellect and skill, consumer health librarianship (CHL) more than many others. In some ways, CHL resembles aspects of public librarianship. Depending on the setting of the service, the library can host everyone from elite individuals, to homeless people, to patients with mental disabilities, and everything in between. Most who make their way to the library will be seeking health information because they have received, or fear they will receive, troubling news. Some will be seeking information for a family member, neighbor, or friend. Others will be seeking information so that they can make an informed decision about treatment. Some may have tried looking for information themselves on the Internet and have questions about what they have found. Still others may come because they are interested in health and appreciate being able to peruse current information sources like newsletters, medical textbooks, or medical dictionaries. Assessing information need, the level at which the client can best process the information, and the best format for the client to receive the information are all basic skills of any reference librarian. The difference in a CHL setting is that the topic of the request will be health related.

In the 1990s, a prescient medical librarian named Alan Rees observed the need for librarians to be involved in patient education and consumer health, and he worked closely with Joanne Gard Marshall, who in the 1980s spearheaded the opening of a consumer health library service at the Toronto Reference Library, part of the public library system in that city. Other early programs were those in Planetree clinics, the CHIPS project in Los Angeles, and learning centers at comprehensive cancer centers. An overview of the consumer health information movement from 1900 to 2010 in the United States can be found in my and Dr. Jeff Huber's article entitled "Knowledge /Power Transforming the Social Landscape: The Case of the Consumer Health Information Movement."[1] The explosion of information available via the World Wide Web in the mid-1990s excited librarians, but they were also well aware of the pitfalls. As part of the Consumer and Patient Health Information (CAPHIS) section of the Medical Library Association (MLA), Rees chaired a task force that developed a statement defining and distinguishing the librarian role in patient education and consumer health. The definitions that the task force devised and published in 1996 remain relevant today:

> Consumer health information (CHI) is information on health and medical topics provided in response to requests from the general public, including patients and their families. In addition to information on the symptoms, diagnosis and treatment of disease, CHI encompasses information on health promotion, preventive medicine, the determinants of health and accessing the healthcare system.
>
> Patient education is a planned activity, initiated by a health professional, whose aim is to impart knowledge, attitudes and skills with the specific goal of changing behavior, increasing compliance with therapy and, thereby, improving health.

CHI and patient education overlap in practice, since patient behavior may change as a result of receiving health information materials. Patient education and CHI often differ in terms of the setting in which the process occurs, rather than in terms of the subject matter.[2]

The task force identified librarian roles as falling under six broad categories: collection management, knowledge and resource sharing, advocacy, access and dissemination of information, education, and research. The entire statement is useful to include in a "key documents" section of a consumer health library's policies and procedures.

As the consumer health information revolution matured through the early years of the twenty-first century, health literacy was identified as a vital but often missing component in consumer health library programs. The reality of low literacy among U.S. adults generally had been a growing concern for several decades. In 2004, the Institute of Medicine published the seminal report *Health Literacy: A Prescription to End Confusion,* in which it defined health literacy as "the degree to which individuals have the capacity to obtain, process, and understand basic health information and services needed to make appropriate health decisions."[3] Such a definition expanded the traditional meaning of literacy—the ability to read words and sentences at a specific grade level—to include more complex skills, including analysis, synthesis, and evaluation. Studies indicated, however, that significant numbers of adults could not even read and follow directions on bottles of prescribed medication,[4] much less comprehend written material or even verbal explanation of disease processes such as common arrhythmias, cancers, or respiratory ailments.[5] Ultimately, the American Medical Association determined that "poor health literacy is a stronger predictor of a person's health than age, income, employment status, education level, [or] race."[6]

The Medical Library Association began an initiative focused on health literacy in the early 2000s. In a document written by Penny Glassman, MLA noted that the demands of increasing health literacy among the American public could be partly met by expanding the role of consumer health librarians. Glassman observed that "consumer health initiatives are geared towards technological access to health information or rewriting existing health materials at a simpler language level" and that both "are important, but limited. Easy-to-read materials and access to technology are only pieces of a process that must be placed in a larger community context."[7] Glassman wrote that consumer health librarians should engage in outreach to community constituencies, including public schools and libraries, organizations providing literacy training, senior citizen centers, and others. She also recommended that consumer health librarians become part of research projects around health literacy and generally advocate for all health consumers, including in their collections and in their culturally appropriate, multilingual programming. Finally, CHLs were charged with teaching consumers how to evaluate health materials, especially those gleaned from the Internet.

The definition and role of consumer health libraries and librarians continues to evolve, even as all libraries and librarians are finding new ways to be relevant and of service in a rapidly changing world.

Venues

Consumer health information (CHI) is provided in both formal and informal settings. Informal settings include person-to-person contact, support groups, online moderated discussion lists, chat rooms, and similar venues. Discussion in this chapter is limited to formal, in-person situations, particularly those that occur in a hospital, a public library, a health organization library that serves the public, or an academic health sciences library that provides a special area and collection for members of the public. Libraries in community-based organizations, clinics, or storefronts may also be considered formal situations and can benefit from the presence or regular input of a consumer health librarian.

Are there advantages to one venue over another, in terms of (1) customer service; (2) stable, long-term funding; or (3) career advantages to librarians? The answer to all three questions is positive. At its core, librarianship remains a profession that requires excellent interpersonal skills from its practitioners. No matter the customer base, the highest level of service must be provided if the library is to be successful. In terms of consumer health, excellent customer service demands not only knowledgeable, friendly staff, but also easy accessibility. Ease of access to the physical space is paramount to sustainability.

Stable funding sources are another key to sustainability. Organizations change over time, so securing as much funding as possible in the beginning is vital. Something like a three-year grant can provide seed money to establish a service, but before such a proposal is even written, leaders must think ahead to the years beyond that funding. Where will the budget come from? This is a place where venue really makes a difference. A large academic medical center, teaching hospital, or even health organization is more likely to have the resources to sustain funding over time than a small community-based organization, for example.

In a time when more and more people feel competent accessing health information online, own personal computers or mobile devices, and have their own networks for gathering information, the question of whether consumer health librarianship is a viable career option is important to consider. For any aspiring medical librarian, knowledge of consumer health and patient education librarianship is useful, since especially if the library is open to the public, questions are likely to arise. For example, many academic health sciences libraries that are attached to private institutions are open only to their faculty and students. State-supported medical schools, however, since they are tax-supported, are required to allow public access. As a result, many of these institutions set aside a space designed specifically for laypeople, with a librarian dedicated to serving that population or reference and education staff rotating through for coverage.

Both the location and type of venue that is seeking a CHL, as well as the career aspirations of the individual, must be taken into account. Some librarians prefer public library settings, while others go the special library, hospital, or academic route. Most positions can be shaped by employees to career advantage, but the right "fit" matters. Librarians just beginning their careers are well advised to build in as much of an experimental period as possible, one that recognizes some moving around may be necessary to find the match that is best for both the individual and the organization. For those who like working with people, would like to experience a clinical setting, and want to make a difference in patient care, CHL is an excellent choice if a position is available.

Importance of Consumer Health Librarianship

But is it important? All one need do is query a person of any age who has survived a serious illness or trauma. If the individual is an information seeker, and a health library service is available, he or she will certainly use it and benefit greatly from interaction with a librarian. The reality is that information on the Internet appears to be moving toward a fee-based model, though at the time of this writing, that question is still unsettled. A great deal of very good information for certain diagnoses—such as Alzheimer disease, diabetes, and cancer—is available for free, if people know how to find it. What if the customer wants to go more deeply into a topic, however? What if he has a rare disorder or even a so-called orphan disease? What if her case is complicated by comorbidities, such as lupus, Parkinson disease, or meningioma? Searching for information in these sorts of situations requires more than typing a couple of key words into Google as well as some direction as to where to go next, what questions to ask the doctors, and so forth. Another important consideration is that *age is not a factor in need for information*. What matters is the severity of the condition, from the patient's perspective, and whether the person deals with crises by seeking information. Consider the following scenario:

> A 35-year-old male survivor of two primary cancers (Stage III melanoma at age 14 and non-Hodgkin lymphoma [NHL] at age 31) approached a librarian in the grocery store.
> "You're that lady from the public library, right?"
> "Yes, I am. Did you need some help?"
> With tears welling up, he replied, "Yeah, I guess so."
> The librarian made an appointment to see N privately later that day at the library. Through conversation, the young man expressed a willingness to seek help for "getting my life back on track," but with no job, no insurance, and no money beyond what he used to meet his basic needs, he had no idea where to turn.
> The librarian provided him with the name and contact information for a local agency that offers services to people with few resources as well as a private psychotherapist who sees people on a very generous sliding scale. The librarian inquired about family support, friends, sleep patterns, and eating habits. She printed an information sheet from MedlinePlus about male depression and another one regarding simple ways to address insomnia, such as retiring at the same time every night, establishing a bedtime routine, and so forth.
> The young man left the library armed with less information than he might ultimately need but the correct amount for him to digest and act on at the time. It is now up to him to take action that will help him move forward with his life.

Could this young man have received information elsewhere? Yes, of course he could have, but after just emerging from three years of treatment for his cancer, his thinking was disorganized. He really had no idea of where to begin to seek help; all he knew was that he was miserable, greatly feared a recurrence of NHL or the emergence of another primary cancer, and wanted to move forward by finding employment and rebuilding a social life. A dedicated consumer health librarian in a public library provided him a lifeline.

Sometimes intervention by a consumer health librarian can make a significant difference in outcome. For example, one reaction that patients sometimes exhibit to a serious diagnosis is anger. If the anger is directed inward, depression may result; if it is directed outward, almost anyone involved with the patient can feel its effects. Hospital librarians who serve patients and the public can expect to experience this anger periodically. With the proper resources, however, the anger can sometimes be redirected, as in the following scenario.

> There was no mistaking V's arrival in the library. She made sure to slam the door, rudely shrug off a volunteer greeter, and loudly demand to "see somebody in charge." The library manager was immediately summoned.
>
> She took V to a private room and closed the door. She permitted some venting and then began asking questions to ascertain the situation. Gradually she learned that V had just received a diagnosis of Stage IIb breast cancer. V protested the unfairness of such an event, since she was living with relatives; her husband was in prison; and her son, a resident of a state in another part of the country, was fighting leukemia. Agreeing that the situation was indeed unfair, the librarian encouraged V to speak with someone from supportive oncology. V refused to go back to "that cancer place." She had not seen anyone else there of her ethnicity and was convinced that she had to be the only African American woman to have this disease that "they say I have."
>
> Fortunately, the library's collection contained an important work for people like V. The librarian retrieved *Celebrating Life*,[8] handed it to V, and suggested that she begin looking through it. For the first time since entering the library, V calmed down a bit. *Celebrating Life* contains photographs on almost every page, photographs of women who looked like V. V hugged the book, looked at the librarian, and burst into tears. She had a long road still to travel, but this moment marked the beginning of acceptance.

On that very day, V went back to the cancer center, arranged for her series of appointments, and kept them faithfully. She emerged successfully from treatment, an outcome that was partly possible because of the library and its collection.

Is CHL important in this time of floods of information? Does it make a difference in the lives of patients and to their disease outcomes? Professionally delivered and institutionally supported, consumer health librarianship is vitally important to the delivery of healthcare. The best advocates can be physicians, nurses, and ancillary care providers who see the impact of library services on patients from a different perspective. Forward thinking hospitals, public libraries, and other venues will find ways to provide such services, if only on a part-time basis. The results speak for themselves.

HOW?

Online or Face to Face?

If you are using this book as part of a graduate class, you may be taking your class online. If you still subscribe to a paper newspaper, you almost certainly occasionally read it online and perhaps also through a tablet or smart phone. You may occasionally communicate with your physician via email, and you may sign in to a patient portal to view the results of medical tests. You likely use at least one form of social media, and you may not only follow certain blogs, but may host one yourself. As Gordon Pask predicted long ago, digital technologies have become extensions of us.[9]

Librarians seized new technologies almost as soon as they became available. So did patients. During the AIDS crisis in the 1980s, activists in New York City, San Francisco, and Los Angeles developed bulletin board systems, or BBSs, to communicate anonymously. In the early 1990s, faculty at the University of Wisconsin–Madison and Indiana University–Bloomington developed a computer-based information system designed to deliver health education and information, allow for anonymous interaction among users, and decrease risky behaviors and adverse outcomes. The system was devised as a "shell" that would allow for the development of future content, what today would be called modules. The researchers developed programs in five topic areas: academic crisis, adult children of alcoholics, HIV/AIDS, breast cancer, and sexual assault. The system was developed prior to the general release of the World Wide Web and the first web browser, Mosaic, and the researchers noted:

> Information required to make many decisions regarding medical issues is often inaccessible. Local libraries seldom have current or in-depth medical information. Medical libraries usually have the information but don't encourage public use. Geographic distance and limited hours often create additional barriers. A computer system, available in the home or in public sites such as libraries, community centers and clinics could provide a single convenient source for in-depth, accurate, up-to-date information.[10]

The system has evolved, has embraced advances in technology, and is still providing support for patients; publications of studies using the system appear regularly every two to three years, and sometimes more often. The success of the Comprehensive Health Enhancement Support System (CHESS), multiple channels of online information support for patients with HIV/AIDS, and increasing levels of comfort with and access to the Internet spawned additional resources. The Association of Cancer Online Resources (ACOR) evolved from a portal site for discussion lists to a "unique collection of online cancer communities designed to provide timely and accurate information in a supportive environment."[11] Hundreds of other such resources, making use of social media like Facebook, exist, and for general reference questions, many public and academic libraries offer "chat reference."

At least for now, there is room and need for both face-to-face consumer health library services as well as digital ones. Personal preference determines which method clients choose, with consumer choice being the arbiter of service delivery. N, for example, did not seek information about his diagnosis beyond what was provided in the cancer clinic where he received his treatment. What he needed was help with issues of survivorship, a growing area of cancer care as many patients live longer beyond their diagnosis than was once the case. V would probably have recovered from her initial shock and realized that breast cancer is not uncommon, especially in African American women, but without the library, she would not have found the book that provided her comfort and strength throughout her treatment and recovery. M could not even fill out forms for the sleep clinic, much less use a computer. All of these instances illustrate the importance of a mixture of technological and personal approaches. Discovering the best mix of the two and monitoring closely for adjustment as needed is part of the job of a consumer health librarian. The combination will provide the greatest good for the greatest number of patients, caregivers, and families.

The Embedded Librarian

One answer to funding challenges faced by libraries everywhere is to embed consumer health and patient education librarians into healthcare teams that are either clinic based, community based or public library based. In a clinic, the librarian would be focused on delivering patient education, either with a nurse or medical assistant or alone, depending on the topic and physician direction. Clinical medical librarians (CMLs) are well established in several academic and research centers; typically, however, they support the work of a physician or research team, not patients or families.

How might this work? Here is an example from an electrophysiology (EP) department in a large academic medical center. *Electrophysiology* is a subspecialty within cardiology that tests for, diagnoses, and treats diseases and conditions that affect the electrical system of the heart. The electrical impulses inside the heart regulate heart rhythm. If the heart beats too slowly, too quickly, or irregularly, the patient is said to have an *arrhythmia,* such as atrial fibrillation, the most common of these afflictions. If a cardiologist detects a heart rhythm problem, he or she refers the patient to an electrophysiologist, who will conduct an EPS (electrophysiologic study). An EPS is an invasive procedure that requires the insertion of electrodes into the heart through either the groin or the neck. As such, it requires informed consent and significant patient education.

At the medical center in this example, electrophysiologists worked with the Patient Education Department to develop a video designed to provide the information necessary for informed consent. The librarian spent three days in the EP lab, observing EPSs, radiofrequency ablation (elimination of the heart tissue causing the abnormal rhythm), and insertion of pacemakers and ICDs (implantable cardioverter defibrillators). The librarian was supplied with spare pacemakers and ICDs so that patients who were about to undergo such a procedure could touch and hold the devices.

Electrophysiologists met with patients and explained the procedure. Then they referred the patient to the embedded librarian. He showed the video, answered questions, explained the meaning of informed consent, secured necessary signatures, reviewed relevant patient education materials, and provided contact information should the patient have further questions. He then wrote up the interaction in the electronic medical record, noting any questions the patient asked and any reservations he or she expressed and thus closing the loop on the preprocedure process. Such a program saved physician and nurse time, allowed for greater personal interaction with the patient, and gave the patient an additional touch point, theoretically increasing satisfaction and lessening anxiety. Similar programs were developed for patients with newly diagnosed type two diabetes mellitus, patients with newly diagnosed adult asthma, and patients interested in developing advance directives. In cases like these, the librarian is specially trained and functions as a part of the health-care team.

A more traditional librarian role can be fulfilled by a consumer health librarian who is part of a public library reference staff. Outside of larger city or metropolitan area, it is probably not cost effective to have a staff member who handles only health questions. However, one person on staff can fulfill a "specialist" role in answering health questions, which studies have shown constitute a large percentage of queries in public libraries. Across the United States, such embedded librarians have formed networks and meet regularly to exchange information. As with online and face-to-face service delivery, it may be that a combination of separate libraries, embedded librarians, and other configurations may best meet the needs of the customers.

BUILDING A PROGRAM

Fortunate is the librarian who has the opportunity to build a consumer health library (or any other type) from its inception. Such opportunities do arise. This section of the chapter will provide an outline of how one might proceed. Every library is different—because every organization has its own unique culture, ethos, demands, and expectations—but some basic principles are true across all cases. Following are first steps:

- Request a copy of the needs assessment report. If such an assessment has not been conducted, determine the feasibility of completing one now *or* determine how the need for a consumer health library was revealed.

- If it has not already been done, articulate the mission and vision of the library, ensuring that both align with institutional priorities. This is an opportunity to develop a few key statements that encapsulate the librarian's philosophy and vision, and define the environment of the library, that is, the "feel" every visitor will experience upon walking into the space.

- Identify key individuals, departments, and divisions within the organization. With the person to whom the library reports, visit these people, explaining the mission and vision, and seeking their input and support. Then stay in touch.

- Identify how the collection will be catalogued, who will be responsible for this task, and how users will gain access.

- Begin developing an outline for a website, preferably one that is part of the larger institutional site.

- Define the scope of the collection and the scope of the service during its first full year of operation. In a hospital, request a report of the top diagnosis-related groups

(DRGs) for inpatient admissions over the past three to five years. If a single disease is the focus of the service (e.g., cancer, heart disease, or physical medicine and rehabilitation), scope will still be an important consideration. Will health professional materials be included? What about resources for family members and caregivers? Will the focus be only on the treatment journey for the condition, or will survivorship issues be included as well? What about risk reduction materials? Will resources for children be included?

- Determine the formats in which materials will be collected. Will there be overlap, that is, if a resource is available online, will it be available in print as well?

- Develop a technology plan that includes provision for growth. With proper planning for space, furnishings, and electrical and network outlets, it is possible to expand to meet demand over at least 20 years. Representatives from the institution's information technology department should be integral to this effort.

- Write basic policies and procedures, such as ones for collection development, circulation (yes or no?) and access, telephone use, and others deemed essential for opening day. Include a relevant documents section, which should include, at a minimum, the CAPHIS statement, the code of ethics for medical librarians, and any essential documents from the institution. Include also a statement of philosophy that will serve as a touchstone for continuity, regardless of changes in personnel.

- Work with institutional partners to develop a marketing plan.

- Identify quantitative and qualitative measures for formative evaluation of operations, develop forms for keeping the data, and determine to whom data will be reported.

All this sounds like a great deal of effort, in addition to everything else that must be done, and it is, but having these pieces in place will ensure a smooth opening and provide a strong foundation for growth and support.

Collections

Whether starting a new service or coming to work in an established one, librarians realize that collections form the core of any library. One of the most difficult questions faced today is how much (if any) print to collect. The brief remarks that follow assume that multiple formats are available, including books and other resources placed on eReaders and checked out like any other material to patrons.

If budget is available, it is helpful to both staff and visitors to have a current edition of a core medical textbook for each body system in the collection. For example, every health or medical library, as well as public libraries, should hold *Harrison's Principles of Internal Medicine* and *Goldman's Cecil Medicine.* Consult *Doody's Core Titles* for a general surgery textbook and include one or more atlases of anatomy and a physiology textbook. These books provide detail and depth not available through booklets and leaflets written for laypeople, and they will be used extensively. A medical dictionary is also an essential purchase. For excellent medical encyclopedias written in nontechnical language, consider the Gale Encyclopedias. *Primer on the Rheumatic Diseases* covers a host of afflictions for which consumers search for information. Another essential purchase is *Fitzpatrick's Color Atlas & Synopsis of Clinical Dermatology: Common & Serious Diseases.*

A category of book, print or electronic, that might be overlooked is that of the patient narrative. Because of the quantity of works published in this genre over the last 20 years, one must be highly selective. A carefully curated collection, however, can bring great comfort and insight to individuals facing serious illness, loss, or a completely changed life as the result of trauma. Works such as *The Noonday Demon, A Life Shaken, Borrowed Time,* and *Elegy for Iris* are classic works forming part of the canon of this literary genre. Older classics such as *The Diving Bell and the Butterfly* or, from the nineteenth century, *In the Land of Pain,* are other examples that can be considered for inclusion.

Some fiction can be part of this collection as well. Works such as *The Curious Incident of the Dog in the Night-Time* and *The Diagnosis* are two relatively recent examples of works of fiction that address medical concerns. They are two among hundreds that have been published over several hundred years. (Think *Journal of the Plague Year* by Daniel Defoe.) Other resources can be added as needed. For a full discussion of resources, especially reference sources, consult *Introduction to Reference Sources in the Health Sciences.*[12] Searching the online catalogues of other libraries will reveal gems as well.

A Word about Personnel

In a clinical setting, or even in a freestanding space that is dedicated solely to consumer health information services, the operation will be greatly enhanced by the employment of an interdisciplinary staff. Much depends on the scope of service and definitely on the venue, but for the consumer health equivalent of continuity of care, having a dedicated team of differently trained professionals will meet many more information needs than most librarians can manage alone. This model is much easier to implement in a hospital or large clinic than in the community, but through networking and collaboration, professionals like these can be on call for the librarian and staff. This approach to scope, service, and staffing will not work everywhere, but if a librarian is engaged in planning a new program, the option should be considered. Here are some examples:

- *Health educators* bring an additional layer of richness and expertise because of their skill and knowledge of educational methods and approaches, coupled with their understanding of anatomy, disease processes, wellness, and risk reduction for common conditions. They can plan public programs, work one-on-one with patients referred from physician offices, and assist with outreach to the community.
- *Social workers* know about networks of services within a community and how to gain access to them. They can provide limited counseling in a library setting and assist with both outreach and public programs. Sometimes, social workers can be hired by an outside agency, like the American Cancer Society, the March of Dimes, or a similar group, and be contracted to provide some of their direct care service in the library, where a built-in clientele will await them. Social workers are independent practitioners who can provide a large array of services to both individuals and families, depending on the need.

- *Dietitians* are essential to helping laypeople lead healthier lives, ones that are focused on risk reduction for heart diseases, stroke, osteoporosis, and some cancers. Cooking demonstrations form part of the programming for some of the top consumer health libraries in the United States, and one of these programs is even led by a registered dietitian who directs a multidisciplinary staff.

- *Registered nurses* bring clinical skills that none of the other players possess. If consumer health libraries partner with a hospital or clinic to provide screenings, nurses can be brought in for blood pressure readings, blood draws for cholesterol or blood glucose analysis, and so forth. They can also be responsible for the follow-up and referral for individuals that have abnormal test results.

- *Pharmacists* also provide invaluable expertise in terms of identifying the potential for drug interactions and other vital issues concerning medication. Just as a library can probably not hire a nurse or social worker, it can also not hire a pharmacist, but collaborating with one can add richness to community classes, some individual services, and annual events like a health fair or an "Ask the Pharmacist" day. An example of the use of a pharmacist collaborating with a hospital-based library is space being provided in the library for immunization of adults taking a new baby home. This collaboration occurred in a large Midwestern birthing center, a joint offering of a national pharmacy chain and the library.

- In a hospital setting, a close collaboration between the library and chaplaincy is essential. *Hospital chaplains* are not necessarily ordained clergy, though they may be. They are specially trained, however, to attend to the needs of patients, families, and staff. They usually form part of the ethics committee at hospitals and play an important role in providing spiritual guidance to all involved in day-to-day hospital operations.

- *Volunteers* are ubiquitous in consumer health libraries. When properly trained, they are true "librarian extenders" and can gain great satisfaction from spending their time in such a setting. In a well-run volunteer program, applicants are interviewed and "hired"—or not—just the same as a paid employee would be. There should be a formal job description. Newly "hired" volunteers participate in both institutional and departmental orientation; ideally, for the first one to three months, they are paired with a partner, a senior volunteer, who can help them feel comfortable and competent to do the work. A program like this, while time intensive to establish, will ensure years of smooth operation and great satisfaction on the part of both staff and volunteers.

EXAMPLES OF EXEMPLARY CONSUMER HEALTH LIBRARIES IN THE UNITED STATES

Lists of the "best" of anything are necessarily subjective. Certainly not all outstanding examples can be included here, but the ones highlighted represent a sampling of both excellence and longevity.

A few institutions and organizations established consumer health libraries early on, some in the 1980s, and have evolved with the times so that they now serve all sorts of clients who have health concerns. At least one of these institutions even provides veterinary information for visitors concerned about their pets. Two large organizations, both founded in California, led the way toward a different kind of healthcare delivery, one that included providing patients with information. One is Planetree,[13] and the other is Kaiser Permanente.[14] Planetree facilities are now scattered throughout the United States and several other countries. Two venerable Planetree libraries are the Planetree Health Resource Center[15] in The Dalles, Oregon, and the Planetree Health Library[16] in Los Gatos, California.

All comprehensive cancer centers have "patient learning centers," or some variant of this name. The Learning Center at the University of Texas M.D. Anderson Cancer Center[17] in Houston is one such library, as is the Cancer Learning Center[18] at the University of Utah's Huntsman Cancer Institute. The Patient Family Education Resource Center (PERC) at the University of Michigan Comprehensive Cancer Center is another noted library for persons interested in cancer information.[19] The Cardiovascular Center at the same institution offers the Mardigian Wellness Resource Center to "patients, families and the general public [so that they can] make informed decisions about their health and communicate effectively with clinicians."[20]

The Stanford Health Library[21] is in a class by itself. With five sites located throughout the Stanford campus and Palo Alto, California, the librarians, educators, and volunteers who staff these centers serve a wide variety of health information needs. More than most other centers, the Stanford Health Library has kept abreast of technology changes. Besides the services they offer in person, resources like EBSCO eBooks, the Gale Resource Center, Gale eBooks, and many more are available to anyone with an Internet connection. Moreover, even if interested users are not in Palo Alto to participate, it is possible to subscribe to a newsletter called "Notes from the Doc Talks," wherein the contents of lectures are summarized.

What about pediatric hospitals and pediatric services? These institutions understandably focus on creating a family-centered environment. Since the very sick children who are cared for in these hospitals will generally transition to care at home, most children's hospitals provide skills labs for parents. This is especially true for the most vulnerable population of all, infants in the neonatal intensive care units (NICUs). The Children's Hospital of Philadelphia (CHOP) has a well-known program, the Connelly Resource Center for Families,[22] where parents can acquire information, support, and skills to care effectively for their child.

Another specialty institution with a long-standing commitment to health information and education is National Jewish Health, located in Denver, Colorado. Founded originally to help patients with respiratory diseases, National Jewish Health still treats these conditions as well as cardiac, immune, and related disorders. Their section of Library & Knowledge Services devotes space and personnel to resources for consumer health information.[23]

Community hospitals often do not have the resources to establish and support a consumer health library, but with the right leadership, and in the right place, such a community resource can arise and thrive. This is the case with an exceptional program among community hospitals for these libraries, the Community Health Education Center (CHEC)[24] in Salem, Oregon. Salem Health, a two-hospital health system based in the Willamette Valley, serves a broad swath of mainly small-town and rural residents, yet it operates the busiest emergency department in the state. Its combination of a librarian, a library assistant, nurses, and health educators provides services that contribute to the improved health of the people in their community, the primary goal for any consumer health information library anywhere. To locate libraries throughout the United States that provide consumer health information, a good starting point is the "Find a Library" page on MedlinePlus : (http://www.nlm.nih.gov/medlineplus/libraries.html). One can also call the National Network of Libraries of Medicine (800.338.7657) to receive a referral.

IS CONSUMER HEALTH LIBRARIANSHIP RIGHT FOR ME?

As should be clear by now, a position in consumer health librarianship requires high levels of interpersonal and collaborative skill. It may demand a more hands-on, intense engagement with patients and families than some librarians are comfortable with. Moreover, fewer job openings are likely to be available than for public, school, or academic librarianship. CHL is a niche market.

So, why even consider it? Why bother? One good reason to develop a skill set in CHL is that this type of service can be built into other positions. Not everyone is interested in or knows the field, so if health information service to patients, families, and consumers becomes a new priority in a workplace, it may be possible for a staff librarian with the skill set to fill that gap. Because it is so specialized, CHL is a bit like holding the knowledge base of a bioinformatics librarian. Not every medical librarian has that desire or expertise. For individuals coming to health sciences librarianship as a second or third career, especially from nursing, education, or a similar field, the fit with CHL is often a natural one. If you are thinking about developing a concentration or skill set in CHL, ask yourself the following questions:

- Are you comfortable dealing with people who are frequently worried, distracted, stressed out, or confused about which way to turn? Can you help them with information without getting too close to the situation?
- Do you enjoy networking, constructing coalitions, and reaching across boundaries to create new programs and services?
- Do you have knowledge of, or are you willing to learn, the basic principles of adult education?
- Are you comfortable working in a position that in the beginning may be funded with "soft" money?
- Are you passionate about creating warm, welcoming environments where the focus is on health improvement, risk reduction for lifestyle diseases, and quality of life?

Careful consideration of these points and others will help you hone your approach to your job search. As you apply and interview for positions, a mantra to remember is: "The jobs people love are made, not found." Shane J. Lopez, a scientist for the Gallup organization, wrote the following about his research: "By studying people who love their work, I came to realize that almost none initially landed the jobs they loved; rather, they landed ordinary jobs and turned them into extraordinary ones."[25]

If the subject matter and possibilities of consumer health librarianship excite you and make you want to seek a position in this field, remember that you may have an opportunity to do this even in a position that at first seems out of scope. The patients, families, and healthcare consumers of the world need dedicated, caring librarians to help them navigate the maze of biomedicine. With personalized medicine coming increasingly to the fore, specialists who can assist with navigation through new vocabularies, tests, and procedures will be essential. One can achieve a position as a consumer health librarian in many ways, including creating a niche for oneself within a public, school, special, hospital, or other library organization. For people who want more than anything else to bring laypeople together with health information they need, no other area of health sciences librarianship offers the opportunity to achieve this goal as directly and effectively as CHL.

FUTURE OF CONSUMER HEALTH LIBRARIANSHIP

In a time of wholesale budget slashing and great uncertainty in healthcare, the idea of expending scarce resources on a consumer health library strikes some decision makers as unnecessary. Others will opt to provide solely an online experience, as some institutions have done to good effect. Yet many of the most prestigious medical organizations in the United States, like Stanford, M.D. Anderson, and others, continue to fund a "clicks and bricks" approach to the provision of consumer health information. More often than not, the decision to establish or continue a consumer health library comes down not to money, but to a champion. If an individual or group of individuals who believe passionately in the library can be part of the decision making, then a positive outcome is likely.

The librarian must do his or her part as well, however. Fundamental to success is consistently and clearly reporting meaningful statistics to the appropriate audiences. Establishing and maintaining a warm, welcoming environment filled with highly trained, competent staff is another fundamental. Networking throughout the organization, participating in outreach efforts to strategic partners, and ensuring library representation on key committees and work groups will demonstrate commitment to the organization and its mission, as well as the way the library can enhance both.

Absent from a champion or a culture in which the library is firmly embedded, a new medical librarian who wants to work in consumer health could do well to develop that as a specialty within the reference department of a public library. Hospital librarians who have traditionally served only medical and nursing staff can lay the groundwork for reaching out to patients and families to let them know that information assistance and some resources are available. Some medical librarians who are very interested in delivering information to laypeople move into entirely nontraditional positions with healthcare or patient education service companies. Or, within hospitals, they work within marketing departments, adding content to or developing web pages; contribute to quality efforts; or make a difference within the patient safety realm. An example of a library initiative for enhancing patient safety is the PPECA Project, Empowering Public Health/Patient Safety Outreach through Community Partnerships (http://hosted.lib.uiowa.edu/ppeca/index.htm). Some librarians act as independent contractors, as is the case with the person at the head of Zipperer Project Management (http://www.zpm1.com/).

In librarianship as in every other field, today's workplace demands expertise, flexibility, adaptability, and continuous learning. Consumer health librarianship rewards its practitioners in countless ways, large and small. The general skills of librarianship applied to this niche field offer the means to improve access and understanding while easing the burden of caregiving, disease, or uncertainty that characterizes the lives of so large a part of our population.

NOTES

1. Huber, Jeffrey T. and Mary L. Gillaspy. "Knowledge/Power Transforming the Social Landscape: The Case of the Consumer Health Information Movement." *Library Quarterly* 81, no. 4 (Fall 2011): 405–430.

2. Rees, A., J. Marshall, M. Bandy, K. Lindner, L. McCormick, and J. Schneider. "The Librarian's Role in the Provision of Consumer Health Information and Patient Education." *Bulletin of the Medical Library Association* 84, no. 2 (1996): 238–239. Available at: http://caphis.mlanet.org/chis/librarian.html.

3. Nielsen-Bohlman, Lynn, Allison M. Panzer, David A. Kindig, and Institute of Medicine Committee on Health Literacy. *Health Literacy: A Prescription to End Confusion.* National Academies Press. Accessed July 9, 2013. http://www.nap.edu/catalog.php?record_id=10883.

4. Davis, Terry C., Michael S. Wolf, Pat F. Bass, Mark Middlebrooks, Estela Kennen, David W. Baker, Bennett. Charles L., et al. "Low Literacy Impairs Comprehension of Prescription Drug Warning Labels." *Journal of General Internal Medicine* 21, no. 8 (2006): 847–851.

5. McCarthy, D. M., K. R. Waite, L. M. Curtis, K. G. Engel, D. W. Baker, and M. S. Wolf. "What Did the Doctor Say? Health Literacy and Recall of Medical Instructions." *Medical Care* 50, no. 4 (2012): 277–282.

6. Weiss, Barry D., Joanne G. Schwartzberg, and American Medical Association. *Health Literacy and Patient Safety: Help Patients Understand Manual for Clinicians.* Chicago: AMA Foundation, 2007. Accessed July 9, 2013. http://www.ama-assn.org/ama1/pub/upload/mm/367/healthlitclinicians.pdf.

7. Glassman P. "Health Literacy." National Network of Libraries of Medicine. Accessed July 9, 2013. http://nnlm.gov/outreach/consumer/hlthlit.html#A8.

8. Dunnavant S. 1995. *Celebrating Life: African American Women Speak Out about Breast Cancer.* Dallas, TX: US Forms Inc. (USFI).

9. Pask, Gordon. *Microman: Computers and the Evolution of Consciousness.* New York: Macmillan, 1982.

10. Gustafson, D. H, K. Bosworth, R. P. Hawkins, E. W. Boberg, and E. Bricker. "Chess: A Computer-Based System for Providing Information, Referrals, Decision Support and Social Support to People Facing Medical and Other Health-Related Crises." *Proceedings of the Annual Symposium on Computer Applications in Medical Care* (1992): 161–165.

11. "Association of Cancer Online Resources." Accessed August 19, 2013. http://www.acor.org/.

12. Huber, Jeffrey T. and Susan Swogger. *Introduction to Reference Sources in the Health Sciences,* 6 ed.. Chicago, IL: ALA Neal-Schuman, 2014.

13. "About Us: What Is Planetree, and Where Did it Come From?" Columbia Memorial Hospital. Accessed August 31, 2013. http://www.columbiamemorial.org/about-planetree.aspx.

14. "Kaiser Permanente: More Than 60 Years of Quality." Kaiser Permanente. Accessed August 31, 2013. http://xnet.kp.org/newscenter/aboutkp/historyofkp.html.

15. "Mid-Columbia Medical Center: Your Health Information Connection." Mid-Columbia Medical Center. Accessed August 31, 2013. http://www.mcmc.net/PatientsAndVisitors/HealthResources/LibraryServices.aspx.

16. "Planetree Health Information Center @ the Cupertino Library." Planetree Heath. Accessed August 31, 2013. http://www.planetree-sccl.org/.

17. "The Learning Center." M.D. Anderson Center, University of Texas. Accessed August 31, 2013. http://www.mdanderson.org/patient-and-cancer-information/guide-to-md-anderson/places-to-visit/the-learning-center.html.

18. "Cancer Learning Center." Huntsman Cancer Institute, University of Utah. Accessed August 31, 2013. http://www.huntsmancancer.org/cancer-information/cancer-learning-center/cancer-learning-center.

19. "Patient Family Education Resource Center." Comprehensive Cancer Center, University of Michigan. Accessed August 31, 2013. http://www.cancer.med.umich.edu/support/patient_education_resource_center.shtml.

20. "Mardigian Wellness Resource Center." Cardiovascular Center, University of Michigan. Accessed August 31, 2013. http://www.med.umich.edu/cvc/pat_vis/wrc.html.

21. "Stanford Health Library." Stanford University. Accessed August 31, 2013. http://healthlibrary.stanford.edu/.

22. "The Connelly Resource Center for Families." Children's Hospital of Philadelphia. Accessed August 31, 2013. http://www.chop.edu/visitors/family-support-and-resources/connelly-center.html.

23. "Library & Knowledge Services: Consumer Health Resources." National Jewish Health. Accessed August 31, 2013. http://www.nationaljewish.org/professionals/research/support/library/health-information-for-patients/.

24. "A Place for Learning: Community Health Education Center." Salem Health [Salem, Oregon]. Accessed August 31, 2013. http://www.salemhealth.org/chec/.

25. Lopez S. J. "Hone the Job You Have into One You Love." *New York Times,* May 26, 2013. Available at http://www.nytimes.com/2013/05/26/jobs/honing-the-job-you-have-into-one-you-love.html.

Chapter 12

HEALTH LITERACY

Robert Shapiro

WHAT IS HEALTH LITERACY?

Origins of the Term

Although the term was not formally coined until the early 1970s, the concept dates back, at least in published literature, to the late 1940s, postwar United States. Soldiers were coming home, and the military quickly realized that there was many health issues that it needed to educate its soldiers about. This led to the distribution of health information and the subsequent realization that the information it was distributing was not readable in some cases, and in others, if it was readable, it may not have been necessarily understandable.

Decades later, in a paper entitled "Health Education as Social Policy," a sociologist used the term "health literacy" to describe the minimal health education that grade school children ought to receive. Scott Simonds was arguing that social policy and health education had an impact on how our healthcare system operates.[1, 2] Though the term largely fell out of use until the 1990s, the concept that a health literate population, or lack thereof, will have an impact on the health of individuals and the operation of the healthcare system did not.

Development of the Concept

It would not be until 1999 that the American Medical Association (AMA) formally defined the term "health literacy" as "a constellation of skills, including the ability to perform basic reading and numerical tasks required to function in the healthcare environment."[3] To be sure, though the recognition by the AMA was significant—perhaps even pivotal—scholars had been using the concept and defining the term for years. Take, for instance, Kickbush's definition: "Health literacy implies the achievement of a level of knowledge, person skills, and confidence to take action to improve personal and community health by changing personal lifestyles and living conditions."[4] Nutbeam and the World Health Organization defined the concept as "the cognitive and social skills which determine the motivation and ability of individuals to gain access to, understand, and use information in ways which promote and maintain good health"[5, 6] Ratzen and Parker, writing for a bibliography produced by the National Library of Medicine (NLM), define health literacy as "the degree to which individuals have the capacity to obtain, process and understand basic health information and services needed to make appropriate health decisions."[7] Ratzen and Parker's definition, and the AMA's, would influence our understanding and measurement of health literacy during a burgeoning time for the field of health literacy research and application. The U.S. Department for Health and Human Services would adopt it for the Healthy People 2010 objectives; the Institute of Medicine (IOM) would adopt it for its essential piece on health literacy, "Prescription to End Confusion"; the National Action Plan to Improve Health Literacy adopted it; and the 2010 Patient Protection and Affordable Care Act, signed by President Obama, utilized the same definition.[8, 9, 10, 11]

A Growing Field

As the field of health literacy grew, so too did its application outside the traditional primary care setting. Public health literacy, arguably the original conception of the term, is defined as "the degree to which individuals and groups can obtain, process, understand, evaluate, and act upon information needed to make public health decisions that benefit the community."[12] "Mental health literacy" is understood as the public's ability to recognize mental disorders and their beliefs about various treatment modalities.[13] The American Dental Association defined health literacy in dentistry similarly to the Ratzen and Parker definition but added "...to make appropriate oral health decisions."[14] Indeed, in its current state, nearly every aspect of the healthcare system is engaged in the health literacy field in one way or another.[15]

In a recent systematic review of the field, Sorensen and colleagues identified 17 definitions and 12 conceptual frameworks of health literacy in order to produce an integrated definition and model.[16] Based on content analysis, they arrived at the following definition, which will be utilized for the remainder of this chapter: "Health literacy is linked to literacy and entails people's knowledge, motivation and competences to access, understand, appraise, and apply health information in order to make judgments and take decisions in everyday life concerning healthcare, disease prevention and health promotion to maintain or improve quality of life during the life course."[17]

Sorensen and colleagues also articulate a typology of health literacy that has been utilized by scholars such as Nutbeam and those who generally take a more critical or meta perspective of the field.[18, 19] This typology divides health literacy into three categories: functional, interactive, and critical.

Functional health literacy often refers to a set of basic skills (reading, writing, numeracy) that one needs to have, or to be taught, to be considered health literate. The AMA definition is often used as an example of functional health literacy. *Interactive health literacy* expands the functional definition to include social and advanced cognitive skills. Its name implies that in situations wherein health literacy skills are needed, an individual is more proactive and communicative; in turn, this implies that the healthcare provider is an active participant and is equally responsible for miscommunication and misunderstandings as well. *Critical health literacy* broadens the scope of health literacy further. As Nutbeam has indicated, critical health literacy has both individual and social implications as well as direct and profound implications for how we practice it. Critical health literacy moves the conversation from a specific event to an individual situated in a particular social and political environment. It argues that health literacy is more than simply being able to understand a prescription bottle; that in fact, critical health literacy makes us aware of what are often called social determinants of health and encourages and empowers individuals to make the necessary changes to better health outcomes.

Although Mancuso adds temporal language and an implication of chronology, she summarizes the current question quite succinctly. She states:

> Health literacy has originated from the necessary skills of reading and numeracy to one of critical thinking, problem-solving, decision-making, information-seeking and communication, along with a multitude of social, personal, and cognitive skills that are imperative in order to function in the healthcare system. In addition, health literacy has expanded into the realm of culture, context, and language.[20]

DEMOGRAPHICS, RESEARCH, AND APPLICATION

Demographics

The body of health literacy literature allows us to describe, with a fair degree of certainty, the prevalence and demographics of health literacy. The collection of literature is also robust enough that it includes "demographic" studies of the literature itself. We begin this section with those studies: bibliographies, bibliometric analyses, and citation analyses.

Bibliographies

The first two attempts to summarize the literature on health literacy were conducted by NLM—one in 2000 and one in 2004.[21, 22] The Harvard Department of Society, Human Development, and Health (HDSHDH) has conducted five reviews of literature beginning with a deep retrospective from 1970 to 1999. This study was followed by a 10-year review from 1990 to 2000 and three subsequent, consecutive years.[23, 24, 25, 26, 27]

Selden and colleagues were the first to attempt to collocate health literacy literature. The authors state the purpose of the bibliography was to "help define and describe the evidence base for advancing health literacy programs by examining theories, strategies, and tactics in the published literature."[28] Though the methods are vague, the bibliography provided a substantial collection of literature indicating, even for just the 10 years investigated between 1990 and 1999, there was a significant evidence base for this growing field.

It is important to recall that the AMA operationalized the term in 1999; in this light, it seems more of a capstone than a beginning to the field. Led this time by Zorn, NLM released a complimentary Current Bibliographies in Medicine to Health Literacy in 2004. This one was more limited in time—in that it searched from 1998 to 2003—but broadened its search, stating also, "so much had been added to the literature, it was clear the time had come for another bibliography."[29] Writing the introduction to the bibliography, Allen and Horowitz are clear that whereas the purpose of the first bibliography was to define the problem of health literacy and examine potential strategies for resolving it, the second bibliography sought to provide literature regarding the barriers that surround implementing those strategies.[30] However, the authors may be being too humble here. That is, the stated boundaries of the bibliographies seem not to be limiting features, but rather organizational in nature.

The effort to summarize the literature on health literacy by the Harvard Department of Society, Human Development, and Health stands as the other significant attempt in this small but important group of papers. Similar to the NLM bibliographies, the authors of the Harvard reports arrange the citations into meaningful categories. The HDSHDH authors, however, add annotations not only to the topics—and subtopics—but to each item cited. In both cases—NLM and Harvard—the authors take the opportunity to summarize briefly the current state of the field, but it is not until the bibliometric studies on health literacy that any inference is drawn from collections *about* the literature *as* literature.

Bibliometric Analyses

To date, there have been four formal bibliometric analyses conducted on the field of health literacy. Two of the four published articles intended to provide a comparison of health literacy research conducted in Europe to that conducted in the United States. Kondilis, Steraides, and Falagas determined that there was considerable neglect of health literacy research in Europe.[31] Later, Kondilis and colleagues would expand the initial analysis by utilizing more comprehensive searches and also by adjusting research productivity by factoring in gross domestic product for each country.[32] They found that the 25 European Union countries produced an amount of health literacy research comparable to 16 percent of the total health literacy research in the United States.

In an exploratory bibliometric analysis of health literacy, Bankson found that PubMed indexed the majority of health literacy articles and that there was an upward trend in articles produced each year.[33] Bankson also found four spikes in production in 2002, 2003, 2004, and 2007, which she attributed, respectively, to MLA defining their role in health literacy, MLA's efforts to highlight health literacy research, the release of the 2003 National Assessment of Adult Literacy data, and health literacy finally reaching a broad audience.

Building off suggestions provided by Bankson to include citation analysis—as well as remove length, time period, and publication type limitations—Shapiro conducted the most comprehensive bibliometric analysis of the field to date.[34] His research found that from 1980 to 2010, SciSearch (Web of Science), in fact, provided the most complete indexing of health literacy research, followed closely by PubMed and Social SciSearch, then Academic Search Premier, CINAHL, and EMBASE (full lists of database coverage, author frequency, and journal rank can be found at http://uknowledge.uky.edu/gradschool_theses/71/).

In terms of journal titles, *Patient Education and Counseling* published the most health literacy articles, followed by the *Journal of Internal Medicine*, the *Journal of School Health*, the *Journal of Health Communication*, the *Australian & New Zealand Journal of Psychiatry*, and the *Journal of the American Medical Association*. The database coverage and journal frequency speak to the multidisciplinary nature of the field of health literacy research. Indeed, the top 20 journals represent patient education and health promotion, internal medicine, nursing, communication, psychiatry, library and information science, and public health. The frequency of such a diverse group of journal titles, combined with the co-authorship data provided by Shapiro, seems to indicate health literacy research is being conducted in disciplinary silos. Interestingly, though, co-citation data seem to imply there is a clear core set of literature that each discipline pulls from when conducting its own work. These works are authored by Wolf, Davis, Parker, Jorm, Schillinger, Paasche-Orlow, Baker, Williams, Gazmarian, and Dewalt—all familiar names for anyone well read in health literacy research.[35]

Research

The breadth of research on the topic has allowed scholars to develop a profile of individuals with low health literacy. Women and individuals who spoke English before starting school tend to have higher measures of health literacy. White and Asian/Pacific Islanders have higher averages than black, Hispanic, American Indian, Alaskan Native, and multiracial adults. Older adults tend to have lower health literacy than their younger counterparts. Adults with lower educational attainment and those living below the poverty line tend to display lower than average health literacy.[36]

Furthermore, a clear link has been shown to exist between low health literacy and poor health status and health outcomes.[37] More specifically, individuals with low health literacy are more likely to omit preventive services and are often sicker when they enter the healthcare system[38, 39]; they are more likely to have chronic conditions and are less able to manage them effectively[40, 41, 42, 43]; they have higher hospitalization rates and use of emergency services[44, 45, 46]; and they are more likely to report their health status as poor.[47, 48, 49]

The National Action Plan to Improve Health Literacy points further to psychological costs, perhaps most importantly, a sense of shame that one could easily see as perpetuating an already difficult situation.[50] A recent systematic review conducted by Berkman and colleagues updated and reconfirmed much of the seminal review conducted by the Agency for Healthcare Research and Quality (AHRQ) in 2004 that linked low health literacy to poor health outcomes.[51, 52]

The United States is not alone in its struggle against low health literacy. New Zealand, for instance, reports 56.2 percent of adult New Zealanders have poor health literacy skills[53] while 59 percent of Australian adults and 60 percent[54] of Canadian adults have poor or low health literacy.[55] Writing for the IOM, Pleasant identified literature regarding health literacy from Australia, the United Kingdom, Canada, the Netherlands, Germany, Japan, Spain, South Africa, Sweden, Brazil, China, Iran, Israel, New Zealand, Nigeria, Taiwan, Argentina, Belgium, India, Malaysia, Norway, Singapore, Switzerland, and Thailand.[56] He states, "mapping the number of peer-reviewed articles in 2011 by country clearly indicates that health literacy has spread around the world and is definitely not a U.S. only phenomenon."[57]

A driving force in the health literacy movement has been the immediate and future cost individuals with low or limited health literacy will incur as a result of their literacy levels. In fact, Clark and others have argued that it is likely cost concerns that have been and will continue to be the motivating factor in developing policies will result in the kind of reforms needed to address low health literacy.[58, 59] Current estimates claim limited health literacy costs the United States economy between $106 and $236 billion annually, and that it may well be in the range of $1.6 to $3.6 trillion annually when accounting for future costs that could result from inaction.[60] The National Assessment of Adult Literacy (NAAL) found that adults who received Medicare or Medicaid and adults who had no health insurance had, on average, lower health literacy than adults who were covered by other types of insurance.[61] In a systematic review published in 2009, Eichler and colleagues found that limited health literacy may be between 3 and 5 percent of the total healthcare cost, amounting to $143 to $7,798 per person.[62]

It is worth noting before moving on that from a substantial core of health literacy research has risen a truly interdisciplinary field of research, one that, for the first time since its conception in 1974, warranted its own conference. The Health Literacy Annual Research Conference (HARC) in 2009 was the first to bring scholars from all aspects of health literacy together to converse about the pressing issues surrounding health literacy, form measurement and definitional problems to the role health literacy plays in reducing health disparities.[63] Now the conference is past its fifth year and continually stands as one of the most significant gatherings of health literacy scholars (For more information on the annual HARC, visit http://www.bumc.bu.edu/healthliteracyconference/).

Application

If the HARC conference is the annual pinnacle of health literacy research, its complement from the practice side is the Institute for Healthcare Advancement's

Annual Health Literacy Conference, which is in its twelfth year (For more information on the IHA and its annual conference, visit http://www.bumc.bu.edu/healthliteracyconference/). The IHA conference regularly features icons of the health literacy field with programs on best practices, toolkits, and practical strategies for addressing low health literacy in a variety of environments.

Although no one which overwhelmingly utilized health literacy intervention has emerged, certainly some programs have been more successful than others.[64] Broadly, health literacy programs fall into the three-tiered framework articulated by Sudore and Schillinger for classifying health literacy interventions. Those categories are clinician-patient level interventions, system-patient level interventions, and community-patient level interventions.[65]

Sheridan and colleagues recently conducted a systematic review of interventions for individuals with low health literacy.[66] Although they found that effects of interventions were often limited or mixed, they did find support for discrete message design features such as presenting essential information first or adding video to verbal narratives. In a few studies, they found consistent, direct, fair, or good-quality evidence that interventions such as intensive self-management and intensive self- and disease-management interventions were effective. Clearly, much work needs to be done.

Three popular interventions that stand out among the rest are the teach back method, Ask Me 3, and what is commonly referred to as universal precautions.

Teach Back

The teach back method, also called the show me method or closing the loop, is a way to ensure that patients and/or their caregivers understand the information being communicated by healthcare providers. After introducing a new concept, decision, or instructions to a patient, the provider will ask the patient to demonstrate his or her understanding by recalling the information just given. The provider is then able to revise, clarify, or tailor the explanation given the response from the patient, and the cycle continues, thus "closing the loop."[67] This process can immediately confirm whether the information was understood and if and where there were gaps, and it recognizes that health literacy is not only about the skills and actions of the patient, but also the ability of the provider to communicate in an effective way. Indeed, the Iowa Health System Health Literacy Collaborative states that the teach back method is not a way to determine if the patient understood the provider, but whether the provider communicated well enough. The teach back method and its underlying principles (e.g., recalling and restating information) have been well scrutinized by scholars from a variety of fields.[68, 69, 70, 71, 72]

Ask Me 3

In 2002, the Partnership for Clear Health Communication (PCHC) formed to expand awareness and educate about health literacy, to develop and advocate for the use of patient-provider communication solutions, to conduct an advocacy program around health literacy policy and funding, and to conduct nationally coordinated health literacy research. Five years later, the PCHC would join with the National Patient Safety Foundation (NPSF) to become the Partnership for Clear Health Communication at the Patient Safety Foundation. The PCHC, both as an independent entity and, while at the NPSF, is known for its work developing and implementing the Ask Me 3 campaign.[73] Ask Me 3 was a patient-provider communication campaign that encouraged patients to ask three questions: (1) What is my main problem? (2) What do I need to do? and (3) Why is it important for me do this?[74] The goal of the program was to "help patients better understand their health condition and be able to follow [the physician's] instructions."[75] Sudore and Schillinger classify the Ask Me 3 campaign as "Creating an Empowering Environment."[76] Ask Me 3 has shown positive results in numerous settings and has been linked to improved patient outcomes.[77]

Universal Precautions

By far the most utilized method for addressing low health literacy is universal precautions, which is a method that arose from the general practice of universal precautions in medicine, which advocates taking specific actions to minimize risk for all individuals when it is unclear who is/could be affected.[78] The Agency for Healthcare Research and Quality commissioned the University of North Carolina at Chapel Hill to develop and test a toolkit of practices to use as a quality improvement initiative that could impact the delivery of safe, timely, efficient, effective, equitable, and patient-centered care.[79] One of the limitations to implementing the universal precautions toolkit is that it, like many quality improvement initiatives, may take a long time to see results; however, this is also a testament to how comprehensive the toolkit is.

Beginning with a self-assessment, this toolkit walks users through how each aspect of the specific healthcare system can be adjusted to account for universal precautions. The universal precautions toolkit, in fact, incorporates the teach back method into its "Tools to Improve Spoken Communication" and suggests Ask Me 3 as a way to encourage questions and improve self-management and empowerment.[80] Broadly, the categories of tools are:

- Tools to Start on the Path to Improvement
- Tools to Improve Spoken Communication
- Tools to Improve Written Communication
- Tools to Improve Self-Management and Empowerment
- Tools to Improve Supportive Systems

The push for universal precautions is echoed in the American Medical Association's recommendation that physicians ought not to be determining the health literacy of individuals—even with a variety of "rapid" assessments at hand—during routine clinical practice.[81, 82] Aside from the time it would take to cater to each individual's personalized needs, health literacy scholars have argued against measuring health literacy in practice due to the stigma associated with being classified as "low literate."

Further complications arise when one considers what to do with the information collected. Should it be included in the patient's medical record? Does that mean that health literacy is a static measurement? And if not, should it be measured at each visit like other vital signs?

Although sometimes there seem to be simple answers to these questions, and although debates about definitions and subtle conceptual nuances seem to distract from pragmatic innovations, Sheridan and colleagues encourage us to move cautiously, citing studies that have shown no benefit to populations with low health literacy,[83] or that appeared to have the potential to harm.[84] Nevertheless, but perhaps as a direct result of those limitations, they encourage keeping an eye to the untested intervention..[85] Both research and practice must move in tandem—with research informing practice and practice informing research—for the field to move forward in a meaningful way. As it happens, health sciences librarians are perfectly situated at the confluence of these two paradigms.

WHAT IS THE RELATIONSHIP BETWEEN HEALTH LITERACY AND HEALTH LIBRARIANSHIP?

The relatively sparse collection of literature indexed with both librarianship and health literacy belies the involvement health science librarians have had with the concept. One could easily argue that librarians have been involved in the provision of appropriate information—in this case to health consumers—for decades, certainly long before the concept of health literacy was articulated. If one were to look only as far back as the early 1990s, one would find standards being developed for the display of information on web pages and the authenticity of the information contained therein (see, for instance, the Health on the Net Foundation at http://www.hon.ch/). These efforts were undertaken with the goal of providing patients—as well as their families and other loved ones—with access to understandable information. At the same time, there were two major tracts of research and practice underway.

The first was primarily concerned with health information. This research would seek to identify a particular population or health condition, evaluate the average health literacy levels of that population or condition, determine if the material being provided to those individuals was understandable, and bridge the gap between the two.

The second direction was focused on the individual. Schulz and Nakamoto state that "a large body of research has focused on the development of interventions to improve health literacy or to limit the problems posed for people with low health literacy, most of the literature advocating education as a key to health promotion and disease prevention."[86]

Perhaps the greatest representation of libraries' and librarians' involvement in health literacy is in the Medical Library Association's *Guide to Health Literacy*.[87] Nearly every chapter in the text contains examples of or suggestions for how libraries and librarians have and ought to be involved in health literacy initiatives. Wilson cites the need for multidisciplinary and collaborative approaches to explore new methods for patient education, patient assessment, and changing health policy, among others.[88] Martin and Wathen use information literacy to frame their discussion on librarians' roles in health literacy.[89] They point to the clear information gap that exists between patients and health information, and again encourage librarians to form partnerships to address the issue. Martin and Wathen state that in addition to developing health literacy programs and promoting health literacy to health professionals, "the central role for librarians is to provide accessible and understandable health material, whether this is in a public library, consumer health resource center, or clinical setting."[90] Bibel's chapter on public libraries and health literacy supports the call for collaborative efforts between health sciences (whether hospital or academic-medical) libraries and our public counterparts.[91]

Although she writes about health literacy and senior citizens, Brown provides general suggestions for future directions for libraries and librarians with regard to health literacy. She suggests plain writing and awareness campaigns, developing partnerships, and using known toolkits for specific populations.[92] Brown also points to the lack of a single repository of information on health literacy programs and their respective data, a concern echoed by others as well.[93, 94] Librarians seem well qualified for this task. In a chapter on health literacy interventions, Pappas suggests similar initiatives to others in the MLA guide, namely, educating health professionals and collaborative efforts in conjunction with local academics and hospital officials as well as the public.[95] Citing Allen, Matthew, and Boland,[96] she also advocates for partnerships with Area Health Education Centers, public health departments, clinics, managed care programs, and local branches of other organizations.

Perhaps the most natural and logical collaboration, as well as the most obvious example of the relationship between health sciences librarianship and health literacy, can be seen in consumer health services. The chapter by Gillaspy in this text provides much more detail than can be given here, but the subject is so vast it warrants, at least briefly, discussion here as well. Citing Perryman,[97] Esparza claims the first hospital libraries established in the mid-1800s in fact aimed to provide nonfictional educational materials to patients.[98] It can be argued that the consumer health library has not evolved much in the interim. That is, even with health information being integrated into electronic medical/health records and provided at the point of care, provision of health information remains at the core of the consumer health library or health education center. These libraries are now places to fill "information prescriptions," gather information for a family member or other loved one, and to meet with health professionals who can make sense of often overly complicated information. An emerging role for health sciences librarians that finds a natural home in the consumer health library is as part of the healthcare navigation team.[99, 100, 101] Participation in healthcare navigation teams places the health sciences librarian directly at the intersection of health librarianship and health literacy by purposefully taking advantage of the specific skillsets librarians have.

CURRENT TRENDS AND ISSUES

Although the concept of health literacy would seem to have solid definition and operationalization, much work still needs to be done in this area, with scholars as recently as 2009 calling for revisions to definitions. Consequently, measurement of health literacy is often cited as a current issue.[102] Pleasant, McKinney, and Rikard go so far as to claim that "building a comprehensive approach to measurement of the social construct called health literacy may well be the most significant task facing health research and practice."[103]

The use of universal precautions is an unmistakable trend that bears repeating. The AMA's statement about stopping patient assessments solidified the use of universal precautions and, until another universal method is adopted to address low health literacy, we can assume that it will continue to be the default.

Interest in pushing the scope of health literacy to public and population health continues to grow, and a great deal of opportunity has arisen in the area. Public health literacy is a concept that has been discussed at length and for quite some time,[104, 105] but interestingly, this segment of the discipline tends to focus on only two approaches. Either it is the conceptualization of individuals critically evaluating their health concerns in a community context, or it is health literacy as a practice for public health professionals.[106] Neither approach, however, is necessarily preventative. To be sure, the Universal Precautions Toolkit was modeled after the broader conception of universal precautions and was a preventive measure. However, universal precautions, and likewise the toolkit, are preventive only in that they prevent risk *from* low health literacy; they are not intended to *prevent* low health literacy. The need to develop preventive measures for addressing health literacy in this context is a critical issue that warrants attention.

As discussed earlier in this chapter, the field of health literacy is a truly multidisciplinary endeavor, with scholars and practitioners from a wide range of academic backgrounds contributing. In this respect, one will find solo discussions of discipline-specific concepts, for instance, mental health literacy or oral health literacy. Two themes, or concepts, however, have emerged that seem to span multiple disciplines: oral communication and numeracy. The focus on oral/aural communication developed in response to the recognition that the patient-provider interaction, and indeed the patient-system interaction, was not an entirely written phenomenon. And although the *Prescription to End Confusion* describes literacy as a multifaceted concept consisting of five interrelated skills (reading, writing, speaking, listening, and calculating), health researchers have only recently begun turning their attention to these matters.[108] Similarly, the concept of numeracy, also called quantitative literacy, has only recently begun garnering appropriate attention. Numeracy skills apply not only to complex risk-benefit calculations, but to more routine healthcare interactions such as prescription labels, the purchase of health insurance, and even scheduling appointments. The prevalence of low numeracy is as widespread as low health literacy. Over 50 percent of Americans measure at or below "basic" levels of quantitative literacy, and only 13 percent qualify as "proficient."[109] Berkman and colleagues' recent systematic review of health literacy interventions and outcomes concluded that there was insufficient evidence to connect numeracy with health outcomes such as knowledge, risk perception accuracy, and accurate interpretation of information, but that it did appear to mediate some health disparities.[110, 111] The issues surrounding both oral/aural literacy and numeracy—and the relative lack of literature on the subjects—warrant further investigation and highlight the need to consider not only what information is presented, but also the format in which it is being presented.[112]

A clear need exists for studies examining the cost of low health literacy to both the healthcare system and to the patient, as well as cost-effectiveness research regarding health literacy interventions. In a systematic review on the cost of health literacy, Eichler and colleagues found that cost-effectiveness studies of health literacy were "scarce."[113] Further support for more studies comes from Sheridan and colleagues who, in their systematic review on health literacy interventions, identified only one study that examined the effects of mixed-strategy interventions on cost and none that examined the effects of single-strategy interventions on cost.[114]

Probably the most significant current trend in health literacy is that of local communities, often entire states, forming coalitions to address low health literacy in their areas. These coalitions are made up of healthcare providers (e.g., nurses, physicians, psychologists), adult educators, health information specialists (e.g., librarians, health educators), health communication professionals, private industry (e.g., insurance companies) and not for profits, and academics (not just faculty, but academic administrations as well). They are engaging stakeholders from far beyond the purview of their traditional outreach efforts. Since these coalitions are often truly multidisciplinary collaborations, they are perfectly positioned to address health literacy holistically and, almost by their very nature, with participatory methods.

CONCLUSION

Low health literacy has been a historical problem, it is a current issue, and a universal solution does not seem imminent. Interest in this field has waxed and waned with political motives and economic eras. Both its corpus of literature and its effect are seen across demographics, health conditions, and disciplines. And health sciences librarians are situated directly at the nexus of all the integral parts. Not only are health sciences librarians able to act as a bridge between researchers and practice, but we also act as a bridge between providers and patients, between private industry and academics, and between disparate aspects of our own field. At this particularly central moment in the field of health literacy—with a tremendous history behind us and a seemingly endless future—the opportunities for librarians are limitless.

NOTES

1. Simonds, S. K. "Health Education as Social Policy." *Health Education Monographs* 2 (1974): 1–10.

2. Ratzan, S. C. "Health Literacy: Communication for the Public Good." *Health Promotion International* 16, no. 2 (June 2001): 207–214.

3. Ad Hoc Committee on Health Literacy for the Council on Scientific Affairs, American Medical Association. "Health Literacy: Report of the Council on Scientific Affairs." *JAMA: Journal of the American Medical Association* 281, no. 6 (February 10, 1999): 552–557.

4. Kickbusch, I. "Think Health: What Makes the Difference?" *Health Promotion International* 12 (1997): 265–272.

5. Nutbeam, D. "Health Literacy as a Public Health Goal: A Challenge for Comptemporary Health Education and Communication Strategies into the 21st Century." *Health Promotion International* 15, no. 3 (2000): 259–267.

6. Smith, B. J., K. C. Tang, and D. Nutbeam. "WHO Health Promotion Glossary: New Terms." *Health Promotion International* 21, no. 4 (2006): 340–345.

7. Selden, Catherine, Marcia Zorn, Scott C. Ratzan, and Ruth M. Parker. "Health Literacy." National Library of Medicine, 2006. http://www.nlm.nih.gov/archive/20061214/pubs/cbm/hliteracy.html.

8. Institute of Medicine. *Health Literacy: A Prescription to End Confusion*. Washington, D.C.: Institute of Medicine, 2004.

9. U.S. Department of Health and Human Services. "Healthy People 2010: Understanding and Improving Health." Washington, D.C.: U.S. Department of Health and Human Services, 2000. http://lccn.loc.gov/00300124.

10. Office of Disease Prevention and Health Promotion. "National Action Plan to Improve Health Literacy." Washington, D.C.: U.S. Department of Health and Human Services, 2010. http://health.gov/communication/HLActionPlan/pdf/Health_Literacy_Action_Plan.pdf.

11. "Patient Protection & Affordable Care Act, Public Law 111-148." In *Title IV, x4207, USC HR*, 2010.

12. Freedman, D. A., K. D. Bess, H. A. Tucker, D. L. Boyd, A. M. Tuchman, and K. A. Wallston. "Public Health Literacy Defined." *American Journal of Preventative Medicine* 36, no. 5 (May 2009): 446–451.

13. Jorm, A. F., A. E. Korten, P. A. Jacomb, H. Christensen, B. Rodgers, and P. Pollitt. " 'Mental Health Literacy': A Survey of the Public's Ability to Recognise Mental Disorders and Their Beliefs about the Effectiveness of Treatment." *Medical Journal of Australia* 166, no. 4 (February 17, 1997): 182–186.

14. Podschun, G. D. "National Plan to Improve Health Literacy in Dentistry." *Journal of the California Dental Association* 40, no. 4 (April 2012): 317–320.

15. Shapiro II, R M. "Health Literacy: A Bibliometric and Citation Analysis." [Thesis] University of Kentucky, 2010, http://uknowledge.uky.edu/gradschool_theses/71/.

16. Sorensen, K., S. Van den Broucke, J. Fullam, G. Doyle, J. Pelikan, Z. Slonska, H. Brand, and European Consortium Health Literacy Project. "Health Literacy and Public Health: A Systematic Review and Integration of Definitions and Models." *BMC Public Health* 12 (2012): 80.

17. Ibid.

18. Nutbeam, *op. cit.*

19. Sorensen et al., *op.cit.*

20. Mancuso, J. M. "Assessment and Measurement of Health Literacy: An Integrative Review of the Literature." *Nursing & Health Sciences* 11, no. 1 (March 2009): 77–89.

21. Selden et al., *op. cit.*

22. Zorn, Marcia, Marin P. Allen, and Alice M. Horowitz. "Understanding Health Literacy and Its Barriers." National Library of Medicine, 2004. Accessed September 5, 2013. http://www.nlm.nih.gov/pubs/cbm/healthliteracybarriers.html.

23. Mancuso, *op. cit.*

24. Greenberg, Jennifer. "An Updated Overview of Medical and Public Health Literature Addressing Literacy Issues: An Annotated Bibliography of Articles Published in 2000."

Harvard School of Public Health, 2001. Accessed September 5, 2013. http://www.hsph.harvard.edu/healthliteracy/lit_2000.html.

25. Rudd, Rima E., Tayla Colton, Robin Schacht, and Educational Resources Information Center. "An Overview of Medical and Public Health Literature Addressing Literacy Issues: An Annotated Bibliography." In *National National Center for the Study of Adult Learning and Literacy Reports*. Cambridge, MA; Washington, D.C.: National Center for the Study of Adult Learning and Literacy, Harvard Graduate School of Education; U.S. Department of Education, Office of Educational Research and Improvement, Educational Resources Information Center, 2000.

26. Zobel, Emily. "An Updated Overview of Medical and Public Health Literature Addressing Literacy Issues: An Annotated Bibliography of Articles Published in 2001." Harvard School of Public Health, 2002. Accessed September 5, 2013. http://www.hsph.harvard.edu/healthliteracy/lit_2001.html.

27. Zobel, Emily, Karen Rowe, and Carmen Gomez-Mandic. "An Updated Overview of Medical and Public Health Literature Addressing Literacy Issues: An Annotated Bibliography of Articles Published in 2002." Harvard School of Public Health, 2003. Accessed September 5, 2013. http://www.hsph.harvard.edu/healthliteracy/lit_2002.html

28. Selden et al., *op. cit.*

29. Zorn et al., *op.cit.*

30. Ibid.

31. Kondilis, B. K., E. S. Soteriades, and M. E. Falagas. "Health Literacy Research in Europe: A Snapshot." *European Journal of Public Health* 16, no. 1 (February 2006): 113.

32. Kondilis, B. K., I. J. Kiriaze, A. P. Athanasoulia, and M. E. Falagas. "Mapping Health Literacy Research in the European Union: A Bibliometric Analysis." *PLoS One* 3, no. 6 (2008): e2519.

33. Bankson, H. L. "Health Literacy: An Exploratory Bibliometric Analysis, 1997–2007." *Journal of the Medical Library Association: JMLA* 97, no. 2 (April 2009): 148–150.

34. Shapiro, *op. cit.*

35. Ibid.

36. Huber, Jeffrey T., Robert M. Shapiro II, and Mary L. Gillaspy. "Top Down Versus Bottom Up: The Social Construction of the Health Literacy Movement." *Library Quarterly* 82, no. 4 (October 2012): 429–451.

37. DeWalt, D. A., N. D. Berkman, S. Sheridan, K. N. Lohr, and M. P. Pignone. "Literacy and Health Outcomes: A Systematic Review of the Literature." *Journal of General Internal Medicine* 19, no. 12 (December 2004): 1228–1239.

38. Scott, T. L., J. A. Gazmararian, M. V. Williams, and D. W. Baker. "Health Literacy and Preventive Health Care Use among Medicare Enrollees in a Managed Care Organization." *Medical Care* 40, no. 5 (May 2002): 395–404.

39. Bennett, C. L., M. R. Ferreira, T. C. Davis, J. Kaplan, M. Weinberger, T. Kuzel, M. A. Seday, and O. Sartor. "Relation between Literacy, Race, and Stage of Presentation among Low-Income Patients with Prostate Cancer." *Journal of Clinical Oncologyl* 16, no. 9 (September 1998): 3101–3104.

40. Schillinger, D., K. Grumbach, J. Piette, F. Wang, D. Osmond, C. Daher, J. Palacios, G. D. Sullivan, and A. B. Bindman. "Association of Health Literacy with Diabetes Outcomes." *JAMA: Journal of the American Medical Association* 288, no. 4 (July 24–31 2002): 475–482.

41. Schillinger, D., J. Piette, K. Grumbach, F. Wang, C. Wilson, C. Daher, K. Leong-Grotz, C. Castro, and A. B. Bindman. "Closing the Loop: Physician Communication with

Diabetic Patients Who Have Low Health Literacy." *Archives of Internal Medicine* 163, no. 1 (January 13, 2003): 83–90.

42. Williams, M. V., D. W. Baker, R. M. Parker, and J. R. Nurss. "Relationship of Functional Health Literacy to Patients' Knowledge of Their Chronic Disease: A Study of Patients with Hypertension and Diabetes." *Archives of Internal Medicine* 158, no. 2 (January 26, 1998): 166–172.

43. Williams, M. V., R. M. Parker, D. W. Baker, N. S. Parikh, K. Pitkin, W. C. Coates, and J. R. Nurss. "Inadequate Functional Health Literacy among Patients at Two Public Hospitals." *JAMA: Journal of the American Medical Association* 274, no. 21 (December 6, 1995): 1677–1682.

44. Baker, D. W., J. A. Gazmararian, M. V. Williams, T. Scott, R. M. Parker, D. Green, J. Ren, and J. Peel. "Functional Health Literacy and the Risk of Hospital Admission among Medicare Managed Care Enrollees." *American Journal of Public Health* 92, no. 8 (August 2002): 1278–1283.

45. Baker, D. W., R. M. Parker, M. V. Williams, W. S. Clark, and J. Nurss. "The Relationship of Patient Reading Ability to Self-Reported Health and Use of Health Services." *American Journal of Public Health* 87, no. 6 (June 1997): 1027–1030.

46. Gordon, M. M., R. Hampson, H. A. Capell, and R. Madhok. "Illiteracy in Rheumatoid Arthritis Patients as Determined by the Rapid Estimate of Adult Literacy in Medicine (Realm) Score." *Rheumatology (Oxford)* 41, no. 7 (July 2002): 750–754.

47. Baker et al., 2002, *op.cit.*

48. Baker et al., 1997, *op. cit.*

49. National Center for Education Statistics. *The Health Literacy of America's Adults: Results from the 2003 National Assessment of Adult Literacy.* Washington, D.C.: U.S. Department of Education, 2006.

50. U.S. Department of Health and Human Services, Office of Disease Prevention and Health Promotion. "National Action Plan to Improve Health Literacy." Washington, DC: Author, 2010. http://www.health.gov/communication/hlactionplan/.

51. Agency for Healthcare Research and Quality. "Literacy and Health Outcomes." In *Evidence Report/Technology Assessment.* Washington, D.C.: Agency for Healthcare Research and Quality, 2004.

52. Berkman, N. D., S. L. Sheridan, K. E. Donahue, D. J. Halpern, A. Viera, K. Crotty, A. Holland, et al. "Health Literacy Interventions and Outcomes: An Updated Systematic Review." *Evidence Report/Technology Assessment (Full Report),* no. 199 (March 2011): 1–941.

53. New Zealand Ministry of Health. *Korero Marama: Health Literacy and Maori Results from the 2006 Adult Literacy and Life Skills Survey.* Wellington, New Zealand: Ministry of Health, 2010.

54. Australian Bureau of Statistics. *Health Literacy, Australia.* Canberra, Australia: Australian Bureau of Statistics, 2006.

55. Canadian Council on Learning. *Health Literacy Canada: Initial Results from the International Adult Literacy and Skills Survey, 2007.* Ottawa, Ontario: Canadian Council on Learning, 2007.

56. Pleasant, A. "Health Literacy around the World: Part 1, Health Literacy Efforts Outside of the United States." Tuscon, AZ: Institute of Medicine, Roundtable on Health Literacy, 2012.

57. Ibid.

58. Huber, Shapiro, and Gillapsy, *op. cit.*

59. Clark, B. "Using Law to Fight a Silent Epidemic: The Role of Health Literacy in Health Care Access, Quality, & Cost." *Annals of Health Law* 20, no. 2 (Summer 2011): 253–327, 5p preceding i.

60. "National Action Plan to Improve Health Literacy," *op. cit.*

61. Kutner, Mark, Elizabeth Greenberg, Ying Jin, and Christine Paulsen. *The Health Literacy of America's Adults: Results from the 2003 National Assessment of Adult Literacy.* Washington, D.C.: National Center for Education Statistics, 2006.

62. Eichler, K., S. Wieser, and U. Brugger. "The Costs of Limited Health Literacy: A Systematic Review." *International Journal of Public Health* 54, no. 5 (2009): 313–324.

63. Paasche-Orlow, M. K., E. A. Wilson, and L. McCormack. "The Evolving Field of Health Literacy Research." *Journal of Health Communication* 15, suppl. 2 (2010): 5–8.

64. Sheridan, S. L., D. J. Halpern, A. J. Viera, N. D. Berkman, K. E. Donahue, and K. Crotty. "Interventions for Individuals with Low Health Literacy: A Systematic Review." *Journal of Health Communication* 16, suppl. 3 (2011): 30–54.

65. Sudore, R. L., and D. Schillinger. "Interventions to Improve Care for Patients with Limited Health Literacy." *Journal of Clinical Outcomes Management: JCOM* 16, no. 1 (January 1, 2009): 20–29.

66. Sheridan et al., *op. cit.*

67. Schillinger et al., 2003, *op. cit.*

68. Esquivel, J., M. White, M. Carroll, and E. Brinker. "Teach-Back Is an Effective Strategy for Educating Older Heart Failure Patients." *Circulation* 124, no. 21 (November 2011): 2.

69. Fara-Erny, A. M. "Innovative Strategies for Patient Medication Education: The Evaluation of Nurse's Teach-Back Technique Using Kirkpatrick's Levels of Evaluation." *Clinical Nurse Specialist* 27, no. 2 (March–April 2013): E37-E37.

70. Flowers, L. "Teach-Back Improves Informed Consent." *OR Manager* 22, no. 3 (March 2006): 25–26.

71. Santiago-Rotchford, L. "Incorporating the Teach-Back Method into Nursing Practice to Prevent 30-Day Readmissions: An Innovative Collaboration Led by a Clinical Nurse Specialist." *Clinical Nurse Specialist* 27, no. 2 (March–April 2013): E33–E34.

72. Wilson, F. L., A. Mayeta-Peart, L. Parada-Webster, and C. Nordstrom. "Using the Teach-Back Method to Increase Maternal Immunization Literacy among Low-Income Pregnant Women in Jamaica: A Pilot Study." *Journal of Pediatric Nursing* 27, no. 5 (October 2012): 451–459.

73. MacReady, Norra. "Read Your Patients: Health Literacy and Its Effects on Quality of Care." *Hospitalist,* February 2007.

74. National Patient Safety Foundation. "Ask Me 3." National Patient Safety Foundation, 2013. Accessed August 17, 2013. http://www.npsf.org/for-healthcare-professionals/programs/ask-me-3/.

75. Pfizer. "Phch/Ask Me 3." Pfizer, 2012. Accessed August 17, 2013. http://www.pfizerhealthliteracy.com/physicians-providers/PchcAskme3.aspx.

76. Sudore et al., *op. cit.*

77. Six-Means, Amy, Thomas K. Bauer, Reba Teeter, Denise Segraves, Lisa Cutshaw, and Louann High. "Building a Foundation of Health Literacy with Ask Me 3™." *Journal of Consumer Health on the Internet* 16, no. 2 (2012): 180–191.

78. Dewalt, D. A., L. F. Callahan, V. H. Hawk, K. A. Broucksou, A. Hink, R. Rudd, and C. Brach. *Health Literacy Universal Precautions Toolkit.* Rockville, MD: Agency for Healthcare Research and Quality, 2010.

79. DeWalt, Darren A., Kimberly A. Broucksou, Victoria Hawk, Cindy Brach, Ashley Hink, Rima Rudd, and Leigh Callahan. "Developing and Testing the Health Literacy Universal Precautions Toolkit." *Nursing Outlook* 59, no. 2 (2011): 85–94.

80. Ibid.

81. Pleasant, A., J. McKinney, and R. V. Rikard. "Health Literacy Measurement: A Proposed Research Agenda." *Journal of Health Communication* 16, suppl. 3 (2011): 11–21.

82. Elliot, V. S. "Experts Debate Value of Assessing Health Literacy." AMedNews.com, 2008. http://www.amednews.com/article/20080602/health/306029968/7/.

83. Greene, J., E. Peters, C. K. Mertz, and J. H. Hibbard. "Comprehension and Choice of a Consumer-Directed Health Plan: An Experimental Study." *American Journal of Managed Care* 14, no. 6 (June 2008): 369–376.

84. Peters, E., N. Dieckmann, A. Dixon, J. H. Hibbard, and C. K. Mertz. "Less Is More in Presenting Quality Information to Consumers."*Medical Care Research and Review: MCRR* 64, no. 2 (April 2007): 169–190.

85. Sheridan et al., *op. cit.*

86. Schulz, P. J., and K. Nakamoto. "Health Literacy and Patient Empowerment in Health Communication: The Importance of Separating Conjoined Twins." *Patient Education and Counseling* 90, no. 1 (January 2013): 4–11.

87. Kars, Marge, Lynda Baker, and Feleta L. Wilson. *The Medical Library Association Guide to Health Literacy,* Medical Library Association Guides. New York: Neal-Schuman, 2008.

88. Wilson, F. L. "Impact of Patient Low Literacy on the Individual and Family." In *The Medical Library Association Guide to Health Literacy*, edited by Marge Kars, L. M. Baker, and F. L. Wilson, 93–102. New York: Neal-Schuman, 2008.

89. Martin, H. J., and N. Wathen. "The Association between Literacy and Health: Providing Health Information to Adults with Low Literacy." In *The Medical Library Association Guide to Health Literacy*, edited by Marge Kars, L. M. Baker, and F. L. Wilson, 103–116. New York: Neal-Schuman, 2008.

90. Ibid.

91. Bibel, B. "Public Libraries and Health Literacy." In *The Medical Library Association Guide to Health Literacy*, edited by Marge Kars, L. M. Baker, and F. L. Wilson, 197–208. New York: Neal-Schuman, 2008.

92. Brown, M. "Health Literacy and America's Senior Citizens." In *The Medical Library Association Guide to Health Literacy*, edited by Marge Kars, L. M. Baker, and F. L. Wilson, 139–160. New York: Neal-Schuman, 2008.

93. Sheridan et al., *op. cit.*

94. Brown, *op. cit.*

95. Pappas, C. "Intervention Programs for Health Literacy." In *The Medical Library Association Guide to Health Literacy*, edited by Marge Kars, L. M. Baker, and F. L. Wilson, 259–280. New York: Neal-Schuman, 2008.

96. Allen, M., S. Matthew, and M. J. Boland. "Working with Immigrant and Refugee Populations: Issues and Hmong Case Study." *Library Trends* 53, no. 2 (Fall 2004): 301–328.

97. Perryman, C. "Medicus Deus: A Review of Factors Affecting Hospital Library Services to Patients between 1790–1950." *Journal of the Medical Library Association: JMLA* 94, no. 3 (July 2006): 263–270.

98. Esparza, J. "Consumer Health Services in Hospitals: The Front Line of Health Literacy." In *The Medical Library Association Guide to Health Literacy*, edited by Marge Kars, L. M. Baker, and F. L. Wilson, 217–242. New York: Neal-Schuman, 2008.

99. Huber, Shapiro, and Gillapsy, *op. cit.*

100. Attwood, C. A., and K. E. Wellik. "Collaboration, Collegiality, and Cooperation: Consumer Health Library Services and the American Cancer Society Navigator Role." *Clinical Journal of Oncology Nursing* 16, no. 5 (October 2012): 487–490.

101. Huber, J. T., R. M. Shapiro II, H. J. Burke, and A. Palmer. "Enhancing the Care Navigation Model: Potential Roles for Health Science Librarians." *Journal of the Medical Library Association: JMLA* 102, no. 1 (January 2014): 55–61.

102. Paasche-Orlow, Wilson, McCormack, *op. cit.*

103. Pleasant, *op. cit.*; Nutbeam, *op. cit.*

104. Baur, C. "New Directions in Research on Public Health and Health Literacy." *Journal of Health Communcation* 15, suppl. 2 (2010): 42–50.

105. Ibid.

106. Institute of Medicine, *op. cit.*

107. Rosenfeld, L., R. Rudd, K. M. Emmons, D. Acevedo-Garcia, L. Martin, and S. Buka. "Beyond Reading Alone: The Relationship between Aural Literacy and Asthma Management." *Patient Education and Counseling* 82, no. 1 (2011): 110–116.

108. Kutner et al., *op. cit.*

109. Berkman et al., *op. cit.*

110. Peters E., L. Meilleur, and M. Tompkins. *Numeracy and the Affordable Care Act: Opportunities and Challenges.* Bethesda, MD: Roundtable on Health Literacy, Institute of Medicine, 2013.

111. Peters, E., J. Hibbard, P. Slovic, and N. Dieckmann. "Numeracy Skill and the Communication, Comprehension, and Use of Risk-Benefit Information." *Health Affairs (Project Hope)* 26, no. 3 (2007): 741–748.

112. Eichler, Wieser, and Brugger, *op. cit.*

113. Sheridan et al., *op. cit.*

114. Ibid.

Chapter 13

OUTREACH SERVICES

Julie K. Gaines and *Meredith Solomon*

INTRODUCTION

Health sciences libraries have a rich history of outreach that has evolved over time to encompass all healthcare professionals, patients, and a variety of settings (urban, rural, etc.). However, outreach has multiple definitions, with the definition dependent on the roles libraries and their partners assume in the outreach relationship.[1] A common theme in the literature presents outreach as the library's activities that extend beyond the "traditional library structure."[2] Libraries provide outreach programs in many different forms and to many different populations. The library's mission, funding capacity, and partnerships influence its ability to conduct outreach and the nature of these activities.

While outreach may be defined differently in various settings, most librarians refer to their outreach services as the activities they do outside the walls of their library. The audiences may vary at different institutions, and in some settings, outreach may refer only to affiliated faculty, staff, and students on a medical school campus or at a hospital, while in other instances, libraries may focus their outreach efforts only to healthcare professionals and the consumers in the community who are not affiliated with a university or hospital. Some libraries consider outreach a part of public relations and marketing or their public mission, but most libraries consider on-campus outreach a more targeted approach to customer service, assisting users with their information needs. For example, if there are academic departments not located on the main campus, having a librarian provide reference hours at the satellite campus is a way to reach students.

More recently, technology and the digital age have both enabled and driven librarians to reach outside the walls of the library to access their customers more easily than ever before.[3] A decrease in the number of in-person reference questions and the evolution of "library as place" have attributed to the increased efforts of libraries toward outreach activities. The evolution of outreach in libraries can be directly compared to that of the library building.[4] This evolution, coupled with the National Library of Medicine's outreach plans,[5, 6, 7] has driven health sciences libraries to add outreach services to their mission statements and strategic plans.

Two critical factors play a role in reaching the target population: location and creating relationships. When providing outreach, librarians need to meet the users where they are and where they need the information. With the evolution of library services, librarians can still maintain a role in learning and education, but they often have to use methods outside of the physical library space to do this. Fortunately, with the advent of online resources and mobile technologies, librarians have been freed to move outside of the library building to provide robust outreach services.

Building relationships often leads to outreach partnerships, which can come in many different forms. These partnerships may be with groups such as nonprofit organizations and academic departments, or with individuals such as a social worker or a physician in a rural area. Collaborating with a partner outside the library is often essential for a successful outreach project. The partner knows the population and is able to guide the librarian in the way to best reach the targeted population. Optimally, the relationship between the library and its partners should be one that includes open communication, shared resources, a thoughtful exchange of ideas, and a common vision for reaching a common goal.[8]

More importantly, it is essential that the partners set goals together that they will be able to attain as a team and ensure everyone is on the same page.[9] In addition, these goals help guide the evaluation and the outcome measurements of the outreach program. Building these partnerships helps when working with health professionals and with the public in the community. Similarities and differences exist in both the public and the health professional communities. It is important for the outreach librarian to meet the audience where it needs the information and to present information at its literacy level. As a result, the methods and goals of these programs should be revisited continuously.[10]

Several challenges are inherent in outreach programs, and these challenges affect the success of the programs. Time and funding are two major challenges.[11] Often, attendees at outreach events or partners do not have time to participate in outreach efforts, whether it is for training or assistance with a research project. Many outreach programs are grant or contract driven, so when the funding runs low, the outreach project has to end. Often, no additional funds are available for long-term sustainability of the project after the initial funding has ended. In addition, personnel can be a challenge.[12, 13] Furthermore, libraries or their partners may not have enough personnel to assist with a project, or there can be a personnel change during the project. Communication between partners is another challenge that can affect the outreach efforts. If everyone is not on the same page, the goals of the project are often not achieved. Therefore, time, funds, and communication are issues that need to be addressed in any outreach program.

HISTORY OF OUTREACH

The Beginning

After World War II, the declining state of biomedical libraries across the nation negatively affected the libraries' ability to provide medical information to healthcare professionals.[14] At that time, an increase in funding for medical education and research, but a decrease in funding for health sciences libraries, resulted in their decline. In 1960–1961, Harold Bloomquist, a medical librarian at Harvard University, conducted a National Library of Medicine (NLM)–funded study on the status and needs of medical school libraries. He found that in most cases, the medical school library was "woefully inadequate to meet the demands placed upon it as an agency of biomedical communication."[15] Based on this study, Bloomquist made recommendations to improve medical libraries, including a system of regional libraries that would be supported by the NLM.[16] This support would include funding and equipment, and the result would be an enhanced communication network.[17]

In early 1964, the President's Commission on Heart Disease, Cancer and Stroke, chaired by Michael E. DeBakey, investigated communication problems among researchers and healthcare professionals who were working on three specific diseases (heart disease, cancer, and stroke) and recommended better resources, legislation, and facilities.[18] That same year, Martin Cummings, the director of the National Library of Medicine, recommended that the future role of the NLM should include programs to strengthen medical libraries in the United States.[19] He felt that the NLM should have regional and local interrelationships that would allow for shared resources to achieve the goal of responding "more effectively to the information needs of the health professional."[20] Taking into account the recommendations of both Bloomquist and Cummings, and the President's Commission on Heart Disease, Cancer and Stroke, the NLM drafted legislation entitled the Medical Library Assistance Act (PL 89-291 MLAA) of 1965. As a result of this act, the Regional Medical Library Program was developed, and it fostered the beginning of extramural outreach in academic health centers.

The Regional Medical Libraries (RMLs) served as a network that allowed the NLM and medical libraries across the nation to respond more efficiently and more effectively to the local information needs of health professionals.[21] Originally, there were 11 RMLs in 11 geographic regions, with each RML established within an existing institution's health sciences library. In 1982, the number of regions was reduced to seven, and later the regions increased to eight when the Greater Northeastern region divided to form the Middle Atlantic Region and the New England Region.[22]

1970s

Circuit riding librarians started providing outreach services such as searching, document delivery, and collection development to health professionals in rural areas as early as the 1970s.[23] The Medical Library Assistance Act (MLAA) was extended in 1970 to assist with the development of the RML network. At the time, outreach services, supported by the RMLs, were primarily interlibrary loan (ILL), search formulation of the NLM's Medical Literature Analysis and Retrieval System (MED-LARS) biomedical literature database, and reference services.[24] In 1971, MEDLINE (MEDLARS Online) became available online, and tapes of the data were available by subscription to universities.[25, 26]

Outreach efforts associated with MEDLINE became more concentrated on improvement of technology rather than just focusing on access to the new technology.[27] Because of MEDLINE's complex interface, researchers often sought librarians' help in searching MEDLINE. Thus, in that era, outreach to health professionals included servicing their remote reference questions and providing them with copies of articles.

While the physician was the focus of outreach services in the early years of the RMLs, the 1970s brought outreach services to a broader audience. This audience included all health professionals, and more specifically, community hospitals and their healthcare teams.[28] The NLM and the Regional Medical Library community hospital outreach efforts included training staff, improving library collections, and increasing library staff knowledge and skills.[29] The development of the Area Health Education Centers (AHEC) and the Health Education Training Centers (HETC) also enhanced outreach to community-based health professionals. In 1971, Congress developed the AHEC program in response to the findings of the Carnegie Commission on Higher Education's report *Higher Education and the Nation's Health: Policies for Medical and Dental Education*.[30] The Carnegie report recommended partnerships between community agencies and university health centers. These collaborations were ultimately designed to help educate healthcare professionals, to increase the number of professionals, and to improve the delivery of healthcare to underserved communities.[31]

Today, AHECs employ librarians and partner with libraries to provide outreach to area health professionals by training them to access reliable health information. The AHECs often provide access to health information resources, including journals, databases, and eBooks for health personnel working with underserved and rural populations. "The strength of the AHEC Network is its ability to creatively adapt national initiatives to help address local and regional healthcare issues."[32] Nationally, there are 56 AHEC programs and 235 centers, which work with approximately 120 medical schools and 600 nursing and allied health schools.[33] These AHEC programs collaborate with the schools to provide health career information to high school students, training for health professional students, and continuing education to practicing health professionals.

1980s

The MLAA Authority helped build the RML Network and focused on the "resource building and sharing among institutions."[34] In 1988, The U.S. Senate Appropriations Committee confirmed the need for improvement in outreach to health professionals, especially in rural and isolated areas, who would likely have challenges as they sought to access the biomedical literature.[35] The committee recommended that the NLM create programs to reach health professionals in rural and isolated areas.[36] The NLM Outreach Planning Panel, chaired by Michael E. DeBakey, reported its findings in the 1989 report titled *Improving Health Professionals' Access to Information*. The panel's recommendations were reported in four categories: (1) The Individual and the Regional Medical Library Network, (2) Strengthening Hospital Access to National Information Sources, (3) Training in Health Information Management, and (4) A New Generation of Information Products and Services. This NLM Outreach Planning Panel report, part of the NLM Long Range Plan, was a pivotal report that changed the landscape of health sciences outreach, specifically the RML Network. In particular, this report emphasized the need for the RML Network and health sciences libraries to improve their outreach to individual health professionals and provide access to biomedical information resources.[37] The report also specifically recommended that the RML Network change its name, which resulted in the network rebranding itself as the National Network of Libraries of Medicine (NN/LM).

1990s

In the early 1990s, NN/LM contracts with the NLM and with other libraries focused on two main outreach components: (1) GRATEFUL MED and Online Services Support and (2) Unaffiliated/Rural/Minority Health Professionals.[38] The GRATEFUL MED projects' main purpose was to teach health professionals in rural and underserved areas how to access biomedical information easily by using GRATEFUL MED, software developed by the NLM for use with personal computer systems.[39] Health sciences libraries focused their library outreach efforts on teaching GRATEFUL MED, providing resources via Loansome Doc (NLM's system for ordering articles), and providing reference services to health professionals who did not have access to the biomedical literature or to a medical library.

The birth of the Internet contributed to the growth of consumer health databases and the ease of access to health information for everyone. Health librarians became promoters of reliable consumer health and also assisted with the evaluation of reliable health information. In the 1990s, the NLM began responding to these shifts in consumer health services by developing new outreach initiatives and resources. The resulting NLM Long Range Plan,[40] titled *The NLM Track Record*, was a turning point for outreach in the health sciences. According to this plan, the NLM and the NN/LM would expand their outreach to the public. This mandate would be built on the NLM's launch of its new consumer health database, MedlinePlus, in October 1998. Thus, the NLM began efforts to publicize this resource and funding for the creation of other reliable consumer health information resources for patients and the public.

2000 to Present

The period from 2000 to the present has seen significant growth in outreach, with the expansion of outreach to public health professionals along with environmental and toxicology fields, representing a shift toward special populations. The NLM's Long Range Plan for 2000 to 2005 called for the NLM to increase its understanding of the evolving information needs of health professionals and the public.[41] The knowledge gathered about information needs assisted in strengthening and improving access to the NLM's digital collections of information resources. With this improvement came more publicity about the NLM's information resources, with raised awareness among a wider array of health professionals and the public.[42] The new millennium has led to new collaborations with federal agencies and health organizations, which has helped to decrease missed opportunities to provide understandable content for the public.[43]

The beginning of this decade also saw an increase in partnerships with public health professionals. The most notable partnership among government agencies, public health workers, and health sciences libraries was the development of the public health outreach portal, PHPartners.org. Today, each RML now has a staff member dedicated to public health outreach.[44, 45] The NLM's Long Range Plan for 2006 to 2016 emphasized this natural partnership between health sciences librarians and public health professionals.[46] This alliance is currently leading to improvements in the provision of health literacy, disaster information management, and public health informatics outreach.[47]

Information outreach in this current decade promotes increased outreach efforts to reach minority and culturally diverse populations and the health professionals who work with them. The NLM and the NN/LM, continuing their partnerships with public libraries, public health professionals, and community-based organizations, have created new strategies for underserved and minority communities' access to health information.[48]

The rich history of outreach by the National Library of Medicine and its organized network of regional health sciences libraries influenced the outreach endeavors of health sciences libraries today. The Internet has allowed health professionals and the public to easily access the NLM's biomedical information resources, which has improved research, education, and patient care.

OUTREACH SERVICES IN PRACTICE

Outreach to Professionals and Students

As the previous section of this chapter has shown, providing outreach to health professionals has been part of health sciences libraries' services for many years. Outreach services have evolved over the decades to include the whole healthcare team, healthcare professional students, healthcare professionals in rural areas, and unaffiliated healthcare professionals (without ties to a health sciences library). Perhaps unique to health sciences librarianship, health sciences librarians have found they need to meet the faculty, staff, students, and even the public, where they are located. The library's mission, the users' needs, and the users' requests determine and drive each library's outreach model. Outreach to healthcare professionals and students can take on different forms, which can range from on-campus activities to reaching out to unaffiliated healthcare professionals in a rural or urban area. While differing models for providing outreach to health professionals exist, most models fit into one or more of the following three categories: (1) reference and instruction, (2) liaison work, and (3) embedded. Outreach efforts aimed at health professionals and students affiliated with the university or healthcare center can often be combinations of these three types of services, and all variations can be seen in one library.

Reference and instruction outreach can lead to a librarian's presence in online classes; virtual reference by chat, text, or email; and continuing education classes as well as the more traditional face-to-face teaching or reference interactions. Librarians often offer classes that "train the trainer" to teach a particular subject, such as finding consumer health information through NLM's MedlinePlus resource. Librarians also teach health professionals and students how to find biomedical literature through the use of online search tools such as PubMed® or to locate information through factual databases such as MedlinePlus and ClinicalTrials.gov.

Providing a liaison to an academic department or group is another outreach model that librarians use to provide outreach services to health professionals and students. The liaison, often a subject specialist, encourages faculty to participate in collection development and facilitates communication between the library and the department.[49] Effective liaisons from outreach programs attend departmental meetings, participate in committees in the department, and meet with faculty in their offices.[50]

The embedded librarian outreach model has at its core the liaison model but takes it a step further by allowing the librarian "to move from a supporting role into partnerships with their clientele, enabling librarians to develop stronger connections and relationships with those they serve."[51] In health sciences libraries, the clinical librarian is a good example of how a librarian becomes embedded into the academic departments, groups, and clinical practice. In clinical librarianship, the clinical librarian is embedded in one or more patient care teams, often doing real-time reference work while on rounds in the hospital or clinic.

With all of the outreach models, partnerships serve as the foundation for success. Partnerships with academic departments, healthcare professionals, students, and faculty lead to stronger outreach efforts, which often turn into collaborative projects between the professionals and health sciences librarians. Since health sciences information outreach often takes librarians outside the library to meet and serve users, the type of outreach services can take on different forms depending on the type of setting. For example, a librarian partnering in hospitals can be seen on the floors doing rounds with the patient care team and organizing or attending journal clubs for faculty, house staff, and students. Being embedded into the patient care team, the clinical librarian teaches and serves as an expert searcher and a patient information advocate.[52] (Other outreach librarians meet students in their classrooms, or even in the student center.)

Outreach to community-based health professionals who are not affiliated with an academic health center or hospital is another example of a potential outreach partnership. Librarians at the University of Texas Health Science Center at San

Antonio partnered with area public health dental teams. The librarians taught team members how to search for biomedical research literature to support their clinical and public health practice, and also how to find information for their patients.[53] The dental health team, in turn, used the newly gained information to enhance its care of patients.

Partnerships can also exist with health professionals who serve animals. Texas A&M University librarians who are embedded in clinical programs in veterinary medicine often join students and faculty as they examine "patients" in small and large animal clinics.[54] In fact, a growing number of librarians are serving on institutional animal care and use committees (IACUCs) in addition to institutional review boards (IRBs). The location may vary, but librarians providing outreach services to professionals, students, and the public have to be flexible and open in their efforts to meet their audience's information needs and to foster the partnerships needed to develop and sustain successful outreach programs.

Outreach Programs to the General Public

As previously mentioned, historically, librarians focused their outreach projects on engaging healthcare professionals, but today, a large share of outreach services are reserved for partnerships with existing community groups.[55] When deciding on community-based outreach activities, the outreach librarian must be sure to critically read and assess the organization's mission and vision statements. The librarian must also be sure all goals and objectives for the outreach project are in alignment with both. Also, it is imperative for the librarian to look at the strategic plan for both the community organization and the librarian's parent institution. Buy-in from both entities will be stronger if the project at hand embodies the mission and vision of the partnering organizations as a whole.

Olney and Barnes outlined the necessary steps to organize community-based outreach, and to gather and interpret the needs of a community.[56] Conducting a needs assessment is the first and best way to identify target populations and/or communities of interest and what an outreach project can offer in return. There may already be connections with members of certain communities who, when approached, will be interested in ways to improve the health of their constituents. Successful outreach programs require goals and objectives combined with methods for satisfying them.[57] Goals and objectives will differ from project to project due to population changes, the different needs of a population, varying financial resources, equipment, and time. Additional differences among the goals and objectives will be identified from the assessment. Access should not be the only goal, as there are several areas that librarians can target, including outreach focused on changing community member behaviors.

Once the goals and objectives of the project are identified, planning strategies and activities to implement these goals is the next step. Try to be aware of potential barriers to achieving goals and objectives. Examples of barriers to be anticipated when conducting outreach related to effective information seeking are lack of time, insufficient financial resources, and lack of or cost of equipment.[58] Some community-based outreach activities can be promotional to increase interest and awareness, logistical to increase adequate onsite access, or educational to develop knowledge or skills in accessing information.[59] Community-based health information outreach projects seek to provide information and technology to members of the general population who often do not seek out information resources on their own. The combination of librarians and community members can assist in training a targeted community in how to navigate the health information landscape and disseminate these lessons among their peers.[60]

COMMON OUTREACH MODELS AND THEORIES

Health Belief Model

The health belief model (HBM) is one of the most commonly used models for changing health behavior for the better.[61, 62] The model, developed by social psychologists in the 1950s, was "designed to explain health behavior by better understanding individuals' beliefs about health."[63] They developed the HBM to help explain why people participate in immunization and health screening programs, but it has since been applied to many outreach and behavioral intervention programs.

The health belief model consists of five major concepts that predict if individuals will take action to prevent specific health behaviors and promote or protect their health (see Figure 13.1): (1) perceived susceptibility to a condition or problem, (2) perceived severity of a health threat, (3) perceived benefits of a recommended course of action, (4) perceived barriers of a recommended course of action, and (5) cues to action. If individuals perceive themselves to be susceptible to a condition or if they believe the condition could have potentially serious consequences, they will be more likely to undertake a course of action to reduce their risk. Individuals will also be more likely to take a course of action when they believe it will reduce their susceptibility or the severity of a condition and when they believe the benefits of taking action outweigh the costs or barriers to action.[64] Cues to action can be external (e.g., television commercials, magazine articles) and/or internal (e.g., psychological or physiological symptoms), and these cues can increase one's perception of susceptibility to or the severity of a certain disease, which can weigh barriers and benefits against each other.[65]

However, the health belief model does not consider specific parameters. The model focuses on attitudes and beliefs that can influence an individual's behavior but does not take into consideration the social, economic, and environmental barriers that can also impact an individual's health decisions.[66]

The REACH 2010: Charleston and Georgetown Diabetes Coalition, which was formed in response to Centers for Disease Control and Prevention's (CDC) funding for the development of community coalitions to combat diabetes, is an example of the health belief model in action. The coalition consisted of a diverse group of partners from the Charleston, South Carolina, community and was coordinated by the Diabetes Initiative of South Carolina at the Medical University of South Carolina.[67] The 28 partner organizations focused on reducing disparities, including

Individual Perceptions   Modifying Factors   Likelihood of Action

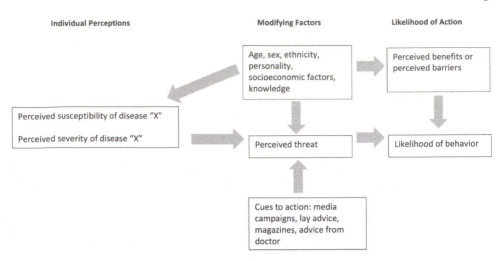

Figure 13.1   Health Belief Model and Linkages

health information and access to healthcare among African Americans who had been diagnosed with diabetes. To reduce these disparities, the coalition took a multipronged approach by educating nurses, librarians, and community health advisors (CHAs) to serve the needs of this special population.[68]

Early in this project, the coalition focused on improving screenings, education, and testing, the components that comprise diabetes management control.[69] Ideally, patients with diabetes would get annual screenings to ensure their diabetes was not leading to complications such as blindness, foot ulcers (which, untreated, could require amputations), or kidney disease. For this program, the medical librarian led education sessions about diabetes screenings and prevention topics. Some of these sessions likely motivated participants to attend or find out about these complication-related screening sessions, rendering the information they received into action.[70] The education and screening partnerships among nurses, librarians, and CHAs helped ensure that participants were made aware that these tests (i.e., foot screening, eye exam, A1C test, annual lipid profile, and an annual kidney [urine] test) would help alert them if they were more susceptible to additional complications but would also emphasize the importance of managing their diabetes.[71]

The coalition wanted to expand diabetes educational opportunities in the Charleston area to promote ownership by the community and raise the likelihood of long-term sustainability.[72] To reach this goal, it chose to focus on decreasing the economic barriers that prevented community members from receiving appropriate screenings and treatment for control of their diabetes, as well as help raise awareness of the status and severity of the disease.[73] As the health belief model states, these barriers can often hinder someone from gaining access to screenings.

Transtheoretical Model of Behavior Change

Developed by DiClemente and Prochaska, the transtheoretical model of behavior change is based on research from the field of behavioral psychology, particularly the

Table 13.1 Stages of Change Model

Variable	Concept	Outreach Application
Precontemplation	Not thinking of changing a behavior	Introduce awareness of health information sources
Contemplation	Thinking about using the Internet for information access	Increase awareness of the need for change
Preparation	Making plans to learn information seeking skills via the Internet	Facilitate computer access, offer skills training with varied formats personalized to local need
Action	Using Internet sources when seeking new information	Assist with technical support, publish articles about search tips, train onsite liaison to offer support or provide intermediary searches
Maintenance	Continuing new information seeking behaviors	Offer advanced and refresher classes, continue to partner with opinion leader advocates to reinforce new behaviors

mechanisms for changing behaviors.[74] The premise of this model is that behavior change is a process, not an event, and individuals have varying levels of motivation or readiness to change.[75] Some examples of behaviors that have been studied using this model are smoking cessation, sun protection, condom use, and medication adherence.[76]

This model is also known as the *stages of change model*, which states there are five stages of change, as shown in Table 13.1: precontemplation, contemplations, preparation, action, and maintenance.[77] Principles of this theory can be easily turned into successful outreach and educational events. However, one mistake that can be made by outreach workers is assuming that participants want to change.[78]

Some iterations of this model incorporate a sixth stage: termination. This stage exists when an individual no longer has any temptation toward the negative behavior.[79]

The behavior change mentioned as part of this model is intentional. An advantage of the stages of change model is that it describes behavior change as a process, not as an event. The process is then broken down into stages, so variables along the continuum are associated with an audience's progress or setbacks. The findings from these stages can also help with intervention design. Many individuals may move in somewhat predictable ways—some may move quickly through the different stages, while others may get hung up within one stage because of their lack of confidence in their ability to change their behaviors.[80] The major concept to understand about the stages of change model is that individuals do not move linearly from stage to stage. Some individuals advance and then recycle back.[81] From a practitioner's perspective, this model provides a useful framework for advising patients and clients, and understanding their compliance. From a program planning perspective, this model helps illustrate how the different stages of change can influence programming and activities.[82]

Numerous analyses and reviews have studied the effectiveness of using the transtheoretical model of behavior change. A recent example is Robinson and Vail's

"Integrative Review of Adolescent Smoking Cessation Using the Transtheoretical Model of Change."[83] The purpose of this review was to evaluate the effectiveness of this model in modifying adolescents' smoking behaviors. The authors searched for randomized, controlled trials or observational studies of adolescent smoking cessation attempts that used the transtheoretical model of behavior change. Cigarette smoking among adolescents is strongly associated with numerous co-morbidities and problem behaviors, including a well-documented link with externalizing disorders, such as conduct, behavior, and anxiety disorders. Using the transtheoretical model of behavior change, practitioners attempt to utilize existing motivation for positive change by facilitating movement through the stages of change.[84]

One limitation to this review was that it did not include smokeless tobacco. The review was limited to programs using the transtheoretical model of behavior change for cigarette smoking only. After careful searching and excluding, the sample yielded six studies that offered a fair representation of adolescents' behavior in the United States. The authors utilized both qualitative and quantitative methods in their analysis of the studies. Their findings state that interventions structured on the transtheoretical model of behavior change can be used successfully with adolescent patients to effect changes in smoking behavior, specifically to promote cessation.[85] A significant finding is that the use of the model's motivational interviewing consistently produced "robust results." Therefore, this model has emerged as an effective intervention for this age group.

Social Cognitive Theory

Albert Bandura, known as the originator of social cognitive theory (SCT), also referred to as social learning theory, defines social learning theory as one that assumes that modeling influences produce learning principally through their informative functions and that observers acquire mainly symbolic representations of modeled activities rather than specific stimulus-response associations.[86] In other words, individuals learn behaviors through observing modeling and motivation.

Social cognitive theory has been applied in clinical settings to predict changes in health behavior.[87] Social cognitive theory is a behavior prediction that represents a clinical approach to health behavior change and has been widely applied to health behavior in relation to prevention, health promotion, and modification of unhealthy lifestyles.[88] Another way of understanding this theory is to think of it as behavior having what Redding calls a "triadic reciprocity" among concepts that operate as determinants for each other and "reciprocal determinism," which forms the basic organizing principle of social cognitive theory.[89] Reciprocal determinism describes the way in which individuals, their environment, and their behavior continuously interact and influence each other.[90]

This triadic approach refers to an individual's personal characteristics. The environment can be physical, cultural, emotional, social, or political. Within the environment are situations that can influence behavior, hence, the reciprocal nature of this theory. The relationship between individuals, their behaviors, and their environments is iterative and interactive. Environmental change affects individuals and

Table 13.2 Social Learning Theory

Variable	Concept	Outreach Application
Behavioral capability	Knowledge and skills about recommended action	Provide information and training about recommended actions (e.g., online searching)
Expectations	Beliefs about likely results of action	Demonstrate searches that provide relevant results
Self-efficacy	Confidence in ability to take action and persist in action	Teach skills in small steps, give feedback and encouragement, give in-class exercise problems that provide challenge
Observational learning	Beliefs based on observing others like self	Point out others' experiences, provide demonstrations by role models (e.g., clinician, senior citizen, member of minority population)

thus may also affect individuals' behavior. When their health behavior changes, be it positively or negatively, that behavior has an effect on the individuals as well as their environment, be it their relationship with their family and friends or how they go about their days.[91] Glanz and Bishop described four variables playing a role in behavior change when applying this theory in a health information outreach setting. Table 13.2 explains these variables, as well as ways to apply them to health information outreach.

This theory is one of the most widely used in health promotion, since it addresses both the health behavior of the individual and methods of promoting change. Understanding the individual helps create the proper intervention, and this interaction then influences the person's knowledge, beliefs, understanding, and self-efficacy. In turn, these changes alter the health behavior of the individual.[92] The key concept of SCT is this reciprocal determinism. An individual can be both an agent for change as well as a responder to change. Therefore, role models, encouragement, and feedback can be used to promote changes to healthier behaviors.[93]

An example of social cognitive theory being used in program design is Rogers and colleagues' study "Better Exercise Adherence after Treatment for Cancer (BEAT Cancer) Study: Rational, Design, and Methods."[94] Two hundred and fifty-six survivors of breast cancer who completed primary cancer treatment were enrolled in this two-site study in Illinois. Each group was randomized to receive either BEAT Cancer physical activity behavior change intervention or usual care.

This project had one primary study aim and two secondary aims. The BEAT Cancer intervention was a three-month physical activity behavior change intervention for survivors of breast cancer to gradually increase participants to more than 150 weekly minutes of moderate intensity physical activity.[95] The study's primary aim was to compare the effects of the study on short- and long-term physical activity adherence among study participants. One of its secondary aims was to compare the behavior change on social cognitive factors. The study's other secondary aim was to compare the long- and short-term effects of the intervention on changes in health outcomes.[96]

The study had its own eligibility criteria as well as enrollment randomization. Participants' assessments were performed at baseline and at three, six, and twelve months. Participants were asked to evaluate each assessment period, take a short survey, answer three open-ended questions, and then rate the program overall.

This study addressed the important clinical and public health problems associated with physical activity among survivors of breast cancer. According to the authors, no other behavioral change intervention study among survivors of cancer has reported using both individual exercise sessions and group counseling that tapers the participant onto a self-directed program to optimize changes in physical activity and longer adherence.[97] The result of this pilot study will not be validated until the larger trial is completed. Authors feel physical activity programs should be offered to all survivors of breast cancer without a medical contraindication, given the association between physical activity and a reduction in risk for breast cancer recurrence and mortality of 35 percent and 46 percent respectively.[98]

Diffusion of Innovations Theory

Diffusion of innovations theory addresses how, why, and at what rate new ideas or programs spread within a community or from one community to another. Everett Rogers originated the diffusion of innovation theory, basing it on his research in the social sciences. Diffusion of innovations is one of the most widely used models in health sciences community-based outreach, and it is applied to a variety of fields and a wide range of settings.

Diffusion is the "process by which an innovation is communicated through certain channels over time among members of a social system."[99] An innovation is "an idea, practice, or object that is perceived as new by an individual or other unit of adoption."[100] If an idea is new to an individual, it is considered an innovation. Diffusion of effective outreach programs and successful interventions can be a significant challenge in health sciences libraries. Rogers identified four characteristics that influence the success of new ideas and programs and the rate at which these are adopted into communities:[101]

- The characteristics of the innovation and the rate of adoption
- The characteristics of the potential adopters
- The nature of the social system
- The characteristics of change agents

The rate that innovations are accepted and integrated into a community varies. Some innovations spread broadly and quickly, while other innovations are accepted slowly, accepted only by a few, or are never adopted by the community at all. The rate of adoption refers to how quickly an innovation is adopted by the members of its social system.[102] Five core attributes determine an innovation's rate of adoption (see Table 13.3).

Table 13.3 Five Core Attributes That Determine an Innovation's Rate of Adoption

Attribute	Concept
Relative advantage	The degree to which an innovation is seen as better than the idea, practice, product, or program it replaces
Compatibility	The degree to which an innovation is perceived as being consistent with the values, habits, experience, and needs of potential adopters
Complexity	How difficult an innovation is to understand and use
Trialability	Extent to which the innovation can be experimented with before committing to adopt
Observability	Extent of the innovation's visibility to others

Rogers describes five categories of adopters according to the how long it takes for each group to adopt new ideas:[103]

- Innovators
- Early adopters
- Early majority
- Late majority
- Laggards

Innovation is adopted first by the innovators, which make up 2.5 percent of the individuals in the system. Early adopters are more integrated in the community and make up 10 to 15 percent of the individuals in a community that adopts an innovation. The early majority represents the average of 34 percent of the population that adopt an innovation. They adopt new ideas just before the average members of the community. The late majority also makes up about 34 percent of the community that adopt an innovation, but they adopt the new ideas just after the average members of the community. The laggards are considered the last 16 percent of the community that finally adopt the innovation. Laggards are considered in most cases to be "actively resistant to the introduction of new ideas."[104] Outreach activities should target innovators and early adopters because they help persuade other groups, and their communication can be powerful and influential for others.

In addition, the setting and the nature of the social system where the new idea is being diffused can directly impact the speed and success of the diffusion. Different factors can influence the organization and the community's diffusion process.[105] In some social systems, change is more common than it is in other communities. Geographic settings, societal culture, political conditions, and globalization and uniformity are all features that can influence the diffusion process in a social system.[106]

Diffusion also depends on leadership and communication. Opinion leaders and change agents are individuals who have influence over other individuals in a social system. Opinion leaders, usually influential members of a community, spread information, positive or negative, about the innovation in a community. The opinion leaders are early adopters if their opinions are positive, and they often act as role models for the other members in a community. The change agents in the diffusion process are often individuals outside the community because they bring the innovations to a community.

Critical mass is another important concept in the diffusion of innovations theory. This is the point at which enough individuals in a community have adopted the innovation and any further rate of adoption becomes self-sustaining. "Early adopters are instrumental in getting an innovation to the point of critical mass, and hence, in the successful diffusion of an innovation."[107]

The Med High Peer Tutor MedlinePlus Pilot project demonstrates the diffusion of innovation theory at work. This project was part of the Texas Lower Rio Grande Valley Health Information Hispanic Outreach, which was funded by the NLM and spearheaded by the University of Texas Health Science Center at San Antonio's (UTHSCSA) branch library, the Mario E. Ramirez, M.D. Library at the Regional Academic Health Center (RAHC) in Harlingen, Texas. The Peer Tutor project was part of a two-year outreach project focused on the Hispanic community in the Lower Rio Grande Valley in Texas. The overarching goal of the project was to ascertain the role that MedlinePlus and the RAHC "could play in the strengthening Hispanic awareness and use of health information."[108] The RAHC partnered with the South Texas High School for Health Professions (Med High) in the Lower Rio Grande Valley of Texas to increase the awareness of MedlinePlus in the community. The project was built on the peer tutor model, which the Med High librarians were already using to teach new software and databases to students and faculty.[109] Four peer tutors were trained to use and teach MedlinePlus to their peers and individuals in the community. The RAHC librarians targeted the innovators and the early adopters (Med High librarians and the four peer tutors) in the school community instead of training everyone in the school. As the Med High librarians and peer tutors learned more, they "became the mentors and role models for others in the school community and beyond," by teaching students and faculty how to use MedlinePlus at school open houses and at community events.[110] This innovation, the use of MedlinePlus for health information use, diffused into different facets of the community through the integration of MedlinePlus into the curriculum and students' increasing use of MedlinePlus for school projects. The Peer Tutor Project, which assisted with the diffusion of MedlinePlus to the Med High Students and to the surrounding community, influenced a change in the librarians' roles in the school.[111] The librarians became active members in the curriculum as a result of their roles in the Med High Peer Tutor MedlinePlus Pilot Project.[112]

Evaluation of Outreach Programs

The evaluation of any project is a necessary step in determining its impact. The Outreach Evaluation Resource Center (OERC) is a source for research-based assessment and evaluation tools for medical libraries. The OERC builds capacity for health information outreach evaluation for the National Network of Libraries of Medicine (NN/LM), and offers workshops, free publications, and assistance regarding all aspects of assessment and evaluation. When evaluation is an integral part of an outreach project, participants can identify productive approaches, learn from experiences, make mid-course corrections, and recognize accomplishments. Through evaluation, project coordinators can demonstrate to partners and stakeholders that their efforts have made a difference.[113]

The publication *Measuring the Difference*—developed by the National Network of Libraries of Medicine, Pacific Northwest Region—is a valuable primer on planning and evaluating health information programs. This book walks the reader through the multistage process needed to begin a health information outreach program or project. Stage 1: Conducting a Community Assessment; Stage 2: Developing Goals & Objectives; Stage 3: Planning Activities and Strategies; Stage 4: Planning Evaluation; Stage 5: Gathering Data and Assessing Results; and Stage 6: Utilizing and Reporting Results. The book also contains an appendix and a useful bibliography.[114]

Also available is a three-part booklet series that supplements *Measuring the Difference* and is available from the OERC website (http://www.nnlm.gov/evaluation/guide).

The first booklet, *Getting Started with Community-Based Outreach*, gives recommendations and direction on how project coordinators can get organized, gather information, and assemble, interpret, and act on their findings. This booklet also gives some real-world examples as well as worksheets for organization purposes. The second booklet, *Planning Outcomes-Bases Outreach Projects*, begins with showing how to create a logic model and then explains how to best use the logic model to develop an outcomes assessment plan and how to use the model through different stages of the project. Some examples of data source and evaluation methods are given as are real-world examples. Worksheets also help keep the project on track and organized. The third booklet, *Collecting and Analyzing Evaluation Data*, walks the reader through designing data collection methods, collecting data, and summarizing and assessing the validity of the data. These steps are given for collecting and analyzing quantitative as well as qualitative data. Also included are examples of questions that can be used to collect both kinds of data as well as worksheets on planning interviews and surveys.

These step-by-step booklets are a must for any organization involved or planning to be involved in community-based health information outreach and are available for free online (http://nnlm.gov/evaluation/). Their step-by-step instructions and explanations as well as supplemental worksheets will keep a novice on the right track and will keep a seasoned project coordinator asking the right questions and collecting the right data.

Logic models are tools that have been used for decades by program managers and evaluators to describe the effectiveness of their programs.[115] The models visually narrate or graphically represent the process and activities involved as well as how each builds upon others and leads to a specific result. Another way to think of it is that the logic model needs to articulate the outcomes so that they are measures and can demonstrate the effectiveness of the project. Creating this model improves the likelihood for a successful project because the logic model provides checks and balances throughout the project.[116]

A logic model and the outcome measures within the logic model are what health information projects use to articulate outcomes and demonstrate to participants and/or funders the effectiveness of the project. It also helps coordinators visualize how activities are linked to results.[117] Convincing evidence of the effectiveness of health information outreach projects is essential to ensure their continued funding and support, and project evaluation is the method for obtaining the evidence.[118]

A major challenge of health information outreach is the gap between what researchers and project coordinators would like to measure and what can be realistically measured.[119] Some examples of outreach project outcomes are developing new partnerships, gaining enhanced access to information through technology, increasing awareness of resources, improving health literacy skills, increasing proficiency in health literacy, and establishing search training for professionals and/or the public.

Olney and Barnes have a three-step approach to outcomes-based projects.[120] Step one is to plan with a logic model, step two is to use a logic model for process assessment, and step three is to use a logic model to develop an outcomes assessment plan. Any health information outreach project should have an evaluation component from the start. Creating a logic model will provide an evaluation framework to help process activities and assessment. Evaluation becomes a more meaningful process if goals for assessment are planned and implemented from the beginning; as a result, the data will be more useful to coordinators, participants, and funders.[121]

Huber and colleagues' "Outreach Impact Study: The Case of the Greater Midwest Region" evaluated the impact funding from the NLM has had on health information outreach projects.[122] The methods used in the study to assess the impact of funding were content analysis and surveys. According to the principal investigators of the assessed projects, all felt the outreach attempts were a success and had a positive impact on both professionals and members of the general public who were involved.[123] This is one of many studies regarding evaluation results of health information projects that have been completed. Constant evaluation throughout the project is necessary to improve outreach efforts and objectives.

Funding Sources

Funding for community outreach is an essential component for success. Funding may come from numerous sources such as the workplace; federal, state, county, or local agencies; and public or private foundations. Prospective audiences may also provide ideas about potential funders. It is important to consider all sources of funding, both internal and external. This section will give some specific examples of organizations and funding sources for health information outreach projects. Access to electronic information is becoming more pervasive, so librarians are being deployed outside of the library to improve quality, to reduce the risks associated with inefficient or incomplete retrieval of available evidence, and to do community outreach.[124]

The National Network of Libraries of Medicine is a major funding source for health information outreach support. The mission of the National Network of Libraries of Medicine is to advance the progress of medicine and improve the public's health by providing all U.S. health professionals with equal access to biomedical information and improving the public's access to information to enable them to make informed decisions about their health.[125] This mission is coordinated by the

National Library of Medicine and carried out through a nationwide network of health science libraries and information centers.

The NN/LM is separated into eight regions throughout the United States, with each having a dedicated regional medical library located within an academic health sciences library. These regional medical libraries offer training and funding to interested member organizations. Numerous funding opportunities are available through the NN/LM, and awards differ from region to region. Since the employees at the NN/LM offices are not employees of the NLM, the monies are distributed in the form of awards and contracts, not grants.[126] The exhibit awards allow organizations to exhibit at the local, state, regional, or national level to promote NLM resources as well as the applicants' outreach services. Additional awards are focused on technology improvement, hospital library promotion, health literacy, digitization, health disparities, disaster preparedness, assessment and planning, and others.

The NN/LM is not the only division at the NLM with federal funding available for health information outreach. In addition to the NN/LM, the National Library of Medicine has its own Division of Extramural Programs and Division of Specialized Information Services (SIS), which fund projects in areas important to their mission. Some of their programs are research, career, and training support, and there are also projects relating to emergency preparedness.

Staying up to date on available funding opportunities via the regional medical library is a task that all outreach medical librarians should complete. Librarians should contact the regional medical library for specific questions (http://www.nnlm.gov) or go online (http://www.nlm.nih.gov/ep/) to find out more specific information about what grants are currently available via the NLM Division of Extramural Programs, as well as a list of previously funded projects. Other federal agencies offering funds for health information outreach projects are the Department of Health and Human Services (http://www.hhs.gov/grants/) and state and county health departments.[127] Private foundations and many not-for-profits non-profit organizations offer outreach funding to improve the health of their communities. Librarians need to think about the population being served and then create an outreach project funding plan that fits the needs of the community. Librarians should be creative, interactive, and multidisciplinary to draw attention to their funding applications, attract more attendees to outreach events, and bolster future partnerships.

Most funding, if created for a specific population's needs, will have a positive impact on the population receiving the outreach, the funding organization, and the outreach organization's ability to conduct outreach.[128] "Today's libraries have unprecedented opportunities to contribute to better quality and efficiency in healthcare, education and research. Those who support and lead medical libraries should seize these opportunities. The future is in their hands."[129]

CONCLUSION

"Academic medical libraries and outreach librarians across the country exert great effort to reach beyond the campus walls."[130] As Fama and colleagues describe, there are numerous resources involved in outreach work, for example, money, staff, and time.[131]

Understanding what outreach means is the first critical step in a successful outreach program. All parties involved need to have a clear understanding of what outreach means to their institutions.[132] Some of the definitions found in Fama's study were serving the unaffiliated, extending services beyond the physical library, and activities outside traditional library services on or off campus.

Not all objectives set forth for a project will be met. There will be barriers to the outreach project as well as unexpected outcomes and new objectives as well. As one institution states, "This project . . . helped to improve access to accurate health information to community members and to healthcare providers who serve them in a free health clinic."[133] Outreach projects will also have known limitations such as staffing issues, time constraints, and technology issues. There will also be unexpected limitations, but if outcomes were identified, these unknown limitations become lessons learned for future projects.

Outreach can be conducted in varying forms. Outreach can be as simple as asking to be part of a departmental meeting to educate those in attendance on resources; it can be a training session for a community health center; it can be a multipart training for public health workers; or it can be a booth at a church health fair. Outreach is educating members of your community about health information. The communities touched by these outreach program vary as well. Senior centers, housing authorities, public health departments, and public libraries are just some communities that can be affected by outreach. The needs of each of these communities will also vary, and a proper needs assessment will ascertain their individual needs.

Evaluation is a key factor for the future success of project participants or the librarians. Final reports from project coordinators will help evaluate the success of the project, and they will provide ideas for sustainability or project continuation. "The Outreach Impact Study: The Case of the Greater Midwest Region" discusses what funders expected to see in reports and what the actual findings were. The results did not yield the expected response: The funders expected to hear how the monies received benefited the outreach project. However, many of the responses indicated an increase in community building and networking, and that the projects would never have been achieved without the funding.[134] Health sciences librarians must bear in mind these many factors to ensure the continuation and growth of such programs into the future.

NOTES

1. Fama, J., D. Berryman, N. Harger, P. Julian, N. Peterson, M. Spinner, and J. Varney. "Inside Outreach: A Challenge for Health Sciences Librarians." *Journal of the Medical Library Association: JMLA* 93, no. 3 (2005): 327–337.

2. Scherrer, C. S., and S. Jacobson. "New Measures for New Roles: Defining and Measuring the Current Practices of Health Sciences Librarians." *Journal of the Medical Library Association: JMLA* 90, no. 2 (2002): 164–172.

3. Nixon, J. M., and D. Shumaker. "Who Let the Librarians Out? Embedded Librarianship and the Library Manager." *Reference and User Services Quarterly* 48, no. 3 (2009): 239–242.

4. Rudin, P. "No Fixed Address: The Evolution of Outreach Library Services on University Campuses." *Reference Librarian* 49, no. 1 (2008): 55–75.

5. "The National Library of Medicine Long Range Plan: The NLM Track Record." Bethesda, MD: National Library of Medicine, 1999. Last Accessed March 2, 2013. http://www.nlm.nih.gov/od/trackrecord.pdf.

6. "National Library of Medicine Long Range Plan, 2000–2005/Report of the Board of Regents." Bethesda, MD: National Library of Medicine, 2000. Accessed June 30, 2013. http://www.nlm.nih.gov/od/ohipd/nlm-lrp.pdf.

7. "Charting a Course for the 21st Century: NLM's Long Range Plan, 2006–2016." Bethesda, MD: National Library of Medicine, 2006. Accessed June 30, 2013. http://www.nlm.nih.gov/pubs/plan/lrp06/report/default.html.

8. Corporation for National & Community Service. "Building Successful Partnerships." National Service Knowledge Network. Last modified 2013. http://www.national serviceresources.org/filemanager/download/partnerships/Building_Partnerships.pdf.

9. Ibid.

10. Fama et al., *op. cit.*

11. Banks, R. A., R. H. Thiss, G. R. Rios, and P. C. Self. "Outreach Services: Issues and Challenges." *Medical Reference Services Quarterly* 16, no. 2 (1997): 1–10.

12. Fama et al., *op. cit.*

13. Johnson, Becky McKay. "Grand Rounds: Medical Library Outreach." In *Academic Library Outreach: Beyond the Campus Walls*, edited by Nancy Courtney, 227–239. Westport, CT: Libraries Unlimited, 2009.

14. Rogers, Everett M., and Karyn L. Scott. "The Diffusion of Innovations Model and Outreach from the National Network of Libraries of Medicine to Native American Communities." National Network of Libraries of Medicine. Last modified 1997. http://nnlm.gov/evaluation/pub/rogers/.

15. Bloomquist, Harold, and National Library of Medicine. *The Status and Needs of Medical School Libraries in the United States.* Boston: 1963.

16. Ibid.

17. Ibid.

18. Cummings, M. M., and M. E. Corning. "The Medical Library Assistance Act: An Analysis of the NLM Extramural Programs, 1965–1970." *Bulletin of the Medical Library Association* 59, no. 3 (1971): 375–391.

19. Kennedy, Scott. "Farewell to the Reference Librarian." *Journal of Library Administration* 51, no. 4 (2011): 319–325.

20. Ibid.

21. Cummings and Corning, *op. cit.*

22. Cogdill, K. W. "Progress in Health Sciences Librarianship, 1970–2005." *Advances in sLibrarianship* 30 (2006): 145–177.

23. Pifalo, V. "The Evolution of Rural Outreach from Package Library to GRATEFUL MED Introduction to the Symposium." *Bulletin of the Medical Library Association* 88, no. 4 (2000): 339–345.

24. Bunting, A. "The Nation's Health Information Network: History of the Regional Medical Library Program, 1965–1985." *Bulletin of the Medical Library Association* 75, no. 3 (1987): 1–62.

25. Cogdill, *op. cit.*

26. "175 Years: Our Milestones." National Library of Medicine. Last modified 2011, accessed June 30, 2013. http://apps.nlm.nih.gov/175/milestones.cfm.

27. Pifalo, *op. cit.*

28. Ibid.

29. Ibid.

30. Seibert, E. M. "Area Health Education Centers and Health Education Training Centers: A Well-Kept Secret." *AANA Journal* 73, no. 5 (2005): 345–349.

31. Ibid.

32. "National AHEC Organization: About Us." National AHEC Organization, 2013. Accessed March 2, 2013. http://www.nationalahec.org/about/AboutUs.html.

33. Ibid.

34. DeBakey, Michael E. "Improving Health Professionals' Access to Information: Report of the Board of Regents." Bethesda, MD: National Library of Medicine, 1989. Accessed June 30, 2013. http://www.nlm.nih.gov/archive/20040721/pubs/plan/ih/contents.html.

35. Wallingford, K. T., A. B. Ruffin, K. A. Ginter, M. L. Spann, F. E. Johnson, G. A. Dutcher, R. Mehnert, et al. "Outreach Activities of the National Library of Medicine: A Five-Year Review." *Bulletin of the Medical Library Association* 84, no. 2 (1996): 1–60.

36. Ibid.

37. DeBakey, *op. cit.*

38. Wallingford et al., *op. cit.*

39. Ibid.

40. "The National Library of Medicine Long Range Plan: The NLM Track Record."

41. "National Library of Medicine Long Range Plan, 2000–2005."

42. Ibid.

43. Ibid.

44. Cogdill, *op. cit.*

45. Cogdill, K. W., A. B. Ruffin, and P. Z. Stavri. "The National Network of Libraries of Medicine's Outreach to the Public Health Workforce, 2001–2006." *Journal of the Medical Library Association: JMLA* 95, no. 3 (2007): 310–315.

46. "Charting a Course for the 21st Century: NLM's Long Range Plan."

47. Humphreys, B. L. "Building Better Connections: The National Library of Medicine and Public Health." *Journal of the Medical Library Association: JMLA* 95, no. 3 (2007): 293–300.

48. "Charting a Course for the 21st Century: NLM's Long Range Plan."

49. Tennant, M. R., L. C. Butson, M. E. Rezeau, P. J. Tucker, M. E. Boyle, and G. Clayton. "Customizing for Clients: Developing a Library Liaison Program from Need to Plan." *Bulletin of the Medical Library Association* 89, no. 1 (2001): 8–20.

50. Scherrer and Jacobson, *op. cit.*

51. Carlson, J., and R. Kneale. "Embedded Librarianship in the Research Context Navigating New Waters." *College and Research Libraries News* 72, no. 3 (2011): 167–171.

52. Tan, M. C., and L. A. Maggio. "Expert Searcher, Teacher, Content Manager, and Patient Advocate: An Exploratory Study of Clinical Librarian Roles." *Journal of the Medical Library Association: JMLA* 101, no. 1 (2013): 63–72.

53. Gaines, J. K., L. S. Levy, and K. W. Cogdill. "Sharing MedlinePlus®/Medline® for Information Literacy Education (Smile): A Dental Public Health Information Project." *Medical Reference Services Quarterly* 30, no. 4 (2011): 357–364.

54. Olmstadt, W., C. L. Foster, N. G. Burford, N. F. Funkhouser, and J. Jaros. "Clinical Veterinary Librarianship: The Texas A&M University Experience." *Bulletin of the Medical Library Association* 89, no. 4 (2001): 395–397.

55. Scherrer, C. S. "Outreach to Community Organizations: The Next Consumer Health Frontier." *Journal of the Medical Library Association: JMLA* 90, no. 3 (2002): 285–289.

56. Olney, Cynthia A., Susan J. Barnes, National Network of Libraries of Medicine Outreach Evaluation Resource Center, and National Library of Medicine. *Getting Started with Community-Based Outreach.* Seattle; Bethesda, MD: National Network of Libraries of Medicine, Outreach Evaluation Resource Center; National Library of Medicine, 2013.

57. Burroughs, Catherine M., Fred B. Wood, National Network of Libraries of Medicine Pacific Northwest Region, and National Library of Medicine. *Measuring the Difference: Guide to Planning and Evaluating Health Information Outreach.* Seattle; Bethesda, MD: National Network of Libraries of Medicine, Pacific Northwest Region; National Library of Medicine, 2000.

58. Marshall, Joanne G. "A Review of Health Sciences Library Outreach and Evaluation." National Library of Medicine, 1997. Accessed June 30, 2013. http://nnlm.gov/archive/pnr/eval/marshall.html.

59. Burroughs et al., *op. cit.*

60. Olney and Barnes, *op. cit.*

61. Witte, Kim. "Theory-Based Interventions and Evaluations of Outreach Efforts." National Network of Libraries of Medicine Outreach Evaluation Resource Center. Last modified 2007. http://nnlm.gov/evaluation/pub/witte/.

62. Nutbeam, Don, Elizabeth Harris, and Marilyn Wise. *Theory in a Nutshell: A Practical Guide to Health Promotion Theories.* North Ryde NSW; London: McGraw-Hill Medical, 2010.

63. Ibid.

64. Champion, Victoria L., and Celette S. Skinner. "The Health Belief Model." In *Health Behavior and Health Education: Theory, Research, and Practice*, edited by Karen Glanz, Barbara K. Rimer, and K. Viswanath. San Francisco: Jossey-Bass, 2008.

65. Witte, *op. cit.*

66. Nutbeam, Harris, and Wise, *op. cit.*

67. Jenkins, C., S. McNary, B. A. Carlson, M. G. King, C. L. Hossler, D. Magwood, D. Y. Zheng, et al. "Reducing Disparities for African Americans with Diabetes: Progress Made by the Reach 2010 Charleston and Georgetown Diabetes Coalition." *Public Health Reports* 119, no. 3 (2004): 322–330.

68. Ibid.

69. Ibid.

70. Ibid.

71. Ibid.

72. Ibid.

73. Ibid.

74. Prochaska, J. O., C. C. DiClemente, and J. C. Norcross. "In Search of How People Change: Applications to Addictive Behaviors." *American Psychologist* 47, no. 9 (1992): 1102–1114.

75. Nutbeam, Harris, and Wise, *op. cit.*

76. Redding, C. A., J. S. Rossi, S. R. Rossi, W. F. Velicer, and G. O. Prochaska. "Health Behavior Models." *International Electronic Journal of Health Education* 3 (2000): 180–193.

77. Burroughs et al., *op. cit.*

78. Ibid.

79. Nutbeam, Harris, and Wise, *op. cit.*

80. Ibid.

81. Redding et al., *op. cit.*

82. Nutbeam, Harris, and Wise, *op. cit.*

83. Robinson, L. M., and S. R. Vail. "An Integrative Review of Adolescent Smoking Cessation Using the Transtheoretical Model of Change." *Journal of Pediatric Health Care: Official Publication of National Association of Pediatric Nurse Associates & Practitioners* 26, no. 5 (2012): 336–345.

84. Ibid.

85. Ibid.

86. Bandura, Albert. *Social Learning Theory.* Morristown, NJ: General Learning Press, 1971.

87. Redding et al., *op. cit.*

88. Ibid.

89. Ibid.

90. Nutbeam, Harris, and Wise, *op. cit.*

91. Burroughs et al., *op. cit.*

92. Nutbeam, Harris, and Wise, *op. cit.*

93. Glanz, K., and D. B. Bishop. "The Role of Behavioral Science Theory in Development and Implementation of Public Health Interventions." *Annual Review of Public Health* 31 (2010): 399–418.

94. Rogers, L. Q., E. McAuley, P. M. Anton, K. S. Courneya, S. Vicari, P. Hopkins-Price, S. Verhulst, R. Mocharnuk, and K. Hoelzer. "Better Exercise Adherence after Treatment for Cancer (BEATCancer) Study: Rationale, Design, and Methods." *Contemporary Clinical Trials* 33, no. 1 (2012): 124–137.

95. Ibid.

96. Ibid.

97. Ibid.

98. Ibid.

99. Rogers and Scott, *op. cit.*

100. Ibid.

101. Nutbeam, Harris, and Wise, *op. cit.*

102. Rogers and Scott, *op. cit.*

103. Rogers and Scott, *op. cit.*

104. Nutbeam, Harris, and Wise, *op. cit.*

105. Oldenburg, Brian, and Karen Glanz. "Diffusion of Innovations." In *Health Behavior and Health Education: Theory, Research, and Practice*, edited by Karen Glanz, Barbara K. Rimer, and K. Viswanath, 313–333. San Francisco: Jossey-Bass, 2008.

106. Wejnert, Barbara. "Integrating Models of Diffusion of Innovations: A Conceptual Framework." *Annual Review of Sociology* 28 (2002): 297.

107. Rogers and Scott, *op. cit.*

108. Warner, D. G., C. A. Olney, F. B. Wood, L. Hansen, and V. M. Bowden. "High School Peer Tutors Teach MedlinePlus: A Model for Hispanic Outreach." *Journal of the Medical Library Association: JMLA* 93, no. 2 (2005): 243–252.

109. Ibid.

110. Ibid.

111. Ibid.

112. Ibid.

113. "National Network of Libraries of Medicine Outreach Evaluation Resource Center." National Library of Medicine. Last modified 2012, accessed March 2, 2013. http://nnlm.gov/evaluation/.

114. Burroughs et al., *op. cit.*

115. McCawley, Paul. "The Logic Model for Program Planning and Evaluation." University of Idaho Extension. Last modified 2001, accessed June 30, 2013. http://www.uiweb.uidaho.edu/extension/LogicModel.pdf.

116. Olney, Cynthia A., Susan J. Barnes, National Network of Libraries of Medicine Outreach Evaluation Resource Center, and National Library of Medicine. *Getting Started with Community-Based Outreach.* Seattle; Bethesda, MD: National Network of Libraries of Medicine, Outreach Evaluation Resource Center; National Library of Medicine, 2013.

117. Olney and Barnes, *op. cit.*

118. Whitney, W., G. A. Dutcher, and A. Keselman. "Evaluation of Health Information Outreach: Theory, Practice, and Future Direction." *Journal of the Medical Library Association: JMLA* 101, no. 2 (2013): 138–146.

119. Ibid.

120. Olney and Barnes, *op. cit.*

121. Olney and Barnes, *op. cit.*

122. Huber, J. T., E. B. Kean, P. D. Fitzgerald, T. A. Altman, Z. G. Young, K. M. Dupin, J. Leskovec, and R. Holst. "Outreach Impact Study: The Case of the Greater Midwest Region." *Journal of the Medical Library Association: JMLA* 99, no. 4 (2011): 297–303.

123. Ibid.

124. Lindberg, D. A., and B. L. Humphreys. "2015: The Future of Medical Libraries." *New England Journal of Medicine* 352, no. 11 (2005): 1067–1070.

125. "NN/LM National Network of Libraries of Medicine." National Library of Medicine. Last modified May 12, 2012, accessed March 13, 2013. http://www.nnlm.gov.

126. Johnson, *op. cit.*

127. "State and Local Health Departments." American Public Health Association. Last modified 2013, accessed February 28, 2013. http://www.apha.org/about/Public+Health+Links/LinksStateandLocalHealthDepartments.htm.

128. Huber et al., *op. cit.*

129. Lindberg and Humphreys, *op. cit.*

130. Johnson, *op. cit.*

131. Fama et al., *op. cit.*

132. Ibid.

133. Huber et al., *op. cit.*

134. Ibid.

Chapter 14

SPECIAL POPULATIONS

Michele A. Spatz

Regardless of whether one is a hospital or medical center librarian, or a public librarian who responds to health reference requests, special populations abound when it comes to providing health information services. Among these special populations are:

- Children and youth
- Seniors
- Cultural minorities
- LGBT community
- People with disabilities
- People who are homeless

As evidenced by our professional library organizations, serving the needs of special populations has had a long history within health sciences librarianship. Founded in 1876, and according to its current mission statement, "the American Library Association *was created* to provide leadership for the development, promotion, and improvement of library and information services and the profession of librarianship in order to enhance learning and *ensure access to information for all*" [emphasis added].[1] To fulfill its mission, the American Library Association (ALA) has a number of organizational offices and member round tables to foster understanding and facilitate action for working with special populations.

Established in 1898, the Medical Library Association declares its mission "is dedicated to the support of health sciences research, education, and patient care."[2] Its current code of ethics states, "The health sciences librarian *works without prejudice* to meet the client's information needs" [emphasis added].[3]

It is clear that deep within our profession's history is an abiding respect for all, and it is upon this fundamental foundation that librarians serve patrons' health information needs, including those of special populations. This professional perspective is important because to make wise decisions about their health, or participate in decisions regarding their medical care and treatment, individuals need sound information. Librarians, upholding the mission and professional ethics of librarianship, are trusted helpmates to individuals seeking to learn more about their own or a loved one's diagnosis or condition.

By definition, "special" connotes unique, meaning the needs of some groups fall outside the mainstream and thus require a different approach than might normally be expected to ensure success. In this chapter, we will explore the essential aspects of serving the health information needs of unique user groups.

CHILDREN AND YOUTH

Children and youth may need health information for a variety of reasons: to learn good health habits, to understand their own diagnosis, to learn about a parent or grandparent's illness, or simply to write a school paper. Many libraries, including health libraries, have a policy on helping students of any age with school papers. Such a policy typically limits the scope of health reference service provided to kindly assist the student with defining his or her topic and then teaching them how to access the library's health information resources.

When the issue is not a health paper, helping children and youth with more personal health information requests requires more important considerations. Understanding the psychological developmental stages of children and youth is important in order to be able to deliver age-appropriate health information. Knowing key developmental attributes will help one determine both how to interact with the child or youth and also what types of materials and resources will best meet his or her needs.

Key Developmental Attributes, Early Childhood through Age 18

Early childhood, ages 3 to 5: This is an age when children are immersed in fantasy yet also begin to learn responsibility. Children this age love stories but may have difficulty distinguishing between the imaginary world and reality. They can be quite fearful. In response to the developmental needs of this age group, it is important to speak simply, yet clearly, and give the child straightforward choices where possible (e.g., This book or that one?). In terms of resources, in addition to factual picture books and preschool-friendly electronic tools, consider hands-on teaching materials such as easy games as well as dolls and puppets for either the child or parent to use when explaining things like necessary tests or procedures.

School-age children, ages 6 to 12: School-age children are active learners and also understand cause and effect. They are developing a greater sense of self while also trying to fit in with their peers, who are becoming more influential in their lives. They can be reluctant to ask questions and may therefore feign understanding. Children this age begin to seek more independence as well as privacy. As a librarian, consider the availability of instructive games as much as possible with this age group or resources with lots of pictures or three-dimensional models. Again, where possible, give the child choices (e.g., Which do you prefer to start with, game A or game B?). Acknowledge the child's growing sense of self by letting him or her help or by giving a task. Ask questions or gently suggest the child's parents ask questions, to ensure the child understands the information shared in the materials.

Youth, ages 13 to 18: Youth are undergoing rapid changes, both physically and emotionally, as their bodies mature and they establish their sense of self-identity. Peer group acceptance is vital, and adults' authority may be challenged in the search for autonomy. Privacy, too, is paramount, as is a deep concern about appearance. Abstract thinking becomes evident, as does the ability to engage higher reasoning and, therefore, consider many choices. When interacting with youth, approach them with genuine respect and a sense of acceptance. Consider their need for privacy by being prepared to move a conversation to quieter voice levels or perhaps a place in the library that affords a bit more confidentiality. Empower youth to do their own research by providing instruction on what constitutes a trusted health or medical resource, including the importance of bias and source date.

The Importance of Health Information to Children

For children fighting acute illness or chronic disease, how important is health information? Britain's National Health Service sought to find out by sponsoring a three-year study of children's (6–18 years old) health information needs to facilitate learning about their illness or condition, aid their choice making, and support their self-care. The study found:

> Children and young people want information conveying health messages in realistic and meaningful ways. They want information that fits with their age, circumstances (family, home, school, college) and differing health needs along differing condition trajectories. Moreover children say they want contemporary information, at the point when they most need it and, importantly, at key information points, for example diagnosis, starting school, changing school, growing up with the condition, lifestyle issues and transition to adult care. Parents and children want greater access to higher quality, timely and relevant information. They also want written information to back up the mass of instructions and advice that is exchanged verbally in clinical encounters.[4]

This study underscores the compelling need for reliable diagnosis- and situation-specific health information at points along the continuum of a child's chronic illness or condition. Organizations such as the American Academy of Pediatrics, KidsHealth from the Nemours Foundation, NIH U.S. National Library of Medicine's MedlinePlus, NIH Eunice Kennedy Shriver National Institute of Child Health and Human Development, NIH National Library of Medicine's Genetics Home Reference, and many other health agencies, foundations, or professional organization websites provide age-appropriate health and medical information resources for kids and parents alike.

Through understanding children's developmental stages and knowledge of age-appropriate resources, health sciences librarians are poised to help meet the compelling health information needs of children and youth.

SENIORS

Seniors (adults aged 65 or older) are a growing demographic group, as the "baby boomer" generation ages. With normal aging, there often comes a natural decline in physical abilities, such as eyesight or hearing. Further complicating life for older adults may be cognitive changes affecting memory or physical conditions, such as arthritis, that affect dexterity or mobility. It is a time in life also marked by many changes in social roles (e.g., retirement, grandparent, widowhood) as well as one where there may be a preponderance of either lifelong or new health issues.

As a librarian, when interacting with seniors, consider good eye contact and, if hearing loss appears to be a concern, make sure they can see your lips while you are talking. Talk a bit slower than you might normally so that the words have time to register. You may find that you need to speak up a bit, but let the senior guide this decision. There is no need to shout, as often happens. Doing so may be perceived as rude or insensitive. However, a slightly amplified voice coupled with slower speech should help a hard of hearing senior participate in the conversation. When providing printed health information to seniors, where possible, include a variety of text sizes—both large and regular fonts—and offer the individual a choice. Other formats, such as DVDs and online videos or audio media, are helpful, as are senior-focused health websites. NIH's SeniorHealth (http://nihseniorhealth.gov/) is one such senior-friendly health website that offers both print and video health information geared especially for those ages 60 or older. Seniors can easily change the size of the font and also the contrast of the site to enhance viewing. Abundant illustrations and photographs accompany the printed information, and NIH SeniorHealth is also rich in videos, a boon for those with low vision because they can listen to the content. The site, developed by the National Institutes of Health's National Institute on Aging (NIA) and the National Library of Medicine (NLM), offers seniors reliable online health information in a senior-friendly format. The American Geriatrics Society's Health in Aging and the Centers for Disease Control and Prevention's Healthy Aging websites also offer reliable senior-specific health information.

CULTURAL MINORITIES

The United States remains the proverbial "melting pot," and 2010 U.S. Census data revealed dramatic growth in both the Hispanic and Asian populations, while non-Hispanic white alone population growth slowed tremendously. The make-up of the U.S. population is changing, with the numbers of minority groups increasing. Broadly, the 2010 census data describes the country's overall ethnic make-up as: 64 percent non-Hispanic white, 16 percent Hispanic, 12 percent black or African American, 5 percent Asian, and 3 percent other.[5]

A recent population-based study called "Racial and Ethnic Diversity Goes Local: Charting Change in American Communities over Three Decades," concluded that "the United States is growing more diverse, not just overall but at the community level. Immigrants from across the globe have fundamentally changed the demographic landscape. The number of all-white communities has shrunk; the number of communities with significant, varied racial ethnic populations has risen. Even in rural areas, and in the nation's heartland cities, diversity has increased, though the most diverse communities continue to be in the West (especially California), the South, and along the coasts."[6]

Our nation continues to be comprised of a rich mixture of people with diverse cultural backgrounds and those who speak a foreign language, a fact that has important implications for meeting their health information needs. To serve these varied needs, it is important to understand what ethnic groups and languages comprise the library's community. From this baseline, appropriate services and collections may be developed. The U.S. Census Bureau's American FactFinder website offers the ability to obtain information on a community's ethnic diversity. Some community Chamber of Commerce or county government websites also post this information. In developing and sustaining ethnically appropriate health information services and resources, consider inviting individuals from diverse community groups to serve in an advisory capacity. They will provide valuable input and feedback to help create successful programs and materials.

Complicating the goal of building local multiethnic and multilingual health resources is a dearth of Western health information produced in foreign languages. Most of what is available is piecemeal, highly localized, or of questionable accuracy. Of course, the Internet has helped make inroads into serving the needs of diverse consumers and patients, but there is still much work to be accomplished. With Hispanics making up the second-largest U.S. population, two notable, trustworthy health websites established by the U.S. government are designed to be bilingual. The National Library of Medicine's MedlinePlus (http://www.medlineplus.gov) and the Centers for Disease Control and Prevention's website (http://www.cdc.gov/) are two such examples. Furthermore, much of the content on MedlinePlus is available in multiple languages, with a link to the diverse choices located at the bottom of the site's home page. Another interesting multiethnic, multilingual site is Healthy Roads Media (http://www.healthyroadsmedia.org/). Started with grant funding from the National Library of Medicine in 2002, the website continues to slowly grow and expand its patient education offerings. Currently, it boasts about 100 health and medical topics provided in 25 different languages and in several different media (e.g., print, video, audio).

In regards to helpful library management practices promoting in-depth services for diverse community members, consider a policy of hiring multilingual staff.

Consider also regular staff development opportunities with insightful presentations about the cultural health beliefs, practices, communication norms, and languages spoken by diverse community members. This is an area where the library's culturally diverse community advisory members could play a significant role.

The American Library Association, through its Reference and User Services Association (RUSA), offers the following helpful resources on its website: *Guidelines for the Development and Promotion of Multilingual Collections* (http://www.ala.org/rusa/resources/guidelines/guidemultilingual) and *Services* and *Guidelines for Library Services to Spanish-Speaking Library Users* (http://www.ala.org/rusa/resources/guidelines/guidespanish).

LGBT COMMUNITY

A 2012 Gallup poll comprising the largest single study of the distribution of the lesbian, gay, bisexual, and transgender (LGBT) population in the United States showed that 3.4 percent of adults self-identify as LGBT.[7] Contrary to portrayals in the popular media, the results of the Gallup analysis showed the LGBT community is not predominately white, highly educated, and very wealthy. What the Gallup analysis revealed is that more nonwhites are likely to identify as LGBT, youth are more apt to disclose than older adults, and that, overall, LGBT individuals tend to have lower educational levels and correspondingly, lower annual incomes.

American culture in social and political discourse has clumped lesbian, gay, bisexual and transgender individuals together, thus the LGBT community acronym, and while they do share some commonalities, the health needs of each subgroup are distinctly different according to the 2011 Institute of Medicine (IOM) report, "The Health of Lesbian, Gay, Bisexual, and Transgender People: Building a Foundation for Better Understanding."[8] Of importance to health sciences librarians are the following IOM findings:

- Self-identification as lesbian, gay, or bisexual and disclosure of this identity may vary by race, ethnicity, income level, or geographic location.
- LGBT individuals live in most geographic areas throughout the United States, but studies have shown higher proportions in urban areas on the East and West Coasts.
- While lesbians and gay men are less likely to be parents than their heterosexual peers, substantial numbers of lesbians and gay men have children.
- Lesbians, gay men, and bisexual and transgender people exist across all age groups.
- LGBT individuals face financial barriers, limitations on access to health insurance, insufficient knowledge on the healthcare provider's part, and negative attitudes on the healthcare provider's part that can be expected to effect their access to healthcare.
- A lack of healthcare provider training may lead to less than optimal care for LGBT adolescents and adults.
- LGBT individuals face barriers to healthcare related to sexual and transgender stigma, and some are further marginalized by additional barriers such as racial/ethnic minority status, low income, immigrant status, and limited English proficiency.

Table 14.1 Urgent Health Issues for LGBT Groups

LGBT youth	**Health services:** Need for LGBT-experienced providers
	Mental health: Suicidal behavior and suicidality; identity-related issues, stigma and discrimination; eating disorders
	Physical health: Obesity and substance use (including smoking and alcohol use)
	Sexual and reproductive health: Sexual development; sexual health; pregnancy; sexually transmitted infections (STIs); HIV
	Transgender-specific health care: Effects, benefits, and risks of puberty-delaying hormone therapy
LGBT adults	**Health services:** Need for LGBT-experienced providers
	Mental health: Eating disorders; depression; suicidality; stigma and discrimination
	Physical health: Substance use; cancer prevention and treatment, especially for breast and anal cancer; cardiovascular disease; obesity
	Sexual and reproductive health: HIV; fertility, infertility, and reproductive health issues
LGBT seniors	**Health services:** Long-term care issues for older LGBT persons; end-of-life issues
	Mental health: Depression; suicidality; stigma and discrimination
	Physical health: Prostate cancer among older gay and bisexual men and transgender women; anal cancer; effects of long-term hormone use among older transgender persons; disabilities
	Sexual and reproductive health: HIV (and the experience of aging with HIV); sexual well-being; sexual dysfunction

Within the IOM report, a number of important findings may inform library service and collection development. These findings, signifying the most urgent health issues identified for each group, are outlined in Table 14.1.

According to its website, the Gay and Lesbian Medical Association (GLMA) is the world's largest and oldest association of lesbian, gay, bisexual, and transgender healthcare professionals. GLMA was founded in 1981 as the American Association of Physicians for Human Rights with the mission of ensuring equality in healthcare for LGBT individuals and healthcare professionals. They offer useful information for both patients and providers on the topics noted in this chapter (http://www.glma.org/).

Another useful resource for health and medical information for this special population is the Centers for Disease Control and Prevention's Lesbian, Gay, Bisexual and Transgender Health website (http://www.cdc.gov/lgbthealth/youth.htm).

Finally, the Human Rights Campaign Healthcare Equality Index (HEI, http://www.hrc.org/hei#.UNJOTORi6So) offers an important resource for LGBT individuals to locate healthcare providers who offer inclusive care and to help educate healthcare providers about how to deliver inclusive care to LGBT individuals.

PEOPLE WITH DISABILITIES

According to "Americans with Disabilities: 2010,"[9] a U.S. Census Bureau report, almost 19 percent of noninstitutionalized U.S. citizens have a disability. The report stipulates that while there are many types of disabilities and an individual may have more than one, it categorized disabilities into three primary types: communicative, physical, and mental. As one might expect, older adults are the largest group with disabilities, as aging takes its toll on the human body.

The surgeon general's "Call to Action to Improve the Health and Wellness of Persons with Disabilities" states, "It is important to recognize that disability is not an illness. Just as health and illness exist along a continuum, so, too, does disability. Just as the same illnesses can vary in intensity from person to person, so, too, can the same condition lead to greater or lesser limitation in activity from one person to another."[10]

From that perspective, the Office on Disability in the U.S. Department of Health and Human Services provides guidance and offers important points about interacting with and serving the needs of the one in five Americans who has a disability,[11] including:

- One of the key challenges for a person with a disability is to be seen as an individual with abilities, not through the lens of his or her disability.
- Most people with disabilities can and do work, play, learn, and enjoy full healthy lives in their communities.

As part of the call to action, the surgeon general's office shared the following basic pointers for interacting with those who have a disability[12]:

- See the whole person, not just the disability.
- Speak directly with the person who has a disability, rather than through a third party.
- Speak with adults as adults, and children as children.
- Ask the person with a disability if he or she needs any help. *Do not assume help is needed.*
- Be aware of and patient with the extra time it might take a person with a disability to speak or act.
- Respect what a person with a disability can do. See the ability in disability.
- Understand that not having access to work, school, healthcare, or fun things to do can cause more problems than a disability itself.
- Be the person who makes a difference.

To meet the healthcare information needs of people with disabilities, health sciences librarians must be prepared to assist them. Of course, compliance with the American with Disabilities Act (ADA) accessibility requirements is essential. The American Library Association (ALA) has a wealth of helpful and practical resources for both ADA compliance and serving the needs of individuals with disabilities. On its website, the ALA's Association for Specialized and Cooperative Library Agencies (ASCLA) provides links to materials on ADA compliance and library issues (http://www.ala.org/ascla/asclaissues/issues).

Additional helpful information for addressing the needs of individuals with specific disabilities may be found in the ALA ASCLA's "Library Accessibility: What You Need to Know" toolkit on the ALA website (http://www.ala.org/ascla/asclaprotools/accessibilitytipsheets). The toolkit is comprised of 15 well-written and practical "tip sheets" covering key disabilities such as deafness, vision problems, physical disabilities, mental illness, learning disabilities, and working with library staff who have a disability.

In building a collection of library resources for those with different disabilities, consider the need to purchase assistive technology to help these individuals access both the physical and virtual library collection. Software solutions can help those with vision or hearing loss successfully utilize any computer or web-based resource, for instance. The ASCLA toolkit provides a tip sheet on assistive technology that offers practical software solutions for librarians to consider. Finally, when purchasing physical materials for the library, look for important resources that are available in multiple formats (e.g., print and multimedia), to accommodate the different needs of library users with disabilities.

PEOPLE WHO ARE HOMELESS

The hard-hitting U.S. recession has altered the landscape of homelessness in America. The "Annual Homeless Assessment Report (AHAR)," issued each year by the U.S. Department of Housing and Urban Development (HUD), provides the results of local point-in-time (PIT) counts of people who are homeless on a single night in January, as well as estimates of the number, characteristics, and service patterns of all people who used residential programs for homeless people during the federal fiscal year (October 1–September 30).[13]

According to the 2010 report, on the night of the January PIT count:

- 649,917 people were experiencing homelessness, an increase of 1.1 percent over 2009.
- 79,446 *family households*—241,951 persons in families—were homeless, an increase of 1.2 percent over the last year.
- 109,812 people were chronically homeless—persons with severe disabilities and long homeless histories—a decrease of 1 percent over the last year.
- More than 1.59 million people spent at least one night in an emergency shelter or transitional housing program during the 2010 AHAR reporting period.[14]

Among the homeless, an estimated one out of every six men and women in our nation's homeless shelters is a veteran, and veterans are 50 percent more likely to fall into homelessness compared to other Americans. Another key group likely to be homeless are people with disabilities. There is a concerted effort underway in the current administration to end homelessness among veterans by 2015 and among children, families, and youth by 2020.[15] These efforts may have impacted the slight downward tick in the number chronically homeless that was noted in the preceding AHAR results.

Serving the health information needs of people who are homeless remains a challenge for health sciences librarians. We are often ill prepared to understand how to serve the needs of this population that is at once both compelling and confounding.

The American Library Association's *Outreach Resources for Services to Poor and Homeless People* (http://www.ala.org/advocacy/diversity/outreachtounderservedpopulations/servicespoor) describes homelessness as a dehumanizing label used to categorize individuals and potentially discriminate against them.[16] The issue brief also invokes librarians' long history of public service by highlighting opportunities that librarians have to change lives by creatively responding to the information needs of individuals who are homeless. Health sciences librarians may play a critical role as that change agent for homeless patrons. Sharing their knowledge about community health and medical services across the continuum of care—from mental health services to primary care clinics, to long term care facilities—and inviting homeless individuals to help identify the best ways to share and inform others of these helpful resources is an ideal place to start. Tolerant library policies will help because the homeless lack "permanent" addresses and also the funds to pay for computer access or library fines. Outreach efforts, such as developing community partnership projects with homeless shelters to provide diagnosis-specific health resources, for example, is a constructive way to live and exemplify the mission of a health or medical library's parent institution. For health librarians practicing in public libraries, a number of examples of partnership projects with the homeless have had a positive impact and, as the ALA encouragingly notes, have "changed lives."[17] Several of these projects are found in the helpful toolkit called "Extending Our Reach: Reducing Homelessness through Library Engagement" that was produced by the American Library Association's Social Responsibilities Round Table and Office for Literacy and Outreach Services (http://www.ala.org/offices/sites/ala.org.offices/files/content/olos/toolkits/poorhomeless_FINAL.pdf).[18]

Perhaps the biggest hurdle to overcome when serving people who are homeless may be addressing our own attitudes and comfort levels in working with this special population. If we are struggling with intolerance, we may want to consider working to build our understanding and compassion by exploring the many resources available to our profession on this issue and also reaching out to colleagues who are successfully addressing the health information needs of the homeless through their library services, policies, and procedures. Doing so may inspire us to take the initial steps to truly engage in meaningful service to this underserved group.

CONCLUSION

This chapter has covered strategies for health sciences librarians to respond to the unique health information needs of several special populations: children and youth, seniors, cultural minorities, the LGBT community, people who are disabled, and people who are homeless. As one begins or expands his or her library's services in these areas, having these helpful tools and resources can be of significant assistance. When interacting with individuals with special needs, it is important to remember we are connected to one another by our humanity. Each of us has the need to feel respected and understood. As a health sciences librarian, reaching out to special populations requires more than good interpersonal skills. It requires us to be self-aware enough to know where we struggle with our biases and to take steps to mitigate these through self-development culminating in a professional practice of nonjudgmental consciousness. Our professional lens of nonjudgmental awareness will lift us out of ourselves, providing a foundation upon which to build valuable library services to those who may benefit most.

NOTES

1. American Library Association. "Mission & Priorities: ALA Online Handbook of Organization." Accessed December 5, 2012. http://www.ala.org/aboutala/missionhistory/mission.

2. Medical Library Association. "Our Mission." Accessed December 6, 2012. http://www.mlanet.org/about/mission.html.

3. Medical Library Association. "Code of Ethics for Health Sciences Librarianship." Accessed December 6, 2012. http://www.mlanet.org/about/ethics.html.

4. Williams, Anne Melita, John Gregory, Davina Ann Allen, Lesley Madeline Lowes, Peter Brocklehurst, Mary Lewis, Simon Lenton, et al. *Children's Health Information Matters: Researching the Practice of and Requirements for Age Appropriate Health Information for Children and Young People. Final Report.* NETSCC, 2011.

5. Humes, Karen R., Jones, Nicholas A. and Ramirez, Roberto R. "Overview of Race and Hispanic Origin: 2010. 2010 Census Briefs. C2010BR-02." U.S. Department of Commerce. Economics and Statistics Administration. U.S. Census Bureau. Last modified March, 2011, accessed December 12, 2012. http://www.census.gov/prod/cen2010/briefs/c2010br-02.pdf.

6. Lee, Barrett A., John Iceland, and Gregory Sharp. "Racial and Ethnic Diversity Goes Local: Charting Change in American Communities Over Three Decades." Department of Sociology and Population Research Institute, Pennsylvania State University, US2010 Project, 2012. Last modified September 2012, accessed December 12, 2012. http://www.s4.brown.edu/us2010/Data/Report/report08292012.pdf.

7. Gates, Gary J., and Frank Newport. "Special Report: 3.4% of U.S. Adults Identify as LGBT." Gallup Intl, October 18, 2012. Accessed December 20, 2012. http://www.gallup.com/poll/158066/special-report-adults-identify-lgbt.aspx.

8. Institute of Medicine, Committee on Lesbian, Gay Bisexual, Issues Transgender Health, Gaps Research, and Opportunities. *The Health of Lesbian, Gay, Bisexual, and Transgender People: Building a Foundation for Better Understanding.* Washington, D.C.: National Academies Press, 2011.

9. U.S. Census Bureau, Economic and Statistics Administration, U.S. Department of Commerce. *Americans with Disabilities: 2010 Current Population Reports; Household Economic Studies.* By Matthew W. Brault, P70-131 (Washington D.C.: U.S. Census Bureau, 2012), Accessed January 4, 2013. http://www.census.gov/prod/2012pubs/p70-131.pdf.

10. U.S. Department of Health and Human Services. "The Surgeon General's Call to Action to Improve the Health and Wellness of Persons with Disabilities: Understanding Disability." Last modified January 8, 2010, accessed January 10, 2013. http://www.surgeongeneral.gov/library/calls/disabilities/understanding.html.

11. U.S. Department of Health and Human Services, Office on Disability. "What Is Disability and Who Is Affected by Disability?" Accessed January 8, 2013. http://www.hhs.gov/od/about/fact_sheets/whatisdisability.html.

12. U.S. Department of Health and Human Services. "The 2005 Surgeon General's Call to Action to Improve the Health and Wellness of Persons with Disabilities: Calling You to Action." U.S. Department of Health and Human Services, Office of the Surgeon General, 2005. Accessed January 10, 2013. http://www.cdc.gov/ncbddd/disabilityand health/pdf/whatitmeanstoyou508.pdf.

13. U.S. Department of Housing and Urban Development, Office of Community Planning and Development. "The 2010 Annual Homeless Assessment Report to Congress." Last modified June 2011, accessed January 11, 2013. https://www.onecpd.info/resources/documents/2010HomelessAssessmentReport.pdf.

14. Ibid.

15. U.S. Department of Housing and Urban Affairs (HUD), HUD Public Affairs. "A Look inside Veteran's Homelessness." HUDdle: U.S. Dept of Housing and Urban Development's Official Blog. Accessed January 11, 2013. http://blog.hud.gov/index.php/2011/10/28/veteran%E2%80%99s-homelessness/

16. American Library Association. "Outreach Resources for Services to Poor and Homeless People." Accessed January 28, 2013. http://www.ala.org/advocacy/diversity/outreach tounderservedpopulations/servicespoor.

17. Ibid.

18. American Library Association's Social Responsibilities Round Table and Office for Literacy and Outreach Services. "Extending Our Reach: Reducing Homelessness through Library Engagement." American Library Association, 2012. Accessed January 14, 2013. http://www.ala.org/offices/sites/ala.org.offices/files/content/olos/toolkits/poorhomeless _FINAL.pdf.

Chapter 15

HEALTH AND BIOMEDICAL INFORMATICS

Prudence W. Dalrymple and *Douglas L. Varner*

Harnessing the power of information technology to improve health status, both of individuals and of populations, is claiming unprecedented attention nationally and internationally as society deals with the effects of recent economic, environmental, and policy changes. Health informatics is the interdisciplinary field that has evolved to bring expertise in information science and technology to the medical and biological knowledge base. The term "informatics" is associated with the massive changes that computer technologies have brought to the delivery of healthcare: many of the core concepts of informatics are easily recognizable by librarians and information professionals. Indeed, the National Library of Medicine has been in the forefront of research, education, and development of biomedical informatics for several decades. As the field of informatics has evolved and expanded, there have been various attempts to explain and define it. Most of these definitions include the premise proposed by Friedman[1]—that people aided by computer technology are essentially more effective than either one is individually. A more distinctive definition that is potentially more relevant to the library and information science (LIS) community is "information science applied to a domain."[2] This definition acknowledges the many variants of informatics such as health informatics, legal informatics, museum informatics, community informatics, nursing informatics—perhaps even the potentially tautological "library informatics" as evidenced by a library informatics program at Northern Kentucky University.[3]

This chapter defines and discusses health informatics—both as a discipline and as an area of practice—and identifies areas of intersection between health informatics and health sciences librarianship in and outside of library organizations. In addition, it includes resources for those who are seeking education and training in health informatics and those seeking to identify sources of funding for informatics research and demonstration in the health sciences.

DATA, INFORMATION, KNOWLEDGE

Using the latter definition—information science applied to a domain, it is easy to use what is known as the informatics pyramid (see Figure 15.1) to examine the parallelism between library and information science and informatics. At the lowest, widest level in the pyramid lay data—the smallest units that are considered in any investigation. Sometimes the data may be individual blood pressure readings, individual medical records, individual scholarly articles, even the 0s and 1s of digital data—the unit measurement of analysis specific to any sector. At the next level, data are processed and organized; we recognize the results as "information"—that which has meaning or enables a decision to be made. To continue with the blood pressure example, single blood pressure readings lack meaning until they are organized to

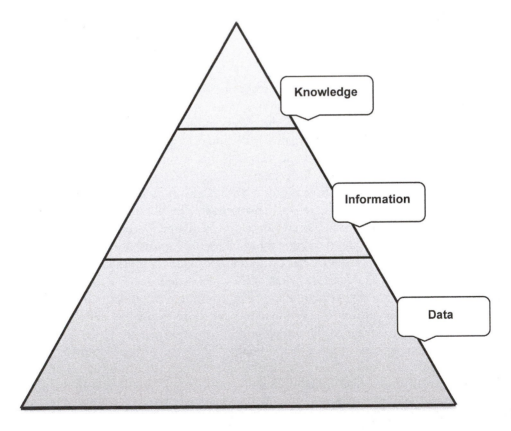

Figure 15.1   The Informatics Pyramid

indicate a trend or direction reflecting an individual's health status at a given moment. Individual scholarly articles become more meaningful when processed in a systematic review or in a meta-analysis, or when visualized through citation graphs. Similarly, aggregating and organizing components of medical records such as diagnostic codes, test results, or medications prescribed can reveal a pattern of disease. This processing, facilitated by computer technology, enables the data to be transformed into information that carries meaning and can support decision making.

In addition, the last decade has brought with it quantum leaps in the generation of data in many fields. In both library and information science and in health informatics, the "data deluge" has presented both challenges and opportunities for applying a growing array of data analysis tools. The adoption of electronic health records and the growth of health information technology applications have made computational methods virtually synonymous with informatics. That is, it is difficult to imagine any discussion of health informatics that does not acknowledge the importance of data science and analytics. Indeed, a strong argument can be made that where biomedical, health, and behavioral health data are concerned, data science and informatics are one and the same.[4] In LIS, movements such as LIBQUAL (http://www.libqual.org/), a service that helps libraries assess and improve library service, provide librarians with examples of the ways in which library practices generate data that can be mined and analyzed to discern meaningful patterns. Bibliometrics, whose roots reach back several decades into library and information science, resemble data visualization applications in biomedicine, to cite another example of the intersection between informatics and information science. While much of the current focus of health informatics is on clinical issues such as the design and implementation of electronic health records and decision support, the field also includes medical ontology construction as well as information organization, storage, and retrieval; artificial intelligence; text mining; data exchange; data standards; natural language processing; and security and privacy. The related field of bioinformatics also includes data curation and modeling of biological functions. Information professionals who have experience with quantitative analysis (or who are interested in acquiring such skills) as well as those who have knowledge in related domains may find health informatics an attractive career direction. (See the section on education and training later in this chapter.) All of these activities have been the focus of research and development in libraries as they have sought to develop new services, foster cooperation, and ensure persistent access to materials.

But what about the topmost level of the pyramid—knowledge? Once again, processing takes place, but with the addition of greater human intervention. The trends in blood pressure, once a diagnosis has been determined (i.e., a disease state), can be treated through a human intervention. Done frequently enough and with appropriate monitoring, the repeated treatments can become the basis for knowledge in the field from which protocols may be standardized into clinical practice guidelines. Health sciences librarians are familiar with this process through the creation and implementation of evidence-based practice—in medicine, in nursing, or in library and information science. It is the field of evidence-based medicine that was an early example of the informatics pyramid and that was one of the first ways in which information professionals played a key role, an involvement that continues today. For a more extensive discussion of evidence-based practice, see Chapter 4.

Having examined the informatics pyramid, it may be useful to take a broader look at the domains of informatics and how they relate to one another. If one imagines the health sciences as being arrayed along a continuum, from the cellular level to the population level, it is easy to envision each with its associated area of informatics—from bioinformatics to public health informatics. If one overlays the basic methods, techniques, and theories that are used in both basic and applied research to solve problems at various levels within these domains, a clear picture of the scope and methods of current biomedical informatics emerges. Indeed, readers of this text will also see parallels between this representation and that proposed by Marcia Bates in her landmark article "The Invisible Substrate of Information Science."[5] While Shortliffe's schematic[6] still characterizes the domains of biomedical informatics in their strictest sense, the field now includes nursing informatics and consumer informatics, two rapidly growing areas. The "traditional" medical model in which patients are diagnosed and treated in episodic encounters with physicians has evolved to an approach in which the goal is as much disease prevention as it is disease treatment. In this model, activities and decisions are embedded in the context of daily living; thus, health informatics problems are not solely those arising from clinical practice, but also those that arise from the needs of individuals in their social environments, thus serving as an underlying construct for the practice of integrated medicine. From this perspective, it is easy to see potential areas where information professionals who have long been concerned with information use in the context of everyday life can contribute to health informatics, especially in the realm of knowledge-based resources.

AN INTERDISCIPLINARY FIELD

Because informatics is an emerging field—and one that is intensely interdisciplinary—most informaticians have migrated from other careers, and physicians, computer scientists, librarians, systems analysts, information professionals, pharmacists, and nurses all can be found working in health informatics. Informaticians must be flexible and innovative broad thinkers who are able to analyze problems from multiple perspectives. Successful informaticians—also referred to as informaticists—integrate their previous experience with their new knowledge and skills, and are willing to move beyond their comfort zone to take on new challenges. Those who enter health informatics from the library and information sciences will find that their knowledge of information organization and database structures serves them well, as does their experience with user-centered information systems and the construction and use of information standards. The barriers and facilitators for acquiring and applying data, information and knowledge to decision making, and familiarity with data from the molecular to the population level are important topics for librarians to acquire expertise in to facilitate a transition to informatics.

As information professionals, librarians have an interest in studying the ways in which professionals access, appraise, and apply information in practice, and they are aware of the multiple barriers facing the busy clinician who desires to apply the latest knowledge to patient care. Beginning with the earliest instance of Literature Attached to Charts (LATCH), through initial clinical librarian activities, to the current use of embedded librarians,[7, 8] librarians have exercised both creativity and expertise in designing new ways to facilitate the application of information and evidence into practice. Informatics offers additional options for providing knowledge support to clinicians; information professionals who are able to bring their understanding of user needs, the structure of information resources, and ways of improving access represent an optimum blending of health sciences librarianship and health informatics. This field of research and development also exists in both the private sector where companies are developing new products and the academic sector where researchers are designing and testing new approaches—as well as in collaborations between business and academia.

THE LIBRARY'S ROLE IN INFORMATION MANAGEMENT

Probably the single seminal event that illustrates the convergence of the common origin of health sciences librarianship and health informatics was the 1982 publication of a supplement to the *Journal of Medical Education* titled "Academic Information in the Academic Health Sciences Center: Roles for the Library in Information Management" and authored by Nina W. Matheson and John A. D. Cooper.[9] This report—subsequently known as the Matheson-Cooper report—proposes the integration of the health sciences library into the information management enterprise of the academic medical center. It describes the shift from paper to digital as an efficient means for management of information and proposes methodologies for transforming the library from "a repository to an interactive information transfer and management system."[10] It places the library at the nexus of networked academic information systems that would dismantle silos of discrete knowledge to create systems that are "integral to the discovery, transmittal, and utilization of knowledge in the service of science and medicine."[11]

The call to action statements in the Matheson-Cooper report were operationalized into a request for proposals in 1982 administered by the National Library of Medicine under the title "Integrated Academic Information Management Systems (IAIMS)."[12] The IAIMS grants were designed for health organizations, private and federal, to assist academic health centers in creating integrated information systems to cope with the growing biomedical knowledge base and to improve information management. Four competitive grants were awarded for pilot projects at the following institutions:

- University of Utah to fund development of the HELP hospital information system[13]
- Columbia University for deployment of computer terminals at the bedside to enhance the availability of clinical information[14]

- Georgetown University to development a patient database management system[15]
- University of Maryland at Baltimore to fund an information utility environment, including decision support systems[16]

At all four institutions, the academic health sciences library director served as the principal investigator for the projects, collaborating with senior administrative and informatics staff to develop and implement the networked systems. Subsequent grants enabled more institutions to effect major changes based on IAIMS principles, thus advancing the central role of the library in the management of biomedical information resources and services, which has continued and expanded ever since that initial catalyzing report.

Decision Support: Integrating Evidence into Practice

Clinical decision support systems are designed to provide "real-time" guidance to physicians at the point of care in making appropriate patient care decisions.[17] Bates and colleagues described the importance of evidence-based practice and the linkage between decision support systems and the point-of-care operationalization of the evidence.[18] Teich, reporting for the Clinical Decision Support Workgroup of the American Medical Informatics Association, discussed the importance of an enhanced knowledge base to formulate rules for electronic prescribing, a well-known implementation of a clinical decision support system, and the incorporation of standard terminologies for medication ordering into the electronic prescription system.[19]

Librarians have played a vital role in the integration of evidence-based content into clinical information systems. Probably the best-known example of integrating evidence into the electronic health record is an application known as the infobutton. The infobutton was originally designed as a static "button" that launched the bibliographic database MEDLINE from a clinical information system interface.[20] The infobutton has evolved into the "infobutton manager," which matches contextual information appearing in the clinical systems interface with the information needed by a clinician and generates a dynamic link to relevant resources.[21] The infobutton manager continues to evolve[22] and in a recent study was used as a method to study clinician information seeking behavior.[23]

Peshek and colleagues developed criteria-based, interactive order sets in a computerized physician order entry system to facilitate the ordering of evidence-based medications. This process represents an efficient and effective method to implement clinical practice guidelines rapidly across multiple clinical settings.[24] Using a different approach, through their evidence-based order set support service, librarians at Vanderbilt University Medical Center Eskind Biomedical Library play a key role in ensuring that order sets reflect the latest evidence.[25] Additionally, a number of clinical systems vendors sell turnkey evidence-based order sets for use in computerized physician order entry systems.[26]

Librarians excel in their knowledge of the evidence and in teaching evidence-based medicine to healthcare professionals. The preceding examples of infobuttons, order sets, and clinical decision support systems all require the incorporation of the latest evidence and standardized terminology into the underlying operational algorithms. Librarians will make significant contributions moving forward into the future as key members of the development, implementation, and operational teams for these clinical systems endeavors.

The Information Professional as Research Partner

The librarian's role as research partner throughout the information life cycle is becoming ever more prominent and crucial. Both the National Institutes of Health (NIH) and the National Science Foundation (NSF) require that a data management plan be included in all grant proposals. These plans must address the organization, preservation, access, and reuse of all data generated as part of federally funded research, and librarians are beginning to position themselves as members of the research team who can provide this service. The role of research partner may be best described as an informationist who is "embedded" in the research enterprise, rather than in the library or the clinical environment. In both instances, the informationist develops a relationship of varying duration with a group of individuals outside the library and contributes expertise to accomplishing a task. The research informationist becomes familiar with the topic being investigated, acquires an understanding of the culture and expectations of the discipline, and can work both as a team member and also as an individual responsible for the organization, management, and preservation of the data generated in the course of a research project.[27, 28, 29]

Because society increasingly carries out its activities using digital appliances of one sort or another, the potential for data generation is virtually unlimited. This "data deluge" can be captured and analyzed to answer a multiplicity of questions, but it is essential to formulate thoughtful and informed queries in order for the analytic tools and techniques to be used to advance knowledge. Managers of health information organizations—typically (but not limited to) libraries—can harness informatics tools to answer questions about their organizations, just as healthcare administrators and researchers can use data to ask and answer questions about their operations and their outcomes. Both process and outcome variables can be discerned from data analytics, which are rapidly becoming more accessible.

While librarians have led in the development and implementation of traditional information retrieval systems, knowledge management systems represent a convergence of both the knowledge base and the information sources, including system architecture, taxonomy, and structure. The organization of data and information to facilitate access and use is a fundamental component of library and information science (see standard I.2.1 at http://www.ala.org/offices/accreditation), and informatics offers the opportunity to apply those same skills to areas beyond the library. Similarly, the library community has sought to share data and materials by creating standards for their organization and representation. One of the great accomplishments of the National Library of Medicine is the creation of the UMLS (Unified Medical Language System), which facilitates the mapping of more than 200 terminologies and vocabularies. This mapping preserves the unique character of each of the terminologies, which makes them easy to use by each field while enabling the exchange of data and information across systems. Interoperability of health information systems is a significant challenge to realizing seamless access to individual health data while protecting personal privacy, and the expertise resident in the library and information science community is another way that information professionals can offer insight and experience to health informatics. Whether they are providing metadata for images to enable subsequent retrieval, text and data mining, or data extraction, librarians can augment their foundation to participate in the transformation of the information life cycle. When acting in these roles, librarians are practicing the informatics skills embodied in the informatics pyramid, transforming data into information and knowledge.

INFORMATICS EDUCATION AND PROFESSIONAL TRAINING

Health sciences librarians play a significant teaching role in informatics. Linton outlined several important factors librarians bring to the teaching of informatics:

- Extensive experience teaching faculty and students
- Strong knowledge of technology to support workflows
- Expertise in standards and vocabularies
- High comfort level in the electronic environment
- Understanding of user needs, effective user interfaces, and needs assessments
- Strong familiarity with health sciences education and the healthcare environment[30]

King demonstrated, following a survey of informatics programs across the United States and Canada, that of the 26 institutions with informatics training programs that participated in the survey, 22 have library involvement.[31] King goes on to stress the value librarians provide to informatics training by demonstrating the importance of the human-centered approach to a field that places heavy emphasis on technology.[32]

The National Library of Medicine has been a leader in education and training for biomedical informatics, having sponsored multiyear training fellowships for over two decades. An excellent overview of the field is offered twice yearly at the weeklong Woods Hole Marine Biology Laboratory. Admission to the program is competitive and open to applicants from a wide variety of professions, including librarians.[33] The learning objectives for this course reflect a broad perspective of the field and include many topics that are familiar to librarians such as database structures, information retrieval, controlled vocabularies, research and evaluation methods, and Web 2.0 and social networks. Seeing their placement within the informatics context serves as a good way to understand linkages between the two fields.

Librarians have numerous opportunities to learn more about informatics. In addition to the formal education programs mentioned earlier in this chapter, continuing education courses are available in multiple locations or online and can be found through a simple Internet search. The International Medical Informatics

Association is an "association of associations" and provides additional listings and resources both inside and outside of North America.[34] The National Network of Libraries of Medicine's regional offices and the Medical Library Association and its regional chapters offer numerous educational programs, many of which deal with informatics-related topics. Fees are charged for some of the offerings, while others are freely available.

Numerous professional societies hold conferences. The two major health informatics organizations are Healthcare Information and Management Systems Society (HIMSS) and the American Medical Informatics Association (AMIA). HIMSS has many local chapters that sponsor regular educational and networking events, and their annual convention and trade show offers an extraordinary display of technological solutions. AMIA (formerly Symposium on Computer Applications in Medical Care [SCAMC]) is the leading scholarly organization that attracts informatics professionals from many diverse backgrounds working in varied organizations and institutions, including libraries. Of special note to health sciences librarians are the outstanding librarians who have received the association's highest accolade, election as a fellow of the College of Medical Informatics. AHIMA (American Health Information Management Association) has played a leading role the adoption of electronic medical records and is an excellent source of information about the adoption of ICD-10 standards (International Classification of Disease, 10th edition). Some of them have been mentioned already, including AMIA, American Health Information Management Association (AHIMA), HIMSS, and International Medical Informatics Association (IMIA). The Association for Information Science and Technology (ASIS&T) has an active health informatics group. If one is contemplating a career shift to informatics, it is wise to attend one or more professional conferences to network and become acquainted with the field. Health sciences librarians can also get a taste of informatics through the activities and programs of the Medical Informatics Section of the Medical Library Association. In addition to MLA, a number of informatics societies hold conferences, and more are being added all the time. The Association for Computing Machinery (ACM) Workshop in Interactive Systems in Healthcare (WISH), now held in conjunction with AMIA, is attracting attention from those who are interested in human-computer interaction.

In addition to formal education and conference participation, there are other avenues to staying abreast of developments in the field. A quick search of PubMed will identify well over 50 scholarly journals in health informatics. Quite a few quality health informatics blogs and Twitter feeds exist, and among the most important is the Office of the National Coordinator for Health Information Technology (http://www.healthit.gov/buzz-blog/), which is a primary site for remaining abreast of current health informatics developments. At the international level, the International Medical Informatics Association maintains an informative website (http://www.imia-medinfo.org/new2/).

Several lists allow prospective students to identify formal education in informatics. Programs located in institutions that are members of AMIA's Academic Forum are listed online (http://www.amia.org/inside/initiatives/acadforum/

members.asp), and a list of medical informatics programs worldwide through the end of 2010 is also available (http://www.hiww.org/se.html). Librarians' experience and expertise in teaching has played a significant role in the inception of training programs such as those outlined in this chapter. Indeed, Murphy postulates that informatics training programs originated from training courses librarians developed and taught in the areas of information retrieval, critical appraisal, and systematic reviews arising from the significant growth of digital information resources.[35]

HOW INFORMATICS PROJECTS ARE FUNDED

The growth and development of any field takes resources, and informatics is no exception. As mentioned, the U.S. National Library of Medicine (NLM) has been a visionary leader in biomedical informatics for several decades. It offers education and training programs as well as a range of grant programs to support informatics-related projects. NLM's listing of previously funded projects (https://www .nlm.nih.gov/ep/Grants.html) provides an historical record of the evolution of research in the field. The page also offers a window into future directions as it lists projects that have been recently funded and are still in progress; its listing of funding opportunities also gives an indication of its priorities for the future. A search of NIH's Reporter (http://report.nih.gov/) can also identify projects in other NIH Institutes that have informatics components.

Internal funding is often available for informatics projects as organizations explore ways to leverage digital technologies to improve their services and outcomes, such as funding to purchase iPad Minis for use by physicians in the neonatal intensive care unit (NICU). A key ingredient of successful applications is demonstrable involvement of all stakeholders; at a minimum, librarians must collaborate with clinicians and/or researchers throughout the project, from inception to conclusion. The longer and more established the relationship, the better the chances for support and the greater the likelihood of a successful outcome. Searching the informatics literature for examples of successful collaborations is a first (and obvious) step, looking especially at institutions where there is an active health sciences library. As well, the Clinical and Translational Science Awards (https:/www.ctsacentral.org/committee/informatics) very often include budget line items for informatics support, which is coordinated through the informatics key function committee.

Because informatics is an applied, interdisciplinary field, it has become more common for federal agencies such as the NIH and NSF (National Science Foundation) to partner on funding initiatives. The most recent example is the Smart and Connected Health Initiative, which is co-sponsored by NSF and NIH and which fosters interdisciplinary collaboration. And with the recent creation of the Patient Centered Outcomes Research Institute (http://www.pcori.org/), a focus on research by and for patients may stimulate librarians and information professionals to contribute their expertise related to how information needs and behaviors contribute to health outcomes.

Finally, a growing source of funding for informatics initiatives originates from provisions in the Health Information Technology for Economic and Clinical

Health (HITECH) Act. The HITECH Act authorizes incentive payments through Medicare and Medicaid to clinicians and hospitals when they use EHRs privately and securely to achieve specified improvements in care delivery.[36] The Medicare EHR Incentive Program provides incentive payments ranging from $44,000 to $63,750 to eligible healthcare practitioners and hospitals that demonstrate meaningful use of certified EHR technology.[37] Meaningful use is determined by a set of standards defined by the Centers for Medicare & Medicaid Services (CMS) Incentive Programs that govern the use of electronic health records and allow eligible providers and hospitals to earn the aforementioned incentive payments by meeting specific criteria.[38] Librarians who are aware of these programs are more likely to be able to identify areas of potential collaboration that can bring resources to develop innovative solutions and can further advance the knowledge base of the field.

CONCLUSION

Throughout this chapter, the focus has been on the intersection between the skills and expertise of library and information professionals, and health informatics. Discussion outlined how the convergence of the two information science professions contributes to the trajectory from data to information to knowledge to implementation. While informatics is not synonymous with information science and extends beyond the library as an organization, there are numerous areas in which expertise in each sector can contribute to the betterment of both. This chapter outlined specific examples of librarians' contributions to informatics initiatives, including deploying electronic health record info buttons, integrating evidence into clinical decision support systems and computerized physician order entry order sets, and harnessing the infrastructural foundation for data management in support of research and clinical initiatives. Acquiring additional skills and building relationships are equally important in continuing to augment and define the historical affinity of these two fields, and ensuring their mutual relevance.

NOTES

1. Friedman, C. P. "What Informatics Is and Isn't." *Journal of the American Medical Informatics Association: JAMIA* 20, no. 2 (2013), 224–226.

2. Ibid.

3. Northern Kentucky University. "Bachelor of Science Library Informatics: Northern Kentucky University, Greater Cincinnati Region." Accessed November 8, 2013. http://informatics.nku.edu/departments/business-informatics/programs/bsli.html.

4. Ohno-Machado, L. "Data Science and Informatics: When It Comes to Biomedical Data, Is There a Real Distinction?" *Journal of the American Medical Informatics Association: JAMIA* 20, no. 6 (2013): 1009.

5. Bates, Marcia J. "The Invisible Substrate of Information Science." *Journal of the American Society for Information Science* 50, no. 12 (1999): 1043–1050.

6. Shortliffe, E. H., and A. M. Garber. "Training Synergies between Medical Informatics and Health Services Research: Successes and Challenges." *Journal of the American Medical Informatics Association: JAMIA* 9, no. 2 (2002), 133–139.

7. Sowell, S. L. "LATch at the Washington Hospital Center, 1967–1975." *Bulletin of the Medical Library Association* 66, no. 2 (1978): 218–222.

8. Grefsheim, S. F., S. C. Whitmore, B. A. Rapp, J. A. Rankin, R. R. Robison, and C. C. Canto. "The Informationist: Building Evidence for an Emerging Health Profession." *Journal of the Medical Library Association: JMLA* 98, no. 2 (2010): 147–156.

9. Matheson, Nina, Association of American Medical Colleges, and National Library of Medicine. *Academic Information in the Academic Health Sciences Center: Roles for the Library in Information Management.* Washington, D.C.: Association of American Medical Colleges, 1982.

10. Ibid.

11. Ibid.

12. Broering, N. C., and G. L. Hendrickson. "Integrated Academic Information Management Systems. Introduction." *Bulletin of the Medical Library Association* 74, no. 3 (1986): 235–237.

13. Peay, W. J., K. A. Butter, and N. A. Dougherty. "IAIMS and the Library at the University of Utah." *Bulletin of the Medical Library Association* 74, no. 3 (1986): 238–242.

14. Hendrickson, G. L., R. K. Anderson, and R. I. Levy. "Iaims at Columbia: A Strategic Plan and Model Project." *Bulletin of the Medical Library Association* 74, no. 3 (1986): 243–248.

15. Broering, N. C. "Beyond the Library: Iaims at Georgetown University." *Bulletin of the Medical Library Association* 74, no. 3 (1986): 249–256.

16. Wilson, M. P., M. J. Ball, J. L. Zimmerman, and J. V. Douglas. "The Iaims Initiative at the University of Maryland at Baltimore." *Bulletin of the Medical Library Association* 74, no. 3 (1986): 257–261.

17. Jones, J. B., W. F. Stewart, J. D. Darer, and D. F. Sittig. "Beyond the Threshold: Real-Time Use of Evidence in Practice." *BMC Medical Informatics and Decision Making* 13 (2013), 47.

18. Bates, D.W., G. J. Kuperman, S. Wang, T. Gandhi, A. Kittler, L. Volk, C. Spurr, et al. "Ten Commandments for Effective Clinical Decision Support: Making the Practice of Evidence-Based Medicine a Reality." *Journal of the American Medical Informatics Association: JAMIA* 10, no. 6 (2003), 523–530.

19. Teich, J. M., J. A. Osheroff, E. A. Pifer, D. F. Sittig, R. A. Jenders, and CDS Expert Review Panel. "Clinical Decision Support in Electronic Prescribing: Recommendations and an Action Plan: Report of the Joint Clinical Decision Support Workgroup." *Journal of the American Medical Informatics Association: JAMIA* 12, no. 4 (2005), 365–376.

20. Cimino, J. J., S. B. Johnson, A. Aguirre, N. Roderer, and P. D. Clayton. "The Medline Button." *Proceedings / the ... Annual Symposium on Computer Application [sic] in Medical Care: Symposium on Computer Applications in Medical Care* (1992): 81–85.

21. Cimino, J. J. "Use, Usability, Usefulness, and Impact of an Infobutton Manager." *AMIA ... Annual Symposium proceedings / AMIA Symposium. AMIA Symposium* (2006): 151–155.

22. Cimino, J. J., B. E. Friedmann, K. M. Jackson, J. Li, J. Pevzner, and J. Wrenn. "Redesign of the Columbia University Infobutton Manager." *AMIA ... Annual Symposium proceedings / AMIA Symposium. AMIA Symposium* (2007): 135–139.

23. Hunt, S., J. J. Cimino, and D. E. Koziol. "A Comparison of Clinicians' Access to Online Knowledge Resources Using Two Types of Information Retrieval Applications in an Academic Hospital Setting." *Journal of the Medical Library Association: JMLA* 101, no. 1 (2013): 26–31.

24. Peshek, S. C., K. Cubera, and L. Gleespen. "The Use of Interactive Computerized Order Sets to Improve Outcomes." *Quality Management in Health Care* 19, no. 3 (2010).

25. Vanderbilt University. "Knowledge Management: Order Sets & Pathways." Accessed November 8, 2013. http://www.mc.vanderbilt.edu/km/ebm/ordersets.html.

26. Zynx Health. "ZynxOrder Order Sets: Evidence-Based Hospital Order Sets." Accessed November 8, 2013. http://www.zynxhealth.com/Solutions/ZynxOrder.aspx.

27. Federer, L. "The Librarian as Research Informationist: A Case Study." *Journal of the Medical Library Association: JMLA* 101, no. 4 (2013): 298–302.

28. Hanson, K. L., T. A. Bakker, M. A. Svirsky, A. C. Neuman, and N. Rambo. "Informationist Role: Clinical Data Management in Auditory Research." . *JESLIB: Journal of eScience Librarianship* 2, no. 1 (2013): 25–29.

29. Martin, E. R. "Highlighting the Informationist as a Data Librarian Embedded in a Research Team." *JESLIB: Journal of eScience Librarianship* 2, no. 1 (2013): 1–2.

30. Linton, A., and L. Abate. "Capitalizing on Our Strengths: Teaching Health Informatics Courses." Presentation delivered at the Medical Library Association Mid-Atlantic Chapter Annual Meeting, October 2011.

31. King, S. B., and K. MacDonald. "Metropolis Redux: The Unique Importance of Library Skills in Informatics." *Journal of the Medical Library Association: JMLA* 92, no. 2 (2004): 209–217.

32. Ibid.

33. "Marine Biological Laboratory." Accessed November 8, 2013. http://hermes.mbl.edu/education/courses/special_topics/med.html.

34. International Medical Informatics Association. "IMIA (International Medical Informatics Association)." Accessed November 8, 2013. http://www.imia-medinfo.org/new2/.

35. Murphy, Jeannette. "Health Science Librarianships Legacy to Health Informatics." *HIR: Health Information & Libraries Journal* 27, no. 1 (2010): 75–79.

36. Blumenthal, D., and M. Tavenner. "The 'Meaningful Use' Regulation for Electronic Health Records." *New England Journal of Medicine* 363, no. 6 (2010): 501–504.

37. Centers for Medicare & Medicaid Services. "EHR Incentive Programs." Accessed November 8, 2013. http://www.cms.gov/Regulations-and-Guidance/Legislation/EHR IncentivePrograms/index.html.

38. HealthIT.gov. "What Is Meaningful Use? Policy Researchers & Implementers." Accessed November 8, 2013. http://www.healthit.gov/policy-researchers-implementers/meaningful-use.

INDEX

ABOUT THE EDITORS AND CONTRIBUTORS

EDITORS

JEFFREY T. HUBER is Director and Professor in the School of Library and Information Science at the University of Kentucky in Lexington and received his Ph.D. in Library Science from the University of Pittsburgh. He teaches courses on health information resources and services and health literacy, and has published in numerous scholarly journals. He has served as editor for *Introduction to Reference Sources in the Health Sciences* for the fourth, fifth, and sixth editions (Neal-Schuman, 2004, 2008; ALA Publishing, 2014).

FEILI TU-KEEFNER is an Associate Professor at the School of Library and Information Science at the University of South Carolina. She received her Ph.D. in Library and Information Studies from Texas Woman's University, an M.L.I.S. from Louisiana State University, and a B.A. from Soochow University, Taipei, Taiwan. Her area of expertise for both research and teaching is medical informatics and health sciences librarianship. She has served as the Health Information and Libraries Journal, HILJ Regional Associate Editor for North America since August 2006.

CONTRIBUTORS

JAMES E. ANDREWS is Director and Associate Professor at the School of Information at the University of South Florida. He received his Ph.D. in Information Science from the University of Missouri–Columbia's School of Information Science and Learning Technologies in 2000. He served as co-editor with Rachel Richesson for *Clinical Research Informatics* (Springer-Verlag, 2012).

KEITH COGDILL is Director of the National Institutes of Health (NIH) Library in Bethesda, Maryland. He received his Ph.D. in Library and Information Science with a minor in medical informatics from the University of North Carolina.

PRUDENCE W. DALRYMPLE, AHIP, is a Research & Teaching Professor and Director of the Institute for Health Informatics at The iSchool at Drexel University. She received her Ph.D. from the University of Wisconsin–Madison and serves on the Board of Directors of the American Society for Information Science and Technology. From 2001 to 2002, she served as president of the Association for Library and Information Science Education.

MELISSA DE SANTIS, AHIP, is Deputy Director of the Health Sciences Library at the University of Colorado–Denver. She received her Master's in Library and Information Science from the University of California–Los Angeles in 1995 and holds a B.A. in Psychology.

MICHAEL A. FLANNERY is Professor and Associate Director for Historical Collections at Lister Hill Library of the Health Sciences at the University of Alabama at Birmingham. He holds a Master's in Library Science from the University of Kentucky and an M.A. from California State University–Dominguez Hills. He has published numerous books, including *John Uri Lloyd: The Great American Eclectic* (Southern Illinois University Press, 1998), for which he was awarded the Kremers Award from the American Institute for the History of Pharmacy.

SANDRA G. FRANKLIN, AHIP, is Director of the Woodruff Health Sciences Center Library at Emory University. She received her Master's in Library Science from the University of Maryland–College Park.

JULIE K. GAINES is Head of the Medical Partnership Campus Library at Georgia Health Sciences University/University of Georgia. Her research focuses on mobile technology in medical education, embedded librarianship, and community outreach. She received her Master's in Library and Information Science from the University of South Carolina.

ANNA GETSELMAN is Executive Director of the Augustus C. Long Health Sciences Library at Columbia University.

MARY L. GILLASPY is a consultant and freelance editor. She holds a Master's in Library Science. She has taught courses in health information at the University of Kentucky School of Library and Information Science.

GERALD PERRY is Director of the Health Sciences Library at the University of Colorado–Anschutz Medical Campus in Aurora, Colorado. He received his

Master's in Library Science from the State University of New York at Buffalo in 1986 and holds a B.A. in Anthropology and Journalism from Syracuse University.

CONNIE SCHARDT is adjunct faculty at the School of Information and Library Science at the University of North Carolina at Chapel Hill.

KATHERINE SCHILLING is an Associate Professor at the School of Library and Information Science at Indiana University–Bloomington. She received her Ed.D from Boston University in 2002 and previously served as an academic health sciences librarian at the University of Pittsburgh.

ROBERT SHAPIRO is the Public Health Librarian for the Medical Center Library at the University of Kentucky. He received his Master's of Arts in Library Science from the University of Kentucky School of Library and Information Science. His research interests lie at the confluence of information science, public health, and health communication.

DENISE SHEREFF is Academic Services Administrator at the University Of South Florida School Of Information, a position she has filled since July 2013. Shereff was previously Health Information & Outreach Specialist for the College of Medicine at University of South Florida.

MEREDITH SOLOMON, AHIP, is the Medical Librarian at INOVA Fairfax Hospital in Virginia.

MICHELE A. SPATZ is Business Projects and Intelligence Manager for Planetree, an international nonprofit leader in patient-centered care. Prior to joining Planetree, Michele served as director of a hospital-based consumer health library. She has taught and published on many aspects of providing consumer health information.

SUSAN SWOGGER began her interest in libraries by repairing books as a student worker, eventually going to the University of Texas at Austin for library school. She spent some years as director of a psychology library in Phoenix before joining the University of North Carolina's Health Sciences Library as Collections Development Librarian.

FAY J. TOWELL is the Health Sciences Library Director/Archivist at Greenville Health System at the University of South Carolina School of Medicine in Greenville.

DOUGLAS L. VARNER, DM/AHIP, is Senior Associate Director and the Chief Biomedical Informationist at Dahlgren Memorial Library at Georgetown University Medical Center.